Community and Purpose in America

An Analysis of American Political Theory

McGraw-Hill Series in Political Science

community and purpose in america

an analysis of american political theory

MASON DRUKMAN
Associate Professor of Political Science
Reed College

McGraw-Hill Book Company

New York • *San Francisco* • *St. Louis* • *Düsseldorf* • *London* • *Mexico*
Panama • *Sydney* • *Toronto*

This book was set in Linofilm Caledonia
by Applied Typographic Systems, and printed on permanent paper
and bound by Peninsula Lithograph Company.
The designer was Marie Carluccio.
The editors were Ronald D. Kissack and Michael A. Ungersma.
Charles A. Goehring supervised production.

Community and Purpose in America

An Analysis of American Political Theory

Printed in the United States of America.

Library of Congress catalog card number: 70-116662

1234567890   PEPE   79876543210

17863

Preface

Almost a century and a half ago Alexis de Tocqueville delineated three interrelated aspects of American society. He observed in the first place that Americans were addicted to an individualistic style of life. Such a lifestyle, he indicated, "disposes each member of the community to sever himself from the mass of his fellows and to draw apart with his family and his friends, so that after he has thus formed a little circle of his own, he willingly leaves society at large to itself." Tocqueville also found that individualism in practice was connected to what he called a "passion for physical gratification." Americans, he wrote, "believe . . . that their chief business is to secure for themselves a government which will allow them to acquire the things they covet and which will not debar them from the peaceful enjoyment of those possessions which they have already acquired." Finally, Tocqueville noticed that the propensity towards self-gratification had further political consequences. He remarked that "men who are possessed by the passion for physical gratification generally find out that the turmoil of freedom disturbs their welfare before they discover how freedom itself serves to promote it. If the slightest rumor of public commotion intrudes into the petty pleasures of private life, they are aroused and alarmed by it. The fear of anarchy perpetually haunts them, and they are always ready to fling away their freedom at the first disturbance."

Today, when public disturbances and commotions are anything but rumor, we may reflect on the accuracy of Tocqueville's insight. The conclusions of innumerable investigations into civil disorder, violence, conflict of rights, and racial hostility suggest that much of our difficulty can be traced to a widespread lack of social concern, to a materialistic individualism whose dominance allows mistrust and suspicion to poison relationships within and among various sectors of American society. The recent eagerness of many people to restore an absolute adherence to "law and order," even at the price of restricting civil liberties, demonstrates that Tocqueville's warning about the abandonment of freedom was far from unrealistic.

That weaknesses noted in the 1830's are with us today testifies to more than Tocqueville's powers of perception. We should also know that the current state of affairs in America is in large measure the result of past experience. The way we view and treat questions of social and public significance today is to a great extent a product of how we have thought about such matters in the past.

I wish to provide the reader with an understanding of American political theory, not merely because the subject should be intrinsically interesting to all Americans, but because its categories and its conclusions bear on the largest problems that confront us today. The historical connection between the concept of community and the idea of national purpose should yield a comprehension of political phenomena relevant to the last third of the twentieth century.

At the same time, American political thought is discussed in this book on its own terms, as a body of speculative writing that can be analyzed systematically and with some degree of objectivity. My intention is thus twofold: to explicate the ideas of important American political thinkers as clearly and as precisely as possible, and through this explication, to suggest the overall direction these ideas have taken. We must study the influential expressions of American political theory both to discover the meaning of our past and to give a more salient meaning to our present.

To my knowledge no other contemporary work on American political thought consciously attempts to interpret ideas of the past in the light of current tendencies and current tendencies in terms of previous political theories. Whether the reader is familiar with the mainstream of American thinking, or whether he is confronting it for the first time, he should, if this book is successful, come away with new perspectives on his nation's political tradition and a new outlook on possibilities for the future.

It is a pleasure to acknowledge those who assisted me in one way or another in the preparation of this book. My earliest thoughts about the subject matter were greatly influenced by Professors Norman

Jacobson and John Schaar of the University of California at Berkeley; one cannot help but be stimulated by their penetrating and creative interpretations of American political philosophy. Various parts of the manuscript were read and criticized by Professors David Tyack of Stanford University, Martin Edelman of the Graduate School of Public Affairs at Albany, Edward Dolbeare of the University of Wisconsin, John Rothney of the University of Missouri, and by my colleagues at Reed College, Professors Kirk Thompson, William Peck, and Howard Waskow. I appreciated their criticisms and benefitted from their advice. Special appreciation is due to Professor Matthew Stolz of San Francisco State College, who discussed every chapter with me and saved me from many errors in analysis. I wish to express my belated gratitude to Professor Louis Wasserman of Simon Fraser University, who opened for me the doors to intellectual inquiry.

I was ably assisted in my research by Peter Baucher, Barbara Rockefeller, and Isadora Wecksler, and by Jean Borders, who performed the combined roles of research assistant, typist, literary editor, and content analyst. Thanks also to Susan Thomas, owner of the fastest typewriter in the West. A generous grant from the Rabinowitz Foundation assisted me in completing this work on schedule.

MASON DRUKMAN

For Elaine

contents

Community and Purpose in America

An Analysis of American Political Theory

1

PURPOSE AND COMMUNITY

Views of America

When Dwight D. Eisenhower appointed a President's Commission on National Goals during his second administration, he showed an awareness of a condition that had been disturbing analysts of the American scene at least since the end of World War II. The direction of American society and the quality of its internal life had come to occupy the minds of a large number of writers. These men were concerned with problems related to the confusion and ambiguity inherent in the prevailing ideas about the "national interest," the widespread quest for a sense of community, and the accelerated growth of alienation and anomie among the general public. The President's Commission, with its widely distributed *Goals for Americans*, and the intellectuals, with their essays on national purpose and social deviance,[1] were responding to a sense of aimlessness and estrangement that seemed to characterize much of contemporary American life.

☆

[1] President's Commission on National Goals, *Goals for Americans*, Prentice-Hall, Inc., New York, 1960. Clinton Rossiter, Adlai Stevenson, et al., *The National Purpose*, Holt, Rinehart and Winston, Inc., New York, 1960.

1

The Political Response

Although the more specific problems of poverty, automation, social violence, urban blight, and youthful unrest would not receive concerted attention until the mid 1960's, perceptive social critics were already delineating the lack of purpose and public drift that would allow these problems to become so serious. In his autobiographical novel, *Going Away*,[2] Clancy Sigal raised the anguished voice of a politically active man painfully sensitive to the absence of community and purpose in his native country. For Sigal, America was typified by citizens "going private," retreating to the seclusion of their split-level, glass-walled ranch houses and excluding a troubled humanity from a meaningful place in their lives. In an America gone private, people did not concern themselves with what happened to their fellow citizens. "If only you had the assurance," Sigal declared, "that in those . . . small towns of Moline and Decatur, Davenport and Pocatello, there were just a few who knew and cared." To care *politically* was to join the ranks of the alienated, for politics as defined by America was not relevant to the collective problems of society. For Sigal, possessed by an acute awareness of social inequities, the sense of alienation was total. He was one of a small number intensely in search "of cultural involvement, of personal meaning, of . . . justice and honesty. Why," he asked, "is there no place for us in America?" Feeling out of place in his own country, "sick of a community where you couldn't contribute your share," Sigal in fact exiled himself to England in his quest for a society where "men care for one another."

From a slightly more removed perspective, Norman Mailer pronounced America a "moral wilderness," a frightened society unable to define its historic or ethical meaning. "Very few of us," he observed, "know really where we have come from and to where we are going . . . and if it is even worthwhile. For better or for worse we have lost our past, we live in that airless no-man's land of the perpetual present, and so suffer doubly as we strike into the future because we have no roots by which to project ourselves forward, or judge the trip."[3] For men like Mailer the future was viewed without optimism precisely because the present was so profoundly out of focus.

The inability of public policy to speak meaningfully to the issues raised by Sigal, Mailer, and many others suggested the lack of overriding purpose in American society. There existed no set of national

☆

[2] Clancy Sigal, *Going Away*, Houghton Mifflin Company, New York, 1962.
[3] Norman Mailer, *The Presidential Papers*, G. P. Putnam's Sons, New York, 1963, pp. 95-96.

goals, or at least no consistent or widely shared set of goals, that could capture the imagination of the citizenry and give meaning and direction to its public life. That this lack of purpose did not go unnoticed was only of limited consequence. While a great deal of rethinking took place, it was not of a particularly penetrating variety; it proved unable either to identify clearly or offer acceptable solutions to the problem, and in its very public inadequacy may have exacerbated an already difficult situation.

Conditions that a decade earlier had appeared amenable to correction had by the late 1960's run seemingly out of control. Lyndon Johnson's Great Society program constituted a misguided attempt to create a national purpose from above. It ultimately failed on almost every important count. Precisely because it tried, thereby raising expectations, and then failed, the Great Society program served to escalate the rate and deepen the level of social alienation. As Johnson left the presidency his nation could be described as riddled by mistrust and discontent. While private citizens cried loudly for law and order and began to arm themselves against "criminals" and "insurrectionists," young militants, no longer engaged in the privatism of the 1950's, pledged themselves openly to revolution, violent as well as nonviolent, and confused public officials exorted all citizens to resist the forces of anarchy and disorder. As America moved toward the last quarter of the century, even its most charitable observers would have to admit that the nation stood in genuine danger of falling into total disarray, and that the image it now presented to the world was one that other countries would emulate only with the gravest of doubts and after the most serious consideration.

This had not always been the dominant view taken of America. Until very recently it was customary the world over to think of America as a very special country. This view, shared by native and foreign commentators alike, was usually flattering to America; frequently it bordered on the panegyrical. It first appeared in the seventeenth century and, despite occasional dissentience, it continued into the twentieth century, depicting America as a benign land where individuals could enjoy in large measure the combined benefits of material security, personal freedom, and human equality. In one version or another, as imaginative construct or as descriptive analysis, this concept suggested above all that, due to the unique joining of historical and geographic factors, America could offer the world an opportunity previously unknown to mankind: the chance to establish a society based on entirely new principles, a society that would be free of the oppressive and corrupt influences that had previously been seen as a natural part of the human condition.

American Self-Image

This optimistic vision of the New World has by and large been shared historically by American writers who have turned their special attention to questions of political philosophy. From the time of the Revolution, when the idea of America as a single nation was first contemplated, through the post World War I period and beyond, American political theorists maintained the highest hopes for their country. They conceived of a society that was already, or soon could be, organized in a just and proper fashion. While this outlook has dominated the literature of American political theory, one finds alongside the optimism a simultaneous sense of limitation, an appreciation, usually unspoken, of boundaries that cannot or should not be exceeded. Most noticeable here is that Americans, unlike the French, were unable to treat seriously the idea of community. With the French they could create a revolution in the name of liberty and equality, but the concept of fraternity, the notion of community among men that the French took so much to heart was somehow beyond their ken. To understand why this was so may help us make strides toward understanding the causes that underlie the problems faced by American society today.

Hannah Arendt has written that the conventional liberalism and practical colonial experiences of the American founding fathers allowed them first to keep the Revolution on a well-controlled, business-like basis, and then to institute an orderly republican constitutional system. The French, on the other hand, indulged in excesses of passion and, as a consequence, permitted their revolution to get entirely out of hand, both in terms of its goals and its usual methods.[4] Arendt's point is well taken. Americans did not attempt to stand society totally on its head. The Revolution was conservative in certain respects and it was consequently unnecessary to posit a whole new set of human relationships in order to formulate an idea of social justice. Since much was given and since much could therefore be taken for granted, it might be argued that American thinkers had little cause to seek new emotional responses based on communal sentiments. At the same time, however, one cannot help being impressed by the American's keen awareness, both during the constitutional epoch and for a considerable time thereafter, that he was creating social and political institutions that departed radically from precedent and tradition.

Time and again one is struck by statements that announce the possibility of new ventures in an environment more conducive to change than any in the history of man. Many American thinkers were anxious to give the idea of self-government the widest possible connotation

☆

[4] Hannah Arendt, *On Revolution*, The Viking Press, Inc., New York, 1963, pp. 74-94.

and were thus prepared to experiment with a variety of novel arrangements. It seems reasonable on its face to believe that Americans, had they so desired, could have joined hands to establish a society based on the idea of fraternity, a society that served to bring men closer together. Indeed, it may be that the principle of equality can be sustained only through the existence of communal attitudes. Whether such is true or not, there was surely more at work inhibiting the growth of a national sense of community than the fact that the American Revolution was less passionate in content than the French. To delineate other relevant factors, particularly those germane to nineteenth and twentieth century developments, it may be helpful to examine some of the precepts upon which the founding of the American republic was based.

The National Purpose

In the latter half of *Revolt of the Masses*, Ortega y Gasset developed a theory often overlooked by readers who have been moved by the book's sensitivity to the oppressive potential of mass society. Having treated the phenomenon of the mass man, Ortega then considered the genesis of modern nations. He argued that nations are not formed as the *natural* extensions of smaller human groupings. Rather, they are realized through the development of transcendent purposes that serve to overcome the sense of exclusiveness typically produced by a lack of proximity and by linguistic and racial differentiation. Nations are not born, they are made; they are the creations not of nature but of man. Left to themselves local regions are naturally parochial and ethnocentric. The purpose that generates the creation of a nation must somehow overcome the centrifugal forces of intrinsic parochialism. It must be of sufficient intensity to provide a substitute for the more normal ties of culture, of tradition, and especially of geographic closeness. In short, the purpose must bring a feeling of unity to peoples who are initially distinct and separate. Certain of the newer African countries may present the closest contemporary approximation of what Ortega had in mind. Here there have been constructed national purposes that sometimes work to coalesce entire populations whose internal content is otherwise heterogeneous and fragmented.

It is difficult to know whether Ortega's theory has validity when applied generally. The nations of the world seem to have sprung from a variety of causes, and certainly no single explanation fits all cases. The theory is extremely suggestive, however, when applied to the experience of America. Despite a general awareness of its unique position, America at its inception possessed no national sense of identity.

At the very least it had thirteen separate identities and perhaps many more. The purpose that linked Americans together under the banner of one nation was the idea of liberty. The Revolution had been fought in the name of liberty and the Constitution was seen as embodying the irrevocable principles of a people dedicated to its preservation. A belief in liberty provided Americans with a common set of ideals and a common sense of why they constituted a nation.[5] Liberty meant, above all, personal liberty as understood by the mind of the Enlightenment. This liberty was a natural attribute of each individual. It could be violated by no political authority, foreign or domestic. The individual was complete in himself and governments were formed solely to provide an environment within which the individual could achieve self-fulfillment through means he deemed most appropriate.

In most cases, however, individuals drew little distinction between personal liberty and the economic liberty derived from colonial and English experience. Liberty could thus be defined either "conservatively," as individual rights grounded in the protection of property, or "liberally," as individual rights manifested in material acquisition and commercial speculation. In either instance the tenets of Lockean liberalism could be advanced and both interests would comprehend their language and meaning. Liberty expressed in terms of economic individualism could, for example, attract either agrarian or entrepreneur, for it promised to fulfill the aspirations of both, even when they ostensibly came into conflict. This point will be developed more fully in the next chapter.

Economic Individualism and Community

It is my central argument that the very national purpose that first united America, *liberty defined as economic individualism,* may have worked to prevent the country from achieving a national sense of community. While communal feelings are undoubtedly intensified when individuals share a dedication to a common purpose, and while community frequently emerges from a situation in which men adhere to a common end, the purpose to which Americans held most consistently seems to have had precisely the opposite effect. Fealty to their dominant ideology kept Americans on separate paths, free from the interference of fellow-citizens, and free also from responsibility for the welfare of other citizens. With the diminution of the patrician class

☆

[5] For a theoretical description of American national ideology which differs somewhat from mine, see Yehoshua Arieli, *Individualism and Nationalism in American Ideology,* Harvard University Press, Cambridge, 1964.

after the War of 1812, economic individualism took firm hold in America. Indeed, it is because the sharing in the national purpose was so pervasive that Daniel Boorstin could picture nineteenth century America as operating totally without ideology, relying upon and accepting without question the very facts, the "givenness" of its existence.[6] Just as we find it difficult to distinguish "good" where there is no contrasting "evil," so is it difficult to discern an ideology that is not challenged by conflicting ideological claims. Economic individualism constituted an implicit national ideology, and as such it could appear as the "normal" way of life. At the same time it could justify a competitive mode of behavior that would make the realization of community extremely difficult, if not totally impossible. Why this was the case may better be understood if we look more directly into the nature of community itself.

In their extreme formulations, individualism and community are irreconcilable principles: to lay heavy emphasis on one is to rule out the inclusion of the other. Whereas individualism is best expressed in terms of *in*dependence, community suggests a condition of *inter*dependence. In a communal society the wall that separates citizens from one another is weakened so that men not only enter into each other's lives but come to depend upon each other, or upon the totality of the citizenry—the community—for social, economic, and even psychological support. Interdependence implies a system of mutual reliance that to a large degree must be taken for granted. At its furthest reach, community involves psychological attitudes, the ability to depend upon others and feel assured that others will respond in a more or less appropriate way; as a corollary, community requires that individuals feel in some way responsible for what happens to other members of the society. If there is serious doubt about either of these requisites, then the existence of community is placed in jeopardy.

Interdependence, it must be noted, is not the logical opposite of independence. The antonym of independence is *dependence,* a quality that implies an absence of mutuality, a one-way, hierarchical relationship that, however close and satisfying, leaves some individuals subservient to others and therefore in a weakened and powerless condition. Interdependence, on the other hand, suggests feelings of strength and sufficiency born of the knowledge that the individual is not alone, that he is supported by society at large, and that society in turn accepts him as a useful and legitimate member. Although individuals depend upon others, they do so not from a position of inferiority but as

☆

[6] Daniel Boorstin, *The Genius of American Politics,* University of Chicago Press, Chicago, 1953.

fellow countrymen who know that the relationship is reciprocal. They consequently retain personal autonomy even as they rely upon others for support. They relate as citizen to citizen, not as servant to master.

There are innumerable problems in choosing the term "community" for the relationships described here. In the first place, there has never been a clear or consistent definition of community in the history of political and social thought. The concept has been used as vaguely and as variously as any in the literature of political theory.[7] To some extent this ambiguity is unavoidable, for when one speaks of a sense of community one refers to a feeling not readily apparent, that, once seen, tends to melt under the glare of close analysis, a feeling that must itself be sensed by the observer and unconsciously expressed by the members of the society. Psychological interdependence is not presented as a definition of community nor as a description of communal organization. With the possible exception of Sebastian de Grazia,[8] writers have tended to define community in ecological or environmental terms. The notion of interdependence is suggested here as an analytical precept that has relevance to the possibility of community in all contemporary societies.

In one meaning of the word, most political entities, towns, cities, nations, and occasionally even groups of nations, may be called communities. If a functional distribution of tasks, a mutual consensus on certain rules and regulations, and a shared belief in prescribed values exist in some combination, then a community may also be said to exist. Such a constellation of factors must not be taken lightly, for it describes a situation where peace, security of rights and position, and the rule of law may obtain. For many, these factors describe the optimal social condition; any development of closer, more integrated patterns is seen as either accidental or illusory. Moreover, a kind of interdependence exists in such a situation. When there is a functional distribution of labor, citizens, especially those in a complex society, rely on each other far more than in more simply organized societies. In this day of technological coordination modern man cannot exist without the work of those who perform necessary social functions; he is dependent upon them as no peasant or rural dweller ever was. But it is the strength of fraternal sentiments that matters, and without these strong feelings the most functionally interconnected society does not

☆

[7] For the variety and lack of clarity in the theoretical treatment of community, see Carl J. Friedrich (ed.), *Community* (Nomos II), The Liberal Arts Press, Inc., New York, 1959.

[8] Sebastian de Grazia, *The Political Community*, University of Chicago Press, Chicago, 1958. For a distinction similar to mine, see Scott Greer's essay, "Individual Participation in Mass Society," in Roland Young (ed.), *Approaches to the Study of Politics*, Northwestern University Press, Evanston, Ill., 1958.

possess a true sense of community. Thus, from the period of its founding, America, with a general consensus on many values and a functional organization of social tasks, constituted a viable political system. Without deeply ingrained feelings of closeness, however, it did not constitute a community of interdependent citizens.

Anticommunal Factors

America did not, of course, occupy an entirely unique position with respect to a lack of community. In his classic study, *Gemeinschaft und Gesellschaft,* Ferdinand Toennies pointed out that a movement away from community (Gemeinschaft) was characteristic of all of Western civilization. With the breakdown of medieval cooperative life and the rise of urban centers and modern technology, the older communal relationships gave way to a more rationalized and individualistic existence (Gesellschaft), where men were no longer tied together through inherited traditions or common beliefs. As the ties that bound them together weakened, men were forced to rely much more on their own resources to make their way in life. They entered a world of mobility where the individual and his relationships to society became a central consideration. They left a static world where the individual as part of the community was the starting point for human understanding.

What distinguished America from other nations was more a matter of tempo and circumstance than of direction or conscious intent. At its commencement as a nation, America was without those older institutions that might have reshaped economic individualism or at least tempered its force somewhat. Louis Hartz has argued that because America had no feudal tradition to rebel against, it constituted an almost pure embodiment of Lockean liberalism.[9] Hartz's argument is extremely compelling. It was equally important, however, that liberalism in practice enjoyed enormous success in America—economic individualism not only dominated as a way of life but, at least until the end of the nineteenth century, it worked. Because of its favorable environment, America could be conceived of as the "land of plenty," a nation whose wealth was available for many in fact, for all in promise. America was thus suited to an insatiable liberalism that Europe, with its problem of scarcity, could never achieve. Whereas in Europe men were often forced into a state of total dependence simply in order to survive, America offered the promise that each man could reap benefits solely as a result of his own efforts. If the breakdown of

☆

[9] Louis Hartz, *The Liberal Tradition in America,* Harcourt, Brace and Company, Inc., New York, 1955.

community was a worldwide phenomenon, for the reasons given, the advent of Gesellschaft was clearly more rapid and more total in America than elsewhere.

While economic individualism may have been the single most influential force, there were other factors that militated against the development of community in America. The relatively weak role of tradition is one prime example. Americans were keenly aware that they were breaking with tradition in constructing their new society. But it is one thing to leave the Old World behind physically and quite another to celebrate this event so that the break with the past becomes a virtual rejection of history itself. Community cannot be instituted overnight. Communal ties evolve over time and are nurtured by long experience. When experience itself is no longer a valid measure of values, when the American is looked upon as a new Adam and America as his Eden, then the usual arguments for community find little in the way of a receptive audience.

Americans in the post-revolutionary generations were constructing a new nation, a nation whose government would constitute a dramatic departure from older methods and institutions. Their eyes were naturally turned to the future, to a release from a time-worn bondage that had held men fixed to class or status for centuries. History and tradition, considerations relevant to community, are normally part of the conservative's rhetoric, and while Americans could be conservative in certain legal and economic spheres, in terms of overall perspective they were intensely progressive, even radical in propensity. If they stood as Adam on the threshold of their history, they could be audacious enough to think that by their own hand they could erect institutions which would permanently guarantee happiness and beneficence to that history. This Adamic quality did not die with the founding. It ran through the nineteenth century to the closing of the frontier and into the twentieth century, receiving intellectual expression in the idea of progress and popular support from the Horatio Alger myth. Many today still speak of America as a young country whose destiny lies in the future.

Perhaps the greatest barrier to community was geographical rather than psychological: the enormous size of America itself. Mutual responsibility and interdependence are not always present in the smallest of face-to-face societies, let alone in a country where citizens are often separated by vast distances. The problem of a population whose members are remote from each other, serious at the time of the founding, was later aggravated by the multiplicity of distinct nationalities that came to occupy separate and self-contained corners of American territory throughout the nineteenth century. In the face of these factors Americans may be seen as having accomplished a signal feat in evolving, both in theory and in practice, a system of governance which brought some semblance of unity and order to a new world that was perhaps in danger of disruption if not outright dissolution.

The Impact of Abundance

It is precisely this accomplishment that Arendt attributes to the founding generation. She argues that because Americans did not know poverty and deprivation they could, in contrast to the French, remain realists. They could develop concepts of free institutions that would be protected from passion; that is, from the excesses of desire and interest. The French Revolution went awry because it gave a free rein to passion; it tried to construct a government based on feelings of pity and compassion. Eventually passion and compassion were equated and this equation was made the foundation of the new regime. Since the door was opened to the expression of passion, and since the worst excesses could be justified in the name of pity, the bloodletting and eventual tyranny were, as Burke noted, inevitable and predictable. America had the good fortune of abundance, and the good sense to make proper use of its advantage.[10]

But the absence of scarcity in America cut both ways; it was precisely this fact that differentiated America from most of the other nations of the world. America could start from a condition of relative plenty, a condition that was in fact enhanced by the great size of the country. Far from being in competition with each other, Americans could, if they so chose, link arms and mutually benefit from their good fortune. There were space and resources enough so that all might prosper. Americans could free themselves once and for all from the relentless demands imposed by a state of scarcity. They could, in short, take their fortunate starting point and give their revolution a totally new dimension, a dimension that would permit compassion the possibility of legitimate public standing.

There were, of course, instances when Americans were able to form communal connections, at least for periods of time. On the frontier and in many small towns, for example, men could sometimes establish intimate and meaningful relationships of a communal kind. In the country as a whole, however, the prospect of individualistic gratification moved men in the opposite direction. Alexis de Tocqueville caught perfectly the compulsive nature of the economic quest. Americans, he wrote, "can never attain as much as they desire." Their goal "perpetually retires from before them, yet without hiding itself from their sight, and in retiring draws them on. At every moment they

☆

[10]Arendt, *op. cit.*, pp. 74-94.

think they are about to grasp it; it escapes at every moment from their hold. They are near enough to see its charms, but too far off to enjoy them; and before they have fully tasted its delights they die."[11]

Tocqueville's perception was shared by innumerable visitors to the United States. While most domestic writers would contend over procedural or legalistic matters, foreign observers from Dickens to Chevallier were impressed immediately by the quality of American life, characterized as it was by what they called the American's "restless desire for wealth." What Mrs. Trollope referred to as the "giddy passion of money-getting," Francis Grund saw as "the very soul of an American."[12] And while incapable of generalizing from evidence as Tocqueville would do, even American writers occasionally displayed a consciousness of this powerful tendency. Thus, writing in 1864, Thomas Low Nichols attacked those who found America abounding in happiness. "I never thought America *was* a happy country," he wrote, "only that it ought to be. In all the years of peace and plenty we were not happy." The main source of unhappiness was readily apparent. "The first element of happiness . . . is contentment. There is no such thing in America as being contented with one's position or condition. The poor struggle to be rich, the rich to be richer. Everyone is tugging, trying, scheming to advance — to get ahead. It is a great scramble, in which all are troubled and none satisfied." Underlying this scramble was the very nature of American society. "Why," Nichols asked, "the universal struggle for wealth? Because it is the only thing needful; the only secure power, the only real distinction. Americans speak of a man being *worth* so many thousands or millions. Nowhere is money sought so eagerly; nowhere is it so much valued; and in no civilized country does it bring so little to its possessor." In this circumstance Nichols looked longingly at the warmth of domestic affection to be found in the Old World. "America," he felt, "is strangely destitute of these affections . . . It would be too much to say that Americans were without natural affection; but it is strange how little they appear to have."[13]

If these observations are even partially accurate, and there is considerable additional evidence to the same effect (see Chapter 5), then Americans in the Jacksonian era already manifested certain tendencies that later in the century Emile Durkheim would define as anomic.

☆

[11] Alexis de Tocqueville, *Democracy in America*, Reeves-Bowen text, revised and edited by Phillips Bradley, Vintage Books, Inc., Alfred A. Knopf, Inc., New York, 1957, vol. II, p. 147.

[12] See Chapter 5 in this volume for a more complete treatment of this theme.

[13] "Forty Years of American Life: 1821-1861," in George E. Probst (ed.), *The Happy Republic, A Reader in Tocqueville's America*, Harper & Brothers, New York, 1962, pp. 29-31.

And if in fact anomie was rife in American society, the realization of community would have been almost entirely out of the question.

Durkheim held that men cannot tolerate a condition in which desires are continually "threatened" by the prospect of imminent gratification. Men must have a sense of limitation or else they lose their bearings, they become perpetually dissatisfied with what they have and seek always to gain something more, something new. The tensions produced by such concupiscence, when spread throughout society and when perceptible gaps develop between certain wants and their satisfaction, result in a generalized state of anomie, a condition of unclarity, rootlessness, and personal disorientation. By definition such a society cannot constitute a community. It can only hope to maintain social balance and avoid serious dislocations.[14] To the extent that economic individualism kept Americans agitated in this way, their relations may be described as anomic rather than communal.

The argument is not that America was totally anticommunal or that it never bore the slightest resemblance to community. If de Grazia is correct, no people can be entirely without community since their infantile experiences of complete dependence tend to create communal behavior patterns that are never entirely left behind. Generally speaking, however, it may be said that communal feelings in America were relatively weak and that little in the way of support was provided for the development of what de Grazia implied was a "natural sense of community." The (debatable) fact that with the exception of the Civil War period America grew and prospered more or less harmoniously throughout most of the nineteenth century is not necessarily evidence of high communal feelings. Turner's argument that the frontier long provided a safety valve in the form of an ever-expanding area for indi-

☆

[14] Following the logic of this argument, it may be necessary to reevaluate certain analyses of contemporary American life based upon judgments made of nineteenth century America. David Riesman and others, for example, have contended that the other-directed, conforming citizen of today represents a departure from the nineteenth century citizen who tended to be independent of mind and spirit and nonconforming in behavior. The modern American, so the argument runs, confronted by a complex, confusing, and fragmented world of industrialization and mass assembly lines, becomes bewildered and uncertain of his own position of worth. He feels, one might say, very much like the anomic man described by Durkheim, and as a result he looks beyond himself for leadership and direction and conforms rigidly, almost desperately, to what he feels are the values deemed acceptable by his society. But it may be that dramatic social and industrial changes have produced differences in degree only and not differences in kind. For, if we can believe the reports of countless foreign observers, nineteenth century Americans were frequently conspicuous in their conformity and in their intolerance of innovative or unpopular opinion. The problem is unquestionably more severe in the twentieth century, and the pressures and demands of contemporary life have undoubtedly contributed to this situation. It may be, however, that it has been more of a case of adding to an old problem than of creating an entirely new one.

vidual exploitation may be more to the point. The open frontier may simply have had the effect of keeping internal frictions to a minimum and of giving the nation the appearance of overall harmony. But as far as community is concerned, appearances can be very deceiving. As Toennies pointed out, Gesellschaft and Gemeinschaft resemble each other insofar as people live peacefully within both; but, he cautioned: "in the Gemeinschaft they remain essentially united in spite of all separating factors, whereas in the Gesellschaft they are essentially separated in spite of all uniting factors.[15] In America the factors that kept men apart tended to outweigh those that held them together.

The important point in this study is not the low level of community in America, but that by and large American political theorists remained impervious to this phenomenon. It may have been the case that, irrespective of the individualistic national purpose, demographic and/or ecological pressures would ultimately preclude the growth of a national sense of community. Notwithstanding this eventuality, American writers might have started with the givens of economic abundance and perhaps have imagined a communal society emerging therefrom. At the very least they might have displayed a conscious awareness that the absence of such a possibility constituted something of a problem. For the most part, however, one finds neither the construction of a theory nor a treatment of the issue in the literature. Whatever the categories of American political discourse, ideas of community or fraternity were not primary among them. For most writers America would be a land where interest and ambition would dominate and where interdependence, to the extent that it was comprehended, would be defined as a strictly private business. Why this was the case is partly the result of the character of American political thought itself.

The Nature of American Political Theory

American political thought differs in important ways from traditional political theory. The greatest figures in the tradition, those, in fact, whose writings worked to establish the tradition, typically possessed two very powerful and interrelated skills: the capacity to stand off, at least for a time, from their immediate environment, and the ability to let their imaginative faculties carry their speculations beyond the demands of historical circumstance. Possessed of these skills, a Hobbes, a Plato, or a Rousseau could begin by treating genuine problems of the day, but could not rest at this level for long. Soon their speculative

☆

[15] *Fundamental Concepts of Sociology (Gemeinschaft und Gesellschaft)*, translated by Charles P. Loomis, American Book Company, New York, 1940.

impulses moved their arguments into more abstract realms, into considerations of generic meaning or universal application. Sometimes their analyses soared onto an artistic plane where aesthetic concerns rivaled those of logic or consistency. At other times the focus turned to matters that were epistemological and often metaphysical in nature. In all events the tradition has been essentially esoteric and most of its contributors have been involved in what I should like to call "dialectical myth-making."

Their endeavors were dialectical in that they began by responding to specific problems of their times. Their responses consequently cannot be fully understood unless one examines their particular historical contexts. On the other hand, they were engaged in myth-making in that they transcended the imperatives of the immediate and allowed their work to range far and wide and to reflect upon the largest of political questions. At this level no amount of contextual analysis can prove very revealing of the writer's intentions. A two-level format is exhibited as well by the "realist," Machiavelli, whose Prince is finally an Olympian figure of mythological proportions, as it is by Plato, whose Republic is a fabulous land, the mythical proportions of which are readily apparent. It is the creative power of myth-making and not the ability to propound "political wisdom" that has kept the tradition alive and provided intellectual satisfaction to those who study the history of political theory.

Generally speaking, this cannot be said about American political theory, for American thought has seldom reached heights of imaginative creation. More often it has been the extension of political action, the legalistic rationalization of, or apologetic for, various short-range political programs. American political theory has seldom risen far above the level of action and has been inextricably related to the facts of American history in a way uncharacteristic of its more philosophical antecedents. The most renowned American theorists have in fact been themselves political actors, men whose ruminations could never stray far from the object at hand. The very relationship between thought and action has been something of a problem for American thinkers, a serious problem for the political scholar who would make sense of the history of American thought. Robert McCloskey has perhaps come closest to delineating accurately the proper dimensions of American political theory. The following remarks are roughly based on his argument.[16]

American political thought tends to be reflective (as a mirror is reflective) and uncritical. It typically expresses and reaffirms the

☆

[16]Robert McCloskey, "American Political Thought and the Study of Politics," in Roland Young (ed.), op. cit.

political and cultural norms of the society. Unlike traditional political theory, it is most often *non*dialectical: that is, it begins, not by critically analyzing the bases of institutions and procedures, but by accepting as given much of the political and social order of the time. It is usually closely related to particular historical facts and for this reason is normally studied to gain a better comprehension of actual political currents in various periods. One can engage in a similar study of Plato only dialectically, by deducing from his propositions what it was that he was responding to. And even this effort is intellectually perilous, for one can never know with absolute certainty where the Platonic critique ends and the myth-making begins.

History, Thought, and Action

Of course this argument about American theory cannot be pushed too far. It applies more directly to eighteenth and nineteenth century writings than it does to those of the twentieth century. Even prior to 1900 there were occasional American political thinkers who critically analyzed the going concern in a fundamental way, and others whose thought transcended the peculiar boundaries of American life. As a general assessment, however, McCloskey's position has much to recommend it, and American theory may plausibly be taken as at least a partial index of American political experience.

It is easy to make this case and then, as some do, to write American theory off as nontheory or, at best, as collections of ideological statements. It is true that American thought is usually close to action and often expressed as ideology, but it does not fail entirely and in all respects to reach the level of theory. It is perhaps best seen as *partial theory*, attenuated statements that, while giving a somewhat fragmented and piecemeal picture, frequently contain explanations and propositions of considerable theoretical importance. This is certainly true of the early American writers who were in some ways the most creative in American history. Their creativity, however, while genuine, was of a practical sort: it took what was given and sought to rearrange or reconstitute it into a new but by no means original structure. It was hardly a Platonic or Hobbesian creativity that begins with particular questions and culminates in the formulation of entirely new mental constructs. This is not unexpected, for Adams, Jefferson, et al., had to confront the oppressively real task of establishing an actual state. They were essentially men of action who had to operate the very system they helped design. They could never alienate or remove themselves from the reality about them as men of thought often do. Thus it has been for most American political thinkers. Preoccupied with the facts of American life, they have been unable to stand off and entertain questions that might go to the very foundations of political order. Consequently, their theory generally remains unfulfilled. It tends to encompass some, but rarely all, of the variables of a more comprehensive political theory.

While this has been the shortcoming of American thought (for it has produced few, if any, superior contributions), from the perspective of the contemporary scholar it is also its singular advantage. Its very proximity to the realm of action suggests that we can learn something both about theoretical formulations *and* about the genesis of those political ideas that Americans espouse today. Thus, while we may not experience the elevation of mind or the expansion of imagination derived from reading traditional theory, we receive much compensation in the form of a new understanding of where we have been, where we are today, and why we believe what we do. American political thought provides, at least for the American student, a kind of material generally unavailable to the student of traditional European political philosophy. For the most part one does not read Plato to understand Athens, nor Marsilio to understand the Italian republican city-state, but one does and must read Jefferson, Madison, and Hamilton in order to understand early America. And, it should be added, it is only through such an understanding that we can begin to comprehend a contemporary American reality whose roots lie deep in the past.

The student of American political theory is consequently placed in a unique position. He has the best, or the worst, of two possible worlds, depending upon how one views the situation. He must, if he respects his subject matter, treat it as real theory, material that, despite its inadequacies, merits in its own right careful and thoughtful consideration. On the other hand, he must, because of the nature of the material, read it as commentary upon and embodiment of significant patterns in the polity at large. This dual focus is probably impossible to maintain for very long. It soon must give way either to double vision or to a completely blurred picture. It is therefore necessary to make use of alternating modes of analysis; one must be prepared to shift the perspective from theory as theory to theory as reflection, from ideas as ideas to ideas as symbols, as common denominators, as ideological particles. Commentaries on American political thought have characteristically taken the latter tack exclusively and have thereby tended to depreciate the value of the endeavor.

The proximity of American political thought to historical events suggests reasons why American writers were largely unable to develop a theory of community. In one way or another they were closely connected to the nation's institutions, especially to its national purpose, and while their ideas were sometimes radical when measured by continental standards, they could not be radically communitarian with respect to potentialities and possibilities of their own country. One should perhaps put this in the form of a paradox, for it may have been the case that the most radical political component of the national purpose ruled out of consideration the only possible vehicle for the realization of community. This paradox can be unravelled by constructing a hypothetical case for community that might have been relevant to eighteenth and nineteenth century circumstances.

Community and Government

While mindful of the pitfalls inherent in historicism, it does not seem unreasonable to argue that central to any modern theory of community would have been a positive concept of government. And since one of the essential ingredients of community would be a concern on the part of most citizens for society as a whole, government would perhaps have been the only institution capable of carrying such a concern. It is certainly difficult to imagine alternatives to government once one notes the final passing of folk society and acknowledges that religion provided a less meaningful bond among men than had previously been the case. If in an earlier period Christian philosophers could posit generalized notions of a "gathered community," it was both because religious bonds were firmer *and* because civil authority could be counted upon to supply those fundamental needs of subsistence and order which the religious fraternity could either take for granted or largely ignore. With the advent of religious pluralism, any new conception of community would have to deal directly with problems of order and subsistence. In this connection government seems the only collective institution capable of representing the aspirations of a society in which interdependence would matter. Acting on behalf of the entire society, government could serve to retain the idea of a larger community to which all belonged. It could reach across wide distances to bring isolated citizens somewhat closer together.

We have already seen how the American experience ran counter to other components of community. To support communal feelings, a nation must seek to preserve certain cherished institutions as well as engage in creative innovation; it must value collective responsibility as well as individual incentive; it must espouse goals over and above those of economic self-aggrandizement. If a commitment to the ends of economic individualism prevented Americans from adopting these views, this commitment constituted an even stronger barrier to *political* aspects of community. Government could act as a transmitter and protector of communal values only if the people were willing to invest it with the authority necessary to accomplish these tasks. This above all Americans were unprepared to do.

The dramatic changes in outlook attending the shift from folk to modern society everywhere involved an explicit deposition of established authority and the gradual rise of egalitarianism. Americans were in the forefront of this change. Having felt what they took to be the heavy hand of political oppression, they understandably looked askance at all manifestations of political authority. They sought, insofar as possible, to relegate government to a secondary level where it would be unable to act repressively with respect to society as a whole. This attitude, radical in itself, was powerfully reenforced by the intensely individualistic national purpose. There is a distinction to be made between the rejection of old structures of authority and the repudiation of political authority per se. Liberty as defined by the national purpose demanded that economic individualism be allowed to run its course free from all political constraints. It insisted that, except when serving the interests of liberalism as such, government should be held in severe confinement and should be regarded as an institution whose legitimacy is scarcely defensible.

This radical perspective dominated not only the thinking of most citizens, but also much of American political philosophy; consequently, it worked to prevent the development of community in theory as well as in practice. The intensity of American liberalism placed all government in an unfavorable light, cast immediate doubt upon the motives of political actors, and ultimately deprived the political sphere of the authority needed to act for the whole citizenry.[17] American writers were unprepared to deal from this position with a large number of difficult problems connected with the issue of community.

Logical Corollaries

Had they given communal possibilities serious attention they would, for example, have had to distinguish its new formulation from that which obtained in earlier times. Clearly articulated distinctions between community of the older, small-society variety and the communal potentialities of a large modern nation would have been essential, as would the question of whether community was feasible in the first place in the New World. By the same token, it would have been impor-

☆

[17]At the Philadelphia Convention the founding fathers struck a somewhat middle position with respect to political authority. Their constitutionalism allowed for a vague kind of authority that emanated from a system of sanctioned rules and procedures. It was not, however, of sufficient strength to lend legitimacy to political action, either by the government or by the populace. Moreover, it was subject to the serious qualifications of Madisonianism (see Chapter 2).

tant to notice that previous communalism, whether a function of the extended family, church organization, the guild system, or the feudal manor, always involved a significant degree of interpersonal subordination, frequently the imposition of outright servitude. To replicate older models would have been either to ignore entirely the question of equality or to announce a willingness to expend the principle of equality as the necessary price for building community.

American writers would also have been forced to make clear where or whether community and political action came together. Whereas in medieval times the communal order was often a pre-political function of associational life, and where for Aristotle the social and political realms coalesced in the forum—thereby creating a "natural" kind of public community—the contemporary mode of civilization that divided society into social, political, and economic functions, into public and private spheres, would be faced with the logical problem of delineating and perhaps of reconciling governmental activity and communal aspirations. If in the process American theorists found themselves involved in establishing subtle boundary lines in the manner that Rousseau distinguished between the general will and the will of all, this would not be surprising, for such a process of differentiating is inherent in approaching problems of national community.

An attempt to relate community to other factors would have had the added effect of concentrating attention on certain problems intrinsic to the American system as already constructed; namely personal equality and public authority. As already indicated, the latter was largely ruled irrelevant in the context of economic individualism. But though irrelevant as far as the ideology was concerned, the development of concentrated power was a political fact of life and, since it was conceptually beyond the pale, it went its natural course unchecked by conscious norms of legitimacy. Thus when Andrew Jackson extended the purview of the executive branch in the 1830's, the only possible negative response by popular critics was to accuse him of becoming a monarchist; that is, of undermining the entire republican system. At the same time, the theoreticians engaged in a totally artificial legal dispute over the stretchability of the elastic clause in the Constitution. The fact was that executive power, responding to nationwide difficulties, continued to expand throughout the nineteenth century without theoretical justification for its authority. A discussion of communal goals and the political means of reaching such goals would have forced political thinkers at least to address this problem-laden area.

The question of equality might have been dealt with similarly. The contemplation of community would inevitably have led to a full consideration of what it really means to be treated fairly in a society where it is truly believed that men are created equal. Without this, equality was either left as a residual category, the lowest common denominator among men, or was defined procedurally as equality of opportunity. Neither approach gave substantial meaning to equality. The former simply indicated, as Tocqueville noted, that to strive for equality meant to enforce a repressive levelling process on society. The latter represented a direct extension of economic individualism for it implied a competitive quest for material gain and the eventual acceptance of inequality, provided that an approximate equality of position existed at the starting point. And since America itself, in its very expanse and abundance, could be seen as imposing a natural equality of opportunity—all could succeed who really tried—the grossest inequalities could, and ultimately would, be sanctioned.

The attempt to construct a theory of community based on political action might finally have had the effect of directing American writers to their own past. Communal experience, perhaps even a theory of community, had, after all, existed in early America in the form of New England Puritanism. It might have been enormously useful to attempt a transformation of Puritan community, which on its own was theocratic and somewhat totalitarian in propensity, into a modern shape appropriate to the demands of egalitarianism and the new republican institutions. But, with the possible exception of certain utopian settlements in the 1820's and 1840's, this was not done, and one senses that in certain important respects the growth of America along individualistic lines constituted a semiconscious effort to escape from Puritanical influences, an endeavor to avoid confronting the nation's own origins. It is probably no accident that Puritanism remained alive only in the repressed regions of the bleak and essentially irrelevant New England conscience or, following the reasoning of Tawney and Weber, as sheer moral rationalization for capitalist acquisitiveness.

The Contemporary Legacy

More important than possible theoretical ellipses connected with the lack of speculation about community, however, is the absence of communal thought per se. The customary mode of American theory has left us ill-equipped to think effectively about the situation before us *today*. And the current situation is far more serious. Not only do social and political factors carry infinitely more explosive potential than in the past, but the nation confronts these factors in a context possessed now of neither community *nor* purpose. Economic individualism began to lose currency at the turn of the century as collective enterprise by both public and private agencies began to dominate society in a massive way. As the national purpose lost effect no new ideology was developed to take its place, no twentieth century purpose appeared to take hold of and direct men's aspirations and activities. Since economic individualism had worked to discourage movement toward community, America was now plunged fully into the modern internationalized world, with neither a sense of community to promote internal solidarity nor a national purpose to guide the exercise of public policy.[18] As we face this reality today we find that American political thought has not provided us with useful or satisfying ways of responding.

While theoretical expositions of community by eighteenth and nineteenth century writers may not have been able to shift national directions, they may at least have had the effect of establishing an intellectual tradition that would provide starting points for critical analysis. But, for reasons already given, American political theory could not adopt a very critical stance. Thus, when such twentieth century writers as Croly and Dewey began to deal with these issues, they found they could reach the heart of the matter only by repudiating or drastically reinterpreting the entire line of theory that preceded them. This is still very much the case for the political commentator today. He will understand the reasons for contemporary conditions better, or perhaps only, by exploring earlier theories; but the attempt to deal positively with problems of community and purpose will perforce constitute an effort at philosophical creativity.

Theoretical Qualifications

This post hoc discussion of considerations related to the theory of community is, of course, highly abstract and therefore subject to criticisms from various perspectives. The most obvious is that of reading into history problems and definitions that bear only contemporary significance. I know of no way to meet this objection except to say that I am aware of this danger and have tried hard to avoid it. In many respects the arguments in subsequent chapters will attempt, however indirectly, to validate the chosen categories of analysis.

As to the particular communal notions outlined, many points of contention are relevant. It could be argued, for example, that community born of a more collective national purpose might threaten the existence of pluralism, the political and social rights of groups and individuals, and that it might encourage an excess of nationalist emotion, and possibly even the development of totalitarianism. These are im-

☆

[18]For a somewhat fuller explanation of this transition, see the concluding pages of Chapter 8 in this volume.

portant considerations and, since the problems of community and purpose are *consciously* before America today, they will be dealt with systematically in the final chapter, which is addressed to contemporary affairs. It is perhaps enough at this point to note that, insofar as this retrospective treatment is concerned, few, if any, American writers confronted these conceptual conflicts; since community itself was beyond their frame of reference, the possible "dangers" of community were scarcely to be appreciated.

It is the primary aim of this book to use the community-purpose dichotomy as a touchstone for the analysis of American political thought. This means that no explicit attempt will be made to demonstrate a causal relationship between these two central concepts. It will not be "proven" beyond a doubt that the presence of the national purpose led ineluctably to the absence of community. As already noted, many factors may have contributed to weak communal sentiments in America. On the other hand, if the *logical* distinction between community and economic individualism is valid, then used as a point of departure it ought to yield fresh insights into the character and direction of American political philosophy. It is precisely these new insights that this book seeks to lay before the reader. The argument about purpose and community will prove useful to the extent that it permits a more meaningful interpretation of political theory in America than heretofore presented.

Because the argument concerns the mainstream of American life, the writers selected for analysis are with few exceptions drawn from the mainstream itself. This being the case, intellectual, social, and political impact of some noticeable significance constitutes the chief criterion for inclusion. Excluded on this ground are some writers whose thoughts on a variety of counts may rival or surpass those of the men chosen for consideration.[19] Notably missing are black writers whose ideas until very recently have not been afforded the respectful attention of literate white America. There is a bitter logic to the typical absence of black people in historical studies of American ideas. Intellectual histories are based upon the recorded reflections of men who have mattered. Since they were denied the opportunity to be men, let alone men who could matter, black contributors to the historical record of American ideas have naturally been limited. Politically speaking, those blacks who refused to be silenced understandably

☆

[19] Excluded as well, for obvious historical reasons, are those American thinkers who wrote during the colonial period; that is, prior to the time the country became a single nation. Mainstream considerations also preclude treatment of utopian communities based on the ideas of Owen and Fourier that were established in the 1820's and 1840's. I am currently investigating the possibility of whether a uniquely American theory of community emerged from these experiments.

concentrated on the effort to gain freedom for themselves and their people. Broader speculations on the nature of political society were a luxury they could seldom afford. Only in very recent years have black intellectuals been able to theorize about comprehensive political considerations. The history of their American political philosophy is perhaps only now beginning to get underway.

In keeping with the argument about the limits of American political theory, the reader will note that many of the expositions run a similar course. This goes somewhat as follows: (1) a painful awareness by the particular theorist of certain social and political problems; then (2) a forceful, sometimes radical, critique of important institutions and procedures; followed by (3) a tempering or narrowing of the argument so that in the end it does not break too drastically from accepted norms. This format was not predetermined and then imposed on the subject matter so that it would conform to one of the book's principal theses. Rather it emerged "naturally" as the materials were probed and analyzed. At the same time it undoubtedly does serve the purpose of demonstrating the powerful limitations on American thought. Yet many writers tried manfully to transcend their American environment, and from time to time a few were at least partially successful in the endeavor.

Since theoretical statements in America have been used largely as historical data, I have found it necessary at times to use the writers' own words in some detail to present their views as accurately as possible.[20] Unlike the history of political philosophy, one cannot take for granted an educated familiarity with the literature at hand. There are in American political discourse no instrumentalities as well known as Plato's cave, Hobbes' Leviathan, or Rousseau's noble savage. One of the hopes of this book is to redress this situation somewhat by giving American political thought the close attention it manifestly warrants.

☆

[20] For the most part quoted materials appear entirely in their original form. I have made no effort to indicate or to correct errors of spelling or syntax and have taken only an occasional liberty with commas and capital letters for purposes of clarification.

2

THE CONSERVATIVE EXPRESSION
JAMES MADISON
JOHN ADAMS

The Lockean Tradition in America

In a famous passage in *The Second Treatise on Government*, John Locke wrote: "in the beginning all the world was America." For Locke, America symbolized that state of nature wherein land abounded and the simple process of mixing human labor with nature's soil produced a right to property approximately equal for all men. But the founders of the American nation lived a century after Locke, and, if one were to follow a Lockean sequence of events, it might be proper to say that their America had come to resemble Locke's state of nature-become-corrupt, ready for and in need of the rules and regulations of civil society. In this condition property is no longer disproportionately greater than population; men have by this time acquired property in unequal portions, and as the absolute quantity of land diminishes, there can be envisaged a day when one man's gain inevitably involves another man's loss. For those who have established ownership, government becomes a necessary instrument of protection, and the protection of property is understood as directly relating to the defense of liberty, order, and stability. Although this interpretation refers to America only metaphorically, for many Americans it provided, consciously or unconsciously, whether they had read Locke or not, a most important application of Lockean principles. Armed with these convictions, they could give conservative expression to an economic individualism that, in the view of some, threatened to close the door on the more liberal or acquisitive side of the national purpose.

Liberals and Conservatives

The terms "liberal" and "conservative" are used here for want of better ones, for there existed in America an early consensus on some very fundamental points that, by comparative standards, was liberal in the extreme. For example, neither the early conservatives (Madison and Adams) nor the early liberals (Jefferson and Paine) accepted traditional doctrines of governmental legitimacy based on older ideas of national sovereignty. In fact, the usual practice, time-honored in Europe, of construing and redefining the concept of sovereignty, was completely abandoned by the Americans, who turned directly to establishing principles for a society founded on individual rights. Such a society would involve a profound adherence to the idea of liberty, and implicit in this conception was a contractual notion of citizenship. Thus, whereas the European, even the European of the French Revolution, could speak of a sovereign nation to which the individual surrendered certain basic rights to obtain the peace, justice, and fraternity afforded by civil society, the American thought in terms of a compact wherein citizens maintained *all* natural rights and where government remained a legitimate party to the compact only so long as those rights persisted. Both the conservative and liberal positions focused on the independent individual and his attendant rights and freedoms; from such a perspective neither could countenance a consolidation of political power that by definition would jeopardize the status of individual rights.

The difference between the two lay more in how personal rights were made operational than in how they were conceived. The liberal, with a general faith in enlightened human nature, required a more equalitarian starting point where the right to life, liberty, and property was seen as natural to all members of society. Government consequently had for the liberal the distinct function of ensuring that the starting gates remained open and that no one began the race with an excessively disproportionate handicap. In economic terms, government had the dual obligation of rendering society secure for the ownership of property and of maintaining an approximate condition of equality so that no one was permanently denied the right to acquire property. Beyond these areas government was expressly forbidden to trespass.

The conservative, unable to ignore the painful lessons of history, emphasized the rights *of*, rather than the right *to*, property.[1] Liberty and independence, the cornerstones of republican government and the theoretical possessions of all men, were fragile elements that could survive only under the watchful care of those members of society best able to use the powers of reason. Property ownership, both because it invested men with a sense of responsibility and attested to a man's capability and resourcefulness, engendered a more or less natural class of reasonable men which could be expected to maintain constant guard over republican virtues. Hence, property rights were seen as having logical priority over other rights, for no rights could be regarded as safe unless the rights of property were initially secured. This was especially true in the state of American civil society (as opposed to the theoretical state of nature) where the incipient problems of scarcity could already be appreciated. In such a situation government must perforce be so constructed that the fixed interests of the propertied class receive in perpetuity adequate representation. This could best be done by erecting a system that would guarantee conservative rules and regulations by building the interests of property directly into the legislative process.

In neither the liberal nor the conservative formulations was the citizenry forged into a social unity. Both emphasized individual independence and accomplishment, and if the conservatives could find a cohesion of sorts in property ownership, it was a very weak cohesion that seemed to supply little more than a common fear of radical egalitarianism. Conservatives, in fact, posited a rather rigid set of economic interests between which there was often competition, if not open hostility. The liberal, on the other hand, theoretically abolished all classes and with them the bonds of connection that in the Old World supplied a social cement of common heritage and status. Man was now left alone to pursue his interests as he saw fit. Both the liberal and the conservative believed in economic individualism, but with the added qualification that in property the conservative found an economic interest in need of special attention. While the full economic content of the national purpose would not be completely furnished to either side until the Jacksonian period, a reliance on an individualism based on economic arguments could be seen even at this early period. These arguments tended to turn on the concepts of property held by each side.

☆

[1] For an insightful discussion of early ideological similarities see Richard Hofstadter, *The American Political Tradition*, Alfred A. Knopf, Inc., New York, 1948, Introduction, chaps. I and II.

Conservative Individualism and the Problem of Property

These liberal and conservative delineations of American purpose in the 1780's and 1790's must be seen as extreme ends of a continuum, and the ideological dispute that took place at the center was often confused by a mixture of contradictory principles. Even in retrospect, however, there seems to have been good cause for confusion. It has often been pointed out, for example, that eighteenth century man did not always distinguish between property rights and the rights of person: "who said property," writes Hannah Arendt, "said freedom, and to recover or defend one's property rights was the same as to fight for freedom."[2] There is much to be said for this argument, but it is also clear that for many early American thinkers, property and liberty were not indistinguishable concepts. James Madison, for one, was entirely capable of separating the two. And the ability to make this distinction also had its analogue in Lockean writings, for in the *Second Treatise* we find the same division: property on the one hand defined as "real" property, and property seen as the repository of life and liberty as well. To miss this distinction in America is to miss the conservative side of economic individualism. Hans Morgenthau, in his stimulating book, *The Purpose of American Politics,* is somewhat insensitive to this conservatism, and consequently his interpretation of American purpose is, I believe, slightly misconstrued.

Morgenthau's basic concept of national purpose is very close to my own. He sees America dedicated to freedom, which he defines as equality of opportunity and the minimization of governmental control. America, according to Morgenthau, got into difficulty when it attempted to expand this "equality in freedom" to other parts of the continent. Here the large Southern reservation to the common ideology asserted itself and resulted in "The Denial"; that is, in a restrictive interpretation of freedom that actually denied the principles of equal opportunity for all.[3] But it may be erroneous to attribute the "negative" side of the ideology to one particular class or section. Conservative individualism existed side by side with liberal individualism, sometimes in the mind of the same person. Even diehard Federalist Fisher Ames could touch both sides of the equation. "All cannot be rich," he wrote, "but all have a right to make the attempt; and when some have fully succeeded, and others partially, and others not at all, the several states in which they then find themselves become their condition in

☆

[2] Hannah Arendt, *On Revolution,* The Viking Press, Inc., New York, 1963, p. 180.
[3] Hans Morgenthau, *The Purpose of American Politics,* Alfred A. Knopf, Inc., New York, 1960, pp. 27-34, 36-39.

life; and whatever the rights of that condition may be, they are to be faithfully secured by the laws and government."[4] While Thomas Jefferson could never agree with Ames' doctrine, he too found it necessary to concern himself with the rights of property. Whereas property could under no circumstances be the sole defining characteristic of personal freedom for Jefferson, neither could he visualize a man with genuine freedom, that is, social independence, who did not own a substantial amount of real property. Thus in the proposed 1776 constitution for Virginia, Jefferson stipulated that every person not already in possession of fifty acres of land should be ceded this amount by the state.[5] While Jefferson shared the general conviction that property rights were crucial, he sometimes spoke as though property ownership were instrumental, that it provided a means without which men could not protect their more personal rights. Moreover, his distribution recommendation presupposed a land supply still far in excess of demand. For these and other reasons his conception of property possessed distinctly liberal connotations.

This was not quite the case with John Adams. Morgenthau further argues that because it consciously moved toward complete innovation, the American Revolution was a self-perpetuating, evolving, institution with no definite beginning or end; and he uses the words of John Adams to support this position. But Adams had another side. It was Adams who compared the revolutions of 1776 and 1789 by saying, "Ours was resistance to innovation, theirs was innovation itself."[6] Although the particular "innovations" referred to in this case were restrictions imposed on America by the Crown, Adams' animus against sheer innovation had general application. As late as 1820 he was able to recommend to a Massachusetts constitutional convention that there be a property qualification for voting. The fact was that the founding generation contained elements that stoutly resisted equalitarianism, even as it applied to the area of economic opportunity. Their commitment was always paradoxical in that it encouraged freedom for all while at the same time it sought to protect, at least to a limited extent, the distribution of property that obtained at the present moment. It was not John Adams, however, who most clearly expressed this position, but James Madison, whose feelings about property rights tended to color most of his other reflections on political matters.

☆

[4] "Equality," no. II, 1801, Seth Ames (ed.), *The Works of Fisher Ames,* Boston, 1854, vol. II, p. 211.

[5] Julian Boyd et al. (eds.), *The Papers of Thomas Jefferson,* Princeton University Press, Princeton, N.J., 1950–, vol. I, pp. 343-344, 352, 362.

[6] Page Smith, *John Adams,* Doubleday & Company, Inc., Garden City, N.Y. 1962, vol. II, p. 955.

James Madison

This is perhaps an unconventional description of Madison, who is often best remembered for his liberal leadership of the Jeffersonian Republican movement and his lifelong defense of civil liberties. Madison tended to stress the conservative half of the national purpose, and this emphasis had a formative impact on the remainder of his theory. While firmly believing in popular government and majority rule, and fully sensitive to the multifarious causes of disorder, he was compelled by his concern for property rights and his fear of attacks on property to construct a theory that emphasized competition and combat, and that would "create" a nation broken into self-contained fragments of interest.

The Threat to Property

Thus in *The Federalist*, Madison offered theoretical justification for a form of government that fractured society into autonomous segments so that a majority faction either would not be able to form behind a unifying interest or, once unified, would not have an opportunity to exert power in behalf of its interest. "If the impulse and the opportunity be suffered to coincide," Madison admonished, "we well know that neither moral nor religious motives can be relied on as an adequate control."[7] Though Madison referred to many factional interests, it is clear that the faction which dominated his thinking is the one that represented a threat to property. Not only was the unequal distribution of property seen as "the most common and durable source of factions" and "an insuperable obstacle to a uniformity of interests," but when Madison came to list those "improper or wicked" acts that a majority faction might attempt, he specified only three: "a rage for paper money, for an abolition of debts, for an equal division of property;"[8] that is, acts detrimental to the rights and security of the propertied class.

Madison was critically concerned about the general problem of order and he consequently worried about factions of every description. Thus, simply by looking at some of his strictures in *The Federalist*, No. 10, it may seem somewhat unfair to suggest that he concentrated narrowly on property rights, especially since Madison was often capable of rising above his material and of balancing, as prudence would dictate, all sides of the questions at issue. Yet, when Madison's

☆

[7] Jacob E. Cooke (ed.), *The Federalist*, Wesleyan University Press, Middletown, Conn., 1961, no. 10, p. 61.

[8] *Ibid.*, pp. 58, 59, 65.

other writings are consulted, one finds that when he specifies what a pernicious faction might do to threaten the rights and liberties of the citizenry, he almost always lists, as in *The Federalist*, No. 10, only those actions that property interests regarded as dangerous to their security. Madison's commitment to order based on prudence automatically placed property at the forefront of his theory, for he felt that prudence itself was best expressed by that element of society that had lawful possession of the land.

His argument had many dimensions, ranging from an apparent moral conviction of the superior wisdom of property, to an appreciation that ownership produced social stability because it gave men a stake in an orderly society. Madison could be very hard on those who opposed property interests. In *The Federalist*, No. 44, he indicted the purveyors of paper money with an uncharacteristic vehemence. He instructed his countrymen that "the loss which America has sustained . . . from the pestilent effects of paper money, on the necessary confidence between man and man; on the necessary confidence in the public councils; on the industry and morals of the people, and on the character of Republican Government, constitutes an enormous debt against the States chargeable with this unadvised measure, which must long remain unsatisfied; or rather an accumulation of guilt, which can be expiated no otherwise than by a voluntary sacrifice on the altar of justice, of the power which has been the instrument of it."[9] Paper money, then, must be extirpated, for it corrupts the soul of the entire society. Madison's positive argument *for* property rights was usually made on less emotional grounds and to understand it we must turn to his other works.

Madison invariably started from the same position: namely, that irrespective of the quantity of land initially available or of the kinds of mitigating devices subsequently employed, all societies must eventually divide into two groups, those who possess property and those who do not—or in Madison's own words, "the owners of the soil, and the other inhabitants."[10] There is, of course, a clear difference between an America that possesses a superabundance of land at the present time and a Europe that has a surplus of population and has long since passed into a fixed and closed system of proprietorship. In 1786 Jefferson wrote to Madison from France commenting on the wretched conditions of the French poor. To remedy this situation and give every Frenchman at least a parcel of land, Jefferson recommended the abolition of primogeniture and the establishment of a taxation system that

☆

[9] *Ibid.*, p. 300.

[10] "Speech at the Constitutional Convention," Gaillard Hunt (ed.), *The Writings of James Madison*, G. P. Putnam's Sons, New York, 1900-1910, vol. IV, p. 124.

would exact contributions exclusively of the wealthy. Madison replied that while certain measures might prove meliorative, an equal distribution of land could not be expected to work in a nation that is "fully peopled."[11] The idea of this future condition, when land would no longer be plentiful enough for a fully peopled America, played a central role in Madison's thinking.

Protection for the Propertied Class

Madison hoped to create institutions that would give to property a perpetual and influential increment of political power. The Senate, he thought, might be such an institution, elected as it would be by the more substantial part of society and possessing an absolute check on the popularly elected and therefore potentially immoderate House of Representatives.[12] Madison thus felt that it would be entirely proper for a senator to serve a nine-year term in office, and he argued strenuously for this provision in the Constitutional Convention. "The landed interest, at present, is prevalent," Madison told his colleagues, "but . . . when we approximate to the states and kingdoms of Europe [the] increase of population will of necessity increase the proportion of those who will labour under all the hardships of life, & secretly sigh for a more equal distribution of its blessings. Will not the landed interest be overbalanced in future elections, and unless wisely provided against, what will become of your government?" Evil things might indeed occur in the event that property lost its justified proportion of power, for, as Madison saw it, property itself represented the lasting interests of the nation. "Our government," he said, "ought to secure the permanent interests of the country against innovation. Landholders ought to have a share in the government, to support these invaluable interests and to balance and check the other. They ought to be so constituted as to protect the minority of the opulent against the majority."[13]

Another means of securing the interests of property could be furnished by a wise dispensation of voting right, and Madison, in a long note appended to his record of the Convention, gave his "full & mature view of the subject." He acknowledged at the outset that the right of

☆

[11] "To Jefferson," June 19, 1786, *ibid.*, vol. II, pp. 246-248.

[12] Madison actually wanted the checking system between the branches to go even further than the plan ultimately approved by the Convention. He argued that all bills should go before the President and the Supreme Court. If vetoed by both branches, a three-fourths vote in Congress would be necessary to override. *Ibid.*, vol. IV, p. 208.

[13] Max Farrand (ed.), *Records of the Federal Convention of 1787*, Yale University Press, New Haven, 1911-1937, vol. I, pp. 422, 431.

suffrage was fundamental to the justly constituted republican government. A problem arises, however, when suffrage is extended to comprehend the rights of persons *and* the rights of property. Both must be effectively protected, but property is in the greater danger from the enfranchised indigent, for "as the holders of property have at stake all the other rights common to those without property, they may be the more restrained from infringing, [and] less tempted to infringe, the rights of the latter." This problem becomes particularly grave when the potential for equitable land distribution is greatly reduced. Then we may expect to see majority injustices, such as agrarian laws, cancelation of debts, violation of contract, and other "levelling schemes." The rights of property are permanent and thus deserve, insofar as possible, permanent protections. In stating this case, Madison followed Locke and carried the argument, which in Locke remained implicit, to a clear and unqualified conclusion.

He began, as always, with the reminder that all nations divide into the owners of property and those who own none. "In a certain sense the country may be said to belong to the former. If each landholder has an exclusive property in his share, the Body of Landholders have an exclusive property in the whole. As the Soil becomes subdivided . . . the principle of natural law . . . vests in individuals an exclusive right to the portions of ground with which he has incorporated his labour & improvements." Others may have rights derived from birth, from their interest in the public domain, or from their support of the government, but they do not have the right to legislate over landed property without its explicit consent. How then can voting be so organized as to insure security both to property and to persons, since each has a justified claim to this security?

There are, according to Madison, five possible modes of suffrage. (1) Only the freeholders and those capable of purchasing property should vote. This plan is at once unjust, since it deprives large numbers of people of representation, and unpropitious, since it would make permanent the struggle between those who have and those who do not have property. (2) One branch of the government should be elected by proprietors, the other branch by the propertyless. This would be unfair to those with property "because the rights to be defended would be unequal, being on one side those of property as well as of persons, and on the other those of persons only." (3) One branch should be elected by property interests, the other by a combination of propertyowners and the rest. This would be the most appropriate method, for "if the holders of property would thus have a two-fold share of representation, they wd. have at the same time a two-fold stake in it, the rights of property as well as of persons, the two-fold object of political Institutions." (4) If universal suffrage must come about, then property can be protected through the establishment of enlarged districts whose representatives serve long terms in office. (5) If enlarged districts and extended tenure are also overruled, then property must fall back on (a) its "ordinary influence," including superior information, (b) a popular sense of justice resulting from a broadened education, and (c) the difficulty in combining for and effectuating attacks on property in an extensive country.

Madison could resign himself if necessary to accepting the last solution, for if there ever came an absolute choice it would be dangerous indeed to deny a voice to the masses in making the laws and in choosing the magistrates. "It is better that those having the greater interest at stake namely that of property & persons both, should be deprived of half their share in the Govt. than, that those having the lesser interest, that of personal rights only, should be deprived of the whole." It is to be hoped, however, that America will never have to choose between these alternatives, for although "the freeholders of the Country would be the safest depositories of Republican liberty," it is possible both to grant universal suffrage and to organize the political society so as to protect property rights.[14] To see how Madison went about this task we must turn again to *The Federalist*.

The Meaning of Property

But before returning to *The Federalist* a more elaborate discussion of Madison's conception of property is called for. When Madison spoke of property he usually meant substantial landed property, exclusive of financial and industrial interests. In his Convention remarks on the qualifications for elected representatives, he offered a clearly restricted definition of property (and perhaps an equally restricted definition of citizenship). He argued that representatives should not have to meet property qualifications, because "every class of Citizens should have an opportunity of making their rights be felt & understood in the public Councils. The three principal classes into which our citizens [are] divisible, [are] the landed the commercial, & the manufacturing."[15]

Property, to repeat, was at that time in no great danger in America: "The U. States have a precious advantage . . . in the actual distribution of property . . . and in the universal hope of acquiring property." Madison was in fact so sanguine about present circumstances that when Gouverneur Moris rose in the Convention to propose a plan of representation based on population and wealth, he replied that in America the two could be considered to coincide, the value of labor

☆

[14] Hunt (ed.), *op. cit.*, vol. IV, pp. 120, 122, 124-127.
[15] *Ibid.*, vol. IV, p. 76.

could be used as the principal criterion of wealth. And similarly Madison later supported liberal immigration policies because of the comparative abundance of land in America available to new settlers.[16] This was in sharp contrast to Europe where the situation was such that property and other interests were inevitably at swords point. When American conditions begin to change, as they will, property will stand in danger from either of two sources: the masses will either launch a direct attack on property rights, or "they will become the tools of opulence & ambition" in an attack on property from the other side. "In either case liberty will be subverted; in the first by a despotism growing out of anarchy, in the second, by an oligarchy founded on corruption." The control of the many by the few is in some countries a product of the relations between landlords and tenants, and in other countries a product of the "relations between wealthy capitalists and indigent labourers." In America the latter condition can be expected to develop because free institutions often allow great wealth to accumulate in the hands of individuals.[17] Property rights, then, for all of these reasons are endangered by both the jealous man of the masses and the pursuits of the power-seeking man of wealth.

This concept of property helps explain why the cautious Madison could join hands with Jefferson in the attack against Hamiltonian economic policies, policies that might yield precisely that combination of capital and labor which Madison so dreaded. At certain times Madison could, in fact, equal Jefferson's zealous support of the virtuous, self-sufficient man of property.[18] But for the most part he was incapable of Jefferson's more rhapsodic sentiments. He usually argued the necessity for the preservation of property rights in more prudential language. Whatever their individual proclivities, property owners as a whole would provide the core of a reasonable and reliable citizenry. They could be counted upon to act with moderation and prudence because they have "a sufficient stake in the public order" to make such behavior obligatory. "Having given hostages to fortune," Madison explained, they "will have given them to their Country also."[19] To show how this essential social component might be protected from majority faction was in large measure the intention of Madison's *Federalist* essays.

☆

[16] *Ibid.*, vol. IV, p. 123, vol. III, p. 405. "Population and Immigration," *National Gazette*, November 21, 1791, *ibid.*, vol. VI, pp. 43-66.

[17] *Ibid.*, vol. IV, pp. 120, 123. "Observations on Jefferson's Draft of a Constitution for Virginia," October, 1788, Boyd et al. (eds.), *op. cit.*, vol. VI, pp. 310-311.

[18] "Republican Distribution of Citizens," *National Gazette*, March 5, 1792, Hunt (ed.), *op. cit.*, vol. VI, p. 98.

[19] Note During the Convention for Amending the Constitution of Virginia, December, 1829, *ibid.*, vol. IX, p. 359.

The Fragmented Society

Rather than present a detailed analysis of the oft-treated *Federalist*, No. 10, I will summarize Madison's argument as briefly as possible. Madison's chief concern was to devise means of controlling the harmful *effects* of majority faction. The *causes* of faction cannot be eliminated because they stem from the natural diversity of human passion and opinion, especially that diversity which flows from the unequal ownership of property. Madison believed the American constitutional system had devices built into it that would either prevent the majority from developing a single, common interest or, failing that, would render the majority unable to carry its interest into effect. In the first place the delegation of authority to a small number of representatives who will govern a large territory will result in better men being elected, better for example, than in a small republic where the number of elected officials is proportionately greater. Secondly, since the representatives are chosen by a large number of voters they will be unable to sway all segments of the population to their evil purpose. A large territory will require republican authority to cover a greater variety of parties and interests, making it difficult for common majorities to develop or, once developed, to act in concert.

But distance alone will not always prevent governmental excesses perpetrated in the name of the majority. The people, therefore, cannot be left entirely to their own devices, even in a large republic. While "a dependence on the people is no doubt the primary control on the government," Madison noted in *The Federalist*, No. 51, ". . . experience has taught mankind the necessity of auxiliary precautions.[20] These "auxiliary precautions" would take the form of institutional checks which guarantee areas of power to the minority in the event of threatened majority aggrandizement. Thus the famous American constitutional system was devised, a system that would "first enable the government to control the governed," and then "oblige it to control itself."

Madison was little concerned about the control of the governed. The federal government had been granted authority sufficient, especially for a limited government, to perform this task. The control of government over itself was the central object of his attention, and by self-control he meant a government structured to prevent a tyrannical majority from occupying simultaneously all or most seats of political power. Protection against such an evil was afforded, since governmental power would be broken into three distinctly autonomous departments, each of which would jealously guard itself against encroachments by either of the other two. In the case of the more powerful

☆

[20] Cooke (ed.), *op. cit.*, p. 349.

legislature, a further check was instituted via the principle of bi-
cameralism. Madison took very seriously the idea that the men in each
branch of government would, following the universal imperatives of
human nature, invest themselves personally in their offices and therefore defend the system of separated powers and checks and balances
with their very beings. "The great security against a gradual concentration of the several powers in the same department," he wrote, "consists in giving to those who administer each department the necessary
constitutional means and personal motives to resist the encroachments
of the others . . . ambition must be made to counteract ambition. The
interest of the man must be connected to the constitutional rights of
the place."

Madison thus not only pitted administration against administration, but he reduced public service to a socioeconomic function
wherein a man's office became his property, another object of his interest and measure of his status. This counterchecking system was aug-
mented by a power distribution broken along a vertical as well as a
horizontal plane. The principle of federalism added important pockets
of power on the state and local levels and, by so doing, further divided
the totality of power already fragmented on the national level. Thus,
in order to oppress the minority, a majority faction would have to in-
sinuate itself in all compartments of this enormously complex edifice,
a monumental task, since the new system would tend to encourage
an already deep-seated American pluralism and thus make it all the
more difficult for a majority to form in the first place. "Whilst all authority . . . will be derived from and dependent on the society,"
Madison pointed out, "the society itself will be broken into so many
parts, interests and classes of citizens, that the rights of individuals or
of the minority, will be in little danger from interested combinations
of the majority. In a free government, the security for civil rights must
be the same as for religious rights. It consists in the one case in the
multiplicity of interests, and in the other, in the multiplicity of
sects."[21] In short, Madison's response to the threat to property rights,
those civil rights most commonly in danger from majority factionalism,
was an accentuated pluralism of interest and the careful fragmentation
of power.

The Possibilities of Community

One thing stands out very clearly in Madison's picture: if his theory
were to have its full impact on American society, then the development
of a national community would be very unlikely. Madison did not in
fact believe in the possibility of community. In 1829, near the end of

☆

[21] *Ibid.*, pp. 348-349, 351-352.

his life, he wrote: "The propensity of all communities to divide when not pressed into a unity by external danger, is a truth well understood. *There is no instance of a people inhabiting even a small island . . . who are not divided into alien, rival, hostile tribes.*" [22] For Madison there was no hope of preventing this condition; one could only attempt to control it, and Madison's method of control involved the construction of a theory which, in its logical extreme, would give rise to a system of atomized individualism.

The interesting point here, one not always noticed by commentators, is that individualism could follow from conservative as well as from liberal principles. Madison's individualism was born not of a profound conviction in the capacities or reason of the individual, but of the sorrowful appreciation that individuals cannot live an orderly existence unless they are kept apart. His individualism was the child of a Hobbesian pessimism, not of the benign optimism of a Paine, or even the qualified optimism of a Jefferson. Madison reached his conclusions, then, for precisely the "wrong" reasons; that is to say, for reasons directly opposite those given by most spokesmen of the ideology. Thus, while it may seem strange at first to see a Madisonian and a Jeffersonian walking hand-in-hand, upon reflection one can understand why they failed to realize that they disagreed on important fundamentals; their goal of individualism was commonly shared and Madisonian means for the realization of this goal suited one position as well as the other.

The Boundaries of Conservatism

Having placed Madison in the ranks of the conservatives, further clarification of his position is necessary. First, although conservative, Madison was no Fisher Ames. He knew that governments had to perform many functions and he could not without qualification say, as Ames said: " . . . the essence, and almost the quintessence, of a good government, is to protect property and its rights." And while Madison had shared the conservative concern over Shay's Rebellion in 1786, he would not years later still tremble at the mere mention of it, as did Ames in his 1800 eulogy on George Washington. Nor did he distrust the popular mind to the extent that Ames did. When Ames beheld the increased power of the demos, he flew into paroxysms of fear: "Our days," he wrote, "are made heavy with the pressure of anxiety, and our nights restless with visions of horror. We listen to the clank of chains, and overhear the whispers of assassins. We mark the barbarous dissonance of mingled rage and triumph in the yell of an

☆

[22] "Outline," September 1829, Hunt (ed.), *op. cit.*, vol. IX, pp. 355-357.

infatuated mob; we see the dismal glare of their burnings and scent the loathsome steam of human victims offered in sacrifice."[23] To the always prudent and usually placid Madison, such an outburst must have seemed nothing short of maniacal.

Madison's personal brand of conservatism can be illuminated somewhat by looking a little more closely at the mechanics of his system. He suggested that if the House and the Senate represented the interests of the two main social classes, an impartial third force would be needed to mediate between them and protect the overriding national interest. The presidency would be perfectly suited for this task. At the same time, Madison felt that presidential power must be severely restricted. He feared that the presidency might be the vehicle through which majority factionalism would assert itself. For this reason the executive should under no circumstances be permitted to assume the role of national leader.

We find in fact no explicit discussion of leadership or of political energy in Madison. Interests appear simply to be played off against each other, producing an equilibrium that is truly static. Madison argued, however, that if a temporary standoff between interests could be effected, *reason* might ultimately emerge and triumph over passion and narrow-mindedness. Unfortunately, he made no direct reference to the source of this ultimate reason. Consequently, we can only assume that the Senate, the institution that represented the wisdom and prudence of property, would, when functioning free of factional disputation, constitute an American wellspring of reason. Madison felt that political reason could not normally be produced by the masses, whose tranquility would be disturbed and whose passion would be dangerously aroused if involved in fundamental issues. Nor would reason be likely to rise from the states, whose legislation Madison would subject to a potential federal veto.[24] Property, as represented in the Senate, would eventually tip the scales in the right direction. It is for this reason that Madison could ask for a nine-year senatorial term of office and for a House of Representatives of which fifty per cent would represent property interests.

Committed as he was to the idea of property rights as a starting point for political theorizing, there is considerable irony in Madison being regarded a Jacobin by some of his more undiscerning contemporaries. It is fair to note, however, that Madison was, and to some extent has remained, difficult to assess, in part because of the dual nature

☆

[23] Seth Ames (ed.), *op. cit.*, vol. II, pp. 76, 166, 354.

[24] Cooke (ed.), *op. cit.*, no. 49, p. 340. Adrienne Koch (ed.), *Notes of Debates in the Federal Convention of 1787 Reported by James Madison,* Ohio University Press, Athens, Ohio, 1966, p. 88.

of his role. The thinking of all writers during this period was "corrupted" by their involvement in political action, but this was especially true of Madison. He was usually more the politician than the systematic thinker. Although attached to certain theoretical principles, he was, to put it mildly, totally undoctrinaire in the application of these principles. The unexpected shifts in his various positions are sometimes quite startling. Hamilton seems to have had at least a little justification for regarding Madison's opposition to the Report on Public Credit as "a perfidious desertion of the Principles which he [Madison] was solemnly pledged to defend."[25] Similarly, it surprised many when Madison opposed the United States Bank, since in the Convention he had proposed that Congress be given power to charter such corporations.[26] But most astonishing was his authorship of the Virginia Resolutions, which suggested the state's right to nullify "unconstitutional" federal laws. This proposition completely contradicted his Convention argument for a federal veto of state legislation.[27] Despite these and other changes in viewpoint, Madison probably felt perfectly free to adapt and alter his political stance, confident in his own mind of a continued dedication to the fundamental precepts of constitutional republicanism.

The Problem of Thought and Action

Nevertheless, his adaptations sometimes went very far in the direction of recantation. This leaning is seen most clearly in a series of essays Madison wrote in 1791 and 1792 in Philip Freneau's *National Gazette* in an effort to muster nationwide support for the emergent Jeffersonian party. In the course of these essays Madison advocated "brotherly affection" in a "consolidated nation"; argued that mass public opinion was crucial as a means of national communication, a means that could be used to contract the vast expanse of the American nation, thereby *advancing* the cause of liberty; insisted that constitu-

☆

[25] John C. Miller, *The Federalist Era: 1789-1801*, Harper & Brothers, New York, 1960, pp. 34-36, 41.

[26] *Ibid.*, p. 57. In Madison's defense it might be pointed out that his argument was entirely in keeping with his philosophy of strict constitutional construction: since Congress did not explicitly have the chartering power, it ought not to exercise it. And yet it was Madison, of course, who as President signed into law the bill chartering the Second Bank of the U. S.

[27] While changing conditions may have had something to do with the question, Madison also seems to have altered his views on slavery over the years. In 1791 Madison said that he was "greatly interested in that species of property," and would "not lessen the value by weakening the tenure of it." (*Ibid.*, p. 107n.) In a letter to Lafayette in 1821, Madison comes to advocate the complete separation of Negroes and Caucasians because he can see no hope of white Americans ever accepting Negroes on an equal basis as fellow citizens. (Cooke [ed.], *op. cit.*, vol. IX, p. 85.)

tional loyalty and the belief in liberty must be held with religious fervor by all citizens; contended that popular participation, rather than "principles of operation," constituted the essential core of republican government; and suggested that severe differential in property ownership must be curbed through remedial legislation, and that under no circumstances should any one interest be favored at the expense of another. In short, Madison seemed to ask Americans to violate some of the very principles that only a few years earlier he had placed as cornerstones of republicanism.[28]

Madison could engage in such blatant "revisionism" because he felt that political necessity demanded it. He and Jefferson went to great and some thought questionable lengths to bring Freneau to Philadelphia so that they would have a popular journal for the expression of their views. They were especially interested in gathering public support in their fight against the powerful Hamiltonian faction within Washington's administration. Madison's pieces were, bluntly, exercises in political propaganda. If the defeat of Hamilton required an espousal of Jeffersonian doctrine, then Madison was quite prepared to argue in this vein. As Adrienne Koch has noted: "in these . . . articles, one cannot help being impressed with Madison's determination to show that republican ideology is first and last on the side of 'the people.' The formulation is clearly in terms congenial to Jefferson's democratic version of republicanism."[29] When espousing his own variety of republicanism, Madison seldom employed such Jeffersonian categories.

After his last essay in the *National Gazette* in 1792, Madison did not again engage in theoretical reflection of any importance until the mid-1820's when he was no longer continuously engaged in political life. At this later period he reiterated most of his main arguments. He alluded again to the abuses of paper money and contract violations; he reaffirmed the natural right to the acquisition and protection of property; he lamented anew the danger of majority tyranny and the weaknesses in man that make government necessary; he once more described government as an "Arbiter or Umpire" whose main function it is to settle peacefully disputes between conflicting interests.[30] If this later period saw Madison reenunciate his basic premises, it also afforded him the opportunity to redefine his concept of the American nation.

☆

[28] Hunt (ed.), *op. cit.*, vol. VI, pp. 67-69, 70, 82, 94-95, 93-94, 101-102.

[29] Adrienne Koch, *Jefferson and Madison, The Great Collaboration*, Oxford University Press, New York, 1964, p. 126.

[30] "To (unknown)," 1833, Hunt (ed.), *op. cit.*, vol. IX, p. 522. "Speech in the Virginia Constitutional Convention," in *ibid.*, p. 361. "To Joseph Cabell," September 7, 1829, *ibid.*, pp. 348-351.

America as a Divided Unity

Politically speaking, what was America? Was it a federation of quasi-sovereign states with separate populations? Or was it a homogeneous nation broken into numerous subpolitical units for administrative and representational purposes? This question tortured early American thinkers, as to some extent it does even today, and Madison, as chief architect of the Constitution, was consulted often as to his views.

Madison's answer to this question was by no means clear, and he tried to make the best of both worlds. He often found it useful to speak of the Constitution as a treaty among the states, but it was a treaty that bound citizens as well as state governments together. He repeatedly argued that "the real parties to the constl. compact of the U.S. are the States — that is, the people thereof respectively in their sovereign character." This dichotomy would seem to follow from Madison's discussion in *The Federalist*, where he argued that, while the states would in fact compete with one another as autonomous entities, there would be occasions when the people of the states would act in concert; that is, as a confederacy, to produce *federal* legislation. At other times they would act in unison; that is, as a nation, to produce national legislation.[31] These painful distinctions bespeak Madison's effort to avoid both consolidation and decentralized confederacy. He considered either of these "extremes" dangerous, and he consequently chose neither. Moreover, in his letter to Everett, which was reprinted in the *North American Review*, Madison argued at length to show that the Virginia Resolutions had presented a special case and that the doctrine of nullification was without constitutional foundation. Upon reading this, John Marshall, long an anti-Jeffersonian, was moved to say: "He is himself again. He avows the opinion of his best days . . ."[32]

Madisonian Realism

Madison's case for fragmentation and individualism differed from the liberal argument in yet another way. Although supremely conscious of the creative moment that the period of the founding presented, Madison was, unlike many Jeffersonians, in no sense the American Adam, striking out for novelty and progress on all fronts and holding history in severe contempt. Every individual and every generation is inescapably caught up in history, Madison believed, and cannot be artificially uprooted without the direst consequences. His argument

☆

[31] "To Edward Everett," August 28, 1830, *ibid.*, vol. IX, pp. 383-403. "Outline," 1829, *ibid.*, p. 352. "To Everett," *ibid.*, p. 386. Cooke (ed.), *op. cit.*, no. 46, pp. 316-319. *Ibid.*, no. 39, pp. 254-257.

[32] "To Justice Story," October 15, 1830, John E. Oster (ed.), *The Political and Economic Doctrines of John Marshall*, New York, 1914, p. 131.

for this position can be best appreciated by examining a fascinating exchange between Madison and Thomas Jefferson in 1790.

Jefferson advanced an argument identical to that Thomas Paine would use in *The Rights of Man.* "As the Earth belongs to the living," he wrote, "not to the dead, a living generation can bind itself only . . . A majority of those ripe for the exercise of their will do not live beyond the term of 19 years; to this term, then, is limited the validity of the society, nor can any act be continued beyond this term, without an *express* declaration of the public will." Madison replied with his usual analytical caution. Political acts, he instructed Jefferson, may be divided into three classes: (1) the fundamental constitution; (2) laws that for some reason cannot be revoked by the legislature; and (3) laws that are not irrevocable. A constitutional revision by every generation could only lead to a major disruption of social order. Madison asked: "Would not such a periodical revision engender pernicious factions that might not otherwise come into existence, and agitate the public mind more frequently and more violently than might be expedient?" In considering the second case, laws irrevocable by the legislature, we must take into account the rights of property. The earth may, as Jefferson contended, be nature's gift to the living, but they own "title to the earth in its *natural* state only. The *improvements* made by the dead form a debt against the living, who take the benefit of them. This debt cannot be otherwise discharged than by a proportionate obedience to the will of the authors of the improvements." Nineteen years may not provide enough time to discharge historical debts. Thus, there must be provision for the descent of obligations from one generation to another. "Equity," Madison concluded, "may require it. Mutual good may be promoted by it."

As to the third class of laws, those revocable by legislatures, the rights of property again dictate that even here legislation must often be binding across generations. Unless this is the case, Madison warned, "all the rights depending on positive laws, that is, most of the rights of property, would become absolutely defunct, and the most violent struggles ensue between the parties interested in reviving, and those interested in reforming, the antecedent state of property." In fact, "the very possibility of an event so hazardous to the rights of property could not but depreciate its value."[33] Madison thus rejected Jefferson's radical proclamation as imprudent on all levels, as manifestly dangerous to the cause of order and the rights of property. The only solution, he told Jefferson, must be found in the doctrine of tacit consent that binds all generations to the obedience of those laws consecrated to public order.

☆

[33] "To Thomas Jefferson," February 4, 1790, *Letters and Other Writings of James Madison*, R. Worthington, New York, 1884, vol. I, pp. 503-505.

The Madisonian Legacy

Madison, as chief designer of the Constitution, seemed to build a system in which only the counterploys of interest and ambition would have room for action. If it worked, his ingenious scheme, which pitted interest against interest, individual against individual, could only perpetuate a separateness that was already deeply ingrained in the sectional and personal parochialisms of America. If America lacked a national sense of community before 1787, Madison's plan, which attempted to tie the American to his interest and his area in a nation-wide competitive struggle, could in no way increase whatever incipient communal sentiments were harbored by the society. If institutions have an effect on the behavior of those who inhabit them, then Madisonian institutions, which were anticommunal in character, may have helped develop a noncommunitarian tradition in America.

It is a most curious irony that Madison was carried to his final position because of his special reading of American economic individualism. Recall a statement by Madison cited earlier: "The U. States have a precious advantage also in the actual distribution of property . . . *and in the universal hope of acquiring property.*" [Emphasis added.] It is clear from this remark that Madison understood the spirit of the American ideology. But, because his concept of property rights emphasized landed property, he could not in 1787 understand that a conflict between property holders and all other interests in the society was neither historically nor psychologically inevitable. Economic individualism included within it the desire to attain wealth of all varieties. In 1829 Madison finally realized that the stake-in-society thesis applied to "those, who although not possessed of a share of the soil, are deeply interested in other species of property."[34] But even here he did not seem to grasp the full import of his discovery, for he never tried to piece his new insight together with his earlier arguments for the rights of property.

Americans shared a general interest in individual acquisition, even when their specific aims ostensibly came into conflict. This helps explain why there could so quickly be an "Era of Good Feelings" after the bitter disputes of the early decades, and why the Whigs in the 1830's could unite the very financial, industrial, and propertied interests that Madison had once divided into separate and hostile classes. Madison's fear of "levelling schemes" directed against property in the 1780's led him to a confusion about American tendencies, a confusion that, it must be added, was by no means exclusively

☆

[34] "Note During the Convention for Amending the Constitution of Virginia," 1829, Hunt (ed.), *op. cit.*, vol. IX, p. 359.

his. It characterized the whole history of the times. It is seen in James Wilson, the "constitutional republican" who, along with Thomas Paine, could write panegyrics for the Bank of North America prior to his participation in the Philadelphia Convention. And it is expressed by the strange turn of events that saw Jeffersonians in 1796 charge John Adams with being unfit for office because he was an opponent of Hamilton's economic policies. Perhaps the confusion is best symbolized by the even stranger twist of logic that found the 1826 memorial to Thomas Jefferson delivered to his beloved American Philosophical Society by none other than Nicholas Biddle, president of the Second Bank of the United States.[35] What makes Madison's confusion in particular so crucial is the formative impact it may have had on the style of American life. If a disproportionate stress on the protection of property drove Madison to plant seeds of competition and mutual distrust in American political institutions, as it may have, then successive generations have been left to reap the dubious harvest of this act, and the national sense of community, if it ever existed, is probably the poorer for it.

John Adams

Although a pronounced opponent of Madison's Jeffersonian party, John Adams held views that on many counts were identical to those of Madison. The extent of this similarity is slightly deceptive, however, for Adams had a notion of political life that sometimes placed him beyond Madison's narrower perspectives. In certain ways, in his basic distrust of human motivation for example, Adams' logic dictated conclusions that replicated those of Madison. But at other times Adams expressed a concern for goals and needs of society as a whole, and this concern broadened considerably his understanding of legitimate political activity. On such occasions Adams propounded a theory of government that Madison could only regard with intense suspicion.

Constitutions and Classes

Adams totally agreed that all societies inevitably divide into rich and poor and that the rights of property need strong and lasting protections. Indeed, he ranked property rights among those fundamental to civilized society. In his draft of the 1780 Massachusetts constitution, he

☆

[35] Joseph Dorfman, *The Economic Mind in American Civilization*, The Viking Press, Inc., New York, 1946, vol. I, pp. 260-263. Page Smith, *John Adams*, Doubleday & Company, Inc., Garden City, N.Y., 1962, vol. II, p. 900.

argued that all "men are born [equally] free and independent, and have certain natural, essential, and unalienable rights, among which may be reckoned the right of enjoying and defending their lives and liberties; that of acquiring, possessing, and protecting [their] property; in fine, that of seeking and obtaining their safety and happiness."[36] And like Madison, Adams would build the protections for wealth and property (unlike Madison he did not draw fine distinctions between kinds of wealth or property ownership) directly into his constitutional system. He felt that a constitution should balance in various ways the propensities and forces characteristic of the society at large.

For Adams, the concept of balance contained two closely related principles: (1) significant economic blocs should receive appropriate representation in the legislature—"equal interests among the people should have equal interests in the representative body"; and (2) the political manifestations of these interests should be set in counterpoint within the institutions of government. "When the many are masters," Adams observed, "they are too unruly, and then the few are too tame, and afraid to speak out the truth. When the few are masters, they are too severe, and then the many are too servile."[37] Adams sought a "well-ordered, a well-balanced, a judiciously-limited government." Such a government would equally represent the poor, or democratically oriented element, in the House, the rich, or aristocratic element, in the Senate, with "an intermediate power, sufficiently elevated and independent to control each of the contending parties in its excesses."[38] The latter would be provided by the executive to whom Adams would unhesitatingly give powers entirely adequate to fulfill this function.

But by 1790 Adams felt that the balance had been seriously disturbed. He believed that the pendulum had "vibrated too far to the popular side . . . and horid ravages have been made upon property by arbitrary multitudes or majorities of multitudes." Nevertheless his commitment to the idea of *equal* balance was very deep, and a transitory shift would not cause him to overcompensate on the side of property and thereby deviate from a premise he had always insisted upon. "Equality of representation in the legislature is a first principle of liberty," he wrote fifteen years earlier, "and the moment the least

☆

[36] "The Report of a Constitution, or Form of Government, for the Commonwealth of Massachusetts," 1776, Charles F. Adams (ed.), *The Works of John Adams*, Little, Brown and Company, Boston, 1856, vol. IV, p. 220.

[37] "To John Penn," 1776, *ibid.*, vol. IV, pp. 205-206. "To Thomas Brand-Hollis," June 11, 1790, *ibid.*, vol. IX, p. 570.

[38] "To George Walton," September 25, 1789, *ibid.*, vol. VIII, pp. 495-496.

departure from such equality takes place, that moment an inroad is made upon liberty."[39] Adams would not allow his appreciation of majority excesses to dull his sense of a still greater danger that emanated from other quarters.

The Few and the Many

The fact was that Adams feared the few even more than he did the many. "The rich," he noted, "are seldom remarkable for modesty, ingenuity, or humanity. Their wealth has rather a tendency to make them penurious and selfish." Given free reign and translated into political power, this selfishness could imperil the stability of the republic, for it would mean that political leadership would inevitably attempt to manipulate the masses in order to advance its own ends. "There is nothing in which mankind have been more unanimous," wrote Adams, " . . . than this, that the multitude have always been credulous, and the few are always artful."[40] While Adams would educate the multitude to reduce their credulousness, for two reasons he would not seek to eradicate the political and economic advantages held by the minority. In the first place, such a policy ignored all of the lessons of recorded history. The existence of an upper class, Adams told Jefferson, derives from "the Ordonance of God Almighty, in the Constitution of human nature, and wrought into the Fabrick of the Universe. Philosophers and Politicians, may nibble and quibble, but they will never get rid of it." Not only would it be useless to attempt to eliminate privilege and inequality, it would be counter-productive, for the "most natural substitute for an assembly of the whole, is a delegation of power from the many to a few of the most wise and virtuous." And it was Adams' belief that such rare men would most likely come from the ranks of the few. This "natural aristocracy," as he called it, formed "a body of men which contains the greatest collection of virtues and abilities in a free government, is the brightest ornament and glory of the nation, and may always be made the greatest blessing of society, if it be judiciously managed in the constitution. But if this be not done, it is always the most dangerous; nay, it may be added, it never fails to be the destruction of the commonwealth."[41]

☆

[39] "To Thomas Brand-Hollis," June 11, 1790, *ibid.*, vol. IX, p. 571. "To Joseph Hawley," August 25, 1776, *ibid.*, vol. IX, p. 435.

[40] "Diary," *ibid.*, vol. II, pp. 296-297. "Defence of the Constitutions of Government of the United States of America," *ibid.*, vol. IV, p. 292.

[41] "To Jefferson," August [14], 1813, Lester J. Cappon (ed.), *The Adams-Jefferson Letters*, University of North Carolina Press, Chapel Hill, 1959, vol. II, p. 365. "Thoughts on Government," 1776, Adams (ed.), *op. cit.*, vol. IV, p. 205. "Defence," *ibid.*, p. 397.

Judicious management of this class would primarily be effected through the institution of the Senate. This body would of course guarantee to the minority a permanent seat of power, which is as it should be, but, more importantly, confinement to the Senate would subject the wealthy to the direct check of the House and the other branches and consequently render this class less of an overall threat. Placed in the Senate, the rich would have specified power, but Adams believed that "this, to all honest and useful intents, [constitutes] an ostracism."[42] In addition, the chief executive, acting in behalf of the entire society, would have ample power to wield against a Senate given to excessiveness. Adams distinguished his position in this regard from all Jeffersonians, Madison included. In reflecting on the new Constitution, he wrote Jefferson: "You are afraid of the one — I, of the few. We agree perfectly that the many should have a full fair and perfect Representation. — You are Apprehensive of Monarchy; I of Aristocracy. I would therefore have given more Power to the President and less to the Senate."[43] Thus, while Adams saw the Senate as the preservative and protector of wealth and its attendant power, he also hoped that the exercise of this power would be completely confined within this arena and that, under the constant surveillance of the House on one side and the President on the other, the few would be carefully controlled and effectually domesticated.[44]

Constitutionalism Broadly Conceived

Although there is a connection between the two areas, Adams noticeably differed from Madison less in his conception of the rights and privileges of property than in his generalized understanding of government. Like Madison, he believed in equipoised powers, clearly separated in jurisdiction and function. In fact, it is Adams, and not Madison, who uses the term "equilibrium" in describing his conception of political order.[45] Yet Adams frequently found it difficult to leave the political energy either of the government or of the citizenry restrained by a system of divided powers. He seems to have understood a constitution to be more than just a diagrammatic distribution of authority. A constitution, based on proper principles, has a formative

☆

[42] *Ibid.*, p. 290.

[43] "To Jefferson," December 6, 1787, Cappon (ed.), *op. cit.*, vol. I, p. 213.

[44] In support of this view Adams strongly opposed the idea of serving in public office without salary. He feared that under such an arrangement politics would become the exclusive province of the rich. ("To John Jebb," August 21, 1785, Adams [ed.], *op. cit.*, vol. IX, p. 533.)

[45] "Defence," *ibid.*, vol. IV, p. 380.

impact on the populace: it "introduces knowledge among the people, and inspires them with a conscious dignity becoming freemen; a general emulation takes place, which causes good humor, sociability, good manners, and good morals to be general. That elevation of sentiment inspired by such a government, makes the common people brave and enterprising. That ambition which is inspired by it makes them sober, industrious, and frugal."[46] With this conception of constitutionalism in mind, Adams wrote into the Massachusetts constitution an obligation upon government "to cherish the interests of literature and the sciences," to foster public and private agencies interested in promoting the arts, the sciences, agriculture, commerce, manufactures, and natural history, "to countenance and inculcate the principles of humanity and general benevolence, public and private charity, industry and frugality, honesty and punctuality in their dealings, sincerity, good humor, and all social affections and generous sentiments among the people.[47] Adams, in other words, occasionally inserted into his philosophy of government that ingredient which was for the most part absent in Madison's theory: a conception of political authority. Where Madison pictured government operating essentially on the periphery of people's lives, maintaining order and protecting rights, Adams made the role of government somewhat more central to the personal habits and aspirations of the citizenry, and he foresaw a system in which governmental authority would be legitimized, not just by constitutional stipulation, but also by active popular support and interest.

Participation and Authority

To begin with, Adams rejected the archaic notion that fear lay at the center of political order. "Fear," he told John Penn, ". . . is so sordid and brutal a passion, that it cannot possibly be called a principle, and will hardly be thought in America a proper basis of government." Principles of government, Adams suggested, can be divided into two varieties: "the principles of authority and the principles of power. The first are virtues of the mind and heart, such as wisdom, prudence, courage, patience, temperance, justice, &c. The second are the goods of fortune, such as riches, extraction, knowledge, and reputation."[48] Although the power of riches typically dominates civilized society, this is not the case in the New World. "In America," Adams pointed

☆

[46] "Thoughts on Government," *ibid.*, p. 199.
[47] "Report of Massachusetts Constitution," *ibid.*, vol. IV, p. 199.
[48] "To John Penn," 1776, *ibid.*, vol. IV, p. 204. "Defence," *ibid.*, 427.

out, "the balance is nine tenths on the side of the people. Indeed, there is but one order; and our senators have influence chiefly by the principles of authority, and very little by those of power . . . " This being the case, the legislature, particularly the lower house, must be seen as more than the political reflector of economic interests. The House of Representatives, Adams argued, "gives free access to the whole nation, and communicates all its wants, knowledge, projects, and wishes to government; it excites emulation among all classes, removes complaints, redresses grievances, affords opportunities of exertion to genius . . . and gives full scope to all the faculties of man; it opens a passage for every speculation to the legislature, to administration, and to the public; it gives a universal energy to the human character, in every part of the state."[49] The House, because it represents the people, stands as an agency of legitimation in a constitutional system where ultimate legality and popular sovereignty are largely coterminous. "It is true," Adams wrote, "that laws are neither made by angels, nor by horses, but by men. The voice of the people is as much the voice of men as the voice of a prince is the voice of a man; and yet the voice of the people is the voice of God, which the voice of a prince is not. The government of laws, said Aristotle, is the government of God."[50] Madison would agree that to argue that the Prince speaks with divine authority is specious, but he would also insist that the doctrine of *vox populi, vox Dei* was equally without merit.

So, in moments of less enthusiasm, would Adams himself. The notion of popular participation, however, was basic to his most positive understanding of republicanism. "The social science," he wrote, "will never be much improved, until the people unanimously know and consider themselves as the fountain of power, and until they shall know how to manage it wisely and honestly."[51] As the "fountain of power," the people would stand as the ultimate source of political authority. Adams did not mean that the masses would assume full command. Far from it. Government must provide direction and its leaders should typically come from the dominant class, which has easier access to the seats of power. The masses, moreover, ought to follow their natural leaders and ought never to have a totally unrestrained voice in public affairs. Yet a republican system of governance imposes obligations on all citizens, rich and poor alike. Every citizen, consequently, must to some extent be involved in the political events of his time. He must be able to weigh and balance choices prudently and disinterestedly. "We electors," Adams remarked, "have an important

☆

[49] "Defence," *ibid.*, vol. IV, p. 434. *ibid.*, pp. 288-289.

[50] *Ibid.*, pp. 404-405.

[51] "To John Jebb," September 10, 1785, *ibid.*, vol. IX, p. 540.

constitutional power placed in our hands . . . It becomes necessary to every subject then, to be in some degree a statesman, and to examine and judge for himself of the tendency of political principles and measures."[52] In short, Adams could not always rest content with the idea of fragmented or counterchecked power. When he thought most pointedly about the needs and potentialities of the public interest, he rested his philosophy on a far broader base.

Participation and Morality

The quality of popular participation was ultimately as important for Adams as was its quantity. Where Madison would rely on the neutralized collisions of ambition and power extended over a vast territory, Adams felt that raw ambition without the further controls of moral restraint would lead eventually to the destruction of republican society. Constitutional safeguards are crucial, but in the final analysis "moral principles, sanctified and sanctioned by religion, are the only bond of union, the only ground of confidence of the people in one another, of the people in the government, and the government in the people." With this in mind, Adams could write into the Massachusetts constitution stipulations enjoining legislators to adhere to the principles of piety, justice, moderation, temperance, industry, and frugality.[53] For those who would contaminate political ends with pecuniary motives Adams had the highest scorn. "Politics," he maintained, "are the divine science, after all. How is it possible that any man should ever think of making it subservient to his own little passions and mean private interests? Ye baseborn sons of fallen Adam, is the end of politics a fortune, a family, a gilded coach, a train of horses, and a troop of livery servants, balls at Court, splendid dinners and suppers?" For Adams the "divine science" required that people cast their eyes considerably higher. The very existence of the republic depended upon it. "Our Constitution," he repeatedly noted, "was made only for a moral and religious people. It is wholly inadequate to the government of any other." When public virtue vanishes, when the "national spirit," as Adams called it, proves insubstantial, "the republic is lost in essence, though it may still exist in form"[54]

☆

[52] "On Self-Delusion," no. II, *Boston Gazette*, August 29, 1793, *ibid.*, vol. III, p. 437.
[53] "Address to the Students of New Jersey College," 1798, *ibid.*, vol. IX, p. 206. "Report of Massachusetts Constitution," *ibid.*, vol. IV, p. 227.
[54] "To James Warren," June 17, 1782, *ibid.*, vol. IX, p. 512. "Address to Officers of the Mass. Militia," October 11, 1798, *ibid.*, p. 229. "To Benjamin Rush," September 27, 1808, *ibid.*, p. 603. See also, "To Rush," August 28, 1811, *ibid.*, p. 635; and "To Zabdiel Adams," June 21, 1776, *ibid.*, p. 401.

It was Adams' conviction, or more accurately his hope, that through a process of education and habituation Americans could learn to obey the dictates of virtue. Education was particularly essential if the ancient impulse toward elitism were to be finally eliminated. "It has ever been my hobby-horse," Adams wrote, "to see rising in America an empire of liberty, and a prospect of two or three hundred millions of freemen, without one noble or one king among them. You say it is impossible. If I should agree with you in this, I would still say, let us try the experiment, and preserve our equality as long as we can."[55] Equality could best be preserved by an educated public. "The whole people," Adams instructed John Jebb, "must take upon themselves the education of the whole people . . . There should not be a district of one mile square, without a school in it . . . maintained at the expense of the people themselves. They must be taught to reverence themselves, instead of adoring their servants, their generals, admirals, bishops, and statesmen." Such learning, moreover, cannot be confined to the formal lessons of the classroom. Virtue can be effectively instilled in the citizenry only through a wider process of habituation. "When children and youth hear their parents and neighbors, and all about them applauding the love of country, of labor, of liberty, and all the virtues, habits, and faculties, which constitute a good citizen, that is, a patriot and a hero, those children endeavor to acquire those qualities, and a sensible and virtuous people will never fail to form multitudes of patriots and heroes.[56]

So convinced was he of the utility of habitual training that Adams grafted this idea onto the notion of a written constitution. He informed Jefferson that " 'the Rights of one Generation of Men must Still depend, in some degree, on the Paper Transactions of another.' The Social Compact and the Laws must be reduced to Writing. Obedience to them becomes a national Habit and they cannot be changed but by Revolutions which are costly Things."[57] A written constitution, therefore, was not, as most contract theorists held, merely a legal covenant establishing legitimate political jurisdictions and powers; it was more akin to a talmudic proclamation that enunciated the basic aspirations of all citizens, a social code that all should espouse and all should follow.

The thought of an American Constitution supported by a virtuous public could upon occasions excite Adams' highest hopes. The year of the Revolution struck him as "a time when the greatest lawgivers of

☆

[55] "To Count Sarsfield," February 3, 1786, *ibid.*, p. 546.
[56] "To John Jebb," September 10, 1785, *ibid.*, vol. IX, pp. 540-541.
[57] "To Jefferson," May 11, 1794, Cappon (ed.), *op. cit.*, vol. I, p. 255.

antiquity would have wished to live . . . When," he asked, "before the present epocha, had three millions of people full power and a fair opportunity to form and establish the wisest and happiest government that human wisdom can contrive?" The act of the American founding would have an impact for centuries to come. Adams wrote in 1787, "The institutions now made in America will not wholly wear out for thousands of years."[58] In his inaugural speech in 1797, he cited the eight years under Washington as strong evidence for his optimism. All legitimate governments exist only to represent the people and to seek their good. Adams told the members of Congress that "the existence of such a government as ours, for any length of time, is a full proof of a general dissemination of knowledge and virtue throughout the whole body of the people."[59] In other words, as Adams assumed the presidency, the fact that his countrymen had attained a sufficient level of education and displayed a commitment to the practice of public virtue caused him to look with favor on the long-term chances for a republican government.

Pessimism and Community

To take Adams-as-an-optimist as the typical Adams, however, would be entirely erroneous. The limit of his harmonious view can quickly be discovered when one tries to extend his concepts of political balance and popular participation into a theory of community. In his endorsement of universal public education, Adams imagined the end product as a people amalgamated by virtuous habits and patriotic sentiments in a country where rich and poor lived peacefully together under a system of legal equality, united "in the hands of mutual affection . . . mutually sensible of each other's ignorance, weakness, and error."[60] Community, however, requires something more. It calls for a certain generosity of spirit among citizens of the same country, or at the very least it requires the possibility that self-interest will not always carry the day. It was difficult if not impossible for Adams to discern the attribute of generosity in his fellowman. His works fairly burst with gloomy comments on the degradations found in human nature.

At his mildest, Adams could see a vague possibility of reasonable behavior. He wrote Jefferson in 1813: "I am a Believer in the probable improvability and Improvement, the Ameliorabi[li]ty and Ameliora-

☆

[58] "Thoughts on Government," Adams (ed.), op. cit., vol. IV, p. 200. "Defence," ibid., p. 298.

[59] "Inaugural Speech to Both Houses of Congress," March 4, 1797, ibid., vol. IX, p. 107.

[60] Smith, op. cit., vol. II, p. 801.

tion in human Affairs: though I never could understand the Doctrine of the Perfectability of the human Mind." But the human condition short of improvement and amelioration, to say nothing of perfection, was for Adams melancholy almost to the point of despair. Having announced his belief in probable improvement, he hastened to inform Jefferson that hopes "of sudden tranquility ought not to be too sanguine," for there lay ahead the inevitability of superstition, revenge, cruelty, intrigue, and violence, all connected with attempts to erect aristocratic, monistic, or democratic despotisms of one kind or another. "These and other Elements of Fanaticism and Anarchy will yet for a long time continue a Fermentation, which will excite alarms and require Vigilance."[61]

One is tempted at first to view this outburst as perhaps the retrospective rancor of a former Federalist leader whose party and reputation had become badly tarnished. But Adams' more positive moments were always subject to immediate qualification. Years earlier he had written that men "should endeavor at a *balance* of affections and appetites, under the monarchy of reason and conscience, within, as well as at a balance of power without . . . They were intended by nature to live together in society, and in this way to restrain one another, and in general they are a very good kind of creatures; but they know each other's imbecility so well, that they ought never to lead one another into temptation."[62] Temptation, however, was, as Adams could never forget, irresistible to most men most of the time; imbecility, therefore, was normally par for the course.

In 1787 Adams had reported to Jefferson: "I have long been settled in my own opinion, that neither Philosophy, nor Religion, nor Morality, nor Wisdom, nor Interest, will ever govern nations or Parties, against their Vanity, their Pride, their Resentment or Revenge, or their Avarice or Ambition. Nothing but force and Power and Strength can restrain them."[63] Adams was accurate in describing this opinion as one of long standing. In his early twenties he already understood that "vice and folly are so interwoven in all human affairs, that they could not, possibly, be wholly separated from them without tearing and rending the whole system of human nature and state." Temptation would forever bedazzle society and lead ultimately to its ruin. Adams wrote that we "see every day that our imaginations are so strong, and our reason so weak, the charms of wealth and power are so enchanting, and the belief of future punishment so faint, that men find ways to

☆

[61] "To Jefferson," July 16, 1814, Cappon (ed.), *op. cit.*, vol. II, p. 435.

[62] "Defence," Adams (ed.), *op. cit.*, vol. IV, p. 407.

[63] "To Jefferson," October 9, 1787, Cappon (ed.), *op. cit.*, vol. I, pp. 202-203.

persuade themselves to believe any absurdity, to submit to any prostitution, rather than forego their wishes and desires." If men cannot
learn this lesson from history or experience, he continued, let them
"look into their own hearts, which they will find to be deceitful above
all things and desperately wicked."[64] Precious little could be expected
from a society built upon vice, folly, deceit, and wickedness.

Adams' extreme statement of dolefulness obliterated all reasonable
hope. He believed that "men are at war with each other and against
all living creatures. Beasts, birds, fishes, and insects are at war with
each other and with all other species. It is a militant state in a militant planet." He explained to Jefferson that "human Reason and
human Conscience, though I believe there are such things, are not a
Match, for human Passions, human Imaginations, and human enthusiasm."[65] Adams' comprehension of how far human "Enthusiasm"
could carry things is stunning in its totality. "Such swarms of passions,
avarice and ambition, servility and adulation, hopes, fears, jealousies,
envy, revenge, malice, and cruelty, are continually buzzing in the
world, and we are so extremely prone to mistake the impulses of these
for the dictates of our consciences, that the greatest genius, united to
the best disposition, will find it hard to hearken to the voice of reason,
or even to be certain of the purity of his own intentions."[66] Given this
as the plight of humanity, one could scarcely hold out hope for the
state of civil society.

The Political Effects of Human Nature

It was in this frame of mind that Adams adhered to strict Madisonian
directives. At such times his gravest concern was the multitude. To
Jefferson, who hoped that a natural aristocracy of talent would emerge
to lead the nation, Adams declared: "'Nobility in Men is worth as
much as it is in Horses Asses or Rams: but the meanest blooded Puppy,
in the World, if he gets a little money, is as good a man as the best of
them.' Yet Birth and Wealth together have prevailed over Virtue and
Talents in all ages. The Many, will acknowledge no other αριστοι."
Equal to its ability to establish an ignoble plutocracy was the majority's capacity to institute its own authority and through this means

☆

[64] "Diary," Adams (ed.), op. cit., vol. II, pp. 107. Ibid., pp. 294-295. "On Private Revenge," no. III, Boston Gazette, September 5, 1763, ibid., vol. III, p. 443.

[65] Smith, op. cit., vol. II, p. 1081. "To Jefferson," February 2, 1816, Cappon (ed.), op. cit.,
vol. II, p. 461.

[66] "On Self-Delusion," no. II, Boston Gazette, August 29, 1793, Adams (ed.), op. cit.,
vol. III, p. 435.

impose an equalitarian tyranny over all segments of social life, including the areas of property ownership, commercial intercourse, religious practice, and even personal choice. Checks and balances were therefore absolutely essential if liberty were to be preserved. Adams had only to point to human nature to justify, for example, the need for a divided legislature. *"A single assembly,"* he insisted, *"is liable to all the vices, follies, and frailties of an individual."* [67] Individuals, moreover, alone or in majorities, were dangerous even when "elevated" by exposure to public education. Adams, in his cynical mood, viewed education with intense suspicion, fearing that it would produce an increased number of able and ambitious men, some of whom would, precisely because of their education, now be wily, inflexible, and doctrinaire, as well as more knowledgeable. [68] The depth of Adams' cynicism cast doubt finally on almost every one of his more generous observations.

The politics of involvement and patriotism he tempered with Machiavellian prudence. "I have lived long enough," he wrote in 1783, "and had experience enough of the conduct of governments and people, nations and courts, to be convinced that gratitude, friendship, unsuspecting confidence, and all the most amiable passions in human nature, are the most dangerous guides in politics." American politics in particular held no great promise. "We are not a chosen people that I know of," he suggested. [69] Visions of a long-lasting republicanism could be parodied by pointing to the teachings of radical "enthusiasts." "Many hundred years must roll away before We shall be corrupted," he apprised Jefferson. "Our pure, virtuous, public spirited federative Republick will last for ever, govern the Globe and introduce the perfection of Man, his perfectibility being already proved by Price Priestly, Condorcet Rousseau, Diderot and Godwin." Because of its generative effect, Adams at one point called even the Revolution itself into question. "Have I not been employed in mischief all my days?" he asked Benjamin Rush in 1811. "Did not the American revolution produce the French revolution? And did not the French revolution produce all the calamities and desolations to the human race and the whole globe ever since?" [70] A rhetorical question, perhaps, but one that clearly indicates the farthest reaches of Adams' desolation.

☆

[67] "To Jefferson," July 9, 1813, Cappon (ed.), *op. cit.*, vol. II, p. 352. "Defence," Adams (ed.), *op. cit.*, vol. IV, p. 402. "To John Penn," 1776, *ibid.*, p. 206.

[68] Smith, *op. cit.*, vol. II, p. 757.

[69] "To Secretary Livingston," January 23, 1783, Adams (ed.), *op. cit.*, vol. VIII, p. 27. In Smith, *op. cit.*, vol. II, p. 1080.

[70] "To Jefferson," November 15, 1813, Cappon (ed.), *op. cit.*, vol. II, p. 400. "To Benjamin Rush," August 28, 1811, Adams (ed.), *op. cit.*, vol. IX, p. 635.

Madison and Adams

Comparative evaluations of Madison and Adams cannot, in the final analysis, be made on grounds of consistency or inconsistency. Adams' remark in 1790—"I am so well satisfied of my own principles, that I think them as eternal and unchangeable as the earth and its inhabitants"[71]—is a manifestation of his temperament, and not an accurate testimonial to his philosophical constancy. Yet, for precisely this reason, his political views were often more inclusive than those of Madison. Like the human nature he repeatedly deprecated, Adams was himself a frequent prisoner of emotions and, driven by emotional energy—a fit of pique, a joyful event, a moment of insight, a cause for hope—he would ride a particular feeling to a new position or to a different set of possibilities; and since his feelings were so intensely involved, he invariably found himself in trouble because he could not shift political gears with facility or say what moderation or expedience of the moment demanded. Madison, on the other hand, seems almost never to have allowed emotions to move him very far and, while no mere opportunist blowing in the direction of the strongest wind, he was, as I have indicated, perfectly capable of adapting and altering his ideas to suit the occasion.

None of his contemporaries, as Adams himself well knew, quite understood his intellectual position. When in his "Defence," for example, he theoretically discussed the monarchical principle inherent in the American executive branch (comparable, as Page Smith suggests, to a prominent politician speaking openly today about "American socialism"), he was branded a monarchist, a charge that would haunt him to his grave.[72] It was this same willingness to probe fundamental questions that led Adams beyond Madison to serious consideration of problems arising from the need for national political

☆

[71] "To Alexander Jardine," June 1, 1790, *ibid.*, p. 568.

[72] There remains today some misunderstanding on this point and the issue therefore deserves further attention. While certain early letters to Rush suggest that Adams was willing to think about the appropriateness of an English-type constitutional monarch for America, the following quotations give some indication of his usual position. 1779: "Government is instituted for the common good; for the protection, safety, prosperity, and happiness of the people; and not for the profit, honor, or private interest of any one man, family, or class of men; therefore, the people alone have an incontestable, unalienable, and indefeasible right to institute government; and to reform, alter, or totally change the same, when their protection, safety, prosperity, and happiness require it." 1763: We "can never be secure in a resignation of our understandings, or in confiding enormous power either to the bramble or the cedar; no, nor to any mortal, however great or good." 1776: "there is not in all science a maxim more infallible than this, where annual elections end, there slavery begins." Standing for election every year will teach politicians the "virtues of humility, patience, and moderation, without which every man in power becomes a ravenous beast of prey." ("Report of Massachusetts Constitution,"

cohesion and collective action. The expanse of America, for example, celebrated by most Americans, was not particularly advantageous in Adams' eyes. A country the size of San Marino, for instance, had much to be said for it. "In so small a state," Adams argued, " . . . every man personally knows every other, let the form of the government be what it will, it is scarcely possible that any thing like tyranny or cruelty can take place." In the extensive territory of America, people lose sight of national interest and of each other. The "Prospect of the Future," said Adams, "will depend on the Union: and how is that Union to be preserved? Concordia Res parvae crescunt, Discordia Maximae dilabuntur." Discord might very well tear the nation asunder, for not enough citizens took the public interest sufficiently to heart. Adams reported in 1801 that we "have no Americans in America." And as late as 1815 he could lament: "We are ignorant . . . of one another. We are ignorant of our own nation; we are ignorant of the geography, the laws, customs, and manners and habits of our own country." [73]

While it is true that these sentiments do not exemplify Adams' general position (no single set of his views could) they nonetheless form an important part of his writings and must be seen alongside his arguments for mixed constitutionalism and balanced government. At certain moments Adams gave full recognition to questions of citizenship, authority, and political energy, and though he shared with Madison a philosophy that stressed a defense of property rights, a politics of interest, and a government of equilibrated institutions — in short, the conservative side of economic individualism — he could at the very least be sensitive to qualities of American life that were something

---

ibid., vol. IV, p. 225. "On Self-Delusion," no. II, *Boston Gazette*, August 29, 1763, ibid., vol. III, p. 435. "To John Penn," 1776, ibid., vol. IV, p. 205. "Thoughts on Government," ibid., p. 197.)

If the question of the existence of a bill of rights is relevant to this issue, then Adams' ability to distinguish between property rights and personal rights led him to a position rather more liberal than that of many of his compatriots. He was more liberal on this question than Madison was. He always insisted that a bill of rights was absolutely crucial to a republican constitution. ("To Benjamin Rush," November 4, 1779, ibid., vol. IX, p. 507.)

Madison, on the other hand, was sometimes equivocal on this point. He felt, for example, that the national Bill of Rights would make little difference one way or the other, but that accepting the Bill was an expediential way of appeasing those who resisted adoption of the Constitution. Madison took personal charge of drafting the Bill in Congress so that he could be certain that federal authority would not be seriously curtailed by its passage. It was Madison's opinion that the antifederalists had temporarily settled for the innocuous rights listed in the ten amendments, and that they would attempt fundamental changes relating to treaties, paper money, and contracts at some later time. (Miller, *op. cit.*, pp. 21-22.)

[73] "Defence," Adams (ed.), *op. cit.*, vol. IV, p. 309. "To Jefferson," February 3, 1812, Cappon (ed.), *op. cit.*, vol. II, p. 295. "To Benjamin Stoddert," March 31, 1801, Adams (ed.), *op. cit.*, vol. IX, p. 582. "To James Lloyd," February 11, 1815, ibid., vol. X, p. 116.

less than desirable. Page Smith notes that Adams shared the American obsession about personal independence, and that for this reason he found French practices rather distasteful. But even with this bias, Adams could sense that France possessed certain attributes that were missing in America. Smith summarizes Adams' reaction as follows:

> Peasants depended upon their lords, the lords depended upon the court. One class depended upon another; the whole society was tied together by a complex web of dependencies, of family, of status, of favors, tips, bribes, of sweetenings and *pourboires*. Yet with their dependence there was the "benevolence" and humanity which Adams had noted, the sympathy and responsiveness. In his own land, in his native New England, the treasured independence was bought at the cost of a certain coldness, a reserve, a pinching of the spirit that made people touchy and suspicious and awkward in their relations with their fellows.[74]

Although Adams never used this insight to investigate the possibilities of humanizing a system that had broken the hierarchical ties of the Old World, the very fact that he had such an insight marks him as a singular observer of his time. He was by no means a theorist of community, but he probably came closer to articulating the political dimensions of such a theory than did any writer of that period, closer, certainly, than any other conservative political thinker of his generation.

☆

[74] Smith, *op. cit.*, vol. I, pp. 403-404.

early LIBERALISM

THOMAS Paine
THOMAS JeFFerson

The Liberal Vocabulary

The counterparts to Madison and Adams on the liberal side of early American thought were Thomas Paine and Thomas Jefferson. Although their ideas were dissimilar in certain respects, Jefferson and Paine could agree on many points of fundamental importance. Perhaps even more basic than particular areas of agreement, however, was a mutually held perspective; the two men had a common way of looking at the world and their shared viewpoint invariably influenced their thinking on narrower subjects. Both tended to see things in individualistic terms, and because of this their political thought had truly radical dimensions. If one takes as a serious starting point Jefferson's dictum in the Declaration of Independence that all men, without exception, have a right to liberty and the pursuit of happiness, then many of the more traditional questions of political theory must, as a consequence, be either greatly diminished in importance or considerably altered in meaning.

When everything turns on the individual, problems of order, stability, sovereignty, authority, power, and even justice, are either rendered meaningless or take on dramatically new content. For the most part, Paine and Jefferson simply cast the older vocabulary aside, since it recalled for them all of the oppressiveness of ancient despotism. "Stability" and "order," if worth considering in the first place, were properly to be understood as direct extensions of nature, visible in the universe and thus natural to human society. Apologetics for "necessary" hierarchical institutions made in the name of order or stability would no longer be tolerated. "Sovereignty" and "authority" were merely esoteric phrases that formerly served to cloak the brute force exerted by tyrants and, as such, these terms would be discarded. "Power," on the other hand, *real* power, would be defined dually as that immediate force used to break the chains of tyranny, and as the potential force that remained permanently in the hands of the individual (or the majority of individuals) so that tyranny from above could not resubstantiate itself. "Justice" would now be measured exclusively in individual terms, would be realized only when all individuals were able to assert their basic claim to happiness and were treated equally. This justice would respond to the new Enlightenment *laws of nature,* which placed individual rights and reason at the center of attention, and not to the older *natural law,* which was sometimes used to establish as "cosmically just" inequality and oppression sanctioned by divinely ordained authority. In fact, all of the older arguments used to justify exclusive privilege, power, and property would now be brought into question. For Paine and Jefferson, the questions would primarily be directed at Europe, since in America the Revolution had placed the ancient wisdom in disrepute, and the ways of enlightened men were now comprehended and typically followed.

Thomas Paine

The American Vision

Paine, in almost all instances, reflected first on the situation in America before turning to speculate on political problems in general. America, as Paine perceived it, had already established beyond recall the new rule of individual rights, existed close to nature, was a society where men could live a reasoned life of brotherhood and benevolence in peace and tranquility with spiritual and material needs more than adequately provided for. This American vision constituted a touchstone for Paine's political theory. It provided him with a continual source of illustrations and lessons with which to instruct the anachronistic rulers of Europe. Thus in *The Rights of Man,* where Paine attacked the ancient and accepted system of public corruption in England as defended by Burke, America became the symbol of natural purity, a nation whose principles, if applied to Europe, would rid the Old World of its hoary addiction to artifice and misery. If in the beginning all the world was America for Locke, Paine could posit America simultaneously as the pristine state of nature and the millennial state of the future: America, with its simplified and mild government, most closely approximated man's original condition; with America as an example, all nations might seek a "progressive return" to natural simplicity and friendship.

America would, in fact, stand as a model of community worthy of worldwide emulation. Community for Paine was a natural condition that, at least on theoretical grounds, involved neither the reinforcement of tradition nor the active support of political institutions. Indeed, it was Paine's conviction that the nexus of tradition and government was largely responsible for the contemporary absence of communal sentiments in most areas of the globe.

If America was different in this respect it was because Americans had taken advantage of their environment and their historical opportunity and had consciously cast off the influences of the past. "The case and circumstances of America," Paine wrote, "present themselves as in the beginning of a world." America he designated as "the only spot . . . where the principles of universal reformation could begin." The lesson for all of Europe, and for England in particular, was therefore clear. America demonstrated the possibility of basing society upon absolutely just principles. Contrary historical legacies were to be completely disregarded. Tradition alone would provide no test of legitimacy. "The wrong which began a thousand years ago is as much a wrong as if it began to-day;" Paine remarked, "and the right which originates today, is as much a right as if it had the sanction of a thousand years. Time with respect to principles is an eternal NOW." There could exist no obligations between generations, for each must be free to organize itself with reference to absolute principles of justice, principles that applied equally to all citizens. Paine followed Jefferson in absolving all generations of responsibility to either the future or the past. "Every age and generation," he wrote, "must be free to act for itself, in all cases, as the ages and generations which preceded it . . . Those who have quitted the world, and those who are not yet arrived in it, are as remote from each other as the utmost stretch of mortal imagination can conceive. What possible obligation then, can exist between them?"[1] From this perspective all institutions, no matter how deeply cherished or long-lived, were subject to an absolutely fundamental kind of criticism. For Paine, the institution of government was in greatest need of such criticism for, even more than tradition, it stood in the way of effectuating "the principles of universal reformation."

☆

[1] "The Rights of Man," Philip S. Foner (ed.), *The Complete Writings of Thomas Paine*, The Citadel Press, New York, 1945, vol. I, pp. 251, 352, 376. "Dissertation on First Principles of Government," *ibid.*, pp. 573-574.

Government and Society

Government contributed very little to society, and when it operated badly, as most often it did, it corrupted mankind by engendering hostility and suspicion where before there had existed love and respect. "Man is not the enemy of man," wrote Paine, "but through the medium of a false system of government." "Government," he argued, "like dress, is the badge of lost innocence; the palaces of kings are built upon the ruins of the bowers of paradise." The positive contributions of government were minimal at best and for the most part superfluous. "Government," Paine suggested, "is no farther necessary than to supply the few cases to which society and civilization are not conveniently competent; and instances are not wanting to show, that everything which government can usefully add thereto, has been performed by the common consent of society, without government." In point of fact, government *"is nothing more than a national association acting on the principles of society."* [2] Man would be better off without it: its productive importance is negligible, its influence pernicious, its very existence a constant source of danger.

Since Paine repudiated the binding force of history, he would listen to no defense of government based upon ancient constitutional sanctions. In the first place, constitutions were merely convenient devices that societies employed in order to control and limit the exercise of political power. The extent of these controls and limitations was a function of present circumstances, and could be specified by reference to actual documents, not by invoking customary usage. "A constitution," Paine argued, "is not a thing in name only, but in fact. It has not an ideal, but a real existence; and whenever it cannot be produced in visible form, there is none." [3] Whatever legitimacy government possessed it could not be supported by Burkean appeals to ancient constitutional procedures. All such appeals, Paine believed, were relics of an age of myth and unreason.

The use of reason clearly indicated that it was society, not government, that stood as the natural vehicle for carrying out men's collective desires. It was society that provided man with a life of sufficiency, decency, and equity. Men were held in society by the demands of mutual dependence and reciprocal interest, and, while these relationships involved multifarious needs, the needs themselves could be met entirely by social, as opposed to political, institutions. Moreover, there was in society a natural practice that, without the coerciveness of

☆

[2] "The Rights of Man," *ibid.*, vol. I, pp. 343, 357-358, 361. "Common Sense," *ibid.*, pp. 4-5.
[3] *Ibid.*, p. 278.

political authority, easily governed social intercourse. Man in the pure social condition would find that his needs and interests were completely fulfilled and, at the same time, that order would exist as a natural attribute of a harmonious social life. Those who would impose governmental structures on social institutions were, in Paine's view, at the very best engaged in a totally unnecessary activity. "In fine," he wrote, "society performs for itself almost every thing which is ascribed to government."[4] Society would stand autonomously as that agency which held men together and which solved those few problems that arise when men live in close proximity.

Even though Paine was willing to invest society with the ability to provide order and human satisfaction, one senses that even social interrelation, while vital to man's happiness, was somehow secondary, a derivative of more basic human characteristics. Note in the following quotation that Paine tried to make the best of two worlds: man is seen both as "forced" into society and as naturally endowed with "social affections."

> As Nature created [man] for social life, she fitted him for the station she intended. In all cases she made his natural wants greater than his individual powers. No one man is capable, without the aid of society, of supplying his own wants; and those wants, acting upon every individual, *impel* the whole of them into society . . . But she has gone further. She has not only *forced* man into society, but she has implanted in him a system of *social affections*, which, though not necessary to his existence, are essential to his happiness. There is no period in life when this love for society ceases to act.[5]

One might logically expect that if nature had consigned to man everlasting social affections, there would be no need to force him into society. His social condition would be natural to him whether or not his wants exceeded his capacity to fulfill them. Paine's ambivalence on this point apparently derived from the fact that although he found society far more important than government, it was individual human nature in its unblemished natural state that, in the final analysis, he principally relied upon and that shaped the central tenets of his theory.

To understand man in his social or political condition, Paine argued, one must first understand the controlling principles of nature itself, those precepts that if discovered and emulated, could provide man with correct guidelines for organizing his own existence. Paine believed that once good principles were uncovered and established they could not be altered or eradicated by time. "Forms," he observed, "grow out of principles, and operate to continue the principles they

☆

[4] *Ibid.*, vol. I, p. 357.
[5] *Ibid.*, vol. I, p. 357.

grow from. It is impossible to practice a bad form on any thing but a bad principle." And the important principles for man, namely, those concerning his rights, were to be found in the prepolitical, presocietal state of nature. Indeed, the rights of man may be traced to the creation of man and as a matter of incontrovertible fact, "every civil right grows out of a natural right."[6]

Community, Individualism, and Commerce

It is not necessary here to consider Paine's description of natural rights and the expression or suppression of these rights in civil society. It is sufficient to note that Paine argued the cause of personal freedom and civil liberty more forcefully and more frequently than did any man of his time. For our purposes it is important to notice, however, that the fundamental rights of man derived not from his political or social status, but from his individual essence, from his part in the very nature of things. Paine went even further. He found in nature not just the principles of individual right, but the embodiment of community as well. In a marvelous metaphor in the *Age of Reason,* God is placed on the rostrum to instruct his human audience in the first principles of kindliness. "The Almighty Lecturer," wrote Paine, "by displaying the principles of science in the structure of the universe, has invited man to study and to imitation. It is as if He had said to the inhabitants of this globe, that we call ours, 'I have made an earth for men to dwell upon, and I have rendered the starry heavens visible, to teach him science and the arts. He can now provide for his own comfort, AND LEARN FROM MY MUNIFICENCE TO ALL, TO BE KIND TO EACH OTHER.'"[7] In America no artificial barriers stood between man and the teachings of nature: "In such a situation man becomes what he ought. He sees his species, not with the inhuman idea of a natural enemy, but as kindred; and the example [of America] shows to the artificial world, that man must go back to nature for information."[8] The example of nature, and thus the example of America, then, was to demonstrate to the world that rights *and* community are the natural possessions of man, prior to and irrespective of his involvement in political society.

This perspective constituted Paine's first level of analysis. On this level community and individualism are in no sense contradictory,

☆

[6] *Ibid.,* vol. I, pp. 274, 276, 297.

[7] *Ibid.,* vol. I, p. 490.

[8] "The Rights of Man," *ibid.,* vol. I, p. 354. In this connection Paine argued that, solely because of his experience in America, LaFayette had become an expert in the "science of civil government." (*Ibid.,* p. 302.)

since both are attributes of man in nature. Similarly, neither factor is enriched by tradition nor reinforced by government, since both precede the development of political traditions and are in fact diluted by this very development. Paine set forth a theory of *natural community*, a theory that posited individuals in a primordial state of brotherly affection.

This theory of community presupposed that men could carry on their interpersonal transactions free of friction and disagreement. Paine held this conviction even with respect to commercial transaction. In this connection he advanced a straightforward statement of economic individualism. He argued that commerce, when based on individual interest, was capable of mitigating singlehandedly the injustices of governments, even though commerce did *not* trace its origins to the natural condition of man.

> I have been an advocate for commerce, because I am a friend to its effects. It is a pacific system, operating to unite mankind by rendering nations, as well as individuals, *useful to each other*. As to the mere theoretical reformation, I have never preached it up. The most effectual process is that of improving the condition of man by means of his interest; and it is on this ground that I take my stand. If commerce were permitted to act to the universal extent it is capable of, it would extirpate the system of war, and produce a revolution in the uncivilized state of governments. The invention of commerce has arisen since those governments began, and it is the greatest approach towards universal civilization that has yet been made by any means not immediately flowing from moral principles. [Emphasis added.][9]

Despite Paine's qualification, it seems logically to be the case that the notion of beneficent commerce was in fact based upon moral principles, for it assumed that the individual conflicts of commercial exchange were in no way disruptive of harmonious and brotherly relationships.

Paine's picture of commercial benevolence was apparently predicated on his prior conception of individual benevolence. Economic intercourse was for Paine merely an extension of natural individual behavior, and since the latter was by definition good, the former must necessarily also be good. This is what Paine meant when he wrote: "commerce is no other than the traffic of two persons multiplied on a scale of numbers; and by the same rule that nature intended the intercourse of two, she intended that of all." And such traffic between persons, even when it involved sharp differences of opinion, could not weaken communal ties, especially in a society that, like America, was organized according to the postulates of civil justice. "The United

☆

[9] *Ibid.*, vol. I, p. 400.

States," Paine contended, "constitute one extended family, one imperial Commonwealth, the greatest and most equal in its rights and government of any ever known in the world." Under these auspicious conditions economic disputation would, as long as it did not run to "licentious abuse," be entirely natural and hardly unsettling. "All that is necessary, in a case like this," said Paine, "is calm discussion, and a disposition to agree and be understood. That measures and subjects do not strike every mind alike . . . and that, in a situation so remote as the several parts of the United States are from each other, some misconception may arise, is a circumstance we may naturally expect; but as our interest, like our object, is a united one, there can be no measure which is to operate equally over all, in matters common to all, that can, on a just consideration, be supposed to affect one more than another."[10] But since individualism was now translated into economic terms and since community could count on neither government nor tradition to aid its cause, one wonders how community would stand up under a conflict over precisely this sort of issue: a severe disagreement on a question of the equal application of a particular economic measure.

Commerce in the Real World

This question was put to the test in 1786 when the matter of rechartering the Bank of North America came before the Pennsylvania legislature. The Bank was vigorously attacked by the debtor class in general and particularly by the frontiersmen of Western Pennsylvania. On February 18, 1786, Paine lifted his pen in defense of the Bank in a pamphlet entitled *Dissertations on Government; the Affairs of the Bank; and Paper Money.*

As matter of public policy, the question of the utility of the Bank is not crucial to our consideration; liberals and conservatives could legitimately be located on both sides of the issue. More important is Paine's choosing to preface his practical argument with a presentation of larger theoretical considerations. He began by drawing a comparison between a nation and an army. Where the latter has but one purpose, the former is a composite of multifarious interests and occupations "continually meeting, crossing, uniting, opposing and separating from each other, as accident, interest and circumstances shall dictate."[11] The public good in a nation is thus not something opposed to the individual good; it is simply "the good of every individual collected." The public good is expressed in terms of equal justice, and

☆

[10] *Ibid.,* vol. I, p. 400. "In Answer to the Citizens of Rhode-Island on the Five Per Cent. Duty," Letter II, *Providence Gazette,* December 28, 1782, *ibid.,* vol. II, p. 346.

[11] *Ibid.,* vol. II, p. 371.

when a people forms itself into a republic, it pledges itself to support the rule of equal justice for all.

What did the pledge to equal justice actually mean? Paine's answer was as straightforward as it was surprising. "In this pledge and compact," he argued, "lies the foundation of the republic: and the security to the rich and the consolation to the poor is, that what each man has is his own; that no despotic sovereign can take it from him, and that the common consenting principle which holds all the parts of a republic together, secures him likewise from the despotism of numbers: for despotism may be more effectually acted by many over a few, than by one man over all."[12] Moreover, certain conditions of political and economic life cannot be rightfully changed by the people. Paine insisted that the Bank charter could not be revoked because it constituted a *contract,* as opposed to a *law,* agreed to by an earlier legislature and thus eternally binding on all parties. His defense of this position was made in the language of European metaphysics. "[It] is the state," he contended, "that is bound on one part and certain individuals on the other part . . . Therefore, for the next or any other assembly to undertake to dissolve the state from its obligation is an assumption of power of a novel and extraordinary kind. It is the servant attempting to free his master. The election of new assemblies following each other makes no difference in the nature of things. The state is still the same state. The public is still the same body. These do not annually expire, though the time of an assembly does. These are not new-created every year, nor can they be displaced from their original standing; but are a perpetual, permanent body, always in being and still the same."[13] Paine completed the theoretical argument by suggesting that corporate bodies should not be dependent upon the state for their charters, for this would mean that the citizens who compose these corporations would be discriminated against by government and therefore not be free.

The analysis presented in *Dissertations on Government,* which seems at first to defy explanation,[14] may have been the product of Paine's favorable predisposition toward commercial autonomy. To begin with, Paine did not see the Bank as occupying a particularly dangerous position. It was, he pointed out, merely a "company for the promotion and convenience of commerce." Having once said this, he

☆

[12] *Ibid.,* vol. II, pp. 372-374.

[13] *Ibid.,* vol. II, pp. 380-381.

[14] It has been suggested by some that Paine's pen was for sale and that the tract was produced simply because Robert Morris and other Bank officials hired Paine to write it. Although Paine knew and corresponded with Morris, there is no conclusive evidence to support this contention.

might have let the matter stand, but he was forced to justify this "convenience" to the bitterest critics of the Bank. Had it simply been an issue of accumulated wealth, Paine could have held his usual ground because, as he indicated elsewhere, large stores of individual wealth were entirely acceptable as long as they did not lead to poverty for the rest of society. "I am a friend to riches," he wrote, "because they are capable of good. I care not how affluent some may be, provided that none be miserable in consequence of it."[15] The case of the Bank, however, was at least problematical in this regard, for many Pennsylvanians charged that Bank policies generated affluence for a few and impoverishment for the majority. It is clear that Paine was not unaware of this difficulty since, despite his attempt in a later part of the tract to refute the specific criticisms of the Bank's financial dealings, he felt compelled at the outset to make an entirely novel theoretical argument. Paine was apparently forced to choose between conflicting values, those of commercial "promotion and convenience" on the one hand, and those of "natural justice" on the other.

On purely economic grounds, an argument for justice, if not for *natural* justice, could certainly be made for a commercial arrangement such as that incorporating the Bank of North America. At the heart of Western commercial enterprise, in fact that which made it a "pacific system" and a "cordiliser of mankind," was the concept of contract. Without contracts, scrupulously honored and strictly enforced, the commercial system would produce not only disharmony, but very likely the constant danger of outright violence. Contracts legally drawn and freely entered into must therefore be preserved at all costs. The problem, however, was that the contract in question, the Bank charter, tended to work *against* the political theory that Paine typically propounded. Consequently, if the contractual concept were to be protected in these circumstances, a new political theory would be required. Clearly, the usual arguments would not apply. It would be impossible, for example, to trace the "rights of contract" back to nature; contracts owed their existence to society, and in the case of the Bank charter, to government itself. Without a politically organized society, they would be unimaginable entities.

At any rate, this new statement would also involve a dramatic recasting of the concept of individualism. Corporations were to be protected, Paine noted, because they were composed of people. Therefore, to subject corporations to "arbitrary" controls would be to treat the individual corporation members unequally; it would be to deprive individuals of their rights. Paine was normally interested in preserv-

☆

[15] "Agrarian Justice," *ibid.*, vol. I, p. 617.

ing freedom, not for the privileged few, but for the popular masses who were so frequently dispossessed of their rights. At another time he wrote: "there is no such thing in America as power of any kind, independent of the people. There is no other race of men in it but the people."[16] It was this idea, the concept of "the people," that Paine usually had in mind when he referred to "individuals" in possession of unalienable natural rights. It was clear, however, that the individual as the basic unit of society was one thing, while the individual as the agent of commerce was quite another, and that when a conflict arose between the two the latter might easily carry the day. In such a situation Paine's natural community would be altered beyond recognition. If the society depicted in *Dissertations on Government* could in any sense be conceived of as a community, it would be a community in Burkean terms: duties, obligations, and responsibilities would obtain among the classes, supported by an overall structure of stability and order, the structure itself buttressed by a system of traditional prerogative and political authority.

A Radical View of Property

That Paine had to resort to a Burkean formulation was ironic since he normally regarded Burke as his principal philosophical antagonist. Yet Paine held to a certain analytical distinction that was also held by many who shared Burke's views, a distinction without which the argument in *Dissertations on Government* could never have been made. Like most of his contemporaries, Paine differentiated between the concept of commerce and the concept of property.[17] By the Jacksonian period this distinction would begin to break down: bank holdings would be regarded as a variety of property, not unlike "property" held in the form of land securities. Had Paine attempted to coalesce property and commerce in his own theory, the argument constructed in *Dissertations on Government* would have been tortured beyond belief, for his views on property, advanced primarily in *Agrarian Justice,* were totally unrelated to those on commerce and carried his ideas entirely in another direction.

Paine stated quite bluntly that the concept of personal property, legitimate in itself, implied no right whatever to ownership of land.

☆

[16] "In Answer to the Citizens of Rhode Island on the Five Per Cent. Duty," Letter I, *Providence Gazette and Country Journal,* December 21, 1782, *ibid.,* vol. II, p. 337.

[17] See "On the Five Per Cent. Duty," Letter IV, *Providence Gazette,* January 11, 1783, *ibid.,* vol. II, pp. 353-354.

"Man did not make the earth," he insisted, "and though he had a natural right to *occupy* it, he had no right to *locate as his* property in perpetuity any part of it." The earth in its natural state is the *"COMMON PROPERTY OF THE HUMAN RACE."*[18] All an individual proprietor "owns," if such a term is appropriate, is the value of the improvements created by his own hands. Everything else—the value of the land itself and the value of accumulation beyond that personally produced—is a function of man residing in society, for without society riches could not exist. The proprietor, consequently, must repay society in both respects: for his land he owes a *"ground rent,* for," Paine contended, "I know of no better term to express the idea for the land which he holds;" with regard to his excess accumulation "he owes on every principle of justice, of gratitude, and of civilization,"[19] a percentage of that excess.

The payments of landholders, in the form of heavy inheritance taxes, would be used to create a national fund from which every person would receive fifteen pounds at the age of twenty-one and ten pounds a year for life after reaching the age of fifty. Society, the generating agent of all personal property, would act as common treasurer, dispensing funds equitably so that all citizens would obtain an equal start and all would be provided for in their old age. Paine argued that such a policy was a matter of right and justice and not of charity, for poverty would never have existed if it were not for the unnatural monopoly of land held by the upper classes. Moreover, to rectify fully this situation, to deal effectively with conditions of poverty, action must be taken by the entire society and not by isolated members exercising their personal charity. "In all great cases," Paine wrote, "it is necessary to have a principle more universally active than charity; and, with respect to justice, it ought not to be left to the choice of detached individuals whether they will do justice, it ought to be national and not individual."[20] The final result of this plan, emanating from the entire society, would be to carry to their logical conclusions the doctrines enunciated by the French and American Revolutions. Now the revolutionary ideas that had been applied chiefly to the political sphere would at last be applied to the social order as well.

☆

[18] "Agrarian Justice," *ibid.,* vol. I, p. 611. Paine apparently differentiated among certain kinds of civil rights. While he normally traced legitimate civil rights back to the natural rights of man, the civil right to property he posited as having originated in the social compact. While the compact itself afforded man the security of society, it in no way extended or depleted the scope of his natural rights. ("To Thomas Jefferson," 1789, *ibid.,* vol. II, pp. 1298-1299.)

[19] "Agrarian Justice," *ibid.,* vol. I, pp. 611, 620.

[20] *Ibid.,* vol. I, p. 618.

A Logical Role for Government

The radical changes proposed in *Agrarian Justice* would take place entirely within the confines of society. Paine made it perfectly clear that government would neither play a significant role in effecting these changes nor benefit from them. He stressed that the inheritance revenues "ought always to go to society and not to the government."[21] Despite this remark and despite Paine's usual position on governmental power, there are occasional instances in his writing where government is given the possibility of performing entirely useful functions. In *Common Sense*, for example, Paine acknowledged that, however benign the aspect of society and however malignant the spread of political authority, defects of moral virtue in human nature would make necessary the formation of some sort of government. Furthermore, if properly derived from a legitimate social compact, if simply organized, and if fairly based on the practices of just representation and frequent elections, government can truly embody the will of the people. Such a government "will establish a common interest with every part of the community, they will mutually and naturally support each other."[22] It follows that a government of this sort must have at least a minimal amount of political authority.

From this perspective Paine could in the early days of the American nation insist on the necessity of government control over certain aspects of the economy. He warned that the country's "fairest prospects may fail and the best calculated system of finance become unproductive of its end, if left to the caprice of temper and self-interest."[23] More pointedly, in *The Rights of Man*, after emphasizing the theoretical importance of the individual and society and depreciating the value of government, he argued that a vast program of political action was needed to ameliorate the terrible blight of English poverty. He recommended legislation that would provide compensation for poor families, funds for the elderly, a system of public education, money for funeral expenses, grants to allay the expenses of marriage and birth, employment for the casual poor, abolition of the tax on houses, limited disarmament with allowances for discharged soldiers, and progressive taxation. Paine made it plain, moreover, that these reforms were motivated by an overriding sense of community. He called for nothing less than a full expression of social altruism, a political program that would

☆

[21] *Ibid.*, p. 616.

[22] "Common Sense," *ibid.*, vol. I, p. 6.

[23] "On the Five Per Cent. Duty," Letter IV, *Providence Gazette*, January 11, 1783, *ibid.*, vol. II, p. 356.

touch the "hearts of the humane" and rid society of its centuries-old "instruments of civil torture."

If implemented, this program would end forever the political hostility between classes and, even more striking, it would increase the popular authority of government. "The poor as well as the rich will then be interested in the support of government," Paine declared, "and the cause and apprehension of riots and tumults will cease." He concluded his appeal by attempting to reach the consciences of the wealthy. In biblical prose he exclaimed: "Ye who sit in ease, and solace yourselves in plenty . . . and who say to yourselves, 'Are we not well off,' have ye thought of these things? When you do, ye will cease to speak and feel for yourselves alone."[24] Thus Paine called upon Englishmen to transcend their personal or class interests and come to the aid of their countrymen through the enactment of proper remedial laws. The result of such legislation would not only be social reclamation and class cohesion, but increased support for a government that spoke at last to the needs of the entire population.

Had this been Paine's main line of attack he might have treated the Bank issue far differently. With government established as a legitimate voice of the community, Paine could, as later generations did, posit general rules of incorporation that, under the administration of government authorities, might simultaneously protect the public interest and the legal position of corporations. But Paine's investment in government was grudging at best. In *Common Sense*, writing in behalf of the American Revolution, he had no choice but to accept some minimal form of government, since Americans were basing their differences with England largely on grounds of political procedure. In *The Rights of Man* he turned to political action and governmental support for want of other means of immediate reform. Paine did not in fact give government legitimate theoretical standing and therefore never came to grips with the real question of its genuine uses and abuses. For this reason he could apparently shift his position on certain issues with scarcely a reservation. In 1805 he wrote: "legislators are elected annually, not only for the purpose of giving the people, in their elective character, the opportunity of showing their approbation of those who have acted right . . . but also for the purpose of correcting the wrong . . . of a former legislature. But the very intention, essence and principle of annual election would be destroyed if any one legislature, during the year of its authority, had the power to place any of its acts beyond reach of succeeding legislatures: yet this is

☆

[24] "The Rights of Man," *ibid.*, vol. I, pp. 431-432.

always attempted to be done in those acts of a legislature called charters."[25] With no serious attempt to reconcile governmental limitation and economic individualism, this statement has the appearance of mere capriciousness.

America as Archetype

Much of the difficult work of the political philosopher who wishes to move from the level of theory to the level of action lies in the construction of an intervening level of analysis. Here an attempt must be made to connect large speculations with practical programs. Paine was on most occasions impatient with such attempts. Part of his logical confusion stems from his proclivity to work exclusively on one level at a time and, while each level might be internally consistent, the integration of the formulation as a whole tended to be neglected. In this regard it was Paine's belief that political science need not concern itself with problems of integration, since it was a relatively simple kind of science that merely required discovery of the two or three basic axioms upon which all rightful governments stand. If political science sought to channel its knowledge in the direction of social change, the mechanical aspect of nature provided a model that was as useful as it was uncomplicated. Paine contended that "it is only by organizing civilization upon such principles as to act like a system of pulleys that the whole weight of misery can be removed."[26] If one were to take this idea seriously, one might, as Montesquieu did, embark on an extended investigation of complex, interconnecting social relationships, an investigation that could yield "scientific" findings of a high degree of sophistication. Paine was content merely to state the principle of the model, however, believing that in society, as in nature, its actual operation would take care of itself.

This is not to say that Paine was never able to engage himself in making broad connections. Indeed, at times he was willing to temper his remarks with observations derived from precisely this kind of reflection. At such moments he could acknowledge the *positive* aspects of contemplating the experiences of history. A too "great inattention to past occurrences," he noted, "retards and bewilders our judgment in everything, while, on the contrary, by comparing what is past with what is present, we frequently hit on the true character of both and become wise with very little trouble. It is a kind of countermarch by which we get into the rear of time, and mark the movements and mean-

☆

[25] "Constitutions, Governments, and Charters," *ibid.*, vol. II, pp. 990-991.

[26] "Dissertation on First Principles of Government," *ibid.*, vol. II, pp. 570-588. "Agrarian Justice," *ibid.*, vol. I, p. 618.

ings of things as we make our return."[27] With the past seen in this light, America itself could be viewed in more realistic terms. Paine could admit that "though the cause of America is the most honorable that man ever engaged in, I am not so dazzled by it as not to perceive the faults that are twisting themselves round it, and unnaturally claiming kindred with it."[28] This approach, however, was not typical, and most often America stood unencumbered by unnatural tendencies, a paragon of modern civilization.

Such was especially the case when, as in *The Rights of Man,* Paine addressed his remarks to a European audience. At those times he usually imagined America as beyond reproach, as the only nation on earth where civil life was based on the "love of the people." As early as 1783 he could look back on and describe the growth of America in rapturous terms. "When the cause of America, like a new creation, rose into existence," he wrote, "it had something in it which confounded and yet enraptured the world. The boldness of the attempt, and the extent of its consequences, overawed the conjectures of mankind."[29] Soon after the successful American Revolution, Paine moved to carry this American enthusiasm to England and France and, in so doing, he removed himself from the exceedingly difficult task of establishing normal political institutions in the new nation. For this reason his later comments on America tended to have a slightly disembodied quality. Whereas Crevecoeur, in his otherwise idyllic picture of America, could, even before his final disillusion, find that selfishness, litigiousness, and indifference occasionally blemished the character of the usually noble American, Paine, from European shores, saw America as the happy coincidence of theory and practice, the embodiment and harbinger of universal order and justice.[30]

In this connection we appreciate Paine's failure to understand why, prior to his return to America, he was left languishing in a French prison by a United States government that professed uncertainty about his American citizenship. What Paine really failed to understand was that a considerable difference existed between his exalted descriptions and the actual America of the 1790's, so much so that there were many who regarded Paine as an outcast, a man who advocated

☆

[27] "The American Crisis," III, April 19, 1777, *ibid.,* vol. I, p. 74.

[28] "On the Five Per Cent. Duty," Letter V, *Providence Gazette,* January 18, 1783, *ibid.,* vol. II, p. 357.

[29] "In Answer to the Citizens of Rhode Island on the Five Per Cent. Duty," Letter III, *Providence Gazette,* January 4, 1783, *ibid.,* vol. II, p. 346.

[30] J. Hector St. John de Crevecoeur, *Letters from an American Farmer,* Fox, Duffield and Company, New York, 1904, pp. 51-59. H. L. Bourdin, R. H. Gabriel, and S. T. Williams (eds.), *Sketches of Eighteenth Century America,* Yale University Press, New Haven, Conn., 1925, pp. 75-78.

doctrines that were essentially un-American. Paine misperceived in reality precisely what he misconstrued in his theory: namely, that the imperatives of economic individualism, conservative *or* liberal, would make the realization of the nation as an "extended family" enormously difficult, if not entirely impossible.

America Reconsidered

After returning to America, Paine, in a series of "Letters to the Citizens of the United States," had occasion to reflect on the events that had transpired since 1776. The direction events had taken caused him to feel grave concern for his nation. Time and again he inquired into the factors behind the bitter disputes that plagued the country. "Fourteen years, and something more, have produced a change," he reported in November of 1802, ". . . and I ask myself what it is?" "Why was it," he wondered six months later, "that America, formed for happiness, and remote by situation and circumstances from the troubles and tumults of the European world, became plunged into its vortex and contaminated with its crimes?" Confronted by these painful questions, Paine was not long without a reply. "The answer," he said, "is easy. Those who were . . . at the head of affairs were apostates from the principles of the Revolution." Men of the Federalist stripe had been attempting to undermine the very foundation upon which American society was based. Paine noted: "it requires only a prudent and honest administration to preserve America always in peace . . . But when men get into power, whose heads, like the head of *John Adams,* are filled with 'strange notions' and counter revolutionary principles and projects, things will be sure to go wrong."[31] In short, Paine accused members of the Federalist party of being nothing less than counter-revolutionaries.

That Paine could even consider such a charge cast serious doubt upon his own political theory. With the announcement that things had gone awry, his view of a happy coincidence between the American situation and the fixed verities of natural justice was called seriously into question. Paine acknowledged that "while I beheld with pleasure the dawn of liberty rising in Europe, I saw with regret the lustre of it fading in America . . . Distant symptoms painfully suggested the idea that the principles of the Revolution were expiring on the soil that produced them." From Europe it had appeared to Paine that America was being subverted, "that some meditated treason against

☆

[31]"Letter II," *The National Intelligencer*, November 22, 1802, Foner (ed.), *op. cit.,* vol. II, p. 912. "Letter VI," *The Philadelphia Aurora*, May 14, 1803, *ibid.*, p. 935. "Letter VII," *Trenton True-American*, April 21, 1803, *ibid.*, p. 955.

her liberties lurked at the bottom of her government."[32] With this admission Paine effectively negated his earlier argument that a society based on proper principles would enjoy in perpetuity internal peace and harmony. A society founded correctly could in fact degenerate, just as America, the living example of natural justice, had been degenerating before his very eyes.

If American experience could go wrong, so could Paine's theory, for Paine had made their identification virtually complete. The expression of nostalgia and regret about his "native" country was consequently a commentary on the adequacy of his own political philosophy. He reported that when he had been engaged in pursuits abroad, his anxiety "to get back to America was great for many years. It is the country of my heart, and the place of my political and literary birth. It was the American Revolution that made me an author, and forced into action the mind that had been dormant, and had no wish for public life. [But] by the accounts I received, she appeared to be going wrong."[33] That America had gone wrong meant that Paine had gone wrong; it might even mean that he was incorrect from the beginning. With the benefit of hindsight, he was ready to admit that the Revolution itself represented something other than the final triumph of reason, was something less than the product of an inevitable popular demand for human rights. "Like you," he told Sam Adams in 1803, I "have often looked back on those times, and have thought that if independence had not been declared at the time it was, the public mind could not have been brought up to it afterwards."[34] The idea that revolutionary circumstances presented but an ephemeral opportunity for establishing independence suggests that America was not so far removed from European ways after all. American history subsequent to the Revolution made this suggestion even more convincing.

And yet if Paine had second thoughts about America, he gave no intimation that these thoughts had any general importance as far as his theoretical position was concerned. Neither his having had to resort to means other than the establishment of first principles, nor his being forced to endorse a political — the Jeffersonian — party,[35] caused him to alter a single tenet of his political philosophy. He could still note happily that American independence had marked a total break with corrupt European precedents. "It was," he reiterated, "the

☆

[32] "Letter I," *The National Intelligencer*, November 15, 1802, *ibid.*, vol. II, pp. 909-910. "Letter IV," *The National Intelligencer*, December 6, 1802, *ibid.*, p. 926.

[33] "Letter IV," *The National Intelligencer*, December 6, 1802, *ibid.*, vol. II, p. 926.

[34] "To Samuel Adams," January 1, 1803, *ibid.*, p. 1434.

[35] In "Dissertation on First Principles of Government," Paine wrote: " . . . it is the nature and intention of a constitution to *prevent governing by party.*" (*Ibid.*, vol. II, p. 588.)

opportunity of *beginning the world anew,* as it were; and of bringing forward a *new system* of government in which the rights of *all* men should be preserved that gave *value* to independence." And despite the temporary villainy of Federalist demagogues, Paine could face the future optimistically. "Reason," he proclaimed, "is recovering her empire, and the fog of delusion is clearing away."[36]

The recovery of reason was for Paine signaled by the triumph of Jefferson in the presidential election of 1800, a triumph that was realized through the concerted action of a political party. But in Paine's view the political activity itself could be ignored. The Jeffersonian "party" was not a party in the usual pejorative sense, but a collection of men dedicated to the reassertion of reason in society. Jefferson's victory thus served as "proof" of the lasting nature of Paine's principles; with this victory, Paine's primary teachings could once again be elevated to the level of universal dicta.

Thomas Jefferson

The Jeffersonian Approach

Although it is necessary and proper to deal with Thomas Jefferson in conjunction with Paine for analytical and ideological purposes, this dual assessment is not made without a certain awkwardness. Although originator of many of the most memorable statements of the American liberal creed, Jefferson was not often given to speculative political theory. Such theorizing occupies an astonishingly small place in his voluminous manuscripts, and he wrote no work that is in any way comparable to Paine's *Rights of Man.* Even late in life, when secluded on his Monticello hilltop, Jefferson felt unmoved to pen in systematic fashion a comprehensive political philosophy. Throughout his later years he carefully sidestepped repeated entreaties by Adams to engage in a dialogue on fundamental questions.

One can find in Paine three varieties or levels of thought: (1) the practical—concerned with correct responses to issues of political necessity; (2) the ideal—concerning the enunciation of first principles of social and political justice; and (3) the speculative—involving a theory (in Paine's case a very brief theory) that either embodies or justifies practical and especially ideal pronouncements. Jefferson seldom carried his thought to this third level. Only on rare occasions, and then only in part, did he attempt to give a philosophical synthesis to his supreme values. He was normally content to state his highest

☆

[36] "Letter VII," *ibid.,* vol. II, p. 948. "Letter VIII," *Philadelphia Aurora,* June 7, 1805, *ibid.,* p. 956.

principles, and this he did often, while leaving the argument at that. Despite his vast learning in the tradition and his insatiable curiosity about all forms of human behavior, he was less a political theorist than any of the major political writers of his time. Jefferson was imbued with an Enlightenment philosophy, and this philosophy was continually expressed in his most dramatic arguments in support of political liberty. He was not himself a political theorist, however, and for this reason his pronouncements seem at times rather desultory, and at other times more epigrammatic than philosophical.

Without question Jefferson shared most of Paine's ideals. Indeed, on the question of the standing of the individual in civil society it is the ringing phrase of Jefferson in behalf of freedom, equality, and civil liberty that we most remember. At his best, Jefferson breathed lasting meaning into a rhetoric that in Paine's hands was occasionally lost in philosophical remoteness or in the commonplace of the pamphleteer. But because Jefferson could not move to a third mode of thought—the speculative—*reality*, with its inescapable set of limitations, incessantly crowded his style and, while it may not have altered his fundamental ideals, it often caused him to make serious shifts in perspective. The awareness of reality was not, as it was for Madison, the constant definer of political feasibility; it was rather a lurking presence that hovered continuously on the periphery of his thought, a presence that sometimes forced itself—in moments of singular clarity or acute pessimism—to analytical stage center.

The Limits of Optimism

With respect to America's historical importance, however, Jefferson could match Paine in optimistic enthusiasm. Like Paine he appreciated the creative opportunity afforded by American uniqueness. In comparing the French and American Revolutions, the metaphor of the omnipotent artist came readily to mind. At first Jefferson was exceedingly sanguine about the chances of success for the French Constituent Assembly. "The National assembly," he wrote from Paris in August 1789, "have now as clean a canvas to work on here as we had in America."[37] But in retrospect Jefferson realized that America had occupied a position unparalleled in human history. "Our Revolution commenced on more favorable ground," he noted two years before his death. "It presented us an album on which we were free to write what we pleased. We had no occasion to search into musty records, to hunt up royal parchments, or to investigate the laws and institutions of a

☆

[37] "To Diodati," August 3, 1789, Julian R. Boyd et al. (eds.), *The Papers of Thomas Jefferson*, Princeton University Press, Princeton, 1950–, vol. XV, p. 326.

semibarbarous ancestry." Such historical inquiry could at best provide examples for nonemulation, for it was Jefferson's opinion that "history, in general, only informs us of what bad government is." Thus, unlike France, America could forge ahead unencumbered by negative historical legacies, by a people schooled in the archaic ways of oligarchy and inequality. "Never was a finer canvas presented to work on than our countrymen," Jefferson exulted in a letter to Adams. This was to be the "age of experiments in government,"[38] and the American experiment must assume a transcendent importance for the entire planet.

The very novelty of its existence would startle the imagination. "We can no longer say there is nothing new under the sun," Jefferson declared. "For this whole chapter in the history of man is new. The great extent of our Republic is new. Its sparse habitation is new. The mighty wave of public opinion which has rolled over it is new."[39] Now at last man's reason would provide a basis for enlightened politics. Representative government would, by the sheer force of its correctness, everywhere loosen the grip on the human spirit held so long by "kings, Priests, and nobles." If America alone was first blessed with the new freedom, then this would make the achievement of her success all the more vital. "It is impossible not to be sensible that we are acting for all mankind," Jefferson informed Joseph Priestley, "that the circumstances denied to others, but indulged to us, have imposed on us the duty of proving what is the degree of freedom and self-government in which a society may venture to leave its individual members." Such a nation, as long as it preserved its mild and limited form of government, could demonstrate to the world nothing less than "the perfection of human society."[40]

But for Jefferson, perfection was not automatically achieved by removing the excrescences of society that historically had distorted the individual. To begin, Jefferson could not conceive of individual existence either prior to or exclusive of the institutions of society. He thus found no conceptual disjunction between individual and social values. "Man," he wrote, "was destined for society. His morality

☆

[38] "To Major John Cartwright," June 5, 1824, Andrew A. Lipscomb and Albert Ellery Bergh (eds.), *The Writings of Thomas Jefferson,* Thomas Jefferson Memorial Association, Washington, D.C., 1903, vol. XVI, p. 44. "To John Norwell," June 14, 1807, Paul L. Ford (ed.), *The Works of Thomas Jefferson,* G. P. Putnam's Sons, New York, 1904, 1905, vol. X, p. 416. "To John Adams," February 28, 1796, Lester J. Cappon (ed.), *The Adams-Jefferson Letters,* The University of North Carolina Press, Chapel Hill, 1959, vol. I, p. 260.

[39] "To Joseph Priestly," March 21, 1801, Ford (ed.), *op. cit.,* vol. IX, p. 218.

[40] "June 19, 1802," *ibid.,* vol. IX, p. 381. "To Francis Hopkinson," May 8, 1788, Boyd et al. (eds.), *op. cit.,* vol. XIII, p. 145.

therefore was to be formed to this object. He was endowed with a sense of right and wrong merely relative to this. This sense is as much a part of his nature as the sense of hearing, seeing, feeling; it is the true foundation of morality."[41] And since man is naturally social, his moral sense is at bottom inevitably involved with the well-being of others. Self-interest, when it predominates, is a perversion of man's nature. Helvetius was wrong when he said that we act generously only out of self-gratification. Generous acts occur "because nature hath implanted in our breasts a love of others, a sense of duty to them, a moral instinct, in short, which prompts us irresistibly to feel and succor their distress." The creator would have been a "bungling artist" had he made man otherwise.[42] Man was thus *naturally* social, and consequently individual rights were always situated in a social matrix. Although the propensities of human nature were in their pristine condition always pointed in the appropriate direction, they were at the same time weak propensities that, if left to themselves, could lead to cataclysmic results for all of society.

Education of the Masses

Jefferson's "natural man" could only achieve moral standing by first being "domesticated," through a process of education. Reality, through the example of pre-revolutionary France, made it clear that nature alone was entirely insufficient. Jefferson could look at France in 1786 and see a nation that, for want of education and "notwithstanding the finest soil upon the earth, the finest climate under heaven, and a people of the most benevolent, the most gay, and amiable character of which the human form is susceptible . . . [and] surrounded by so many blessings from nature, [is] loaded with misery."[43] Education by itself might not bring an end to all human misery, but it could certainly contribute significantly to this aspiration. A man with some education was almost by definition in an improved condition. "Education," Jefferson maintained, " . . . engrafts a new man on the native stock, and improves what in his nature was vicious and perverse into qualities of virtue and social worth."[44] The notion of *improvement* was very important to Jefferson, for, although he could not follow some Enlightenment thinkers to the concept of human perfectibility, he could

☆

[41] "To Peter Carr," August 10, 1787, *ibid.*, vol. XII, p. 15.

[42] "To Thomas Law," June 13, 1814, Lipscomb and Bergh (eds.), *op. cit.*, vol. XIV, pp. 141-142.

[43] "To George Wythe," August 13, 1786, Boyd et al. (eds.), *op. cit.*, vol. X, p. 244.

[44] "Report of the Commissioners for the University of Virginia," 1818, Saul K. Padover (ed.), *The Complete Jefferson*, Viking Press, Inc., New York, 1943, p. 1099.

see possibilities of real progress in certain areas. "Although," he cautioned, "I do not, with some enthusiasts, believe that the human condition will ever advance to such a state of perfection as that there shall no longer be pain or vice in the world, yet I believe it susceptible of much improvement, and most of all, in matters of government and religion, and that the diffusion of knowledge among the people is to be the instrument by which it is to be effected."[45]

The connection between "the diffusion of knowledge" and better government was critical, for the wisest political constructions would be wasted on an uneducated public, and in such a situation republicanism could be expected to wither. "Experience hath shewn," Jefferson warned, "that even under the best forms, those entrusted with power have, in time . . . perverted it into tyranny; and . . . the most effectual means of preventing this would be, to illuminate, as far as practicable, the minds of the people at large, and more especially to give them knowledge of those facts, which history exhibiteth, that . . . they may be enabled to know ambition under all its shapes, and [be] prompt to exert their natural powers to defeat its purposes." Government left in the hands of rulers exclusively, as it must be where the public is uneducated, inevitably degenerates. The citizens therefore "are the most legitimate engine of government," must constitute the final repository of power, and "to render them safe, their minds must be improved to a certain degree."[46]

A mass so educated would provide a rock upon which the entire social edifice could rest. Jefferson had in mind a citizenry peacefully following agricultural pursuits, well enough informed so that, when the occasion demanded, a majority could exercise a residual check on those who actually held the seats of authority. Ideally, the principle of majority rule must from the outset be accorded very high standing. "Every man, and every body of men on earth," Jefferson pointed out, "possesses the right of self-government. They receive it with their being from the hand of nature. Individuals exercise it by their single will; collections of men by that of their majority; for the law of the *majority* is the natural law of every society of men." This is the case operationally as well; even where a particular question finds a society evenly divided, a majority victory of only one vote must be regarded "as sacred as if unanimous."[47] But it is especially where the citizen

☆

[45] "To Pierre Samuel Dupont de Nemours," April 24, 1816, Ford (ed.), *op. cit.*, vol. XI, p. 524.

[46] "Bill for the More General Diffusion of Knowledge," presented to the Virginia Legislature, December 1778, Boyd et al. (eds.), *op. cit.*, vol. II, pp. 526-527. "Notes on Virginia," Query XIV, Ford (ed.), *op. cit.*, vol. IV, p. 64.

[47] "Cabinet Opinion," July 15, 1790, *ibid.*, vol. VI, p. 98. "To Alexander von Humboldt," July 13, 1817, *ibid.*, vol. XII, p. 69.

has gained sufficient independence, through a modest possession of property and an adequate education (this would *"require no very high degree of education,"* Jefferson informed Madison), to protect his own interests that Jefferson felt most secure about absolute dominance by the masses. Jefferson saw it "as an axiom of eternal truth in politics, that whatever power in any government is independent, is absolute also," and he argued that "independence can be trusted nowhere but with the people in mass."[48] In a society where the mass is neither propertied nor informed; that is, where the mass is totally without independence, the "will" of the majority must be looked upon with considerable suspicion.

The Primacy of Reason

A society whose populace is possessed both of property and education is capable of making use of man's highest faculty, *reason.* For Jefferson, reason was the ultimate measure of all human activity. "Let us," he exclaimed, " . . . forever bow down to the general reason of the society" and follow its path to the good life. The "general reason of society" was equatable with the will of the majority, an equation that involved Jefferson in a logical difficulty. While repeatedly identifying reason with the dictates of the majority, Jefferson simultaneously insisted that to be right the majority must be reasonable. Even though the majority might make errors (that is, act unreasonably), patience was called for because "its errors are honest, solitary and short-lived" and "it soon returns again to the right way." Logically speaking, of course, to posit the majority as the source of reason is to suggest that it can only act reasonably. Jefferson was, in fact, resting his case more on faith than on logic, for he believed, in true Enlightenment fashion, that reason lay with the individual who, once given the opportunity, was capable of exercising that faculty. "I have so much confidence in the good sense of man," he wrote, "and his qualifications for self-government, that I am never afraid of the issue where reason is left free to exert her force."[49] From this it followed that reason collectively would find its place in the majority, since it was very likely that most men would be right most of the time.[50] With society constructed so that reason is firmly in authority, a

☆

[48] "To Spencer Roane," September 6, 1819, *ibid.,* vol. XII, p. 137.

[49] "Jefferson's Response to the Welcome from the Citizens of Albermarle County," February 12, 1790, Boyd et al. (eds.), *op. cit.,* vol. XVI, p. 179. "To Diodati," August 3, 1789, *ibid.,* vol. XV, p. 326.

[50] This formulation involves another logical problem, for if the many are right most of the time, then the few, the minorities, must be wrong most of the time. And if, as Jefferson appears to have believed, the few and the many are more or less permanently constituted, the civil liberties of the former might be in severe jeopardy.

general felicity will become evident everywhere. "Life is of no value," wrote Jefferson, "but as it brings us gratifications. Among the most valuable of these is rational society. It informs the mind, sweetens the temper, chears our spirits, and promotes health."[51]

Reason and Reality

But while homage would be paid to man's reason, the effects of the passionate, the emotive, the unreasonable side of man must be taken into account as well. It was inevitable that Jefferson would turn to this concern, for his sense of reality forced him to acknowledge that ideals must sometimes be sacrificed to the demands of necessity. "It mortifies me," he wrote in 1802 in reference to the entrenched Hamiltonian system of economics, "to be strengthened by principles which I deem radically vicious, but . . . what is practicable must often control what is pure theory."[52] Paine could never make such an admission, nor could he allow himself to recognize the seamier side of man that frequently haunted Jefferson. Although for Paine the American provided an example of virtuousness for all to emulate, Jefferson could note that "among many good qualities which my countrymen possess, some of a different character unhappily mix themselves." Indolence, extravagance, and infidelity, for example, were readily apparent, and there even existed tendencies "aristocratical, pompous," and "clannish" in nature.[53] With such a mixture of propensities the life of reason, and thus the vitality of the republic, was seen to be in constant jeopardy.

The difficulty was that Jefferson's faith in man's reasonableness, firm and inflexible where the conflict of ideas was involved, frequently weakened under the pressure of his sense of reality. From the very beginning Jefferson betrayed an irresolute confidence in the new nation's ability to maintain the true course of republicanism. That the Founding Fathers failed to stipulate a rule regarding presidential rotation in office filled him with dire forebodings. He saw little hope of an immediate constitutional amendment to correct this defect, "and if it does not take place ere long," he admonished, "it assuredly never will. The *natural progress of things* is for liberty to yield, and government to gain ground."[54] [Emphasis added.]

Earlier, during the Revolution, Jefferson argued in even stronger terms for the necessity of instituting prompt reforms in Virginia (this

☆

[51] "To Madison," February 20, 1784, *ibid.*, vol. VI, p. 550.

[52] "To Dupont de Nemours," January 18, 1802, Saul K. Padover (ed.), *A Jefferson Profile, As Revealed in His Letters*, The Viking Press, Inc., New York, 1956, p. 135.

[53] "To Alexander Donald," July 28, 1787, Boyd et al. (eds.), *op. cit.*, vol. XI, p. 633. "To Marquis de Chastellux," September 2, 1785, *ibid.*, vol. VIII, p. 468.

[54] "To Edward Carrington," May 27, 1788, *ibid.*, vol. XIII, pp. 208-209.

time with respect to religious practice) lest the opportunity for such reform be irretrievably lost. His position merits lengthy quotation. He granted that the people presently would be unlikely to tolerate religious persecutions,

> but is the spirit of the people an infallible, a permanent reliance? Is it government? Is this the kind of protection we receive in return for the rights we give up? Besides, the spirit of the time may alter, will alter. Our rulers will become corrupt, our people careless. A single zealot may commence persecuter, and better men be his victims. It can never be too often repeated, that the time for fixing every essential right on a legal basis is while our rulers are honest, and ourselves united. From the conclusion of this war we shall be going down hill. It will not then be necessary to resort every moment to the people for support. They will be forgotten therefore, and their rights disregarded. They will forget themselves, but in the sole faculty of making money, and will never think of uniting to effect a due respect for their rights. The shackles, therefore, which shall not be knocked off at the conclusion of this war, will remain on us long, will be heavier and heavier, till our rights shall revive or expire in a convulsion.

Jefferson was not here making a relative statement applicable only to the circumstances in Virginia in the 1780's. "In every government on earth," he noted, "is some trace of human weakness, some germ of corruption and degeneracy, which cunning will discover and wickedness insensibly open, cultivate and improve."[55] All men, especially those who possess power, and Jefferson included himself in this category, were prone to such wickedness. "Cherish therefore the spirit of our people," he advised Edward Carrington, "and keep alive their attention. Do not be too severe upon their errors, but reclaim them by enlightening them. If once they become inattentive to the public affairs, you and I, and Congress, and Assemblies, judges and governors shall all become wolves."[56] Jefferson himself, however, could occasionally be severe in the extreme when men displayed only foolishness or apathy in the conduct of their affairs.

At times he seemed to throw up his hands in bitter despair over man's capacity for perverseness. "What a stupendous, what an incomprehensible machine is man!" he exclaimed. "Who can endure toil, famine, stripes, imprisonment or death itself in vindication of his own liberty, and the next moment be deaf to all those motives whose power supported him thro' his trial, and inflict on his fellow men a bondage, one hour of which is fraught with more misery than ages of that which he rose in rebellion to oppose." If man could not be relied upon, Jefferson was prepared to seek amelioration in the form of divine intercession. We "must await with patience the workings of an overruling providence, and hope that that is preparing the deliverance of

☆

[55] "Notes on Virginia," Query XVII, Ford (ed.), *op. cit.*, vol. IV, pp. 81-82. *Ibid.*, p. 64.

[56] "To Edward Carrington," January 16, 1787, Boyd et al. (eds.), *op. cit.*, vol. XI, p. 49.

these our suffering brethren. When the measure of their tears shall be full, when their groans shall have involved heaven itself in darkness, doubtless a god of justice will awaken to their distress, and by diffusing light and liberality among their oppressors, or at length by his exterminating thunder, manifest his attention to the things of this world, and that they are not left to the guidance of a blind fatality."[57] It was frequently the "exterminating thunder" rather than the diffusion of "light and liberty" that seemed to Jefferson most probable. It is for this reason that he could so long ignore the excesses of the French Revolution, a revolution whose thunder appeared divinely inspired. And it is in this context that Jefferson could entertain the possibility of dissolving society every twenty years; in the natural retrogression of things such a dissolution would be positively necessary.

Jefferson's moments of gloom were not exclusively his own, for there existed in the Enlightenment mind something of a contradiction with respect to man's relationship to his universe. While on the one hand enlightened thinkers celebrated the power of reason that could overcome all obstacles—especially, following Locke, authoritarian political obstacles—on the other hand they saw a universe in the control of objective forces that, following Newton, were susceptible of human comprehension, but totally beyond man's power to change or redirect. The discovery of nature's laws, in other words, was a testament to man's reasoning powers, but it also illustrated how inconsequential were his powers to act significantly. In the same letter wherein is recorded his famous remark: "I have sworn upon the altar of god, eternal hostility against every form of tyranny over the mind of man," Jefferson expressed something of this attitude as it applies to human history. "When great evils happen," he wrote, "I am in the habit of looking out for what good may arise from them as consolations to us, and Providence has in fact so established the order of things, as that most evils are the means of producing some good."[58] But Jefferson could push this notion beyond Enlightenment boundaries, to a point where reason was essentially read out of the argument.

America and the Dangers of Unreason

America, it is well to repeat, was in no way immune to the vicissitudes of reason. While unquestionably the only truly just society on the face of the earth, it, like all nations, was vulnerable to decay and degeneration. Jefferson had, for example, seen things occur during the

☆

[57] "To Jean Nicolas Demeunier," June 26, 1786, *ibid.*, vol. X, p. 63.

[58] "To Benjamin Rush," September 23, 1800, Ford (ed.), *op. cit.*, vol. IX, pp. 148, 147.

Revolution that his realism could not allow him to forget. "The mischief done us by our Citizens, plundering one another," he commented sadly in 1781, "has far exceeded what the Enemy did." At this same time, Jefferson, as Governor of Virginia, was forced to issue a proclamation reminding his citizens of their allegiance and obligations to the state of Virginia because so many of them had signed statements promising not to injure the British cause.[59] And he regarded the American propensity for forming private military associations, a propensity that became manifest after the War's conclusion, as dangerous to the very foundations of the society. In the context of attacking the veterans' Order of Cincinatti, Jefferson, in a revealing expression of Hobbesian dolefulness, gave his critique general application. "When men meet together," he wrote, "they will make business if they have none; they will collate their grievances, some real, some imaginary, all highly painted; they will communicate to each other the sparks of discontent; and these may engender a flame which will consume their particular, as well as the general, happiness."[60] It is for this reason as well that Jefferson wanted the American out of crowded cities, independently situated on his own piece of arable land. The problem was whether there would be enough land to go around, for, like Madison, although for different reasons, Jefferson worried about a time when property demand would catch up with or exceed the total supply.

In 1787 such a time appeared very remote, and America's future seemed bright for years to come. "I think our governments will remain virtuous for many centuries," Jefferson informed Madison, "as long as they are chiefly agricultural; and this will be as long as there shall be vacant lands in any part of America. When they get piled upon one another in large cities, as in Europe, they will become corrupt as in Europe." If and when the time should come that trades other than agriculture needed populating, Jefferson would encourage his people to turn first to the sea rather than take up manufacturing, for he considered the "artificers as the panders of vice and the instruments by which the liberties of a country are generally overturned."[61]

Even at this early date, however, Jefferson saw tendencies that threatened his ideals. If he could have had his way, he would have preserved things as they were. "Were I to indulge in my own theory," he wrote from Paris in 1785, "I should wish them to practice neither commerce nor navigation, but to stand with respect to Europe precisely on the footing of China. We should thus avoid wars, and all our

☆

[59] "To Thomas Nelson," January 12, 1781, Boyd et al. (eds.), *op. cit.*, vol. IV, p. 344. "Proclamation Concerning Paroles," January 19, 1781, *ibid.*, pp. 402-405.

[60] "Observations on Demeunier's Manuscript," Spring, 1786, *ibid.*, vol. X, p. 53.

[61] "To Madison," December 20, 1787, *ibid.*, vol. XII, p. 442.

citizens would be husbandmen." Jefferson knew, however, that his ideal was not shared by most of his countrymen, that reality would have it otherwise. "But this is theory only," he confessed, "and a theory which the servants of America are not at liberty to follow. Our people have a decided taste for navigation and commerce."[62] This taste proved decisive, and less than eight years later the easy accession of financial capital to a central position in the economy filled Jefferson with a frenzied horror. He pleaded with Washington to reconsider his decision against running for a second term lest, in the President's absence, the commercial interests completely destroy the accomplishments of the Revolution and the Constitution and cast the nation backward into European despotism. He instructed Washington to the effect "That all the capital employed in paper speculation is barren & useless . . . That it nourished in our citizens habits of vice and idleness instead of industry & morality: That it has furnished effectual means of corrupting . . . a portion of the legislature . . . That this corrupt squadron, deciding the voice of the legislature, have manifested their dispositions to get rid of the limitations imposed by the constitution . . . That the ultimate object of all this is to prepare the way for change, from the present republican form of government, to that of a monarchy, of which the English constitution is to be the model."[63]

Although Jefferson's exaggerated fears of monarchical plots would somewhat subside, his concern about commercial influences would not. He could refer in his First Annual Message to agriculture, manufactures, commerce, and navigation as "the four pillars of our prosperity,"[64] but the distant time when the yeoman farmer would no longer dominate national values proved much less remote than first imagined, and the turn of international events only two decades later compelled Jefferson to declare: "experience has taught me that manufactures are now as necessary to our independence as to our comfort."[65] With this radical change in perspective, Jefferson was suddenly faced with an enormously difficult question: what possible alternative existed, how was republicanism to be preserved now that agriculture was to be regarded as simply one legitimate interest among many?

☆

[62] "To G. K. van Hogendorp," October 13, 1785, *ibid.*, p. 633.

[63] "To the President," May 23, 1792, Ford (ed.), *op. cit.*, vol. VI, p. 488. Jefferson was so afraid of the corrupting influence of paper transaction that for a time after the Revolution he actually looked with favor on the states not having paid their outstanding debts and as a consequence having poor credit in Europe. "I own it to be my opinion," he wrote, "that good will arise from the destruction of our credit. I see nothing else which can restrain our disposition to luxury, and the loss of those manners which alone can preserve republican government." ("To Archibald Stuart," January 25, 1786, Boyd et al. [eds.], *op. cit.*, vol. IX, p. 218.)

[64] "December 8, 1801," Ford (ed.), *op. cit.*, vol. IX, p. 339.

[65] "To Benjamin Austin," January 9, 1816, *ibid.*, vol. XI, p. 504.

The Ward System

Jefferson answered this question by advancing his famous scheme for a national system of political wards. Beginning approximately in 1813, Jefferson, in a series of letters to various correspondents, suggested that the entire nation be divided along a graduated scale of autonomous political units, with the federal government on one end of the scale, state and then county governments next in order, and ward units modeled after the New England townships at the other end. For Jefferson, such an arrangement would have many benefits.

Each unit of government would be entirely separate and distinct and confined to its own functional jurisdiction. "It is by dividing and subdividing these republics," Jefferson maintained, "from the great national one down through all its subordinations until it ends in the administration of every man's farm by himself; by placing under everyone what his own eye may superintend, that all will be done for the best." The wards, as Jefferson conceived them, would be "pure and elementary republics" possessed of total authority to deal with those matters exclusively local in character. Thus organized, "every man is a sharer in the direction of his ward-republic . . . and feels that he is a participator in the government of affairs, not merely at an election one day in the year, but every day."[66] To place under ward purview all decisions pertaining to judgeships, constabularies, military companies, patrols, schools, care of the poor, public roads, jury selection, and district voting for higher offices would "relieve the county administration of nearly all its business, will have it better done, and by making every citizen an acting member of the government, and in the offices nearest and most interesting to him, will attach him by his strongest feelings to the independence of his country, and its republican constitution."[67] Jefferson, by extending the principle of town-meeting government across the nation, would thus invest the concept of American citizenship with a genuinely political content and would place on every local community the unavoidable responsibility for conducting its own public affairs.

Much has been made of Jefferson's ward suggestion. One writer has concluded that "in fact, wards are the token of good faith in Jefferson's political vocabulary . . . They are the proof that he took seriously the principle of majority rule . . . "[68] Another feels that because Jefferson conceived of the idea in his old age and was somewhat

☆

[66] "To Joseph C. Cabell," February 2, 1816, Lipscomb and Bergh (eds.), *op. cit.*, vol. XIV, p. 421. "To Samuel Kercheval," September 5, 1816, *ibid.*, vol. XV, p. 70. "To Cabell, *ibid.*, p. 422.

[67] "To Samuel Kercheval," July 12, 1816, Ford (ed.), *op. cit.*, vol. XII, pp. 8–9.

[68] Adrienne Koch, *The Philosophy of Thomas Jefferson*, Peter Smith, Publisher, Gloucester, Mass., 1957, p. 163.

vague about the exact function of the ward, he created a whole new theory of political space, a theory that does more than merely add a footnote to the Constitution.[69] And recent attention to local politics and community action projects has maintained a keen interest in the possibility of giving Jefferson's idea practical application. Missing from these interpretations, however, is a full appreciation of the premises behind Jefferson's recommendations. Although he saw the wards as areas within which the citizen could involve himself directly in political affairs, he more importantly posited them as defensive weapons to be used against high positions of power, positions that ineluctably would threaten the stability of the republican system.

Why, one might ask, such heavy stress on the wards when, as Jefferson himself insisted to Adams, the existing structure of free elections worked very well? The people, though they occasionally blundered, never did so often or seriously enough to endanger the society.[70] The fact was, however, that despite his repeated espousals of faith in the people, Jefferson simply did not believe that the majority, as politically organized, could sufficiently protect the republic against the incursions of power.

Wards were necessary primarily because of the distance between the seats of power and those over whom power was exercised. This simple fact of remoteness, "by rendering detection impossible to their constituents, will invite the public agents to corruption, plunder, & waste."[71] Because of the imminent possibility of tyranny from above, Jefferson believed that the local communities must consolidate their own power in order to protect themselves. In short, he wanted a revised Madisonian mechanism, with considerably heavier weight placed on the popular side of the fulcrum. Jefferson even used the language of Madison to describe the whole structure. He argued that the gradation of republics would constitute "truly a system of fundamental balances and checks for the government," and with power so divided "there shall not be a man in the State who will not be a member of some one of its councils, great or small." Such a man, Jefferson contended, "will let the heart be torn out of his body sooner than his power be wrested from him by a Caesar or a Bonaparte." The only alternative to this investment of power, in light of the inevitability of political autocracy, was out-and-out rebellion. Jefferson preferred the former course. "Constituting the people, in their wards, a regularly organized power," he argued, "enables them by that organization to crush, regularly and peaceably, the usurpations of their unfaithful

☆

[69] Hannah Arendt, *On Revolution*, The Viking Press, Inc., New York, 1963, p. 258.

[70] "To Adams," October 28, 1813, Cappon (ed.), *op. cit.*, vol. II, pp. 388–389.

[71] "To Gideon Granger," August 13, 1800, Ford (ed.), *op. cit.*, vol. IX, p. 139.

agents, and rescues them from the dreadful necessity of doing it insur-rectionally." [72] The important factor about the ward system, then, was that it provided a device for the organization of power on a local level that would counteract the "natural" abuses of power on the state and national levels. A fuller understanding of what Jefferson had in mind may be obtained by examining some of his views on the administra-tion of justice, for in this connection his doubts about the preservation of republicanism began much earlier.

Political Wards, the Legal System, and Negative Freedom

Again we find Jefferson dismayed at the prospect of a missed oppor-tunity to resist the predictable decline of republican rule. In a formal petition to the Virginia Assembly in 1798, he warned that although civil government was a powerful instrument for order and happiness, "such is the proneness of those to whom its powers are necessarily deputed to pervert them to the attainment of personal wealth and do-minion & to the utter oppression of their fellow-men, that it has be-come questionable whether the condition of our aboriginal neighbors who live without laws or magistracies be not preferable to that of the great mass of the nations of the earth." The allusion to primitive inno-cence might be rhetorical, but the concern for disorder and decline was not. Jefferson urged the Assembly to institute (and thereby pre-serve the principle of) a system of popularly elected juries, chosen first within the local school districts and then on a progressive basis by lot from the county through the federal levels, wherever juries, grand and petty, were required. Time was of the essence, Jefferson insisted, since the moment for action could easily be lost. Protection must be provided against "public functionaries, who never did yet in any country fail to betray and oppress those for the care of whose affairs they were appointed, by force if they possessed it, or by fraud and delusion if they did not"; and this protection must be afforded now while the "legislature . . . are still honest enough to wish the preservation of the rights of the people, and wise enough to circum-scribe in time the spread of that gangrene which sooner than many are aware may reach the vitals of our political existence." [73] That freely elected juries could check that "gangrene" of tyranny Jefferson had little doubt.
☆

[72] "To Joseph C. Cabell," February 2, 1816, Lipscomb and Bergh (eds.), *op. cit.*, vol. XIV, p. 422. "To Samuel Kercheval," September 5, 1816, *ibid.*, vol. XV, p. 71.

[73] "Petition on the Election of Jurors to the Virginia General Assembly," October 1798, Ford (ed.), *op. cit.*, vol. VIII, pp. 451, 453-454.

It is true, Jefferson many times admitted, that the people in mass are incapable of executing the laws themselves, although they certainly are able to choose their own executive; the people are also unqualified to legislate, although, again, they are competent to choose legislators. But whereas most citizens also possess insufficient skill to judge questions of law, their common sense and honesty nicely suit them to judge questions of fact in cases tried before the bar.[74] It was consequently only in the capacity of jurors, judging factual questions, that citizens participated directly in the governmental process. Limited as it was, Jefferson regarded this participation as absolutely essential. "Trial by jury," he informed Paine in 1789, " . . . I consider . . . as the only anchor, ever yet imagined by man, by which a government can be held to the principles of its constitution." Although from an ideal viewpoint Jefferson usually measured the extent of republicanism by the degree of direct popular involvement in legislative procedures, realistically speaking, the jury function was even more important to the maintenance of the republic. Thus Jefferson could conclude: "Were I called upon to decide whether the people had best be omitted in the Legislative or Judiciary department, I would say it is better to leave them out of the Legislative."[75] A graduated system of popularly elected juries, then, would constitute the critical republican safeguard, the ultimate defense against rule by tyrannous outlaws.

This argument closely resembles the argument concerning wards. When the two are placed side by side, one discovers again that Jefferson's main interest was primarily negative in character. He was clearly more interested in *freedom from* (that is, from tyranny, oppression, corruption) than he was in *freedom to* (to engage directly and democratically in deciding issues of public policy). Although he continuously adhered to the concept of the American as citizen, as social activist and political participant, the American as guardsman, antipolitical defender of rights, and protector of personal power tended to dominate his thinking and to color most of his thoughts on other political matters. And Jefferson's commitment to a negative concept of freedom further explains why he and Madison could form a political alliance despite obvious incongruities in their philosophies.

The negative idea of freedom also meant that Jeffersonianism

☆

[74] "To the Abbe Arnoux," July 19, 1789, Boyd et al. (eds.), *op. cit.*, vol. XV, p. 283. "To Pierre Samuel Dupont de Nemours," April 24, 1816, Ford (ed.), *op. cit.*, vol. XI, p. 521.

[75] "To Paine," July 11, 1789, Boyd et al. (eds.), *op. cit.*, vol. XV, p. 269. "To John Taylor," May 28, 1816, Ford (ed.), *op. cit.*, vol. XI, pp. 529-530. "To the Abbe Arnoux," *loc. cit.*

would leave the national purpose essentially unchallenged. Conservative and liberal alike could accept a doctrine that promoted individualism, relegated liberty primarily to a private sphere, and posited government chiefly as a hostile force that must be under constant surveillance. In this connection Jefferson's "failure" to justify Federalist fears of his Jacobinism after he assumed the presidency is not surprising, for he could never have led the masses in a minor revolution if he had harbored doubts about their political competence in the first place. Although Jefferson's ideal position supported neither side of the national purpose, his ingrained sense of caution meant that both sides would be free to run their course. Caution with respect to political activism is most clearly seen in his views on political education.

Political Education

You will recall that for Jefferson education was the necessary link between the naturally moral man and republican society. And as far as the masses were concerned, no great amount of education was required to produce the desired end, republican virtue. This would not be true for those destined to become leaders, however, and Jefferson spent much of his life designing and working for a program of free education that would meet their needs. He wished to extract this leadership element—the "natural aristocracy," as he called it—from the population at large, without regard to considerations of class or status. "It becomes expedient for promoting the public happiness," he reported to the Virginia legislature, "that those persons, whom nature hath endowed with genius and virtue, should be rendered by liberal education worthy to receive, and able to guard the sacred deposit of the rights and liberties of their fellow citizens, and that they should be called to that charge without regard to wealth, birth or other accidental condition or circumstance."[76]

The idea of a liberal education was taken very seriously, and although in curricular terms "liberal" tended to mean a thorough grounding in a utilitarian subject matter rather than an attempt to produce the cultured gentleman-scholar, procedurally speaking, liberal implied an exposure to diverse ideas, a minimum of collegiate authoritarianism, and in general an adherence to what we today call the principles of academic freedom. This would be the case in all instructional areas save one, the study of law, where men would be trained to become

☆

[76]"A Bill for the More General Diffusion of Knowledge," presented to the Virginia Legislature, December 1778, Boyd et al. (eds.), *op. cit.*, vol. II, p. 527.

not merely educated leaders of society, but effective *political* leaders, men who would hold positions of power. Here, and here alone, reality dictated another set of standards.

As founder of the University of Virginia, Jefferson would for the most part leave the methods of instruction and choice of textbooks to those hired to do the job of teaching. "But," he explained to one of his administrative colleagues, "there is one branch in which we are the best judges, in which heresies may be taught, of so interesting a character to our own State and to the United States, as to make it a duty in us to lay down the principles which are to be taught. It is that of government . . . It is our duty to guard against such principles being. disseminated among our youth, and the diffusion of that poison, by a previous prescription of the texts to be followed in their discourse."[77] This prescription would be carried quite far. For example, no political precepts would be taught that ran counter to those contained in either the Virginia or United States constitutions. Such an interdiction was crucial because the stakes were very high. Political dissension within the republic was "a great evil, and it would be as worthy of the efforts of the patriot as of the philosopher, to exclude its influence, if possible, from social life." Of course, such exclusion might not be possible, because politics is unlike other areas of human intercourse; Jefferson doubted "whether we shall ever be able so far to perfect the principles of society, as that political opinions shall . . . be as inoffensive as those of philosophy, mechanics, or any other."[78] But with or without the assurance of success, the effort to oppose incorrect political ideas had to be made, and made immediately, before these ideas had a chance to take firm hold. "I have great confidence in the common sense of mankind in general," Jefferson declared, "but it requires a great deal to get the better of notions which our tutors have instilled into our minds while incapable of questioning them, & to rise superior to antipathies strongly rooted."[79] The tutors must be checked because they gave instruction to those who would someday exercise political authority. To admit noxious doctrine into this area would be to threaten the foundations of the whole nation.

Jefferson was here faced with a painful dilemma. It was vital that leaders be educated, but too much education could itself be a harmful

☆

[77] "To ____," February 3, 1825, Lipscomb and Bergh (eds.), *op. cit.*, vol. XVI, p. 104. See also Leonard W. Levy, *Jefferson and Civil Liberties*, Harvard University Press, Cambridge, Mass., 1963, chap. 7; Daniel J. Boorstin, *The Lost World of Thomas Jefferson*, Henry Holt and Company, New York, 1948, pp. 213-225; David Tyack, "Forming the National Character: Paradox in the Educational Thought of the Revolutionary Generation," *Harvard Educational Review*, vol. 36, pp. 29-41, Winter, 1966.

[78] "To Thomas Pinckney," May 29, 1797, Ford (ed.), *op. cit.*, vol. VIII, p. 292.

[79] "To Jeremiah Moor," August 14, 1800, *ibid.*, vol. IX, pp. 143-144.

influence. On the one hand, educated men were essential to administer the affairs of the nation; the people *en masse* could simply not do the job. By the very virtue of their education, however, such men were potentially corruptible and therefore dangerous. Jefferson put the issue clearly when he pitted the ploughman against the professor in a contest for moral superiority. "The moral sense, or conscience," he wrote, "is as much a part of man as his leg or arm. It is given to all human beings in a stronger or weaker degree, as force of members is given them in a greater or less degree. It may be strengthened by exercise, as may any particular limb of the body. This sense is submitted indeed in some degree to the guidance of reason; but it is a small stock which is required for this: even a less one than what we call Common sense. State a moral case to a ploughman and a professor. The former will decide it as well, and often better than the latter, because he has not been led astray by artificial rules."[80] It was precisely this, the inculcation of "artificial rules," that had to be prevented. Of the many fabrications of artificiality in print, Jefferson feared most the history of England as interpreted by David Hume.

Jefferson was concerned that the felicitous style of Hume's history would entice students into accepting the "false" Tory premises contained therein. In an effort to combat Hume's impact, he tried frequently to interest American publishers in reprinting a revision of Hume by one John Baxter. Baxter's version commended itself because it "gives you the text of Hume, purely and verbally, till he comes to some misrepresentation or omission . . . he then alters the text silently, makes it what truth and candor say it should be, and resumes the original text again, as soon as it becomes innocent, without having warned you of your rescue from misguidance . . . And these corrections are so cautiously introduced that you are rarely sensible of the momentary change of your guide. You go on reading true history as if Hume himself had given it."[81] In other words, Baxter's Hume was especially useful because the editor's adulterations of the text were so skillfully accomplished as to defy detection. Baxter would be required reading in the University of Virginia Law School.

Jefferson's recommendation of a corrupted text was a logical consequence of his fundamental ambivalence about reason. Reason could be regarded as the highest faculty and the possession of all men. But when the security of the republic was in doubt, reason alone could not be trusted. The strictures against Hume are somewhat ironic, for one almost gets the impression that Jefferson's conception of reason had a large Humian component and that, like Hume, he understood that

☆

[80]"To Peter Carr," August 10, 1787, Boyd et al. (eds.), *op. cit.*, vol. XII, p. 15.

[81]"To Mathew Carey," November 22, 1818, in Levy, *op. cit.*, p. 146.

reason was itself morally neutral and could be used by man to achieve either good or bad ends. Ultimately of more importance than reason was habituation: training and practice in right behavior. Time and again Jefferson attempted to hit this lesson home. "Every emotion [conducive to moral feelings]," he wrote, " . . . is an exercise of our virtuous dispositions; and dispositions of the mind, like limbs of the body, acquire strength by exercise . . . exercise produces habit; and . . . exercise . . . of the moral feelings, produces a habit of thinking and acting virtuously."[82]

Virtuous habits, however, were not only vulnerable to corruption by subversive literature, but could also be undermined by exposure to unhealthy environments. For this reason Jefferson, although he could see the intellectual advantages of going abroad, was fearful of the harmful effects of visiting other countries. "Travelling," he wrote to a youthful correspondent, ". . . makes men wiser, but less happy. When men of sober age travel, they gather knowledge which they may apply usefully for their country, but they are subject ever after to recollections mixed with regret, their affections are weakened by being extended over more objects, and they learn new habits which cannot be gratified when they return home." For the inexperienced youth the situation is even more hazardous, for "young men who travel are exposed to all these inconveniences in a higher degree . . . and do not acquire that wisdom for which a previous foundation is requisite by repeated and just observations at home." "These observations," Jefferson remarked, "are founded in experience. There is no place where your pursuit of knowledge will be so little obstructed by foreign objects as in your own country, nor any wherein the virtues of the heart will be less exposed to be weakened."[83] For Jefferson, then, the good citizen was the one drilled in virtue who, because of his training and environment habitually (mindlessly?) responded in the appropriate way when put to the test of temptation.

Philosophical Ambivalence

It was not that Jefferson was a cynic, that his lofty expressions of individual freedom and responsibility were disingenuous; it was rather that he was of two minds on the subject and his ideal conceptions often succumbed to a mentality controlled by the dictates of reality. Jefferson was not always unaware of this dichotomy, and his sensitivity is demonstrated in a memorable letter to Maria Cosway written in 1786.

☆

[82] "To Robert Skipwith," August 3, 1771, Boyd et al. (eds.), *op. cit.*, vol. I, pp. 76-77.
[83] "To Peter Carr," August 10, 1787, *ibid.*, vol. XII, pp. 17-18.

In this letter Jefferson constructed an imaginary dialogue between his head and his heart.

The letter begins with Heart's avowal of affection for Mrs. Cosway and bereavement because she has left Paris for her native England. This is followed by remonstrances from the Head who scolds the Heart for imprudently indulging in emotional display. As the letter continues, the characters voice more general sentiments on both sides of the argument.

> *Head* . . . Everything in this world is a matter of calculation. Advance then with caution, the balance in your hand . . . The art of life is the art of avoiding pain: and he is the best pilot who steers clearest of the rocks and shoals with which it is beset. Pleasure is always before us; but misfortune is at our side: while running after that, this arrests us . . . Friendship is but another name for an alliance with the follies and the misfortunes of others. Our own share of miseries is sufficient: why enter then as volunteers into those of another?
>
> *Heart* . . . This world abounds indeed with misery: to lighten its burden we must divide it with one another. But let us now try the virtues of your mathematical balance, and as you have put into one scale the burthens of friendship, let me put its comforts into the other. When languishing then under disease, how grateful is the solace of our friends! How much are we supported by their encouragements and kind offices! . . . friendship is precious not only in the shade but in the sunshine of life: and thanks to a benevolent arrangement of things, the greater part of life is sunshine . . . When nature assigned us the same habitation, she gave us over it a divided empire. To you she allotted the field of science, to me that of morals. When the circle is to be squared, or the orbit of a comet to be traced; when the arch of the greatest strength, or the solid of least resistance is to be investigated, take you the problem: it is yours: nature has given me no cognizance of it. In like manner in denying to you the feelings of sympathy, of benevolence, of gratitude, of justice, of love, of friendship, she has excluded you from their controul. To these she has adapted the mechanism of the heart.

Thus the issue is joined and, in almost Thomistic fashion, Jefferson gives both positions a fair hearing. But, although the letter illustrates Jefferson's perception of the problem, it also shows that his perception is somewhat muddled. For he has the Head carry the argument beyond reality, beyond caution, balance, and the avoidance of pain, to the "unreal" position of complete estrangement.

> *Head* . . . Those, which depend on ourselves, are the only pleasures a wise man will count on: for nothing is ours which another may deprive us of. Hence the inestimable value of intellectual pleasures. Ever in our power, always leading us to something new, never cloying, we ride, serene and sublime, above the concerns of this mortal world, contemplating truth and nature, matter and motion, the laws which bind up their existence, and that eternal being who made us and bound them up by these

laws. Let this be our employ. Leave the bustle and tumult of society to those who have not talents to occupy themselves without them.

This is not the "natural rhetoric of the Head, who understands fully the necessity of making accommodations to society.

Jefferson's confusion is further suggested by his giving the Heart almost identical lines when describing the attractions of life at Monticello. "And our own dear Monticello, where," asks the Heart, "has nature spread so rich a mantle under the eye? mountains, forest, rocks, rivers. *With what majesty do we there ride above the storms!* How sublime to look down into the workhouse of nature, to see her clouds, hail, snow, rain, thunder, *all fabricated at our feet!"* [Emphasis added.][84] This is the language of neither the Heart nor the Head. It is an Olympian prose, the reflections of a mind disengaged from the usual demands of political reality on the one hand and social sentiment on the other. It is the expression of a condition for which Jefferson, very early in his life, disclosed an ardent longing. "My first wish," he asserted shortly after the outbreak of the war in 1775, "is a restoration of our just rights; my second a return of the happy period when, consistently with duty, I may withdraw myself totally from the public stage and pass the rest of my days in domestic ease and tranquility, banishing every desire of afterwards even hearing what passes in the world."[85] But to withdraw was never consistent with duty; Jefferson was never really able to turn a deaf ear to "what passes in the world," to "ride serene and sublime" "above the storms," to contemplate truth and matter and the laws of nature.

To put it differently, Jefferson, although a committed and erudite intellectual, could never engage himself for long in imaginative speculation. He had neither the spirit nor the patience for such endeavor. It is perhaps revealing that he thoroughly despised and could find no value in the works of Plato, that most eloquent composer of political myth. And he admittedly retreated from intellectual controversies that lacked tangibility and concreteness. On the materialist-spiritualist dispute over the nature of matter, for example, he confessed to Adams that "these . . . are speculations and subtleties in which, for my own part, I have little indulged myself. When I meet with a proposition beyond finite comprehension, I abandon it . . . and I think ignorance, in these cases, is truly the softest pillow on which I can lay my head."[86] Devoid of such "speculations and subtleties," Jefferson's works are comprised of constant juxtapositions of the ideal and the real, what he hoped for and what he realistically expected.

☆

[84] "To Maria Cosway," October 12, 1786, *ibid.*, vol. X, pp. 447-450.

[85] "To John Randolph," August 27, 1775, *ibid.*, vol. I, p. 241.

[86] "To Adams," March 14, 1820, Cappon (ed.), *op. cit.*, vol. II, p. 526.

Property and Community

In the letter to Mrs. Cosway, the Heart has the last word and seems to carry the day. In Jefferson's writings the battle is actually something of a draw. His pessimism — the "darker side," as some have called it — has been stressed to this point because familiarity with the brighter side is commonplace. Jefferson was, in fact, potentially capable of a conception of community which, because it was less radically individualistic, could be more sophisticated than Paine's. At times he seemed to understand, as did no other writer of his time, that liberty as a principle was empty of meaning without the sympathetic support of the society as a whole. In his First Inaugural Address he called upon the nation to "unite with one heart & one mind; let us restore to social intercourse that harmony & affection without which Liberty, & even Life itself, are but dreary things."[87] This call to unity could have a genuine ring to it, for although Jefferson saw himself primarily as the spokesman for the small property-holding class — that class upon which the fate of the republic depended — he, like Paine, dissociated the concept of the right to property from the concept of permanent ownership of land.

Following Locke, Jefferson believed that the individual had a natural desire to accumulate property and a right to such acquisition as long as it did not obstruct similar rights of others. Mere possession of property, however, scarcely testified to a man's intelligence or moral worth. In fact, it sometimes made men illogical. "I find very honest men," said Jefferson, "who, thinking the possession of some property necessary to give due independence of mind, are for restraining the elective franchise to property. I believe we may lessen the danger of buying and selling votes, by making the number of voters too great for any means of purchase: I may further say that I have not observed men's honesty to increase with their riches."[88] Increased riches obtained by increased property ownership ought above all to be discouraged. "Legislators cannot invent too many devices for subdividing property," Jefferson stated, "only taking care to let their subdivisions go hand in hand with the natural affections of the human mind . . . Whenever there is in any country, uncultivated lands and unemployed poor, it is clear that the laws of property have been so far extended as to violate natural right. The earth is given as a common stock for man to labour and live on." We must give just compensation to the dispossessed. "If we do not the fundamental right to labour the earth returns to the unemployed."[89]

☆

[87] "To Dupont de Nemours," April 24, 1816, Ford (ed.), *op. cit.*, vol. XI, pp. 522-523.
[88] "To Jeremiah Moor," August 1, 1800, *ibid.*, vol. IX, pp. 142-143.
[89] "To Madison," October 28, 1785, Boyd et al. (eds.), *op. cit.*, vol. VIII, p. 682.

Jefferson finally left Locke completely and advanced an argument almost identical to that made earlier by Paine in *Agrarian Justice.* "It is agreed by those who have seriously considered the subject," he wrote, "that no individual has, of natural right, a separate property in an acre of land, for instance. By a universal law, indeed, whatever, whether fixed or movable, belongs to all men equally and is common, is the property for the moment of him who occupies it, but when he relinquishes the occupation, the property goes with it."[90] Thus, where Madison found differential property ownership a natural and permanent divisive factor in society, Jefferson saw property-ownership merely providing the satisfaction of a human desire, a phenomenon that could give rise to factionalism only when allowed to go beyond just limitations.

Reason and Community

But despite progressive views on property, a concept of a naturally cooperative society, and an image of national unity based on the principle of liberty, Jefferson's sense of reality never let him move far beyond a rather tepid assertion of community. If community were possible it would be fundamentally based on reason, and with reason itself rendered suspect, the likelihood of community must be greatly diminished. It is true that very late in life Jefferson could still distinguish his party from the Federalists on traditional grounds. "We believed," he wrote in 1823, ". . . that man was a rational animal, endowed by nature with rights, and with an innate sense of justice . . . The cherishment of the people then was our principle, the fear and distrust of them, that of the other party."[91] But one also has the impression that what really distinguished Americans from other people in the world was not so much their innate moral characteristics as their beneficent physical environment. In 1820 Jefferson informed William Short that "the excess of population in Europe, and want of room, render war, in their opinion, necessary to keep down that excess numbers. Here, room is abundant, population scanty, and peace the necessary means for producing men to whom the redundant soil is offering the means of life and happiness. The principles of society there and here, then, are radically different."[92]

If the environment is what mattered most, rather than man's intrinsic rationality, then arguments proceeding from reason alone

☆

[90] "To Issac McPherson," August 13, 1813, in Lipscomb and Bergh (eds.), *op. cit.,* vol. XIII, p. 333.

[91] "To William Johnson," June 12, 1823, *ibid.,* vol. XV, pp. 441-442.

[92] "To William Short," August 4, 1820, *ibid.,* vol. XIII, p. 333.

would not be enough to keep the whole society on one fraternal path. Jefferson finally gave this point ambiguous recognition in 1824. "A government held together by the bonds of reason only," he suggested, "requires much compromise of opinion; that things even salutary should not be crammed down the throats of dissenting brethren, especially when they may be put into a form to be willingly swallowed, and that a good deal of indulgence is necessary to strengthen habits of fraternity and harmony."[93] Men, in other words, were not always reasonable, and if they were to live together peacefully they sometimes had to be appealed to on other grounds.

But Jefferson's notion of habituated fraternity was essentially hollow. Precisely because his ideal view of humanity depended on the reasoned life, he could give the concept none of the historical and cultural substance that came naturally to a writer like Burke, and the talk about sugar-coating offensive policies so that the opposition could swallow them reveals a basic conflict in combining moderation and indulgence in order to obtain harmony. Whereas Burke could speak of fundamental agreements and the unifying spirit of the nation, Jefferson would utilize moderation and indulgence only as long as one's opponents were somehow induced into accepting the "right" view of things. And since men were so often impervious to reasonable argument, harmony was more likely to result from the inculcation and a kind of rote learning of "correct" principles. Jefferson finally left the issue in a totally confused state when he said, "I have learned to be less confident in the conclusions of human reason, and give more credit to the honesty of contrary opinions."[94] Given the fact that Jefferson had offered only morality learned as conditioned reflex as an alternative to the dictates of reason, it is virtually impossible to know what is meant by "contrary opinions." Surely Jefferson meant neither "unreasonable" opinions nor opinions contrary to man's innate sense of morality. It is probably safe to say that he had no precise meaning in mind, and that the statement vaguely expresses an ambiguity that runs throughout his work.

At any rate, a weakened confidence in reason also raises puzzling questions about the role of government. Unlike Paine, Jefferson never saw government, even in exceptional instances, as a vehicle for achieving communal ends. As much as any man, he believed in strictly limiting the functions of government, especially those of the executive. Thus in his 1783 draft of the Virginia Constitution he detailed the powers of and the restrictions upon the legislature and the judiciary, and for the executive—who would be checked by an administrative

☆

[93] "To Edward Livingston," April 4, 1824, Ford (ed.), *op. cit.*, vol. XII, p. 350.
[94] *Ibid.*, p. 349.

"Council of State" elected by and from the ranks of the legislature—
Jefferson was hard put to think of any explicit functions whatever:
"We give him those powers only which are necessary to carry into
execution the laws, and which are not in their nature either legislative or Judiciary."

"The application of this idea," Jefferson felt, "must be left to
reason." [95] What reason would suggest, beyond the further *limitations*
listed later in the draft (recall Jefferson's remark: "The natural progress of things is for *liberty to yield, and government to gain ground.*"),
is by no means clear. Leaving the question open to the use of reason,
however, Jefferson could at least feel secure that, whatever his ultimate
powers, the executive would be constantly checked by the masses
acting rationally through their legislature and the Council of State.

But when reason falls into disrepute, as it inexorably must, the
whole argument is reversed and the safeguards seem logically to
vanish. Thus in 1814 Jefferson could declare that "if our government
ever fails, it will be from this weakness. No government can be maintained without the principle of fear as well as of duty. Good men will
obey the last, but bad ones the former only." [96] If one were to push the
logic of this position very far, all arguments about limited government
based on rational restraint would appear to be seriously vitiated. At
bottom, the idea of government checked by a rational public and the
idea of government imposing its will, even partially, through the use
of fear are incompatible, for once the door is opened to restraining
"bad men" with authority from above, justifications for increased
power will inevitably follow. Jefferson, of course, in his less impul-
sive moments, understood this full well.

The Impact of Reality

But the lurking specter of reality made impulsiveness a prominent
Jeffersonian quality. His very exaltation of America allowed him to
entertain certain thoughts that can be described as at least partially
realpolitik in character. Of America he said: "May it be to the world,
what I believe it will be . . . the signal of arousing men to burst the
chains under which monkish ignorance and superstition had persuaded them to bind themselves, and to assume the blessings and
security of self-government. That form which we have substituted,

☆

[95] "May-June 1783," Boyd et al. (eds.), *op. cit.*, vol. VI, p. 299.

[96] "To John W. Eppes," September 9, 1814, Ford (ed.), *op. cit.*, vol. XI, pp. 425-426.
The context of this remark was a recommendation for compulsory conscription into the
armed forces, a recommendation made because the people were too "easy and happy"
to fight the British voluntarily.

restores the free right to the unbounded exercise of reason and freedom of opinion. All eyes are opened, or opening, to the rights of man."[97] But if in the Western Hemisphere eyes opened too slowly to human rights, Jefferson, in a remarkably early notion of Manifest Destiny, could foresee progress through acquisition rather than through emulation. "Our confederacy," he wrote in 1768, "must be viewed as the nest from which all America, North and South is to be peopled." It was prudent, therefore, to allow and even to encourage the Spanish to maintain their American territories until the time for expansion was ripe. "My fear," Jefferson said, "is that they are too feeble to hold them till our population can be sufficiently advanced to gain it from them piece by piece."[98]

In the realm of international affairs a standard very different from republicanism could also be applied. Regarding the reestablishment of the French monarchy, Jefferson in 1792 wrote: "We surely cannot deny to any nation that right whereon our own government is founded, that every one may govern itself under whatever form it pleases, and change these forms at its own will . . . The will of the nation is the only thing essential to be regarded."[99] Ideally speaking, of course monarchy and the "will of the nation" were totally incompatible, since only in a republic could the national will ever receive genuine expression. But ideals aside, and Jefferson's consciousness of reality often caused him to put them aside, the French monarchy would be accorded its due recognition.

So it typically was with Jefferson when basic theoretical conflicts arose. One is tempted to explain this dualism as more apparent than real, as the result perhaps of a tragic view of life that pervaded Jefferson's thinking. Thus one might argue that Jefferson held out his ideals as the highest goals for mankind, worthy of the greatest expenditure of blood and tears; but because imperfect man is finally incapable of living up to his grandest aspirations, Jefferson understood that the ideals must remain ultimately unfulfilled. I do not believe, however, that such an argument can be sustained. It is simpler and, I am persuaded, more accurate to say that Jefferson, if he was ever fully aware of his divergent perspectives, never engaged in the kind of searching examination of himself and his ideas that might have yielded a fruitful resolution. He remains, therefore, a great, perhaps the greatest, American spokesman of personal liberty, a spokesman, however, who never placed his libertarian ideals within a consistent philosophical framework and who, for this reason, must also be truthfully remem-

☆

[97] "To Roger Wieghtman," June 24, 1826, *ibid.*, vol. XII, p. 477.

[98] "To Archibald Stuart," January 25, 1786, Boyd et al. (eds.), *op. cit.*, vol. IX, p. 218.

[99] "To Gouverneur Morris," December 30, 1792, Ford (ed.), *op. cit.*, vol. VII, p. 198.

bered as a voice capable of considerable narrowness when the over-powering influence of reality seemed to demand it.

Since the demands of reality appeared so frequently, Jeffersonianism could never go so far as to alter the basic directions of the culture. It could do little more than popularize a vocabulary of individual freedom and egalitarianism and, much like the influence of religious instruction that is typically restricted to Sundays only, it received a public allegiance that was often more rhetorical than real. At best, its standards were honored on a general level by a population mindful of the moral superiority of a democratic society. Just as often, perhaps, it was ignored or subverted when its aims conflicted with those of economic individualism. At worst, Jeffersonianism established myths of equality that could be used later in the century to conceal the gross inequalities that not only existed but were on the increase. It is not surprising, therefore, that by the time of his death, Jefferson's words could be quoted by men of widely different political views, and that those who believed in the national purpose, whatever their particular interpretation, could invoke Jefferson in support of their position.

4

a VISION OF GLOrY
aLEXanDer HamILTon

Alexander Hamilton stands strangely alone in the catalogue of early American theorists. Hamilton had a vision of America which differed widely from the America his countrymen saw about them every day. Although many would seek simply to preserve the accomplishments of the Revolution, the stability of the Constitution, Hamilton could not remain satisfied with the mere establishment of republicanism. He would elevate the nation in the eyes of men everywhere; he would have for his country an undisputed place in recorded history.

If Hamilton shared his compatriots' profound adherence to the principles of personal liberty, he wanted that liberty to produce something more than the individualism of the liberal spokesmen or the systematic order of Madison. Hamilton looked at America and dreamed great dreams of a nation energetic and powerful, an American "empire" that would take its place beside, perhaps even above, the traditional powers of the world. Most Americans of his day wished to break forever the ties with Europe. Europe must be escaped, its influence shaken once and for all. Hamilton would break free of European domination only if America could then stand erect and deal with the Old World at the very least on a basis of equality. "It belongs to us," he exclaimed, "to vindicate the honor of the human race, and to teach that assuming brother moderation . . . Let Americans disdain to be the instruments of European greatness! Let the thirteen states, bound together in a strict and indissoluble union, concur in erecting one great American system superior to the control of all trans-atlantic force or influence, and able to dictate the terms of the connection between the old and the new world!"[1]

America as an indissoluble power would require the release of an enormous force within the American political system. In light of given political institutions, where would this force come from? Who would generate it? Or, to put the question a little differently, could an American empire rise from the condition of equilibrium outlined in Madison's *Federalist* essays? Perhaps the best way to begin to answer these questions is to differentiate between the Hamiltonian and Madisonian points of view.

Hamilton and Madison on Political Power

Their point of departure was the role of government, and Hamilton struck this point in a speech before the New York ratifying convention. "When," said Hamilton, "you have divided and nicely balanced the departments of government; when you have strongly connected the virtue of your rulers with their interest; when, in short, you have rendered your system as perfect as human forms can be, you must place confidence, *you must give power.*"[2] [Emphasis added.] Which is to say that you must go beyond the Madisonian restrictive philosophy and give government, not merely enough power to act, but power enough to act vigorously and forcefully, as all great governments have always acted. Hamilton was, in fact, the only political thinker of his day who could approach the question of political power without feeling the need to repress an inward shudder at the sorrowful prospect of power gone wrong. As Hamilton saw it, no one, not even those who most resented it, could dispute the fact that government was at least a necessary institution; and "government," in the Hamiltonian vocabulary, was "only another word for POLITICAL POWER AND SUPREMACY."[3] While there might be differences as to the proper jurisdiction of government, there should be no disagreement over the fact that, whatever its legitimate purview, government must be given power adequate to fulfill its function. "Not to confer . . . a degree of

☆

[1] Jacob E. Cooke (ed.), *The Federalist,* Wesleyan University Press, Middletown, Conn., 1961, no. 11, pp. 72-73.

[2] John C. Hamilton (ed.), *The Works of Alexander Hamilton,* Charles S. Francis & Company, New York, 1851, vol. II, p. 454.

[3] Cooke (ed.), *op. cit.,* no. 33, p. 207.

power, commensurate to the end," Hamilton believed, "would be to violate the most obvious rules of prudence and propriety."[4] Why, Hamilton wondered, such a distorted fear of power in the first place? "What is power," he asked, "but the ability or faculty of doing a thing? What is the ability to do a thing but the power of employing the *means* necessary to its execution?"[5] Surely Americans had every reason to grasp this simple truth.

Perhaps in a unitary form of government one might worry about oppression from the center. In the case of pluralistic America, however, "the danger is directly the reverse. It is, that the common sovereign will not have power sufficient to unite the different members together, and direct the common forces to the interest and happiness of the whole." The danger of divisiveness was especially acute owing to the large expanse of the nation. "And remember also," Hamilton wrote, "that for the efficacious management of your common interests, in a country so extensive as ours, a government of as much force and strength as is consistent with the perfect security of liberty is indispensible."[6] It would be an error of the greatest magnitude for America to shackle its government with the chains of limited power and legalistic restraint. In *The Federalist*, Hamilton warned that "a government, the Constitution of which renders it unfit to be trusted with all the powers, which a free people *ought to delegate to any* government, would be an unsafe and improper depository of the NATIONAL INTERESTS."[7] Without such a trust the government could never become that which Hamilton believed it must become: "THE ROCK OF OUR POLITICAL SALVATION."[8]

On this most crucial point the co-authors of *The Federalist* differed, and yet as they wrote their appeals for the Constitution each perhaps felt secure of his own ground: Madison could be certain in his own mind that federal power was safely fragmented; Hamilton may have felt equally assured that the Constitution was flexible enough in the final analysis to yield a sufficient amount of power to the national government. Small wonder that this difference in attitude led to a post-constitutional split between the two. It was around this fundamental issue that the whole strict-construction/loose-construction controversy revolved.

☆

[4] *Ibid.*, no. 23, p. 149.

[5] *Ibid.*, no. 33, p. 204.

[6] "To James Duane," September 3, 1780, Hamilton (ed.), *op. cit.*, vol. I, pp. 152-153. "Hamilton's Draft of Washington's Farewell Address," August 1796, *ibid.*, vol. VII, p. 584.

[7] Cooke (ed.), *op. cit.*, no. 23, p. 150.

[8] "Examination of Jefferson's Message to Congress of December 7, 1801," January 18, 1802, Hamilton (ed.), *op. cit.*, vol. VII, p. 780.

At any rate, it is clear that Hamilton could not rest content with political equilibrium. The necessary energy for a strong government would not flow naturally from a situation which saw power balanced and contained on all fronts. Safeguards, while exceedingly important, must not prevent government from dealing with the most important issues of the day, issues which directly or indirectly concern every member of the society.

It was precisely this factor, the concern of all members of society, which Hamilton saw as the energizing source of governmental power, for only with mass support and affection could the federal government overcome the seemingly natural resistances to political authority. Consequently the national government must be brought to act directly on the people: "the authority of the union," Hamilton wrote, must be extended "to the persons of the citizens—the only proper objects of government." "The government . . . must be able to address itself immediately to the hopes and fears of individuals; and to attract to its support, those passions which have the strongest influence upon the human heart."[9] The government, in short, must have a vital link with the people and must be able to call upon mass support in situations requiring forceful action. In Hamilton's words, "the fabric of American empire ought to rest on the solid basis of THE CONSENT OF THE PEOPLE. The streams of national power ought to flow immediately from that pure original fountain, of all legislative authority."[10]

This was a general lesson of political science that applied with particular pertinence to the case of America. "All governments," Hamilton argued, "even the most despotic, depend, in a great degree, on opinion. In free republics, it is most peculiarly the case. In these, the will of the people makes the essential principle of the government, and the laws which control the community, receive their tone and spirit from the public wishes." Even the intensely local sympathies of most citizens might be overcome by a federal government administered properly and fairly.[11] Moreover, with generalized popular backing from all levels of society, there was little chance that increased power in the hands of federal officers would pose a threat to individual liberty. "Where in the name of common sense," Hamilton asked, "are our fears to end if we may not trust our sons, our brothers, our neighbors, our fellow citizens? What shadow of danger can there be from men who are daily mingling with the rest of their countrymen; and

☆

[9] Cooke (ed.), *op. cit.*, no. 15, p. 95; no. 16, pp. 102-103.

[10] Quoted in John C. Miller, *Alexander Hamilton: Portrait in Paradox*, Harper & Brothers, New York, 1959, p. 180.

[11] Hamilton (ed.), *op. cit.*, vol. II, p. 438. Cooke (ed.), *op. cit.*, no. 17, p. 107.

who participate with them in the same feelings, sentiments, habits, and interests?"[12] The American government would thus be a government for all, the guardian and protector of the "sacred knot which binds the people of America together," as well as a respected contender in the worldwide contest for international prestige and glory. America as an indissoluble power would require the accumulation and expenditure of considerable political momentum. Would it also require the participation of the indissoluble *community* dedicated to the achievement of Hamilton's lofty goals?

Patriotism versus Community

For all of his unifying sentiments voiced in behalf of government sustention, Hamilton stopped considerably short of a conception of community. While I have argued that positive government is an important prerequisite to the modern realization of community, government itself must be understood as no more than the means through which the entire society acts collectively. For Hamilton, however, government was at once far more and far less than the instrument of aggregate action. On a minimal level he could agree with many liberals that the object of government was merely to keep order. Hamilton asked: "Why has government been instituted at all?" And echoing Madison, he answered: "Because the passions of men will not conform to the dictates of reason and justice, without constraint." In a government of laws, the law must not be disobeyed or even disrespected. "Government supposes control. It is that POWER by which individuals in society are kept from doing injury to each other . . . The instruments by which it must act are either the AUTHORITY of the laws or FORCE."[13] There is no other choice.

    Great governments, on the other hand, are meant to play a majestic role on the international stage, a role that carries them far beyond mere concerns of law and order. To play their part effectively such governments, the United States among them, must have the ardent support of the citizenry. But ardent support does not necessarily lead to community in and of itself. Hamilton, in fact, called his people, not to community, but to *patriotism*. A certain core of agreement must obtain if America were to fulfill her grand destiny; yet this consensus was centered almost entirely around one item: government must possess the power necessary to rule with dignity and strength. Through the lips of George Washington, Hamilton told his countrymen that America

☆

[12] *Ibid.*, no. 29, p. 185.

[13] *Ibid.*, no. 15, p. 96. Hamilton (ed.), *op. cit.*, vol. VII, p. 164.

"claims and ought to concentrate your affections. The name American must always gratify and exalt the just pride of patriotism more than any denomination which can be derived from local discriminations."[14] A feeling of patriotism was desirable and might possibly be inculcated in America; but this feeling, which for Hamilton occasionally bordered on chauvinism, had no necessary internal relevance. Hamilton's vision was essentially directed outward, and his solidarity concept had meaning only when measured in foreign coin. Cohesiveness was thus valuable because it would permit government to exercise adequate power and thereby assure a strong entry in the competition against foreign nations, and not because it might in any way contribute beneficially to the internal life of the society, where Hamilton typically saw only perpetual conflict between rival interests.

There were, in addition, other factors in Hamilton's thought that provided barriers against community. One finds, for example, the same pessimistic view of human nature exhibited by John Adams. When Hamilton spoke of connecting government to the "passions" of the people, he had in mind those passions which derive from the individual's interest. "The safest reliance of every government," he tells us, "is on men's interests. This is a principle of human nature, on which all political speculation, to be just, must be founded."[15] Given the fact that men act principally with their own immediate ends in mind, a "community" of such men taking conjunctive social and political action would be a highly unlikely prospect, particularly when, as Hamilton remarked time and again, "the triumphs of vice are no new things under the sun, and . . . till the millenium comes . . . hypocrisy and treachery will continue to be the most successful commodities in the political market."[16]

There were also important structural reasons why community would not form a part of Hamilton's vision. While Hamilton was convinced that Americans, if they followed their enlightened self-interest, would see that all interests in the society could reside peacefully together to their mutual benefit, he also knew that because these interests typically followed an *un*enlightened path, certain provisions had to be made in order to prevent open conflict. This caveat was particularly important with respect to the masses, for they could seldom be counted upon to act with intelligence or to reach proper conclusions. It was not that the masses were intentionally perverse; it was simply that they were incapable of connecting desired ends to appropriate

☆

[14] "Farewell Address," *ibid.*, vol. VII, p. 578.
[15] "Letters from Phocion," no. I, 1784, *ibid.*, vol. II, p. 298.
[16] "To Harrison," January 5, 1793, *ibid.*, vol. V, p. 543.

means or of protecting themselves against pernicious manipulators. "It is a just observation," Hamilton pointed out, "that the people commonly *intend* the PUBLIC GOOD. This often applies to their very errors. But their good senses would despise the adultor who should pretend that they always *reason right* about the *means* of promoting it. They know from experience, that they sometimes err; and the wonder is, that they so seldom err as they do; beset as they continually are by the wiles of parasites and sychophants, by the snares of the ambitious, the avaricious, the desperate."[17] With such men abroad, the masses, while they must be granted due power (if only to defend themselves), must not be allowed to exercise that power unchecked by cooler spirits and wiser minds, for that power would surely then be used directly against the interests of the higher classes.

Thus, where Adams would "fence off" the plutocracy in the Senate because he feared its excesses, Hamilton, for identical reasons, recommended a similar circumscription of the masses whose representatives would reside exclusively in the House. While congressmen would be popularly elected for a specified period, senators would, if Hamilton were to have his way in the Constitutional Convention, serve during good behavior and be elected solely by property owners. The President, who once chosen would also serve for life, would be even further removed from the people: "His election to be made by *electors* chosen by *electors* chosen by the people."[18] As a final prerequisite the presidential electors would qualify only when in possession of property (land or value) in excess of $1,000. Consequently while the people might constitute "the fountain of legislative authority," this was to be a fountain placed in a political reservoir surrounded by the very high walls of a stratified society. This must inevitably be the case since, even when informed by what seems to be absolute fact, mass sentiment is easily confused and misled. Most men, Hamilton noted, "are governed by opinion: this opinion is as much influenced by appearances as by realities." "A degree of illusion mixes itself in all the affairs of society. The opinion of objects has more influence than their real nature."[19] Given the general untrustworthiness of public opinion, the erection of walls of stratification was unavoidable, and with these walls Hamilton effectively sealed off one constituency from the other.

He established in his political structure a permanent breach between interests which shared only a common pride in national

☆

[17] Cooke (ed.), *op. cit.*, no. 71, p. 482.

[18] Hamilton (ed.), *op. cit.*, vol. II, p. 393.

[19] "To James Duane," September 3, 1780, *ibid.*, vol. I, p. 168. "To Morris," 1779 (?), *ibid.*, vol. I, p. 122.

glory, and he consequently left scant room for the evolution of integrated communality. It is not that national pride works in principle against communal development. As Mazzini would show almost a century later,[20] nationalist and communitarian feelings could theoretically run hand-in-hand and mutually reenforce each other. But in Hamilton's thought the nation—geared as it was primarily for international rivalry—while it might achieve a high place in the annals of diplomatic history or command the respect of the contemporary world, could do little in the way of strengthening bonds of community among its interest-conscious citizens. As John C. Miller puts it, Hamilton's "romanticism was reserved for the nation, not for its citizens."[21]

Power and Commerce

Public and Private Interest

Although Hamilton was anxious to draw the affection of all citizens to the national government, the affection of some was clearly worth more than that of others. In 1779 Hamilton wrote to Robert Morris suggesting that the best scheme of government would link "the interest of the State in an intimate connection with those of the rich individuals belonging to it," and would turn "the wealth and influence of both into a commercial channel, for the mutual benefit."[22] There could be no clearer conservative statement of a stake-in-society thesis. Hamilton thus agreed with Madison that the dominant interest must have a fixed connection with governmental operation. But Hamilton did not pin his hopes on the same interest that Madison favored. While he fully concurred that property with its attendant rights needed the full and continual protection of the laws, he saw no reason why the landed class ought to control the political machinery of the entire nation. Indeed, property rights per se must give way before more essential considerations. Thus Hamilton argued that when property rights ran counter "to the social order and to the permanent welfare of the society," they must be abrogated. The public interest, moreover, might even dictate an "unjust" treatment of property. "Whenever," Hamilton insisted, ". . . a right of property is infringed for the general good, if

☆

[20] See Joseph Mazzini, *The Duties of Man and Other Essays*, Thomas Jones (ed.), J. M. Dent and Sons Ltd., Publishers, London, and E. P. Dutton & Co., Inc., New York, 1907, particularly pp. 221-247.

[21] John C. Miller, *The Federalist Era*, Harper & Brothers, New York, 1960, p. 80.

[22] Hamilton (ed.), *op. cit.*, vol. I, p. 130.

the nature of [the] case admits of compensation, it ought to be made; but if compensation be impracticable, that impracticability ought not to be an obstacle to a clearly essential reform."[23] If America was to be an expanding and active force in the world, it required above all the interest, not of the proprietor, but of that element which commanded qualities capable of impelling the nation forward to greatness. This could only be the entrepreneurial class, that class in possession of the energy and initiative naturally derived from the profit motive.[24] To harness this class to the wheel of government was Hamilton's precious objective.

For Hamilton there was no contradiction between individuals working simultaneously for the public and their own private interest. Indeed, the realization of the former depended in large measure on the pursuit of the latter. "Let it not be said," Hamilton wrote in 1801, "that an office is a mere trust for public benefit, and excludes the idea of a property or a vested interest in the individual . . . Every office combines the two ingredients of an interest in the possessor, and a trust for the public . . . The idea of a vested interest holden even by a permanent tenure, so far from being incompatible with the principle, that the primary and essential end of every office is the public good, may be conducive to that very end, by promoting a diligent, faithful, energetic, and independent execution of the office."[25] While personal interest might be made to point toward the public interest, certain fundamental policies would also be necessary in order to set the entire political-economic process in motion. Foremost among these would be the establishment of a system of public credit.

While usually dependent upon arguments of interest and utility, Hamilton was capable of making the case for public credit on a much higher level. The good faith that underscores public credit is, of course, "recommended by the strongest inducements of political

☆

[23] Quoted in John C. Miller, *Alexander Hamilton: Portrait in Paradox,* Harper & Brothers, New York, 1959, p. 122.

[24] Parrington was mistaken in interpreting Hamilton to combine business and property into one interest. (Vernon L. Parrington, *The Colonial Mind, 1620-1800,* Harcourt, Brace and Company, Inc., New York, 1927, 1930, p. 304.) Hamilton was quite clear on this point. In arguing that the National Bank could not be made into an immediate source of loans to landholders he pointed out that "land is, alone, an unfit fund for a bank circulation . . . Neither is the idea of constituting the fund partly of coin and partly of land . . . These two species of property do not, for the most part, unite in the same hands. Will the moneyed man consent to enter into a partnership with the land-holder, by which *the latter* will share in the profits *which will be made by the money of the former?*" ("National Bank," December 13, 1790, Hamilton [ed.], *op. cit.,* vol. III, p. 133.)

[25] "Examination of Jefferson's Message to Congress of December 7, 1801," February 23, 1802, *ibid.,* vol. VII, p. 796.

expediency." However, "there are arguments for it which rest on the immutable principles of moral obligation," and should these principles be violated the providential connection between public virtue and public happiness would be badly damaged. Hamilton could argue this way because he saw in public credit, not only that motivating force which would drive the whole society forward,[26] but the bedrock of a financial system that could address most of the major issues confronting the new nation. Why do we need public credit? "To justify and preserve . . . confidence; to promote the increasing respectability of the American name; to answer the calls of justice; to restore landed property to its due value; to furnish new resources, both to agriculture and commerce; to cement more closely the union of the States; to add to their security against foreign attack; to establish public order on the basis of an upright and liberal policy . . ."[27] This, by any standard, is an impressive list, and to see that public credit did in fact produce such results, a central agency would be needed that could regulate and control the flow of public credit. That agency would be the National Bank.

It is on the issue of the Bank that Hamilton faced directly the problem of the American purpose, for with the establishment of the Bank he irrevocably cast his lot with the financial and commercial interests. There is no question that Hamilton's hopes for America went far beyond the objectives of economic individualism. Nor is there any question that he thought the Bank capable of mixing private gain and public virtue, with the latter emerging dominant. Although the Bank was a public organ—"a political machine, of the greatest importance to the State"—it must of necessity be run on the profit motive. "Public utility," Hamilton wrote, "is more truly the object of public banks than private profit. And it is the business of Government to constitute them on such principles, that, while the latter will result in a sufficient degree to afford competent motives to engage them, the former be not made subservient to it."[28] But the question immediately arises, how can we be certain that the public interest will result from this tenuous balance? How can we be sure that the commercial class will rise above the imperatives of economic individualism? Hamilton had more than one perspective from which to respond to these questions.

☆

[26] "Finance," January 9, 1790, *ibid.*, vol. III, p. 4. "Public Credit," January 16 and 21, 1795, *ibid.*, vol. III, pp. 524-525.

[27] "Finance," January 9, 1790, *ibid.*, vol. III, p. 5. Hamilton foresaw similar positive results from a national debt, the other side of the financial coin. ("To Robert Morris," April 30, 1781, *ibid.*, vol. I, p. 257.)

[28] "National Bank," December 13, 1790, *ibid.*, vol. III, pp. 132, 128.

The Limits of Commercial Interest

In the first place it is well to notice that while Hamilton relied heavily on the commercial class, he had, unlike Paine, for example, no great faith in the benevolent influence of commerce itself. "Has commerce," he asked, ". . . done any thing more than change the objects of war? . . . Have there not been as many wars founded upon commercial motives . . . as were before occasioned by the cupidity of territory or dominion?"[29] Secondly, the worldly Hamilton in no way believed that the moneyed class had a monopoly on virtue. "Experience," he pointed out, "has by no means justified us in the supposition, that there is more virtue in one class of men than in another. Look through the rich and the poor of the community; the learned and the ignorant. Where does virtue predominate?" All men are tainted by vice, rich and poor alike. The vices of the rich, however, "are probably more favorable to the prosperity of the State, than those of the indigent; and partake less of moral depravity."[30] Hamilton made the remarkable suggestion that one class should dominate, not because of any inherent superiority, but because its private vices were less degenerate and of such a nature as to be somewhat more conducive to prosperity on the public level. A financial class, then, even one manifestly corrupt, would be Hamilton's choice for the position of leadership since, politically speaking, it could do less harm than any other.

At other times, however, one gets the impression that Hamilton settled on the business class because, given his general position, he had no other logical choice. It was the only interest capable of taking a broad view of governmental affairs. In *The Federalist* he wrote that, "the operations of the national government . . . falling less immediately under the observation of the mass of citizens the benefits derived from it will chiefly be perceived and attended to by speculative men. Relating to more general interests, they will be less apt to come home to the feelings of the people; and, in proportion, less likely to inspire a habitual sense of obligation and an active sentiment of attachment."[31] And yet even if one should grant to Hamilton no alternative save the commercial class for energy and understanding, it

☆

[29]Cooke (ed.), *op. cit.*, no. 6, p. 32.

[30]"Convention of New York, Speech on the Compromises of the Constitution," 1788, Hamilton (ed.), *op. cit.*, vol. II, p. 443.

[31]Cooke (ed.), *op. cit.*, no. 17, p. 108. Of course the more widely diffused the entrepreneurial propensity the better it would be for society in general. Such a diffusion would most naturally take place in a complex industrialized economy. "The spirit of enterprise," Hamilton noted in his "Report on Manufactures," "useful and prolific as it is, must necessarily be contracted or expanded, in proportion to the simplicity or variety of

is clear that his own endorsement of that interest was made for more positive reasons as well.

The Bank, although publicly controlled, must be in private hands — "under the guidance of *individual interest*" — of that there could be no doubt. To place the Bank in public hands would be to expose it to the influence of "*public* necessity," that is, to the impulsiveness of the ephemeral majority. Hamilton was convinced beyond argument that the interests of government and commerce could coalesce so tightly that the one could do no otherwise than mutually benefit the other. "The keen, steady, and, as it were, magnetic sense of their own interest as proprietors, in the directors of the bank, pointing invariably to its true pole — the prosperity of the institution — is the only security that can always be relied upon for a careful and prudent administration."[32] Notice, however, that the connection was not entirely mechanical; Hamilton *did* have to depend upon prudential administrators to direct their own interest in a manner beneficial to the government as a whole, even when their personal interests might suffer in the short run. Hamilton was apparently quite prepared to do this. "Those who are most commonly creditors of a nation," he wrote, "are, generally speaking, enlightened men; and there are signal examples to warrant a conclusion, that, when a candid and fair appeal is made to them, they will understand their true interest too well to refuse their concurrence in such modifications of their claims as any real necessity may demand." It was because he believed this that Hamilton could suggest that society would be in no danger of exploitation by the Bank, even though the Bank's directors would be drawn from only one class and would not be responsible to the public at large. The public interest would be guaranteed, he argued, simply by requiring the directors to employ the principle of rotation in office.[33] The directors would, after all, be "enlightened men," and could therefore be expected to behave in a manner beneficial to the general interest.

Romantic Realism

Hamilton's reliance on the commercial class proved to be the tragic flaw in his grand design. It is hard to understand why he expected financial interests to modify their personal demands in the face of

---

the occupations and productions which are to be found in a society. It must be less in a nation of mere cultivators, than in a nation of cultivators and merchants; less in a nation of cultivators and merchants than in a nation of cultivators, artificers, and merchants." (Hamilton [ed.], *op. cit.*, vol. III, p. 210.)

[32] "National Bank," *ibid.*, vol. III, pp. 134-135.

[33] "National Bank," *ibid.*, vol. III, pp. 130-131.

national needs. Of all the sectors of American society permeated by economic individualism, the commercial sector was the first and most thoroughly saturated. No sadder commentary on Hamilton's misplaced confidence can be found than the Hartford Convention, that assemblage of New England mercantilists which stood ready to scrap national policy, if not the Union itself, for the perpetuation of a profitable business arrangement. Moreover, even the Bank of the United States, although having a salutary effect on the economy over the years, was not always free from the enticements of self-aggrandizement. Hamilton was apparently unmoved even by personal exposure to commercial chicanery. In 1792, for example, the dubious speculations of his close friend, William Duer, brought the entire American business world into a state of near-collapse, and brought Hamilton a "bitterness of soul"[34] but not, so it would appear, a change of mind. He put all of his faith, albeit a reserved and qualified faith, in the business class, and his dream faded, in reality and perhaps even for Hamilton personally, as this class pursued its narrow-minded interest. William Miller has accurately summarized Hamilton's predicament. "Hamilton," Miller writes, "had a vision of the future of the United States that was . . . too innocent for his mercenary fellow Federalists . . . Hamilton was concerned with money only as a medium for national, not personal aggrandizement; capital was the heart, the lungs, the bloodstream of power; capitalists the instruments of progress . . . But Federalist capitalists thought, as a rule, on a lower plane, and nursed their substance carefully in the familiar lines of investment."[35]

To say that the business class represented a tragic flaw is to suggest that Hamilton's unrealized dream itself constituted political tragedy. In the classical understanding of tragedy, this was very nearly the case. His dashed hopes for America meant a fall from greatness, at least the potential greatness he saw in his mind's eye. Despite his business-class partiality, it must be acknowledged that at least on the very highest theoretical level, if not in practice, Hamilton's elevated aspirations sometimes carried him above some of the narrower differences found in the political thought of his contemporaries. For example, while he depended foremost on speculative men, he saw — again in theory — that the gulf between their interests and the interests of the proprietor class *ought* not to exist. "Nothing can be more mistaken," Hamilton wrote, "than the collision and rivalship which almost always subsist between the landed and trading interests, for the truth is, they are so inseparably interwoven that one cannot be injured without

☆

[34] "Hamilton to Duer," March 14, 1792, *ibid.*, vol. V, p. 498.

[35] William Miller, *A New History of the United States*, George Braziller, Inc., New York, 1958, p. 134.

injury nor benefited without benefit to the other . . . It is only to be regretted, that [this] is too often lost sight of, when the seductions of some immediate advantage or exemption tempt us to sacrifice the future to the present." Hamilton understood, in an almost Aristotelian sense, the intimate connection among all interests and sections of the society. "Mutual wants," he explained, "constitute one of the strongest links of political connection,"[36] and the wants of some interests could only be supplied through reciprocal exchange among and mutual satisfaction of all interests.

Ironically, Hamilton's grandiose plans were offered in the name of realism. Like Madison, Hamilton was far from the vision of the American Adam. Perhaps even more than Madison he labored under what he considered the realities of his time. America might be endowed with an overflow of the gifts of nature, but these resources could at best serve only to meet the future demands of an expansive nation: *"in the usual progress of things, the necessities of a nation in every stage of its existence will be found at least equal to its resources."* This, along with other unavoidable, if somewhat depressing, facts of life, makes the creation of a strong government with powers of taxation and control an absolute necessity. "Reflections of this kind," Hamilton admitted, "may have a trifling weight with men, who hope to see realized in America, the halcyon scenes of the poetic or fabulous age; but to those who believe we are likely to experience a common portion of the vicissitudes and calamities, which have fallen to the lot of other nations, they must appear entitled to serious attention. Such men must behold the actual situation of their country with painful solicitude, and deprecate the evils which ambition or revenge might, with too much facility, inflict upon it."[37] Hamilton himself, of course, could never shrink from these baneful aspects of the human condition. Even the seemingly good things of life, if uncontrolled, could have the most harmful effects on society. "The precious metals," for example, "those great springs of labor and industry, are also the ministers of extravagance, luxury, and corruption. Commerce, the nurse of agriculture and manufactures, if overdriven, leads to bankruptcy and distress. A fertile soil, the principal source of human comfort, not unfrequently begets indolence and effeminacy. Even liberty itself, degenerating into licentiousness, produces a frightful complication of ills, and works its own destruction."[38] Hamilton might judiciously have added that a business class, whose energy and

☆

[36] "The Continentalist," no. VI, August 30, 1781, Hamilton (ed.), *op. cit.*, vol. II, pp. 196-197. "Manufactures," *ibid.*, vol. III, p. 241.

[37] Cooke (ed.), *op. cit.*, no. 30, pp. 190, 193.

[38] "Public Credit," Hamilton (ed.), *op. cit.*, vol. III, p. 528.

resourcefulness are otherwise dazzling, is likely, when given the reins of power and attracted by the promise of unending profit, to peg the needs of the nation as a whole considerably lower than the immediate fulfillment of its own interest.

To ignore this possibility was to engage in unmitigated idealism, to miss a concrete fact of American life, and thus it is not surprising that Hamilton could occasionally look about in utter bewilderment. When all around him (or so it seemed) opposed his propositions regarding the unsubscribed national debt, he was genuinely confounded. "Am I," he asked, ". . . more of an American than those who drew their first breath on American ground? Or what is it that thus torments me, at a circumstance so calmly viewed by almost every body else? Am I a fool – a romantic Quixotte – or is there a constitutional defect in the American mind?"[39] Bewilderment in 1795 turned seven years later to almost total alienation. Where at an earlier period Hamilton could perceive, along with Jefferson and Paine, the singular opportunity for political change afforded by America – "Our situation is peculiar," he had written, *it leaves us Room to dream as we think proper*" – by 1802 he could remark on a fate which had carried him to such an "odd destiny. Perhaps no man in the United States has sacrificed or done more for the present Constitution than myself; and contrary to all my anticipations of its fate . . . I am still laboring to prop the frail and worthless fabric. Yet I have the murmurs of its friends no less than the curses of its foes for my reward . . . Every day proves to me more and more, that this American world was not made for me."[40]

Although his financial system may have been solidly entrenched, Hamilton's American empire which was to grow from this economic seedbed was nowhere in sight. This, as far as Hamilton was concerned, constituted not merely a personal disappointment but a loss to humanity, for he too wished to advance the cause of republicanism, as he defined it. As things stood, however, *America* and *republicanism* were coterminous, and if American republicanism were not given "due stability and wisdom, it would be disgraced . . . & lost to mankind forever."[41] It was this likelihood, the probability that republican America would remain an inconsequential and therefore disgraceful world power, that more than anything else drove Hamilton to despair and caused him to feel that he and the "American world" were ultimately not meant for each other.

☆

[39] "To _____ King," February 21, 1795, *ibid.*, vol. V, p. 625.

[40] Quoted in John C. Miller, *Alexander Hamilton: Portrait in Paradox*, Harper & Brothers, New York, 1959, pp. 161, 543.

[41] *Ibid.*, p. 153.

5

THE LIBERAL EXPRESSION

RALPH WALDO EMERSON
ORESTES BROWNSON

The Jacksonian Era

The historical epoch commonly known as the Age of Jackson marks a transition in the American ideology, a transition that saw the national purpose move away from both its early-liberal and conservative progenitors. From a theoretical viewpoint, the content of the new ideology can best be understood by analyzing the works of Ralph Waldo Emerson and by contrasting Emerson's views with those of Orestes Brownson. Before turning to Emerson and Brownson, however, it is necessary to say something about their times and about the general attitudes expressed by men of thought during the period in which they wrote. For times had changed radically. The nation, as Thomas Jefferson on the one side and Chancellor Kent on the other could sadly observe, no longer resembled the age known by the founding generation. The country from 1825 to 1850 was undergoing sweeping alterations as Americans sought to develop an indigenous and self-reliant industrial system, a native intellectual force, a self-styled political culture, in sum, a state of national autonomy. Above all, it was a period of enormous activity characterized by a release of intellectual and physical energy on all fronts. Everywhere citizens were involved in multifarious schemes, projects, and experiments, exploring and sometimes exploiting the resources and space of their vast nation.

The Jacksonian era was, from the perspectives of this study, also the time when the conservative side of the national purpose began to fade into the background and acquisitive impulses assert themselves across the nation. While in no way devaluating the importance of other Jacksonian aspirations, we will focus here upon those that had the most to do with problems of community and purpose. The material in the following pages, therefore, is not meant to be taken either as a total definition of the times or as expressing literally the complete thought of the authors cited. They are used merely to provide a setting within which it will be easier to comprehend the meaning and importance of Brownson and Emerson.

Liberal Economic Individualism

The twenty-five years from 1825 to 1850 saw the ascendency of the liberal side of the American purpose. Whatever is to be said of the early theorists and their relationship to economic individualism, it must be noted that their espousal, when made, was always countered by commitments to other cherished values. For Paine and Jefferson, the demands of equalitarian justice theoretically, if not always logically, provided an essential element of social balance. For the conservatives, the rights and duties of property tended to circumscribe and thereby socialize forceful individualistic propensities. This breadth of concern is even more noticeable in the personal lives of these men than it is in their political theories. Irrespective of political affiliation, they were to a man dedicated to the well-being of their nation and they very often sacrificed monetary gain, in some cases financial stability, to engage in a life of national service. George Washington, with his accumulation of material wealth, is not a typical example. More normal were the meager trappings of a John Adams or the ragged and somewhat faded accoutrements of a Thomas Jefferson who, despite his seemingly regal abode, left an estate that had not even the means to meet his funeral expenses. With the Age of Jackson this older way began to yield to a more acquisitive style of economic individualism, a style that tended to cut across all sectors of American life.

Andrew Jackson himself seemed to embody the aggressive spirit of his age. Nothing symbolizes this period better than Jackson, the property-speculating frontier aristocrat, doing battle with the Bank of the United States in the name of equality of opportunity. The quarrel that the Jacksonian had with his patrician forebears was not so much over the high station of the latter, as over the fact that station and its counterparts, financial wealth and property ownership, were being monopolized by the privileged few while the many were denied access to the obvious abundance of America. This in a nation where there was clearly enough for all, and that had come to prize unfettered individual initiative, was intolerable. Jackson sought to break forever what he saw as the stranglehold that financial interests had both on the economy and, through the economy, on the individual. With the destruction of the National Bank, Jackson answered a yearning that seemed to run through all of society, where men desired nothing more than an equal chance to toe the mark for the big race to success and monetary gain. Theophilus Fisk exhorted the laboring classes to look the money monopolists squarely in the eye: "Let our motto be," he exclaimed, "'Take your delicate fingers from our throats.'"[1] Jackson's job was to pry loose those fingers and to extricate the masses from a combination of governmental and financial oppression.

Antigovernment and the American Adam

It is difficult for us today to see how deep the Jacksonian distrust of governmental authority went. We normally think of the *laissez-faire* and corporate-person doctrines as conservative devices aimed at giving business interests a free hand to maximize profits and gain special legal protection, probably at the expense of the worker and the consumer. At the time of Jackson, however, it was simply taken for granted that the political realm had either sold out to or had been entirely occupied by the financial classes. Consequently, *laissez faire* meant for many the separation of the commercial monopoly from government *protection*, and thus the end of sanctioned exclusive privilege. Similarly, the corporate-person doctrine meant that the corporation, rather than being vested with legal rights and protections similar to those of the individual — as would be the case in the late nineteenth century — would at last be brought within the reach of the law, and would no longer enjoy a position before the bar *superior* to that of the individual litigant.[2] Thus, it was entirely natural for Jackson to take on the dual obligation of breaking the financial monopoly and retrenching the power of government. The elimination of the Bank ran hand-in-hand with Jackson's seven consecutive annual messages requesting

☆

[1] "New York Evening Post," August 6, 1835, in Joseph L. Blau (ed.), *Social Theories of Jacksonian Democracy*, The Liberal Arts Press, Inc., New York, 1954, p. 202.

[2] On the need for *laissez-faire* policies, see the essays of William Leggett, in Theodore Sedgwick (ed.), *Political Writings of William Leggett*, Taylor & Dodd, New York, 1840. On the corporate person, see David Henshaw, "Remarks Upon the Rights and Powers of Corporations" (1837), in Blau (ed.), *op. cit.*, p. 163.

that the president be limited to one term in office. Jackson's position is deceptive only because he felt the need to exercise extraordinary power in the endeavor to reinstate minimal government and establish equality of opportunity. His critics accused him of acting unconstitutionally, and when he continually ignored the sentiments of Congress — like the general public, he distrusted "politicians" — his administration, not always without justification, was labeled, "The Reign of King Andrew."

And yet, while he found it necessary to wield what for his times was enormous power to achieve his ends, Jackson never really altered his position on the role of government. In his Veto Message on the Bank he pointed out that government's "true strength consists in leaving individuals and States as much as possible to themselves."[3] Eight months later, in the draft of his Second Inaugural Address, Jackson made the case more strongly. "Let us," he urged the electorate, "extricate our country from the dangers which surround it and learn wisdom from the lessons they inculcate. That people is not best governed who have the most laws . . . Government should treat all alike; and the surest means of attaining that end is to let all alone."[4] *The Democratic Review,* for a time an extremely influential political organ, also shared Jackson's suspicious attitude. In the introduction to its first number, it said, "Legislation has been the fruitful parent of nine-tenths of all the evil, moral and physical, by which mankind has been afflicted since the creation of the world, and by which human nature has been self-degraded, fettered, and oppressed."[5] Even by the end of the Jacksonian era the strength of this conviction had apparently not diminished. A youthful Walt Whitman could restate the argument with resolution and force. "Under a proper organization," Whitman wrote, ". . . the wealth and happiness of the citizens could hardly be touched by the government . . . *Men* must 'be masters unto themselves,' and not look to presidents and legislative bodies for aid. One point . . . must not be forgotten . . . that although government can do little positive *good* to the people, it may do an immense deal of harm."[6] "We have grown in the way of resting on it to do many things which ought to be done by individuals, and of making it answer for

☆

[3] "Bank Veto Message," July 10, 1832, in James D. Richardson (ed.), *A Compilation of the Messages and Papers of the Presidents 1789-1897,* published by authority of Congress, Washington, D.C., 1900, vol. II, p. 590.

[4] "March 1, 1833," John Spencer Bassett (ed.), *Correspondence of Andrew Jackson,* Carnegie Institution of Washington, Washington, D.C., 1926-1935, vol. V, pp. 26-27.

[5] In Blau (ed.), *op. cit.,* p. 27.

[6] "New Light and Old," *Brooklyn Daily Eagle,* July 26, 1847, Emory Holloway (ed.), *The Uncollected Poetry and Prose of Walt Whitman,* Doubleday & Company, Inc., Garden City, N.Y., 1921, vol. I, p. 167.

much that society alone (for government and society are distinct) is in truth the responsible author of."[7] If in the preceding age the attainment of community was rendered difficult by a dubious view of government, the Age of Jackson served to establish an even firmer commitment to noncommunalism with what came very close to being, at least on the level of ideology, a complete rejection of all important governmental authority.

Jackson also made the achievement of community somewhat less possible by representing in full measure the spirit of the American Adam. While the idea of the New Eden predated even the settlement of America, the shadow of Europe, and especially of England, continued to dominate American thought until weakened by the War of 1812 and Jackson's triumphant victory at New Orleans. This was America's first military victory as a national entity, and the defeat of Mother England served to symbolize the final break with the historical past. Jacksonian America therefore not only experienced a democratic revolution, but the leader of that revolution had also been the Hero of New Orleans, the man who had decisively cut the last link with the past, and who by so doing had finally completed the American Revolution. Thus, under Jackson, America was emancipated first from the Old World and then from the old order, and stood finally at the commencement of its individual history. "Our national birth," exclaimed the *Democratic Review* in 1839, "was the beginning of a new history . . . which separates us from the past and connects us with the future only."[8]

The "Laboring" Class

Economic individualism and the release from a plutocratic government were also constant themes in the more critical "labor" literature of the Jacksonian era. It is difficult to generalize about a collection of ideas that ranges from the *laissez-faire* humanism of a Leggett to the more communal notions of a Frederick Robinson. It is equally difficult to make sense out of a Workingmen's movement that, as one observer of the day said, consisted "as well of merchants, lawyers, physicians, and speculators, as of operatives under the cognomen of *working men.*"[9] Yet, despite an almost Marxian consciousness of class differences, the majority of the workingmen and their supporters, when not openly in

☆

[7] *Brooklyn Daily Eagle,* March 27, 1846, in Blau (ed.), *op. cit.,* p. 133.

[8] Cited in R. W. B. Lewis, *The American Adam,* The University of Chicago Press, Chicago, 1955, p. 5.

[9] Quoted by Joseph Dorfman, *The Economic Mind in American Civilization,* The Viking Press, Inc., New York, 1946, vol. II, pp. 643-644.

favor of economic individualism, delivered an attack upon the existing political and economic order in such a way as to leave the door open to a perpetuation of economic self-aggrandizement. Perhaps the title of Edward Kellog's 1849 treatise on the subject best expresses the sentiment most typically found in the workingman's critique. His book was entitled, *Labor and Other Capital: The Rights of Each Secured and the Wrongs of Both Eradicated, or, An Exposition of the Cause Why Few Are Wealthy and Many Poor, and the Delineation of a System, Which, Without Infringing the Rights of Property, Will Give to Labor Its Just Reward.*

For the most part, Jacksonian social critics sought to break the political-economic combine in order to establish equality of opportunity, which is to say, an equal opportunity for the individual to pursue his own interest as he personally saw fit. Thus Stephen Simpson, leader of the Philadelphia Working Men's party, could write about "unjust, despotic, proud, all-grasping government" that has kept the laborer from the rewards that God has spread before him, and about the banking system whose tyrannical power is comparable to the subjugation of the country by a foreign king.[10] Addressing the General Trades' Union of New York City in 1833, Ely Moore stated that "man, by nature, is selfish and aristocratic. *Self-love* is constitutional with man, and is displayed in every stage and in all the diversities of life." Self-love is, moreover, "one of the elements of life and essential to the welfare of society." Having established man's omnipresent "self-love" Moore went on to urge the union members to emulate the great men of American history who, by their own industry, that is, by a correct implementation of self-interest, have overcome humble beginnings and achieved prominent success. The day has come when the American citizen has but to open his own door to fame and fortune. "You have no longer an excuse why you should not prosper and flourish," he informed the meeting, "both as a body and as individuals . . . If mortification and defeat should attend you, blame not your fellowmen; the cause will be found within yourselves. Neither blame your country; the fault will not be hers! No, Land of Genius, Land of Refuge, Land of the Brave and the free! thy sons have no cause to reproach thee! All thy deserving children find favor in thine eyes, support on thy arm, and protection in they bosom."[11]

It was this euphoric picture of America that allowed the proponents of labor to argue that workingmen could achieve their goals without governmental assistance. "The laborer," said Theophilus Fisk, "asks

☆

[10] Stephan Simpson, *Working Man's Manual*, 1831, pp. 9, 13, 28.

[11] In Blau (ed.), *op. cit.*, pp. 289, 300.

no protection . . . the laborer can and does both protect himself and the non-producer into the bargain."[12] Gilbert Vale, the disciple of Thomas Paine, carried this combined argument for economic self-interest and limited government to a theoretical conclusion when he equated personal gain and national well-being. "The wealth of a nation," he argued, "is made up of the wealth of the individuals composing that nation; the increase of an individual's wealth is, therefore a national benefit . . ."[13] The workingman, in short, would advance both his own cause and that of his nation when he devoted himself to the pursuit of economic acquisition. With all workingmen so occupied, political institutions were little needed except to protect the "natural right" of all men to that which they might acquire.

The Restless Desire for Wealth

With government declared irrelevant to the citizen's central concerns, the way was cleared for *all* Americans to go forth in quest of financial reward. That this sentiment often occupied the Jacksonian mind there can be little doubt. To document this assertion one must rely largely on the impressionistic and often divergent accounts found in the travel literature of the day. And while travelers sometimes gave very conflicting reports, from Tocqueville and Francis Grund to Harriet Martineau and Mrs. Trollope, there was consensus on this one point: Americans are driven by the hope of economic advancement. Thus Dickens finds the American incessantly worshipping, in his words, "the almighty dollar;" Francis Grund describes business as "the very soul of an American;" Mrs. Trollope speaks of the "universal and everlasting struggle for wealth," and the "giddy passion of money-getting;" Harriet Martineau is struck by the "prevalent desire of gain;"[14] and Michael Chevallier, one of the most perceptive of foreign observers, notes that "everybody is speculating," and that "from Maine to the Red River, the whole country has become an immense *Rue Quincampoix.*"[15]

Many Americans were also aware of this overriding desire to accumulate. In an editorial in the *Brooklyn Daily Eagle,* Whitman

☆

[12] "Capital Against Labor," in *ibid.*, p. 202.

[13] "From the Supplement to *The Diamond*, Series II," April to August, 1841, in *ibid.*, pp. 258, 244.

[14] For a penetrating analysis of this theme, see Marvin Meyers, *The Jacksonian Persuasion,* Stanford University Press, Stanford, Calif., 1957, chap. 6, from which these extracts are taken.

[15] John W. Ward (ed.), *Society, Manners, and Politics in the United States,* Doubleday & Company, Inc., Garden City, N.Y., 1961, p. 295.

pointed out that "on no particular matter is the public mind more un-healthy than the appetite for money . . . The mad passion for getting rich . . . engrosses all the thoughts and the time of man. It is the theme of all their wishes. It enters into their hearts and reigns para-mount there."[16] It remained, however, for the irrepressible Theophilus Fisk to describe his American world to the ambitious workingmen. "Every man for himself, is the convenient motto of the age," Fisk noted, "and of this age especially . . . There prevails, at this time, a spirit of cold calculation, which is carried into all the relations of society making barter and merchandise of the best feelings of the heart . . . We live in an age of selfishness . . . Everything has its price . . . All are bent with an undivided aim upon schemes of gain."[17] And lest the speculative propensity seem the particular prov-ince of the Jackson Men, it should be noted that certain Whig adher-ents were affected by it as well. Thus a Boston editorial could chide its readers for not opposing Jackson's reelection with more vigor. "We are now so flourishing and prosperous," ran the editorial, "that we can get along perfectly well under any chief magistrate, and it is not worth while for the citizens to leave their own concerns . . .Thus says the optimist and, without even taking the trouble to vote, he goes on quietly increasing the numbers of his dollars."[18] It was precisely this spirit of self-aggrandizement that caught the attention of both Orestes Brownson and Ralph Waldo Emerson.

Tocqueville's America

Before turning to Emerson and Brownson, however, it is necessary to dwell for a moment on Alexis de Tocqueville, whose considerations of American democracy are relevant to the study of community and pur-pose. Tocqueville immediately detected that the Americans lived in a state of Gesellschaft. This he attributed to the transition from an aristocratic society to a society based on equalitarian democracy, a transition that had the effect of relaxing "the bond of human affection."

> Among aristocratic nations, as families remain for centuries in the same spot, all generations become, as it were, contemporaneous. A man almost always knows his forefathers and respects them; he thinks he already sees his remote descendants and he loves them. He willingly imposes duties on himself towards the former and the latter, and he will frequently sacri-

☆

[16] "Morbid Appetite for Money," November 5, 1846, Holloway (ed.), *op. cit.*, vol. I, pp. 123-124.

[17] "An Oration delivered at the Queen-Street Theatre, in the City of Charleston, S.C.," July 4, 1837, p. 7.

[18] *Boston Daily Advertiser and Patriot*, 1832 (reprint), pp. 4-6.

fice his personal gratifications to those who went before and to those who will come after him. Aristocratic institutions, moreover, have the effect of closely binding every man to several of his fellow citizens. As the classes of an aristocratic people are strongly marked and permanent, each of them is regarded by its own members as a sort of lesser country, more tangible and more cherished than the country at large. As in aristocratic communities all the citizens occupy fixed positions, one above another, the result is that each of them always sees a man above himself whose patronage is necessary to him, and below himself another man whose co-operation he may claim. Men living in aristocratic ages are therefore almost always closely attached to something placed out of their own sphere, and they are often disposed to forget themselves . . . In democratic times, on the contrary, when the duties of each individual to the race are much more clear, devoted service to any one man becomes more rare; the bond of human affection is extended but it is relaxed.[19]

Americans had broken free from the restraints of the old order, but the very generality of their new condition made it impossible for them to relate to each other as profoundly or as closely as before. And thus, according to Tocqueville, it is for all "democratic times."

Associations in America

Americans, however, were not without their own mitigating institutions, as one quickly learns from a reading of *Democracy in America*. Tocqueville was enormously impressed by the American's rich political life. The America he described was a beehive of activity, as citizens formed themselves into an endless number of political associations in order to pursue certain common objectives. This associational life was so pervasive and so much a part of the American's routine that, if he "were condemned to confine his activity to his own affairs, he would be robbed of one half of his existence; he would feel an immense void in the life which he is accustomed to lead, and his wretchedness would be unbearable."[20] This is a powerful statement, and it immediately leads one to wonder whether such avid participation in political groups in any way contributed to a feeling of community, a feeling that could offset the normal divisive condition of the new world.

As a matter of fact, ubiquitous associational life could apparently speak to this problem, at least to some degree. Tocqueville specifically indicated that to join groups had the effect of easing the isolation that individuals were forced to endure in an equalitarian society cut off from traditional hierarchical ties.[21] And yet while such participation

☆

[19] Alexis de Tocqueville, *Democracy in America*, Reeves-Bowen text, revised and edited by Phillips Bradley, Vintage Books, New York, 1957, vol. II, pp. 104-105.

[20] *Ibid.*, vol. I, p. 260.

[21] *Ibid.*, vol. II, pp. 104-132.

could somewhat heal personal estrangement, it apparently fell considerably short of a true communal spirit. Certainly no *national* sense of community could flow from group involvement. Associations, or parties (Tocqueville used these terms interchangeably), are always seen as dealing with affairs of a strictly local nature and show no concern for national problems that affect the whole society.[22] Moreover, since the associations were usually formed for trivial, if not totally artificial, reasons, their importance to the individual member was probably never very great, certainly not great enough to overcome the pull of personal interest. Although Tocqueville clearly distinguished between "political" and "civil" associations, and placed each in separate realms,[23] he provided little or no content for the former, other than the realization of what appear to be private or semiprivate goals. Indeed, there existed in many cases a happy coincidence between organizational and personal aspirations, for the sole object of many groups was to satisfy the temporary collective economic interest of their membership. The "political" content of associations, then, seems open to some question.

Although Tocqueville used the term "political," it is often difficult to separate the activity of a political association from that of a more private organization. If to be political means to be related in some way to government, then his political groups fall distinctly outside this category. Tocqueville explicitly stated that "when a private individual meditates an undertaking, *however directly connected it may be with the welfare of society,* he never thinks of soliciting the cooperation of the government; but he publishes his plan, offers to execute it, courts the assistance of other individuals, and struggles manfully against all obstacles."[24] [Emphasis added.] Indeed, some critics of the time could find little hope for developing meaningful political associations. Albert Brisbane, for example, concluded that while "free competition and individual action" could be discerned everywhere, joint political action was scarcely to be found.[25] To a large extent local group participation may be looked upon as the public side of the American's private life, immediately related to the specific objectives with which he was most concerned.

☆

[22] *Ibid.*, vol. I, pp. 95, 185, 259. The one exception to this was the issue of the National Bank, an issue so crucial that it engendered national party action. (*Ibid.*, vol. I, p. 186.)

[23] *Ibid.*, vol. I, p. 98; vol. II, pp. 123-128.

[24] *Ibid.*, vol. I, p. 98.

[25] Summary of Brisbane's views in a review of his "Social Destiny of Man," Philadelphia, 1840, in *Democratic Review*, November, 1840; Yehoshua Arieli, *Individualism and Nationalism in American Ideology*, Harvard University Press, Cambridge, 1964, p. 237.

Historically, it may serve as some measure of the political relevance of these associations that as soon as local government could no longer satisfy their economic demands they were revealed immediately for what they essentially were, pressure groups with specific interests to advance; and, as organized labor was later to discover, sheer economic interest provides poor soil for the cultivation of community. As a matter of fact, given their initial local orientation, the American associations might have had the opportunity to develop and preserve some of the Gemeinschaft qualities that characterized the medieval corporate societies. But because many of their objectives were tinged with economic interest— "A native of the United States," Tocqueville wrote, "clings to this world's goods as if he were certain never to die; and he is so hasty in grasping at all within his reach that one would suppose he was constantly afraid of not living long enough to enjoy them"[26] —they more often than not grew into the pressure organizations described by the modern group theory of politics.

Jacksonian democracy had the effect of bringing the individual partially out of his privacy and into the contest for the prizes of America. Tocqueville sensed this when he wrote: "I have no doubt that the democratic institutions of the United States, joined to the physical constitution of the country, are the cause (not the direct, as is so often asserted, but the indirect cause) of the prodigious commercial activity of the inhabitants." Tocqueville also believed, however, that the average American "sincerely wished to promote the welfare of the country," but was prevented from implementing this desire by a lack of time and knowledge.[27] Sufficient time and knowledge were clearly missing, but it may be that an interest in the larger society was also somewhat lacking. Francis Grund is instructive on this point. One of his "typical Americans" asks: "What man of talent would forsake a respectable position in society, in order to earn eight dollars a day in Washington by making or listening to dull speeches?" Another tells us that "even statesmen like Webster, Clay, Calhoun, Wright, &c. are at home only listened to from complacency, unless they touch upon a subject immediately affecting the interest of their particular state."[28] Because he was so intensely involved in his own private fight for achievement, the Jacksonian American seems little concerned with outside problems, least of all with questions of national public policy.

☆

[26] Tocqueville, *op. cit.*, vol. II, p. 144.

[27] *Ibid.*, vol. I, pp. 261, 208.

[28] Francis Grund, *Aristocracy in America*, Richard Bentley, London, 1839, Harper & Brothers, New York, 1959, pp. 80, 252.

Individualism and Social Institutions

This fact should have been fairly obvious to Tocqueville who, like his fellow Europeans, was repeatedly distracted by the American's monolithic drive toward economic accumulation. In an illuminating essay entitled, "Quinze Jours au Desert," Tocqueville recounted experiences that he and Beaumont had while moving from the Eastern seaboard through the Western frontier. Time and again the Frenchmen encountered expressions of the American purpose. "This world belongs to us," they were told on more than one occasion by the frontiersmen. "God, in denying its first inhabitants the faculty of civilizing themselves, has predestined them to inevitable destruction. The true proprietors of this continent are those who know how to take advantage of its riches." Tocqueville was struck by how daring and adventurous the American could be if money were the object, and how blunted his outlook if something other than money were involved. "To cross almost impenetrable forests," he wrote, "pass deep rivers, brave pestilential swamps, sleep exposed to the damp of the woods: these are efforts the American has no difficulty understanding if it's a question of gaining a dollar, for that's the point. But that one should do such things through curiosity, that's something that doesn't reach his intelligence." Tocqueville could summarize Americans as "a people which, like all great peoples, has but one thought, and which is advancing toward the acquisition of riches, sole goal of its efforts, with a perseverance and a scorn for life that one might call heroic, if that name fitted other than virtuous things."[29]

In light of this analysis, Tocqueville's reference to "democratic times," rather than to American democracy in particular, seems somewhat dubious. The fact was that America had never experienced the transition from aristocracy to democracy, since, by European standards, aristocracy had never existed on American soil. Thus, while the advent of democracy might imply a general loosening of bonds of affection wherever it took place, American democracy, which had none of the restraining influences of older institutions, probably should have been looked upon as a special case, where for peculiarly native reasons

☆

[29] George W. Pierson (ed.), *Tocqueville In America*, Oxford University Press, New York, 1938, pp. 235, 339, 244. In *Ten Years in the United States*, D. W. Mitchell noted similar characteristics on the frontier. "There are no statistics," Mitchell wrote, "which show how many Yankees went out West to buy a piece of land and make a farm and home, and live and settle, and die there. I think that not more than one-half per cent of the migration from the East started with that idea: and not even half of these carried out the idea . . . all classes and people of all kinds became agitated and unsettled . . . by land speculations in some shape or other." Quoted by Harold U. Faulkner, *American Economic History*, 7th ed., Harper & Brothers, New York, 1960, p. 199.

isolation had reached a particularly acute level. Certainly Michael Chevallier, Tocqueville's countryman, found American behavior strangely unique.

In fact, the tumultuous uproar of American society left Chevallier fairly breathless. "An irresistible current," he wrote, "sweeps everything away, grinds everything to powder and deposits it again under new forms. Men change their houses, their climate, their trade, their condition, their party, their sect; the States change their laws, their officers, their constitutions. The soil itself, or at least the houses, partake in the universal instability. The existence of social order in the bosom of this whirlpool seems a miracle, an inexplicable anomaly."[30] Social order seemed even more of a mystery to Chevallier when he discovered in America a totally fragmented structure of political authority. In wonder, he noted: "the American Republic subdivides itself indefinitely into independent republics on various levels. The states are republics in the Union; the cities are republics in the states; a farm is a republic in the county. The banking and canal . . . companies are also distinct republics. The family is an inviolable republic . . . and each individual is himself a little republic in the family."[31] Despite Chevallier's bewilderment, order could exist in this state of apparent derangement for a very simple reason: there was an almost total consensus on precisely this mode of behavior. Everyone seemed to agree that this style of life fitted America nicely, and since the continent provided space and resources for all citizens, men could rest assured that, at least on a minimal level, law and order would be preserved. But if men could feel legally secure as sovereign islands in this sea of turbulence, psychological security might not be so easily attained. Even the Whig leadership was sensitive to this problem.

In a remarkable 1845 article, *The American Review*, Whig counterpart to the *Democratic Review*, noted a coldness of spirit, an "excessive anxiety written in the American countenance." This the *Review* took to be the result of the "restless desire to be better off," a desire that, since it knows no bounds and is common to all classes, can never find satisfaction or contentment. While trade is and has heretofore been a beneficial, even a liberating force, it now bids fair to establish conditions worse than those for which it originally provided a corrective. "The excitement," continued the article, "the commercial activity, the restlessness, to which this state of things has given birth, is far from being a desirable restlessness or a natural condition." "A man's life with us *does* consist of the abundance of things which he

☆

[30] Ward (ed.), *op. cit.*, p. 299.
[31] Quoted in Arieli, *op. cit.*, p. 206.

possesseth. To get, and to have the reputation of possessing, is the ruling passion. To it are bent all the energies of nine-tenths of our population." Given the special nature of American history, this unhappy circumstance should perhaps not be entirely unexpected; that it happened was probably inevitable. Even if this is so, Americans should not delude themselves into thinking that they now live in the best of all possible worlds. "If we are doomed to be tradesmen," cautions the *Review*, "and nothing but tradesmen — if money, and its influences and authority, are to reign . . . over our whole land, let us not mistake it for the kingdom of heaven, and build triumphal arches over our avenues of trade, as though the Prince of Peace and the Son of God were now and thus to enter in."[32] This last piece of imagery brings immediately to mind similar thoughts from the pen of Ralph Waldo Emerson, and it is to Emerson's work that we now turn.

Ralph Waldo Emerson

Emerson's response to the crass materialism of his age is well known. His critique of early-American shabbiness and corruption is incisive and challenging, and Emersonian aphorisms elevating spiritual considerations have become part of a critical vocabulary that is still alive today. I propose to take this side of Emerson for granted — it is widely known and needs no further elucidation from me. There is, I suggest, another side to Emerson, a side that has been largely ignored by students of his work. Emerson's audience, on the other hand, may have been more aware of this side; they may have been more sensitive to those of his remarks that tended to support the system as it stood, lectures that sanctioned a way of life already accepted and firmly entrenched in all areas of the country. Because I am especially interested in the interpretations that his audiences may have made of his philosophy, I will deal almost exclusively with Emerson's public statements, those statements written or delivered orally for the edification of the population at large.

Emerson was an accomplished speaker. His public addresses often moved his listeners very deeply, and the popularity of his lectures carried him to country lyceums throughout the United States. Everywhere audiences were apparently ready and eager to hear the noted Concord philosopher dilate on man and his universe, instruct them in a better, a more natural way of life. Emerson's reception was

☆

[32] "The Influence of the Trading Spirit on the Social and Moral Life in America," January 1845, in Edwin C. Rozwenc (ed.), *Ideology and Power In the Age of Jackson*, New York University Press, New York, 1964, pp. 48-51.

typically enthusiastic, but aside from his rhetorical abilities, the reasons for this enthusiasm are not entirely clear. In fact, though his addresses were inevitably variations on an unchanging theme,[33] there is some reason to believe that his message was not always genuinely understood. Edward Waldo Emerson tells us that "among the persons who attended Mr. Emerson's courses of lectures were many who were attracted by his growing fame. Some among those would have found it hard to follow his thoughts' subtle thread, connecting his periods, or ascend to its higher level."[34] James Elliot Cabot states categorically that many "came . . . to hear Emerson, not his opinions." And according to Oliver Wendell Holmes, "the music of his speech pleased those who found his thought too subtle for their dull wits to follow."[35] But even superior minds sometimes had difficulty remaining in tune with Emerson's rhapsody. Thus, immediately after listening to one of Emerson's addresses, James Russell Lowell wrote that his "oration was more disjointed than usual, even with him. It began nowhere, and ended everywhere, and yet, as always with that divine man, it left you feeling that something beautiful had passed that way, something more beautiful than anything else, like the rising and setting of stars."[36] Even Holmes found that Emerson's intuitive tendencies rendered "him sometimes obscure, and once in a while almost, if not quite, unintelligible;" "he passed from one thought to another not by logical steps but by airy flights, which left no footprints."[37] If his audience had been asked what it was that Emerson was trying to say, his "average" listener would probably not have been able to respond with certainty. A Boston attorney, whose teenage daughters thought they understood Emerson completely, found his lectures "utterly meaningless," while a Concord scrubwoman, who never missed an Emerson oration, admitted that she comprehended "not a word," but liked to

☆

[33] I have deliberately avoided a developmental approach in the presentation of Emerson's thought. I would agree with John Jay Chapman that it matters little where you begin with Emerson. The argument, at least insofar as it relates to the issue of community and purpose, sooner or later takes a familiar turn and occupies traditional ground. This position does not apply to shifts in Emerson's thought that take place in other areas (religion, ethics, and so forth). On these themes see Stephen E. Wicher, *Freedom and Fate, An Inner Life of Ralph Waldo Emerson,* University of Pennsylvania Press, Philadelphia, 1953.

[34] Edward Waldo Emerson (ed.), *The Complete Works of Ralph Waldo Emerson,* Houghton Mifflin Company, Boston, 1904, vol. VI, p. 400n.

[35] James Elliot Cabot, *A Memoir of Ralph Waldo Emerson,* Houghton Mifflin Company, Boston, 1887, vol. II, p. 383. Oliver Wendell Holmes, *Ralph Waldo Emerson,* Houghton Mifflin Company, Boston, 1893, p. 376.

[36] Quoted by John Jay Chapman, Jacques Barzun (ed.), *Selected Writings of John Jay Chapman,* Farrar, Straus & Cudahy, New York, 1957, pp. 165-166.

[37] Holmes, *op. cit.,* pp. 390, 366.

attend because Emerson made people feel that they were as good as he was.[38] And Charles Dickens reports that when he inquired as to the meaning of Emerson's transcendentalism, he "was given to understand that whatever was unintelligible would be certainly Transcendental."[39] Whatever Emerson was trying to communicate, it is clear that many experienced difficulty grasping it, even as they listened with pleasure and gratification. His thought, to use John Jay Chapman's metaphor, was hidden by a high wall, and while Chapman could deduce with confidence where Emerson stood at any given moment from the objects thrown over that wall,[40] most Americans were probably too attracted by the objects themselves to bother with fixing Emerson's exact philosophical or political locus. Without careful study, and perhaps without a spiritual predisposition, Emerson's thought is sometimes unclear and often confusing, and out of this confusion it may not have been difficult to extract a position that was sustaining of the American purpose. On its more fundamental level, Emerson's critique was absolutely devastating, for he told Americans that they were not men. But short of this fundamental level—and Emerson's inconsistent juxtaposition of mystical idealism and common sense made it easy for many, mandatory for some, to stop short—his argument could be taken as a spiritual justification of the American way.

Emersonian Ambiguity

"The Young American," an early address delivered before the Mercantile Library Association of Boston,[41] illustrates both Emerson's general position and the problems one encounters trying to find a surface consistency in his thought. In this address Emerson is mainly concerned with placing America at the forefront of nature's slow but inexorable improvement of human existence. Nature is most evident in the great expanse of the American continent, which provides a natural antidote to the often noxious behavior of man. "The land," Emerson points out, "is the appointed remedy for whatever is false and fantastic in our culture." America, amply endowed with land, is simply the clearest example of a long-run beneficence which nature affords all of mankind: "there is," Emerson notes, "a sublime and

☆

[38] Brooks Atkinson (ed.), *The Complete Essays and Other Writings of Ralph Waldo Emerson,* Random House, Inc., New York, 1940, p. xiv.

[39] Emerson (ed.), *op. cit.,* vol. I, p. 447n.

[40] Barzun (ed.), *op. cit.,* p. 164.

[41] Emerson (ed.), *op. cit.,* vol. I, pp. 361-395. This later appeared as an essay in the *Dial,* vol. 4, pp. 484-507, April, 1844.

friendly Destiny by which the human race is guided—the race never dying, the individual never spared—to results affecting masses and ages. Men are narrow and selfish, but the Genius or Destiny is not narrow, but beneficent. It is not discovered in their calculated and voluntary activity, but in what befalls, with or without their design . . . Genius has infused itself into nature. It indicates itself by a small excess of good, a small balance in brute facts always favorable to the side of reason."[42]

The Genius of nature shows itself with utmost clarity when it counters the feeble attempts of man to "correct" what he takes to be abuses of privilege or disadvantages of status. Thus we pass relief laws for the poor, but the principle of population growth always reduces wages to the lowest possible level of human endurance. We establish currency and credit regulations and these lead ultimately to undiminished bankruptcy. We pass antimonopoly legislation and advocate common granaries for the poor; "but the selfishness which hoards the corn for high prices is the preventive of famine, and the law of self-preservation is surer policy than any legislation can be." In fact, most of the public improvements we attempt do little to change current conditions, but have only a future impact. The only genuine acts of improvement that have present value are those which affect the private individual, and such acts, ironically, can be traced largely to the "beneficent tendency" of commerce.

In this address Emerson showed little patience for the critics of commerce. "The philosopher and lover of man have much harm to say of trade; but the historian will see that trade was the principle of Liberty; that trade planted America and destroyed Feudalism; that it makes peace and keeps peace, and it will abolish slavery." Although it is true that trade may produce a new aristocracy of wealth, we need not fear this development, for the content of the new aristocracy is very impermanent, being susceptible to the fortuitous accumulation and loss factors characteristic of an uncertain market. In sum, "trade is an instrument in the hands of that friendly Power which works for us in our own despite. We design it thus and thus; it turns out otherwise and far better."[43]

To this point, Emerson appears to be arguing that man, the Young American in particular, can and ought to do very little, politically or socially, to improve his condition. Nature, and trade—which seems an extension of nature's largesse to man—will in the end place man in his proper setting, and any attempt by man to take things into his own

☆

[42] Emerson (ed.), *op. cit.,* vol. I, pp. 365, 371-372.
[43] *Ibid.,* vol. I, pp. 378, 379.

hands will very likely have results precisely opposite those anticipated. This is one of the ironies of life. But at this juncture Emerson shifts to a discussion of the communalist and socialist movements that have suddenly appeared on both sides of the Atlantic and are fast superseding trade as the great meliorative force in the world. The motives behind these various movements are many, but common to all is a feeling that the state has fallen down on its job. What function has the state failed to perform? It is, Emerson tells us, "the duty to instruct the ignorant, to supply the poor with work and with good guidance." If the new communities cannot accomplish this task, they can at least provide their own members with economic security; they are not after all to be understood as revolutionary institutions. "The Community," Emerson suggests, "is only the continuation of the same movement which made the joint-stock companies for manufactures, mining, insurance, banking, and so forth. It has turned out cheaper to make calico by companies; and it is proposed to plant corn and to bake bread by companies." But from another perspective, the new communities are indicative of the fact that a revolution is near at hand. Their value lies not in what they have accomplished, "but [in] the revolution which they indicate as on the way. Yes, Government must educate the poor man. Look across the country from any hill-side around us and the landscape seems to crave Government. The actual differences of men must be acknowledged, and met with love and wisdom."[44]

In this revised statement, then, Emerson seems to argue that the communities will either improve upon the beneficial effects of commerce, while retaining the methods of commercial success, or that they will encourage vitally needed government to act as the protector and educator of the poor. But Emerson is by no means recommending an active role for traditional government. Quite the contrary, since he sees America progressing toward a day when select private individuals will themselves lead their society as natural governors, self-styled leaders of men. And the emergence of such individuals is a direct function of the "gradual contempt into which official government falls." Emerson has at this point reached what for him is the most important level of analysis, that of the individual. He no longer speaks of community, but suggests with apparent seriousness that society might adopt a system that delineates natural leaders by affixing to their names vocational titles descriptive of their work, as in commerce: for example, Mr. Smith, Governor. And it would be the obligation of these "patriotic heroes," to lead America to its grand destiny by acts of unexcelled greatness. Principal among these acts would be an attack

☆

[44] *Ibid.*, vol. I, pp. 381, 383, 384.

on the harmful effects of the American commercial system. With some heat Emerson argues that all of the institutions with popular influence — the legislature, the lyceum, the church, the press — are of a piece with regard to capitalism and property. "They recommend conventional virtues, whatever will earn and preserve property; always the capitalist; the college, the church, the hospital, the theatre, the hotel, the road, [all are aboard] the ship of the capitalist — whatever goes to secure, adorn, enlarge these is good, whatever jeopardizes any of these is damnable. The 'opposition' papers, so called, are on the same side. They attack the great capitalist, but with the aim to make a capitalist of the poor man. The opposition is against those who have money, from those who wish to have money."[45] In such a state, laments Emerson, the virtues of heroism go unattended. Notwithstanding this bleak outlook, Emerson concludes on an optimistic note: free of feudalism and European influence, America will go on to achieve its masterful triumph.

Thus we find in "The Young American" a deprecation of human action followed by an endorsement, on one level at least, of concerted communal action and a plea for activity by the involved individual; a minimization of the necessity for government followed by a discussion of the tragic failure of government and the current need for governmental leadership, but not by public men; enthusiastic praise for the positive influence of commerce followed by a passionate attack upon the primacy of commercial values. All of this is delivered with obvious conviction by a man of considerable stature. Small wonder that his audience was sometimes left puzzled. Although an intuitive consistency may lie beneath Emerson's logical contradictions, much of the audience saw the surface only, and this often tended to be fully in keeping with the American ideology. After hearing "The Young American" would his listeners remember commerce as an example of nature's way or capitalism as the destroyer of patriotic heroism?

Harmony in the National Purpose

Emerson's work is replete with statements that Americans could turn to their own purpose. This easy assimilation was not entirely accidental. For all the radicalism implicit in his thought, Emerson could also stand on the typical conservative platform. Cabot tells us that Emerson was of "the party of progress, or at least of aspiration and hope. But he could not help seeing that the existing order, since it is here has the right to be here, and the right to all the force it can exert."[46]

☆

[45] *Ibid.*, vol. I, p. 388.
[46] Cabot, *op. cit.*, vol. II, p. 390.

Yet Emerson's support for the here-and-now stemmed from an even deeper source. It was a natural derivative of his faith in a Nature whose "brute facts" were ultimately "favorable to the side of reason." Indeed, men themselves are often numbered among nature's brute facts. We are told that "the grandeur of our life exists in spite of us — all over and under and within us, in what of us is inevitable and above our control. *Men are facts as well as persons,* and the involuntary part of their life is so much as to fill the mind and leave them no countenance to say aught of what is so trivial as their selfish thinking and doing."[47] [Emphasis added.]

With men as natural facts, Emerson can extend the circle of what is "trivial and selfish" to include much of what normally goes for conventional social and political action. Thus in *Self-Reliance* he can advise his listeners to "accept the place the divine providence has found for you, the society of your contemporaries, the connection of events. Great men have always done so, and confided themselves childlike to the genius of their age . . ." "Shun the negative side," he says elsewhere. "Never worry people with your contritions, nor with dismal views of politics or society."[48] For, in the final analysis, there is no need to worry. There is at work in nature a principle that compensates mankind in general, even individual men in particular, although they may never realize this because of apparent temporary deprivations. This principle of compensation or balance is continually operative and eventually harmonizes all phenomena with nature's divine scheme. For example, "if riches increase, they are increased that use them." If the gatherer gathers too much, nature will have her revenge. "Nature hates monopolies and exceptions . . . There is always some leveling circumstance that puts down the overbearing, the strong, the rich, the fortunate, substantially on the same ground with all other." To illustrate this point Emerson suggests that nature will temper an overly fierce man — "a morose ruffian, with a dash of the pirate in him" — by sending him attractive sons and daughters whose welfare occupies his mind and becalms him. Thus nature "takes the boar out and puts the lamb in and keeps her balance true." Man must learn once and for all that he is "ordinarily a pendant to events, only half attached, and that awkwardly, to the world he lives in."[49]

Occasionally Emerson seems to see man's connection with the world as something even less than "half-attachment;" at such times reality itself is brought into question. "Dream delivers us to dream," Emerson writes, "and there is no end to illusion. Life is a train of

☆

[47] "Poetry and Imagination," Emerson (ed.), *op. cit.*, vol. VIII, p. 75.

[48] *Ibid.*, vol. II, p. 47. "Social Aims," *ibid.*, p. 98.

[49] "Compensation," *ibid.*, vol. II, pp. 98-99. "Character," *ibid.*, vol. III, p. 90.

moods like a string of beads, and as we pass through them they prove to be many-colored lenses which paint the world in their own hue, and each shows only what lies in its focus." "Life itself is a bubble and a skepticism, and a sleep within a sleep."[50] This of course is the final position of mystical alienation from *all* social involvement, and although Emerson touches this point frequently he seldom permits himself to rest there for long. More typically, he tempers his mysticism with traditional New England common sense, arguing that acceptance of nature's correct path is enough to bring man clearer vision and peace of mind. "The lesson is forcibly taught by these observations that our life might be much easier and simpler than we make it; that the world might be a happier place than it is; that there is no need of struggles, convulsions, and despairs, or the wringing of the hands and the gnashing of the teeth; that we miscreate our own evils. We interfere with the optimist of nature . . . we are begirt with laws which execute themselves."[51] What more could a nation already hostile to government and strongly imbued with the idea of progress ask to hear from one of its leading sages? Emerson could in fact be even more pointed in telling his countrymen precisely what they wanted to hear.

If America was overly respectful of the dollar, Emerson could offer natural justification for monetary pursuit. "We cannot," he said, "trade the triumphs of civilization to such benefactors as we wish. The greatest meliorator of the world is selfish, huckstering Trade."[52] Moreover, the energy produced and expended in commercial activity provides a generative force which helps to perpetuate civilized society. Emerson pointed out that "the pulpit and the press have many commonplaces denouncing the thirst for wealth; but if men should take these moralists at their word and leave off aiming to be rich, the moralists would rush to rekindle at all hazards this love of power in the people, lest civilization should be undone." To tamper with trade would be to alter nature's normal course, and this would prove ultimately self-destructive. This holds even for the gross inequalities that result from differentiated commercial success. "There are," Emerson insists, "geniuses in trade, as well as in war, or the State, or letters; and the reason why this or that man is fortunate is not to be told. It lies in the man; that is all anybody can tell you about it . . . Nature seems to authorize trade, as soon as you see the natural mer-

☆

[50] "Experience," *ibid.*, pp. 50, 65.

[51] "Spiritual Laws," *ibid.*, vol. II, p. 135. In a letter to Carlyle in 1841, Emerson wrote: "My whole philosophy—which is very real—teaches acquiescence and optimism." (*Ibid.*, vol. I, pp. 434-435n.)

[52] "Works and Days," *ibid.*, vol. VII, p. 166.

chant, who appears not so much a private agent as her factor and Minister of Commerce."[53]

This notion of the successful entrepreneur as nature's agent had real meaning for Emerson. He could use it by way of analogy to give his followers a valuable lesson in self-respect. "It is disgraceful," he said, "to fly to events for confirmation of our truth and worth. The capitalist does not run every hour to the broker to coin his advantages into current money of the realm; he is satisfied to read in the quotation of the market that his stocks have risen." For the man whose stocks seem never to rise, who is perennially pressed to make ends meet, there is nature's promise of eventual satisfaction. Not only does America provide those of her youth who possess "a turn for business, and a quick eye for . . . investment"[54] with ample opportunity to acquire wealth, but nature itself sees to it that even the most underprivileged will get their chance. "Certainly," Emerson maintains in one of his more compassionate moments, "I am not going to argue the merits of gradation in the universe; the existing order of more or less . . . I know how steep the contrast of condition looks; such excess here and such destitution there . . . such despotism of wealth and comfort in banquet halls, whilst death is in the pots of the wretched . . . But the constitution of things has distributed a new quality or talent to each mind, and the revolution of things is always bringing the need, now of this, now of that, and is sure to bring home the opportunity to everyone." Whether all will succeed or not, it is to be hoped that all will try: "So true is Dr. Johnson's remark that men are seldom more innocently [for innocently read naturally] employed than when they are making money!"[55] By this measure one can find little fault with nineteenth century America, most of whose energy was spent with this end firmly in mind.

With commerce placed securely in the natural order of things, there is, of course, little need for governmental interference in the economic or social spheres. One can, or should be able to, see this, Emerson argues, even when ignorant masses push government far in excess of its natural authority: "there are limitations beyond which the folly and ambition of governors cannot go. Things have their laws, as well as men; and things refuse to be trifled with . . . Under any forms, persons and property must and will have their just sway." Men are governed principally by the laws of nature, and governments above all

☆

[53] "Character," *ibid.*, vol. III, p. 92.

[54] "Social Aims," *ibid.*, vol. VIII, p. 100.

[55] "Aristocracy," *ibid.*, vol. X, p. 46. "Society and Solitude," *ibid.*, vol. VII, p. 23.

should not attempt to do for men what they naturally must do for themselves. "This undertaking for another is the blunder which stands in colossal ugliness in the governments of the world . . . all public ends look vague and quixotic beside private ones. For any laws but those which men make for themselves are laughable . . . Hence the less government we have the better—the fewer laws, and the less confided power. The antidote to this abuse of formal government is . . . the growth of the Individual . . . The appearance of character makes the State unnecessary." Thus true men of character will not pay homage to the state. "Every actual State is corrupt," Emerson tells them. "Good men must not obey the laws too well."[56]

Emerson could carry his hostility toward government to such a degree that he actually looked with enthusiasm upon the rapid deterioration of the federal government just prior to the Civil War. Three days before the bombardment of Fort Sumter he suggested that "the facility with which a great political fabric can be broken, the want of tension in all ties which had been supposed adamantine, is instructive, and perhaps opens a new page in civil history . . . the hour is struck, so long predicted by philosophy, when the civil machinery that has been the religion of the world decomposes to dust and smoke before the now adult individualism; and the private man feels that he is the State, and that a community in like external conditions of climate, race, sentiment, employment can drop with impunity much of the machinery of government, as operose and clumsy, and get on cheaper and simpler by leaving to every man all his rights and powers, checked by no law but his love or fear of the rights and powers of his neighbor."[57] When the private man becomes as the state he will at last realize that "the stream of human affairs flows its own way, and is very little affected by the activity of legislators."[58]

Emersonian Individualism

The idea of man as his own state tells us very much indeed about Emerson's philosophy. His concept of individualism was sometimes pushed to an intractable extreme. In *The American Scholar* he argued that everything which "tends to insulate the individual—to surround him with barriers of natural respect, so that each man shall feel the world is his, and man shall treat with man as a sovereign state with a

☆

[56] "Politics," *ibid.*, vol. III, pp. 204-205, 214-216, 208.

[57] Quoted in Cabot, *op. cit.*, vol. II, pp. 603-604.

[58] "Emancipation in the British West Indies," Emerson (ed.), *op. cit.*, vol. XI, p. 139.

sovereign state—tends to true union as well as greatness."[59] Emerson abhorred nothing so much as man's dependency on man. "It is foolish," he contended, "to be afraid of making our ties too spiritual." By breaking away we may seem to loose some joy, but in the end nature will bestow upon us a joy far nobler than that derived from common affection. "Let us feel, if we will, the absolute insulation of man. We are sure that we have all in us . . . Let us even bid our dearest friends farewell, and defy them, saying 'Who are you? Unhand me: I will be dependent no more.'"[60] Temporary friendships and associations directed at good purposes are excellent things, "but remember that no society can ever be so large as one man . . . In the hour in which he mortgages himself to two or ten or twenty, he dwarfs himself below the stature of one." Emerson can make the case no plainer than when he exclaims: "Hands off! let there be no control and no interference in the administration of the affairs of this kingdom of me."[61] One can imagine his American "congregation" rising as one upon hearing this and shouting, "Amen!"

To seal oneself from other men within one's own kingdom is to impute independence and sovereignty to all other men whether they desire it or not. It follows that one must remain deaf to the importunities of those men who cannot get by on their own devices and of those who would claim your assistance for others apparently in need. Emerson does not shrink from this consequence. "Do not," he admonishes, "tell me . . . of my obligation to put all poor men in good situations. Are they *my* poor? I tell thee, thou foolish philanthropist, that I grudge the dollar, the dime, the cent I give to such men as do not belong to me and to whom I do not belong." For certain meritorious persons Emerson would give all he possesses: "but your miscellaneous popular charities; the education at college of fools; the building of meeting-houses to the vain end to which many now stand; alms to sots, and the thousand-fold Relief Societies—though I confess with shame I sometimes succumb and give the dollar, it is a wicked dollar, which by and by I shall have the manhood to withhold."[62]

To be a true individual requires constant self-appraisal and examination and leaves little time for those external demands that involve an expenditure of personality, even when such demands are made by individuals who have need of more than ordinary attention. "In dealing with the drunken," Emerson advises, "we do not affect to be drunk.

☆

[59] *Ibid.*, vol. I, p. 113.
[60] "Friendship," *ibid.*, vol. II, pp. 213-214.
[61] "New England Reformers," *ibid.*, vol. III, pp. 265, 255.
[62] "Self-Reliance," *ibid.*, vol. II, p. 52.

We must treat the sick with the same firmness, giving them of course every aid—but withholding ourselves."[63] This is after all the way of nature that not only justifies, but makes imperative, our personal isolation: ". . . the gods, in the beginning, divided Man into men, that he might be more helpful to himself . . ." Carried to its final extreme, this position comes very close to the doctrines of Social Darwinism. Emerson reaches this extreme. "Power," he argues, "is, in nature, the essential measure of right. Nature suffers nothing to remain in her kingdom which cannot help itself."[64] When Rousseau divided his citizenry into totally independent and exclusive entities, he drew all men into common cause and affection under the state which would act collectively for all concerned. Emerson leaves the individual alone with nature, a being whose affinity with all other beings stems from the realization that he, like all natural phenomena, is a brute fact, carried along by nature's inviolable laws.

It is essential, however, that we do not miss Emerson's basic point. He tirelessly argued that for the man who can understand and cope with this condition there is ecstatic insight, triumphant power, an individualism that is productive of incomparable greatness, an individualism that molds men who can look the world in the eye and subject it, for a time at least, to their own iron will. Such men can achieve anything: "Nothing is impossible to the man who can will."[65] When one thinks of a brotherhood of such giants, one can easily dispense with the common ties of routine existence. "Ah! seest thou not, O brother, that thus we part only to meet again on a higher platform, and only be more each other's because we are more our own?"[66] This is the individualism that Emerson calls his country to. It is a Nietzschean call to excellence, and Emerson is enraged that America does not heed it. "Leave this hypocritical prating about the masses," he thunders. "Masses are rude, lame, unmade, pernicious in their demands and influence, and need not to be flattered but to be schooled. I wish not to concede anything to them, but to tame, drill, divide and break them up, and draw individuals out of them . . . Masses! the calamity is the masses. I do not wish any mass at all, but honest men only . . . and no shovel-handed, narrow-brained, gin-drinking million stockingers or lazzaroni at all."[67] But to climb from the masses to

☆

[63] "Considerations by the Way," *ibid.*, vol. VI, p. 263.

[64] "The American Scholar," *ibid.*, vol. I, p. 82. "Self-Reliance," *ibid.*, vol. II, p. 70.

[65] "Considerations by the Way," *ibid.*, vol. VI, p. 248.

[66] "Friendship," *ibid.*, vol. II, p. 314.

[67] "Considerations by the Way," *ibid.*, vol. VI, p. 249. Edward Waldo Emerson saw fit to append a note to this paragraph stating that it was not representative of Emerson's usual sentiments regarding the demos. (*Ibid.*, p. 403.)

individuality, as Emerson demands, is to scale great heights indeed.

Emerson's concept of the complete individual is to be found in a volume ironically entitled *Representative Men,* ironic because the figures dealt with do *not* for the most part represent man, with his usual set of good and bad features, but men of unparalleled accomplishment, men of excellence, supermen. None of the "representative men" is American. And Emerson's call to a "brotherhood" of such individuals can have little relevance for normal men involved in common human equations. Emerson's brotherhood meets on a transcendent plane that is itself beyond the social and political condition of most men, and brings to mind the ethereal notions of universal community conceived by Marcus Aurelius and other Stoics in the second century A.D. In *Representative Men,* Plato provides the prototype for complete individualism. "Plato," Emerson writes, "would willingly have a Platonism, a known and accurate expression for the world, and it should be accurate. It shall be the world passed through the mind of Plato—nothing less. Every atom shall have the Platonic tinge; every atom, every relation or quality you knew before, you shall know again and find here, but now ordered; not nature but art. And you shall feel that Alexander indeed overran, with men and horse, some countries of the planet; but countries, and things of which countries are made, elements, planet itself, laws of planet and of men, have passed through this man as bread into his body, and become no longer bread, but body: so all this mammoth morsel has become Plato. He has clapped copyright on the world. *This is the ambition of individualism.*"[68] [Emphasis added.] This indeed is the glory of individualism, rightly understood. And the allusion to Alexander is by no means out of place, for Emerson valued the individualism of the great man of action almost as much as that of the man of creative thought. Holmes noted that of the authorities cited in Emerson's works, Napoleon appears eighty-four times, second only to Shakespeare's one hundred twelve, and ahead of Plato's eighty-one.[69]

Even in his eulogy to Thoreau, Emerson can express disappointment in the man who, by Emerson's own admission, put transcendentalism into practice better than any man alive. "Had his genius been only contemplative," Emerson writes, "he had been fitted to his life, but with his energy and practical ability he seemed born for great enterprise and for command; and I so much regret the loss of his rare powers of action, that I cannot help counting it a fault in him that he

☆

[68] "Plato; Or, the Philosopher," Emerson (ed.), *op. cit.,* vol. IV, p. 77.

[69] Holmes, *op. cit.,* p. 382. But see Emerson's essay on Napoleon in *Representative Men* (*ibid.,* vol. IV) in which Napoleon is presented as the typical man of the masses, with all of his strengths, but especially his weaknesses.

had no ambition. Wanting this, instead of engineering for all America, he was the captain of a huckleberry party. Pounding beans is good to the end of pounding empires one of these days; but if, at the end of years, it is still only beans!"[70] Even Thoreau, America's noblest son, is somehow not completely a man. The other sons of America are for Emerson scarcely worth the mention.

The Emersonian Critique

This, then, is Emerson's radicalism. His criticism states that America is unable to produce real men; its masses stultify and crush true individualism beneath the enormous pressure of their tawdriness and conformity. I must repeat that my interpretation of Emerson is rather one-sided and is made to support a very special argument. Moreover, many of Emerson's remarks have been taken out of context in order to show that his individualism often ran second to more frequent arguments in behalf of the national ideology. To cite Emerson out of context, however, is not entirely unjustified, since, as Holmes tells us, "his paragraphs are full of brittle sentences that break apart and are independent units, like the fragments of a coral colony."[71] Yet for every statement that is either anticommunal or supportive of American purpose, one can find another that goes in the opposite direction. Cabot writes that Emerson's criticisms "were subversive of the common beliefs; and yet, since Emerson could never take the polemical tone, and was not ready with a scheme for reconstruction, he found himself condemned to a way of speaking that seemed vague and ineffective."[72] But as we have seen, Emerson could be very polemical; the problem lay in the fact that his polemics were always tempered by the next paragraph, or perhaps by a restatement of the argument in more positive language. On one point only did he remain consistent: his stress on individualism. But when fitted together with his seeming enthusiasm for everything else American, his individualism, although directed at the highest of achievement, must have sounded a familiar and comfortable note in the ears of his listeners. For America *was* individualistic; Americans already believed in and practiced their own kind of self-reliance, and, unlike Tocqueville, Emerson seems to have missed the causal connection between individualism and mass conformity. Tocqueville could be critical both of American massness and the individual isolation that drives men into mass behavior. Emerson could feel anguish over the mass man, but could offer him only what seemed to be a stronger dose of the individualism he al-

☆

[70] "Thoreau," Emerson (ed.), *op. cit.*, vol. X, p. 480.

[71] Holmes, *op. cit.*, p. 404.

[72] Cabot, *op. cit.*, vol. II, p. 397.

ready accepted.[73] Of course, in the final analysis, Emerson's individualism is of another genre altogether; his self-reliance is the stuff of which great heroes are made, and was not native to American soil. To his average listener, however, confused as well as charmed by the noted philosopher, individualism may have meant only a continuation of an already established pattern.

When Emerson's espousal of the American Eden is added to his individualism, his apparent endorsement of the national ideology is made complete. In 1838 he wrote that "the new man must feel that he is new, and has not come into this world mortgaged to the opinions and usages of Europe, and Asia, and Egypt . . . now our day is come; we have been born out of the eternal silence; and now will we live — live for ourselves . . ."[74] Years later he summed up his feeling: "When I look over this constellation of cities which animate and illustrate the land, and see how little the government has to do with their daily life, how self-helped and self-directed all families are — knots of men in purely natural societies, societies of trade, of kindred blood, of habitual hospitality, house and house, man acting on man by weight of opinion . . . I see what cubic values America has . . ."[75] After such a benediction who would remember Emerson's "moments of truth?" Who would even recall that two pages later in the very same essay he wrote: "And the highest proof of civility is that the whole public action of the state is directed on securing the greatest good for the greatest number." Oliver Wendell Holmes caught Emerson's spirit when he described him as "an iconoclast without a hammer, who took down our idols from their pedestals so tenderly that it seemed like an act of worship."[76] For many Americans it very likely *was* an act of worship and, at least as far as their national purpose was concerned, after hearing Emerson, their idols probably stood as straight and as tall as ever.

Orestes Brownson

One cannot say the same for Orestes Brownson. When Brownson attacked sacred American cows he did so with a bullwhip and his lashes invariably drew pained cries of protest. Yet if Emerson seemed to shift his ground occasionally, Brownson, it is only fair to point out,

☆

[73] It is interesting to note that, though he was influenced to some degree by the "transcendental" side of Coleridge, Emerson appears to have missed entirely the side that was deeply concerned with problems of community.

[74] "Literary Ethics," Emerson (ed.), *op. cit.*, vol. I, pp. 159-160.

[75] "Society and Solitude," *ibid.*, vol. VII, p. 32.

[76] Cited in Cabot, *op. cit.*, vol. I, p. 262. Holmes' remark is perhaps less relevant to the realm of religion where Emerson's "Divinity School Address" shook the foundations of organized Protestantism.

could outdo the most accomplished Sophist in polemical transmutation, and he continually stormed from position to position, even from ideology to ideology. James Freeman Clarke claimed that "no man has ever equalled Mr. Brownson in the ability with which he has refuted his own arguments."[77] And in one of his razor-edged rhymes, James Russell Lowell says of Brownson:

> He shifts quite about, then proceeds to expound
> That 'tis merely the earth, not himself, that turns round,
> And wishes it clearly impressed on your mind
> That the weathercock rules and not follows the wind;
> Proving first, then as deftly confuting each side,
> With no doctrine pleased that's not somewhere denied . . .[78]

These charges are undeniable. But unlike the Sophist, Brownson was not especially interested in winning debates. For much of his life he was engaged in a search for truth, and it was his peculiar bent that, while he could be profoundly certain of a belief at the time he held it, the force of his logic inevitably drove him to further inquiry and thus to still newer beliefs. Hence it appeared to his reader that no sooner was he fixed at a particular point than he was off again exploring entirely new territory. To treat Brownson systematically, therefore, is very unrewarding and, strictly speaking, one can only adopt an historical approach to his work, pointing out transitions in thought as he moved from conviction to conviction. What I should like to do, however, is to take a temporal piece of Brownson's theory and present it as a more or less coherent whole. I do this because it enables me to deal with a critical appraisal of American life unexcelled in this period for candor and cogency. In Brownson's work we find not only a contrast to the more complacent side of Emerson, but a powerful example of the American voice of opposition that, while usually unheard above the roar of popular sentiment, has on rare occasions found a relatively large and attentive audience. For a short time at least Brownson had such an audience, a public that took his proposals with the utmost seriousness. And justifiably so, for from approximately 1836, when he began intensively to delve into economic and political problems, to early 1844, when he was baptized into the Catholic Church, there appears in Brownson's writing an exposition in political theory that must rank among the most serious produced by American thought. One could in fact argue that, with the possible exception of John C. Calhoun, Brownson was the only comprehensive American political theorist to appear in the first half of the nineteenth century.[79]

☆

[77] Cited in Arthur M. Schlesinger, Jr., *A Pilgrim's Progress: Orestes A. Brownson,* Little, Brown and Company, Boston, 1939, p. 191.

[78] Quoted in *ibid.,* p. 278.

[79] Except for certain Catholic writers and the inclusion of parts of the essays called "The Laboring Classes" in historical anthologies, Brownson's work has fallen into relative

The Radical Attack

If Emerson's critique of America was sometimes ambiguous, Brownson, at least at the beginning of this period, levelled an attack that never left the issue in doubt. Where the Jacksonian labor literature tended to leave the argument at the level of equal opportunity, Brownson carried it to a dramatic conclusion. In his two essays on "The Laboring Classes," [80] he brought into question the entire structure of the American political economy. The laborers, the "proletary," he argued, were being exploited by employers everywhere. Although he is the real producer of wealth, the laborer is paid barely enough to subsist, and is systematically excluded from whatever benefits society has to offer. The laborer, in short, is scarcely better off than the slave: "he has all the disadvantages of freedom and none of its blessings, while the slave, if denied the blessings, is freed from the disadvantages." And it matters little what class the employer seems to be a member of: "In all countries," Brownson wrote, "it is the same. The only enemy of the labourer is your employer, whether appearing in the shape of the master mechanic, or in the owner of a factory." [81] In fact, the class that is often strongest in its declamations against labor is the parvenu class, those who, having become successful themselves, find no reason to sympathize with others who remain in an unimproved state. Brownson noted sardonically that "standing now on the shoulders of their brethren, they are too elevated to see what is going on at the base of the social organization." [82]

Brownson's comment, however, is not necessarily to be understood as an adverse moral judgment on the nouveaux riches, for they are simply part of a middle class that is simultaneously playing a liberating and a restrictive role in the historical progression of society.

---

neglect. This is probably due to many factors. First, commentators have very likely been put off by Brownson's later rock-bound, strident conservatism and by the fact that his treatment of social and political questions tended to become "contaminated" by or subsumed under his views on theological matters. There is also the possibility that because his position was formulated in unblushing theoretical language it has met with the usual American resistence to such discourse. Schlesinger, generally speaking a sympathetic biographer, found Brownson's 1843 essays in the *Democratic Review* "long, tedious and misty, shot through with Platonism and several times going up in the smoke of metaphysics." (*Ibid.*, p. 158.) There is clearly some truth in this appraisal, but what Schlesinger fails to mention is that these essays also comprise an inquiry into fundamental questions of political order unmatched by any American whose work had theretofore appeared in print. One wonders also why Parrington excluded Brownson ("regretfully out of regard to space"), when he dealt with numerous other writers who were obviously not Brownson's equal.

[80] *Boston Quarterly Review*, vol. 3, pp. 358-395, July, 1840 (hereafter referred to as Article I). *Boston Quarterly Review*, vol. 3, pp. 420-510, October, 1840 (hereafter referred to as Article II).

[81] Article I, pp. 368, 364.

[82] Article II, p. 461.

"The middle class," he contended, "is always a firm champion of equality, when it concerns humbling a class above it; but it is its inveterate foe when it concerns elevating a class below it." It was the English middle class, for example, and not the nobility, which led the fight against the French Revolution—"that glorious uprising of the people in behalf of their imprescriptible and inalienable rights"—in order to defend trades and manufactures against the assertion of the rights of workingmen.[83] But while Brownson can excoriate the middle class for its social indifference, he cannot escape the conclusion that class itself is derivative of organizational and structural principles inherited from earlier times. "All classes," he observed, "are victims of systems and organizations, which have come down to us from the past. We know not in reality, who suffer the most by the present order of things. If we deplore the condition of the laborer, we by no means envy that of the capitalist. We know not, indeed, which most to pity."[84] Two years earlier Brownson had written that he, for one, could not deprecate "the 'monarchy of the middle classes.' We believe its reign, in a certain stage of social progress, not only inevitable, but desirable."[85]

What Brownson ultimately desired was a classless society. In another 1838 article he argued that "all classes, each in turn, have possessed the government; and the time has come for all predominance to end; for Man, the People to rule."[86] And for the people to rule there must be an end to an economic system that hypostatizes what are fundamentally artificial distinctions between men; there must be "neither the slave nor the proletary. We would combine labor and capital in the same individual. What we object to, is the division of society into two classes, of which one class owns the capital, and the other performs the labor."[87]

The Means of Reform

The road to attaining this end was glaringly obvious, if difficult to traverse. First, it would be necessary to do away with the organization of the Church. Because the Church depends for its sustenance on the system as it stands, it can never be a useful means of reform. It has a stake in the established order and cannot subvert it, even if it wished to, and to eschew such an attack is to help keep the laborer in sub-

☆

[83]Article I, pp. 363-364.

[84]Article II, p. 471.

[85]"Democracy," *Boston Quarterly Review*, January 1838, Henry F. Brownson (ed.), *The Works of Orestes A. Brownson*, Detroit, 1882-1887, vol. XV, p. 25.

[86]"Tendency of Modern Civilization," *Boston Quarterly Review*, April 1838, *ibid.*, vol. I, p. 237. In Schlesinger, *op. cit.*, p. 82.

[87]Article II, pp. 467-468.

jection.[88] Secondly, the banking system must be demolished, for it is simply a mechanism through which the rich consolidate and perpetuate their exclusive control of power. Finally, the dynastical chain of inherited property must be broken, and this can only be done by redistributing the estates of deceased persons among all citizens when they reach legal age of maturity.[89]

Although these steps were clear enough, taking them would be not merely difficult, but extremely hazardous, and would probably be accompanied by violence. The classes in power would simply not give up their prerogatives peacefully. The remedy, Brownson wrote in the first article, "will not be obtained without war and bloodshed. It will be found only at the end of one of the longest and severest struggles the human race has ever been engaged in, only by that most dreaded of all wars, the war of the poor against the rich, a war which, however long it may be delayed, will come, and come with all its horrors." Brownson made it clear, however, that he did not expect the laboring class to initiate the bloodshed; "but . . . the masters may, for the purpose of keeping the proletaries in their present condition."[90] This would be the case because property and power have been so long and so firmly fixed together that they can be pried apart only by the exertion of great force. The problem goes to the heart of society and superficial solutions will simply not work. "No matter what party you support, no matter what men you elect, property," Brownson insisted, "is always the basis of your governmental action. No policy has ever yet been pursued by our government . . . notwithstanding our system of universal suffrage, which has had for its aim the elevation of man, independent of his relation as a possessor of property. In no instance have the rights of the proletary prevailed over the interests of the proprietor. To separate power from property, we hold to be impossible under our present system."[91] The inescapable answer, then, as Brownson saw it, is to effect a change in the system.

Individualism versus Individuality

Brownson's radical proposals naturally brought down storms of protest from religious and political conservatives everywhere. But surprisingly, there were many friendly critics, although most could not follow completely. Their reservations were usually made on conven-

☆

[88] Article I, pp. 374-375, 378-379, 380-382.

[89] This plan was not entirely original with Brownson. More than a decade earlier, Thomas Skidmore made a similar proposal that carried the more radical first requirement of an equal division of the property of citizens now living. (Thomas Skidmore, *The Rights of Man to Property,* Burt Franklin, New York, 1829.)

[90] Article I, p. 366; Article II, p. 507.

[91] Article II, p. 474.

tional grounds. Thus Bancroft approved the attack on the Church, but objected to the doctrines on property. Calhoun, Brownson's acknowledged intellectual hero, was favorably disposed toward most of the essay, but thought that the inheritance proposals ought to be re-examined. Theodore Parker liked "much of his article, though his property notions agree not with my view."[92]

From a theoretical viewpoint, Brownson's critique went even further than the inheritance scheme and the division of property. In his arguments in support of these changes he directly confronted the national purpose and rejected it as undignified and immoral. "It is said," he wrote, ". . . of the proposed change, that its effect will be bad, for it will check the spirit of enterprise, lessen the desire for the accumulation of property, consequently enervate industry, and lead to universal indolence and pauperism . . . Grant, then, that our scheme will check this propensity, this, instead of being an objection, should be regarded as a recommendation. In fact, one of the strongest reasons we have for urging it is, that it will check, in some degree, the action of the propensity to accumulate. Looking at society as it is, we cannot fail to perceive, that the passion for wealth is quite too absorbing." Any economic system that drives individualism beyond reasonable limits is extremely dangerous; such a system, in fact, threatens the very existence of society. Free trade, for example, is desirable in itself, but when "pushed to its last results, it becomes the introduction of a system of universal competition, a system of universal strife, where each man is for himself, and no man for another. It would be a return to the pure individuality of the savage state, the abolition of all government, and the adoption, as the practical rule of conduct, of the maxim, 'save who can.'"[93]

Brownson would by no means abolish individuality per se, for he understood, as did no writer of his time, that community and purpose in America were antithetical only because the latter had been carried beyond sensible limits. *Individuality* was in itself a positive characteristic which only became dangerous when it was distorted into *individualism*. "Community without individuality," Brownson argued, "is *tyranny*, the fruits of which are oppression, degradation and immobility, the synonym of death. Individuality without community is *individualism*, the fruits of which are dissolution, isolation, selfishness, disorder, anarchy, confusion, war . . . What we need, then, is . . . communalism and individuality harmonized . . . atoned."[94] A harmony of these principles would yield a far superior condition

☆

[92] In Schlesinger, *op. cit.*, pp. 106, 103.

[93] Article II, pp. 500, 476.

[94] "Community System," *Democratic Review*, February 1842, in Arieli, *op. cit.*, p. 240.

where man's nature would be expressed through his more generous sentiments. "We would look upon [man] as a brother." Brownson explained, "an equal, entitled to our love and sympathy. We would feel ourselves neither above nor below him, but standing up by his side, with our feet on the same level with his." While these may be Christian values, they have little to do with Christianity as practiced in a corrupt society. Indeed, if all men were made Christians it would accomplish nothing if the present system of trade were not altered. "No man can be a Christian," announced Brownson, "who does not begin his career by making war on the mischievous social arrangements from which his brethren suffer."[95] We can, if we desire, organize a truly Christian society following the equalitarian principles of Christ. Anything short of this called by the name Christian is simply sham.

Brownson and the Conservatives

On examining the specific ends Brownson envisaged for his workers, one is at first struck by their similarity to certain strains of Jacksonian Whiggery. He insisted that "there must be no class of our fellow men doomed to toil through life as mere workmen at wages. If wages are tolerated it must be, in the case of the individual operative, only under such conditions that by the time he is of proper age to settle in life, he shall have accumulated enough to be an independent laborer on his capital — on his own farm, or in his own shop."[96] The notion of the independent laborer operating on his own capital recalls Daniel Webster's picture of a society in which *all* members have a sufficient stake to preserve liberty and order because all own an adequate quantity of property.[97] This conception as offered by Webster was important in its own right, for it signaled the Jacksonian conservative's redefinition of national purpose. "Adequate property" for all did not of course imply an equality of ownership. Far from it. But it did suggest the abandoning of the Madisonian notion of land in limited supply. The conservative now understood that everyone could partake at least in partial measure of American resources, and that in fact the surest way to protect those who already owned substantial amounts was to make modest portions available to all citizens. By this means the class of "owners" would become universal, and ownership as such would constitute a palliative that could work to prevent the making of invidi-

☆

[95] Article I, pp. 360, 376.

[96] *Ibid.*, p. 373.

[97] "First Settlement of New England," delivered at Plymouth, Massachusetts, December 22, 1820, *Works of Daniel Webster*, Little, Brown, and Company, Boston, 1854, vol. I, pp. 34-40.

ous comparisons. In a nation where to some extent all men shared a like interest, there would be no danger of a conflict that might otherwise prove unavoidable.[98] Economic individualism would now have a similar meaning for liberal and conservative alike — the national purpose would now provide an equality of individual opportunity unhindered by the reservations of vested interest.[99]

The similarity between the formulations of Webster and Brownson was not accidental. Each reached his conclusions through reasoning processes that were almost identical: both saw the intimate connection between property and political power, and both knew that exclusive ownership of the former led to tyrannical propensities in the latter. Webster's answer was to make property accessible to everyone so that the dangers of a dispossessed class could not develop. Brownson, in dispensing with the wage system and redistributing acquired estates, would apparently do the same. The difference between the two men was actually a matter of degree, but it was a telling difference nonetheless. Webster shared the conservative's concern for order, stability, and property rights, and his novel egalitarianism was chiefly motivated by this concern. Brownson simply reversed the equation. Where Webster gave equal attention to property rights and to human rights, Brownson specifically stated: "property should be held subordinate to man," and while he claimed in his second article on labor that he did not disapprove in principle of unequal property ownership, his remedial measures suggest that this was not exactly true. If, in fact, the implementation of his proposals did not result in total equalization, it would surely come very close. Moreover, just two years later Brownson could write that "democratic theory . . . requires for its success a community, in which all the citizens have in all respects one and the same interest, and are all substantially equal in position, wealth, and influence."[100]

☆

[98] If Tocqueville was correct, there existed a common stake in society as early as the 1830's. He noted that since Americans "are all engaged in commerce, their commercial affairs are affected by such various and complex causes that it is impossible to foresee what difficulties may arise. As they are all more or less engaged in productive industry, at the least shock given to business all private fortunes are put in jeopardy at the same time, and the state is shaken." (Tocqueville, *op. cit.*, vol. II, p. 167.)

[99] Although Webster's statement was made in 1820, the redefinition of purpose did not receive general conservative endorsement until the 1840's. There is some doubt as to whether they really meant it even then, or whether they were simply forced into voicing those sentiments that would gain popular political support. For an insightful discussion of this issue, see Louis Hartz, *Liberal Tradition In America*, Harcourt, Brace and Company, Inc., New York, 1955, chap. IV.

[100] "Constitutional Government," *Boston Quarterly Review*, January 1842, Brownson (ed.), *op. cit.*, vol. XV, pp. 347-348.

Brownson's plea for laborers who "sustain themselves by laboring on their own capital"[101] is analagous to Jefferson's plan to give all citizens a prescribed portion of free land. In both arguments the aim is the dignity of man, and to the achievement of this end approximate equality is stressed over the establishment of order. In fact, both Jefferson and Brownson would be hard put to erect a defense for stability, since both had built conceptions of social conflict solidly into their theories. On the question of where government would fit into this whole scheme, however, Brownson parted company with Jefferson, and with most other nineteenth century liberals.

The Need for Government

Just because government had become the tool of class exploitation, Brownson could not say that government as such was either an unnatural contrivance of human guile or a parasitic but necessary evil. In the essays on "The Laboring Classes," government receives considerable attention. It is even suggested that government can fill the moral vacuum created by the misbegotten Church. "Our views," wrote Brownson, "if carried out, would realize not a union, but the unity, the identity of Church and State. They would indeed destroy the Church as a *separate* body, as a distinct organization; but they would do it by transferring to the State the moral ideas on which the Church was professedly founded, and which it has failed to realize." And such a government would apparently act as the focal point of a true community, for the individual in this "Christian Commonwealth" would be encouraged to "go out into the highways and byways . . . and labor to recall the erring, to enlighten the ignorant, to comfort the sorrowing, to heal the broken-hearted, to raise up the downtrodden . . . to set at liberty them that are bound . . . to redress all individual and social wrongs, and to establish, in our own hearts and in society at large, the reign of truth, justice, and love."[102]

For all of these sentiments, however, Brownson, too, was occasionally susceptible to the liberal's ever present resistance to strong government. What is interesting about Brownson's position is that the tensions within it are strikingly, almost ingenuously, apparent. "Government," he wrote in the first article, "is instituted to be the agent of society, or more properly the organ through which society may perform its legitimate functions. It is not the master of society; its business is not to control society, but to be the organ through

☆

[101]Article I, p. 371.
[102]Article II, pp. 437-439.

which society effects its will . . . Now the evils of which we have complained are of a social nature . . . This being the case, it is evident that they are to be removed only by the action of society, that is, by government, for the action of society is government." Despite this conviction, Brownson found ample reason for caution. "What shall government do?" he asked, and, striking a familiar liberal note, he replied that "its first doing must be an *undoing*. There has been thus far quite too much government, as well as government of the wrong kind. The first act of government we want, is a still further limitation of itself."[103] While Brownson is obviously ambivalent here, he normally endowed government with a full complement of powers, and in his subsequent writings the qualifications tended to become less and less important as the functions of government became increasingly more essential.

The fact is that, with the exception of Alexander Hamilton, no other significant American writer went as far as Brownson in recognizing the critical role that government had to play in modern society. Indeed, government would provide Brownson with the harmonizing agent that could reconcile the demands of both individuality and community. Two years earlier he had written that "social order . . . demands the creation of a government, and that the government should be clothed with the authority necessary for the maintenance of order. The portion of sovereignty necessary for this end, and, if you please, for the promotion of the common weal, justice delegates to the state."[104] The "promotion of the common weal" soon came to outweigh considerations of maintaining order, and government was seen as the logical extension of man's social instincts, disciples of Thomas Paine to the contrary notwithstanding. "Government," Brownson argued in 1842, "is not, as the author of 'Common Sense' asserts, 'at best a necessary evil.' It has its origin and necessity in what is good, not merely what is bad, in human nature . . . Man was made to live in society . . . It is only in society, and by its aid, that he can grow, and expand, and fulfill the end of his being." "Society is inconceivable without individuals, but it has an existence, a destiny distinguishable, if not separable from others . . . It is not itself an aggregate . . . but a unity, an individuality, leading its own life . . . Society becomes a unity . . . by organizing itself into the state or commonwealth. So organized, it . . . has for its mission the maintenance of . . . natural liberty, and the performance . . . of those labors demanded by the

☆

[103]Article I, p. 391.
[104]"Democracy," Brownson (ed.), *op. cit.*, vol. XV, p. 10.

common-good of all, which necessarily surpass the reach of individual strength, skill, and enterprise."[105]

Brownson found that Americans often did not grasp this positive notion of doing for individuals together what they cannot do alone. "In all their speculations," he noted, "they who differ from us, overlook the important fact that *government is needed for the people as the state, as well as for the people as individuals.*"[106] There are, after all, an enormous number of governmental tasks beyond "maintaining the natural liberty of the individual." Government must "open the resources of the country, construct roads and bridges, railways and canals, open harbors, erect light houses and churches, asylums and hospitals, and furnish the means of universal education, of the highest industrial, scientific, and artistic culture for all the children born into the community."[107] Government, in short, has the inescapable responsibility of carrying out those acts that men in society wish to perform as a collectivity.

Political Authority as an Absolute

Of course, to speak of government as "an individuality leading its own life" is to come dangerously close to a metaphysical statist position and, with this 1843 statement, Brownson helped pave the way for his subsequent shift to political conservatism. For the sake of balance we will take brief note of this later position. In 1841, after the Democratic defeat of 1840 had caused him to reevaluate certain fundamentals, Brownson had already begun to shift his argument from democratic to constitutional grounds, and by 1842 this transition was completed. Schlesinger comments: "he held to his old belief in the sovereignty of the people within the limits of justice; but in 1838 he had insisted on the sovereignty, and now he had come to insist on the limits.[108] And

☆

[105] "Constitutional Government," *ibid.*, vol. XV, pp. 231-232.

[106] "Democracy and Liberty," *Democratic Review*, April 1843, *ibid.*, vol. XV, p. 274.

[107] "Constitutional Government," *ibid.*, vol. XV, p. 232.

[108] Schlesinger, *op. cit.*, p. 114. I have purposely avoided a discussion of Brownson's conception of "concurring majorities" ("Constitutional Government," Brownson [ed.], *op. cit.*, vol. XV, pp. 242 et seq.) because I think it proceeded more from Brownson's general concern about mass society than from his later conservative convictions. As early as 1833 he noted that "the age tends too much to association; people are beginning to act only in crowds, and the individual is fast being lost in the mass." ("Address on Intemperance," February 26, 1833, in Schlesinger, *op. cit.*, p. 47.) The device of a state veto power would simply provide a defense against mass tyranny imposed through the central government. Because he had no particular sectional interest to advance, Brownson's argument strikes me as slightly more objective than the similar position made famous by John C. Calhoun, which we will examine in the next chapter.

once these limits are established the obedience of the citizen becomes firm and inflexible. "The governed," Brownson maintained, ". . . are not only *forced* to obey, but are morally *bound* to obey. Obedience is a duty."[109] This obedience, moreover, is not perpetuated across generations by the fictional notions of tacit consent found in myth-laden contract theory. "The true view to be taken," wrote Brownson, "is to regard government as never beginning, never ending, and considering its legitimacy as transmitted from generation to generation, and from place to place, by a law analagous to that by which the life of the race itself is so transmitted."[110]

It is but a short step from conceptions of elevated government and automatic obedience to a position holding that "human association, is not a mere *association of equals, but a* LIVING ORGANISM." As a living organism, government, though exercised by human resources, comes under the natural domain of God's law; in Brownson's words, government acts under the "FORCE" of the people, but under the "AUTHORITY" of God, and by God's authority he had primarily in mind the sanctions of the Church. With government so established, the people cannot, of course, be granted the right of rebellion. "There is, in fact, no such right."[111]

Through this period of transition, Brownson continued to be critical of economic interests and the inequalities of property. One of the reasons for having strong government is the need to curb economic exploitation. "We are no believers in the sovereign virtue of free competition," he wrote in 1844. "There are times and cases where government is needed to control it; to set bounds to it."[112] But as the years passed, Brownson's outlook grew even more conservative, culminating in an argument that set government as the protector of a right to property that had now become sacred, and that accepted gross inequality as natural and just. In 1846 Brownson argued that poverty could not be cured; "and, moreover, we do not wish it to be cured, for we do not believe that poverty is an evil."[113] And by 1853 rigid stratification was understood as a natural attribute of men in a social state: it is "our duty," Brownson wrote, "to accept the distinction of classes as a social fact, permanent, and indestructable in civilized society."[114]

☆

[109] "Origin and Ground of Government" (a series of three articles), *Democratic Review*, 1843, Brownson (ed.), *op. cit.*, vol. XV, p. 308.

[110] "Origins and Ground of Government," *ibid.*, vol. XV, pp. 326-327.

[111] *Ibid.*, pp. 372, 393, 397.

[112] "The Protective Policy," *Brownson Quarterly Review*, October 1844, *ibid.*, p. 497; cited in Schlesinger, *op. cit.*, p. 165.

[113] Quoted in Schlesinger, *op. cit.*, p. 205.

[114] "Liberal Studies," Brownson (ed.), *op. cit.*, vol. XIX, p. 433.

With this observation the metamorphosis was complete and Brownson, who once challenged the American ideology with boldness and determination, had now become not only a defender of the status quo, but a leading proponent of a return to the past.

Brownson's Contribution

We must not, however, allow Brownson's later views to detract from an appreciation of the contribution he made to American thought. His early ideas were more than just radical, they were often original. He understood in a very modern way, for example, that true freedom did not necessarily mean the complete rejection of all authority. "Men," he wrote, "revolt from one authority, not because it oppresses them, or restrains them in the free use of their persons or property, but because they regard it as illegitimate . . .; they submit to another authority and uphold it, although it impose severe burdens . . . because they hold it to be legitimate, the rightful sovereign."[115] In 1843 Brownson developed what amounted to a pre-Marxian theory of surplus value, and in the same year he offered a conception of property that included within it the right of every individual to be gainfully employed.[116] And, in an area slightly removed from his usual concerns, Brownson long ago seems to have understood those vagaries and propensities of the independent voter that have only recently been discovered by modern social science. "There is," he noted in 1842, "altogether . . . too much nonsense uttered about independent voters. One fourth of your independent voters will not take the trouble to go to the polls, unless called out by more zealous partisans; and the party which can make the most noise, and has the most money to spend for electioneering purposes, will always be able to call out the larger portion of them, and usually enough to decide a closely contested election in its own favor. Nearly as many more make it a rule to vote always with the stronger party . . . Of the remainder, not one in ten has any clear conception of the questions at issue, or any tolerable judgment of what will be the practical operations of one policy or another."[117] But if he is to be remembered at all, it is the radical Brownson of *The Laboring Classes* who will live in people's minds, and rightly so, for from his pen came one of the first, perhaps the very first, of the major challenges to American national purpose, a challenge whose intensity would not be equaled until the Populist revolt at the end of the century.

☆

[115] "Democracy," *ibid.*, vol. XV, pp. 13-14.

[116] "The Present State of Society," *Democratic Review*, July 1843, *ibid.*, pp. 452-453. "Origin and Ground of Government," *ibid.*, pp. 370-371.

[117] "Constitutional Government," *ibid.*, pp. 238-239.

THE SOUTHERN VARIATION

JOHN C. CALHOUN
GEORGE FITZHUGH

The political scene in the post-Jacksonian period was dominated by the issue of slavery and the surrounding tariff and new-state questions, problems that would soon come to divide the nation into warring garrisons. Lincoln would later speak of a house divided, but even as early as 1840 there was serious doubt as to the existence of a unified national house. It may be argued that the Southern defense of its "customs" at this time constituted a direct assault on the national purpose as practiced by most Americans. This view can logically be maintained only if one believes that contemporaneously in the North individualism was being extended to include the Negro, that Negroes were at last being invited by at least a part of the society to participate in the realization of the American dream.

This was precisely one of the announced goals of Wendell Phillips, William Lloyd Garrison, Charles Sumner, and many (although not all) of their fellow Abolitionists. They argued the cause of equal opportunity for all citizens, and their pronouncements expressed a belief in human freedom that often transcended the mere recitation of American liberalism. At the same time, however, they frequently invoked the common ideology of economic individualism, and it was consequently not accidental that Harriet Beecher Stowe saw fit to append to *Uncle Tom's Cabin* nonfictional data describing a number of free Northern Negroes whose substantial assets suggested that, if given the opportunity, Negroes could achieve material success as well as anyone – and if a Negro could succeed in economic terms, on what grounds could he be denied access to the society?

It was to this kind of question that the South had to address itself and, while the Northern arguments are historically interesting, the pre-Civil War period was actually one-sided in favor of the South in its production of political theory. The basic problems, the exceptional hypotheses, were raised not in the North, but by Southerners who found themselves forced to defend Southern institutions in the face of nationwide legal and moral imperatives that seemed to run counter to their local beliefs. The argumentation in the North, however lofty and inspired, tended to be either canonical or polemical, since it was understood that the Northern position occupied constitutional high ground, and that new justifications for a free society were unnecessary. The South, on the other hand, needed a spokesman who could go beyond the resounding rhetoric of a Phillips or a Garrison. It found both a practical and theoretical spokesman in John C. Calhoun, former Vice-President under Jackson, now Senator from South Carolina.

John C. Calhoun

It has been said that, of thinkers in the American political tradition, Calhoun stands almost alone as a genuine and creative theorist, as a writer who not only developed a systematic body of ideas, but who advanced original propositions that go to the heart of political matters.[1] Whether or not this estimate is accurate, it is at least fair to say that Calhoun's ideas were considered novel by many of his contemporaries. If the typical expression of the American ideology, especially in the North, can be said to have extended from a Madisonian base, then perhaps the uniqueness of Calhoun's philosophy, as expressed most notably in *A Disquisition on Government* (1853), can be assessed by examining it against a Madisonian setting. There are more than heuristic reasons for engaging in such an analysis, for Calhoun avowedly challenged the conventional constitutional wisdom of his day, and such a challenge inevitably forced him to consider many Madisonian principles.

☆

[1] See, for example, C. Gordon Post's, Introduction to John C. Calhoun, *A Disquisition on Government*, The Bobbs-Merrill Company, Inc., Indianapolis, 1953, p. vii.

Calhoun's Madisonianism

It should be noted at the outset, however, that Calhoun personally never allowed that his arguments ran counter to the Madisonian tradition. Indeed, his long and labored *Discourse on the Constitution and Government of the United States* was an effort to establish that his own constitutional interpretation was precisely that of the founding generation. He contended, moreover, that his comprehension of the Constitution was influenced "above all [by] the transcendent argument of Mr. Madison himself, in his celebrated resolutions of 1798," an argument "which . . . wrought a great change in [my] views."[2] But since the 1798 announcement of nullification in the Virginia Resolutions played such an ambiguous role in Madison's thought, and since it was customary anyway for political exhortations of the day to claim legitimate descent from the authors of the Constitution—that assemblage of "demi-gods," as Jefferson called them—we can proceed with our comparison, Calhoun's proclamations notwithstanding.

On examining *A Disquisition on Government*, one immediately notes many points of agreement between Calhoun and Madison. Calhoun's appreciation of the unending threat of political factionalism, for example, recalls the graphic realism of *Federalist* No. 10. "So deeply seated," wrote Calhoun, ". . . is this tendency to conflict between the different interests or portions of the community that it would result from the action of the government itself, even though it were possible to find a community where the people were all of the same pursuits, placed in the same condition of life, and in every respect . . . without inequality of condition or diversity of interests. The advantages of possessing the control of the powers of the government, and thereby of its honors and emoluments, are, of themselves . . . ample to divide even such a community into two great hostile parties."[3] This carries the argument even further than Madison, who could at least imagine eliminating faction through the abolition of diversity, even though he rejected such means as self-defeating where liberty was the desired end. And if factionalism per se was viewed as a central problem by both writers, one also finds in Calhoun a Madisonian stress on the majority as faction, a majority that, as in Madison, would become increasingly populated by those in the poorer classes. Calhoun noted that as the society grows, "the difference between the rich and the poor will become more strongly marked, and the number of the ignorant and dependent greater in proportion to the rest of the

☆

[2] "Remarks on the Joint Resolution in Reference to the Madison Papers," February 20, 1837, Richard K. Crallé (ed.), *The Works of John C. Calhoun*, D. Appleton & Company, Inc., New York, 1853, vol. III, p. 41.

[3] "A Disquisition on Government," *ibid.*, vol. I, p. 17.

community. With the increase of this difference, the tendency to conflict between them will become stronger; and as the poor and dependent become more numerous in proportion, there will be in governments of the numerical majority no want of leaders among the wealthy and ambitious to excite and direct them in their efforts to obtain control."[4]

With the problem stated in these terms, the solution falls almost naturally, as it were, into Madisonian categories for, like Madison, Calhoun believed that, of themselves, neither a written constitution nor the principle of separation of powers were adequate safeguards against majority tyranny. Exclusive reliance on the former would be a "great mistake," and institution of the latter "could do little or nothing to counteract . . . oppression and abuse of power."[5] It must be recognized that "power can only be resisted by power," and that political liberty must be secured "by the adoption of some restriction or limitation which shall so effectually prevent any one interest or combination of interests from obtaining the exclusive control of the government as to render hopeless all attempts directed to that end."[6] Madison had hoped that the separation of powers and its concomitant set of checks and balances, the federal division of power, the great size of the nation, the latent pluralism of the society, and the natural proclivity of men to attach themselves to their occupational positions, would combine either to diversify interests or, more realistically, to effect such an arrangement that the majority interest would never assume absolute power. It is at this point that Calhoun exceeded Madisonianism, for as he stood before the blistering anti-Southern attack from the North—that is, from the numerical majority—he could only feel that stronger safety mechanisms would be required if liberty, in the form of minority rights, was to be preserved. These additional safeguards would be provided by introducing into the system the concept of concurrent majorities.

It may be argued that in granting to each significant interest the possibility of an immediate and effective veto over federal legislation, the concurrent majority idea represented a logical extension of Madisonianism, that the Virginia Resolutions constituted an inevitable next step in a theory that spoke of protecting minority interests against the extremes of majority power. In this connection, Madison's subsequent equivocations on the question of interposition must be seen as totally unjustified in light of his earlier arguments. This viewpoint has much

☆

[4] *Ibid.*, p. 46.
[5] *Ibid.*, pp. 31, 34.
[6] *Ibid.*, pp. 12, 24.

to commend it, for if one takes Madison's fragmentation argument seriously, there is no reason why each social grouping should not be able to secure itself against legislative acts it regards as inimical to its interests. This position *does* go beyond Madison, however, even if it follows logically from his fundamental precepts, for correctly or not, Madison at least implied that once a measure had received the Senate's stamp of approval it had stood the full test of legitimacy. What distinguishes Calhoun from Madison more importantly on this issue (and simultaneously makes him a Madisonian) is the nature of the interests he wished to protect.

We saw that when Madison defended minority rights from majority incursions he had primarily in mind the rights of property; since the Senate would represent property interests, it could be regarded as liberty's last line of defense. In a similar vein, Calhoun, although he frequently alluded to unspecified economic interests, equated his minority rights with those of the states, more accurately with the Southern states. His pluralism, like Madison's, was engendered by the need to protect a *particular* minority; and, by the same token, because his minority did *not* receive the kind of guaranteed indulgence that Madison hoped the Senate would provide to property, Calhoun was forced to endorse fully the Madisonian philosophy and then carry it one step further. That the defense of Southern states' rights should have carried Calhoun into the Madisonian camp at all seems in some ways ironic, for at least a few of the components of his theory appear to be distinctly anti-Madisonian in tone and content. We will examine the most important of these before treating the concurrent majority doctrine in more detail.

Governments and Constitutions

Noticeably different was the role that Calhoun cast for government. Whereas Madison and most of his associates were, at best, ambivalent in their attitude toward government, Calhoun announced at the very beginning of the *Disquisition* that, because he understood men as social beings, he regarded government as an absolutely natural and positive agency of human association. He could not conceive of men without society, nor society without positive government, and with this conviction he avoided the usual difficulty in liberalism of somehow rationalizing government as an inconvenient but "necessary evil." Government, however, involves the exercise of power, and since this power is wielded by men and since men are more self-oriented than socially oriented, men in power—that is, the government—must be strictly controlled lest that power get out of control. The mechanism of control, in all societies where controls are in fact applied, is called the constitution.

For Calhoun, a constitution is that means contrived by man which keeps governmental authority within specified limits. While constitutions are "artificial" in that they are man-made, as opposed to society and government, which are of divine origin, and while they differ in content from nation to nation, they exist, by definition, wherever non-absolute rule obtains. But although artifice, the contrivance of man, the constitution is also described by Calhoun as an organism. This seems a strange choice of terms, used as it is to refer to the "principles [on which] government must be formed in order to resist by its own interior structure . . . the tendency to abuse of power."[7] Since the constitution is a human fabrication, and since it pertains to internal governmental structures, one might have thought the mechanistic language of Madison more appropriate. The constitution as organism gives the concept a suggestion of naturalness almost precisely at the moment Calhoun has defined it as derived from nonnatural origins. Is this a paradoxical formulation, or did Calhoun simply mean the word "organism" to have a "nonorganic" connotation, merely (as he himself suggested) as a substitute for the phrase "interior structure"? Whether conscious of it or not, it seems apparent from the rest of his argument that Calhoun wished to have the best of both worlds, that he desired to present the constitution as artificial, and therefore subject to change and interpretation, *and,* at its highest expression, as comprised of elements that are organic and consequently natural.

Calhoun was ambiguous on this point because, although he began with the concept of constitution posited as a rubric beneath which various limiting devices might work to control power, he immediately equated the notion itself with his own idea of the concurrent majority. Even as he spoke in the plural of "constitutional governments, of whatever form," he offered the concurrent majority as *the* "indispensable element in forming constitutional governments,"[8] as that agency which allows society to hear *"the voice of God"* because it grants to the *whole* society the opportunity to express itself without simultaneously stifling the voices of particular interests.

Concurrent Majorities and Compromise

The concurrent majority doctrine itself is characterized by logical simplicity and, if put into effect, would be productive of enormous good. Calhoun did not spell out the exact details of the constitution; but in general terms he argued that there is only one way of effectively limiting political power "and that is by taking the sense of each interest

☆

[7] *Ibid.,* pp. 5, 11.
[8] *Ibid.,* pp. 36, 35.

or portion of the community which may be unequally and injuriously affected by the action of the government separately, through its own majority or in some other way by which its voice may be fairly expressed and to require the consent of each interest either to put or to keep the government in action. This, too, can be accomplished in only one way, and that is by such an organism of the government—and, if necessary, for the purpose, of the community also—as well, by dividing and distributing the powers of government, give to each division or interest, through its appropriate organ, either a concurrent voice in making and executing the laws or a veto on their execution."[9]

The institution of such a constitution in a pluralistic society would not only mitigate factionalism but would generate a high sense of community. "By giving each interest, or portion, the power of self-protection," Calhoun contended, "all strife and struggle between them for ascendancy is prevented, and thereby not only every feeling calculated to weaken the attachment to the whole is suppressed, but the individual and the social feelings are made to unite in one common devotion to country . . . and . . . there will be diffused throughout the whole community kind feelings between its different portions and . . . a rivalry amongst them to promote the interests of each other . . . Under the combined influence of these causes, the interests of each would be merged in the common interests of the whole; and thus the community would become a unit by becoming the common center of attachment of all its parts."[10] Moreover, since public and private morality are so closely allied, the effect of this change would quickly penetrate into the private sphere. With the death of factionalism, political influence would come to those who manifest "knowledge, wisdom, patriotism, and virtue," attributes that would soon "become prominent traits in the character of the people."[11] All these advances would take place, the constitution would become effective, only insofar as the citizenry was able to practice one further virtue, the art of compromise.

Compromise is the quintessential ingredient: it is to constitutional governments what force is to absolute governments. At its highest level of operation, compromise yields unanimity, and it may be likened therefore to the workings of the jury system where unanimity is the product of a compromise born of disinterested argumentation. The unanimous agreement of all interests required by the concurrent majority principle would ensure that each portion would be prepared

☆

9 *Ibid.*, p. 25.
10 *Ibid.*, pp. 48-49.
11 *Ibid.*, p. 51.

to sacrifice part of its interest to the common good, for to do otherwise would be to imperil the very existence of government, and thus to court the most "fatal consequences" and "the evils that would be inflicted on all." "So powerful, indeed, would be the motives for concurring and, under such circumstances, so weak would be those opposed to it, the wonder would be, not that there should, but that there should not be compromise."[12] Although less important than anarchy, the fear of which constitutes a perpetual incentive to compromise, the age-old rewards of log-rolling also provide a strong mediating inducement: in order to gain its own ends, "each portion," according to Calhoun, "would have to conciliate all others by showing a disposition to advance theirs." In the end, the process would be so conducive to the common good as to alter completely old attitudes. Concession would, in fact, "cease to be considered a sacrifice — would become a free-will offering on the alter of the country and lose the name of compromise"[13] — would, one is tempted to add, become "natural" or "organic" to the citizen's nature.

The concurrent majority doctrine, in other words, seems to emanate from interests that are natural to society. But despite its beneficent effects, its naturalness is derived negatively, not from what it accomplishes, but from what it prevents. It avoids anarchy, "the greatest evil of all," the greatest evil because under it men are reduced to an *unnatural* condition, that of society without government. Men are only natural in society, and those societies that partake of *true* constitutionalism (namely, Calhoun's variety) seem finally to have a stronger claim to naturalness than do all others. It is perhaps for this reason that Calhoun wished to have it both ways: the establishment of the constitution both as artifice, so that "it" ("it" meaning the American Constitution in this case) might be reinterpreted and changed, and as "organic," so that Calhoun's particular changes would carry more weight. Since Calhoun provides neither legal tradition nor social custom as wellsprings of conciliation, however, one wonders how he expected the spirit of compromise to work.

Human Nature and Compromise

One naturally turns to Calhoun's delineation of human nature in response to this question, for a predominantly optimistic view of human nature, or even one that strikes a balance between selfish and social tendencies, would provide a reliable precondition for generalized compromise. Calhoun, at the beginning of the *Disquisition*,

☆

[12] *Ibid.*, pp. 37, 66, 68.

[13] *Ibid.*, p. 69.

seems to take somewhat the latter position. He notes that men feel more intensely that which affects them directly, and that usually they act in accordance with these feelings. He will not, however, describe these propensities as "selfish . . . because as commonly used, it implies an unusual excess of the individual over the social feelings in the person to whom it is applied and, consequently, something depraved and vicious."[14] Man's self-interest is natural and not necessarily dangerous, even though it is in all cases stronger than his other feelings. But having stated the case for selfness in morally neutral terms, less than two paragraphs later Calhoun gives way to a cynical rhetoric about human nature that rivals any picture drawn by Madison's pen. In discussing the absolute necessity of government, which exists to control the inevitable conflicts that arise in society, he argues that we are menaced constantly by "the tendency to a universal state of conflict between individual and individual, accompanied by the connected passions of suspicion, jealousy, anger, and revenge—followed by insolence, fraud, and cruelty—and, if not prevented by some controlling power, ending in a state of universal discord and confusion."[15] If these are the tendencies engendered by self-interest, there seems little reason why Calhoun should have been reluctant to use the word "selfish" to encompass them, since these very characteristics are the ones usually associated with selfishness or its by-products. More important, there should have been even less reason to expect the institutionalization of permanent compromise when men behave so dangerously and where the controlling mechanism itself is an additional source of peril.

The fact is that Calhoun provided no adequate justification for hoping that compromise would work effectively—and without this his whole position tends to deteriorate, for the concurrent majority is chimerical at best unless compromise can be grounded on a very firm base. Logical apostrophes of this sort cause Hartz to describe Calhoun as "a profoundly disintegrated political theorist."[16] Although this critique may be a little overdrawn, especially in the American context, one cannot agree with those who place Calhoun at the top of the list either. In the last analysis, Calhoun must be understood, like Madison, in ideological terms, for his elaborate philosophy was constructed primarily in the attempt to advance, or at least to protect, a specific political interest, that of his own slave-holding South.

☆

[14] *Ibid.*, p. 3.

[15] *Ibid.*, p. 4.

[16] Louis Hartz, *The Liberal Tradition in America,* Harcourt, Brace and Company, Inc., New York, 1955, p. 159.

Calhoun's Ideology

Because he referred to various kinds of interests — economic, political, geographic, governmental — Calhoun has been taken by many commentators as the true theorist of American pluralism, as one who sought simply to constitutionalize a diversity of interests that could already be found in the society.[17] Other writers have found a kind of reactionary Marxism in Calhoun because he stressed the notion of struggle between classes and because he saw clearly the exploitative tendencies in industrial capitalism.[18] Calhoun's explication of concurrent majorities is sufficiently vague that both interpretations appear logically defensible. Evidence both within the *Disquisition* and elsewhere, however, strongly suggests that these interpretations are misleading, and that Charles Merrian summed it up nicely long ago when he wrote: "'Concurrent' or 'constitutional' majority is simply the prolegomena to nullification. The interests to be consulted and given a veto power are the separate states of the union. The tyranny to be averted is the enforcement of protective tariff laws or the passage of laws unfavorably affecting slavery interests."[19] Calhoun was, in other words, a philosopher of states rights whose position at its center differs only in degree from those who traditionally have espoused this view.

Calhoun first promulgated the concurrent majority concept on the floor of the Senate in 1833. In a series of very long speeches having to do with North-South disagreements, he made absolutely plain that by a concurrent majority he meant the majority opinion in each of the several states.[20] In one speech he stipulated clearly that a practical way of operating the principle of concurrent majorities would be to require approval of three-fourths of the states before the federal government could put a policy into effect.[21] Indeed, all of the comments on human nature and factionalism that later appear in the *Disquisition*

☆

[17] See, for example, C. M. Wiltse, "Calhoun and the Modern State," *Virginia Quarterly Review*, vol. 13, pp. 396-408, Summer, 1937; P. F. Drucker, "Key to American Politics: Calhoun's Pluralism," *Review of Politics*, vol. 10, pp. 412-426, October, 1948; R. Lerner, "Calhoun's New Science of Politics," *American Political Science Review*, vol. 57, pp. 918-932, December, 1963.

[18] See R. N. Current, "John C. Calhoun, Philosophy of Reaction," *Antioch Review*, vol. 3, pp. 223-234, June 1943. Richard Hofstadter (who follows Current in this interpretation), "John C. Calhoun: The Marx of the Master Class," *American Political Tradition*, Alfred A. Knopf, Inc., New York, 1948, chap. IV.

[19] Charles Merrian, "The Political Theory of Calhoun," *American Journal of Sociology*, vol. 7, p. 584. March 1902.

[20] The concept was introduced in "A Speech on the Force Bill," February 15 and 16, 1833, Crallé (ed.), *op. cit.*, vol. II, p. 250.

[21] "In Reply to Mr. Webster, on the Resolutions Respecting the Rights of the States," February 26, 1833, *ibid.*, p. 304.

are made in these pro-South speeches, and when read in this context their partisan content is readily perceived.

Just as he would in the *Disquisition*, Calhoun argued that unchecked majoritarianism must inevitably lead to tyranny. So true is this that a community of five completely equal men would, if divided into a majority and minority for governing purposes, soon create a system of absolute rule if checks were not introduced at the outset. Contrary to the Madisonian understanding, this baneful propensity is heightened in a large, differentiated society. In a small society "the similarity of the interests of all the parts will limit the oppression from the hostile action of the parts . . . to the fiscal action of the government . . . but in the large community, spreading over a country of great extent, and having a great diversity of interests . . . the conflict and oppression will extend, not only to a monopoly of the appropriations on the part of the stronger interests, but will end in unequal taxes and a general *conflict between the entire interests of conflicting sections,* which if not arrested by the most powerful checks, will terminate in the most oppressive tyranny that can be conceived." [Emphasis added.] Such a degeneration, moreover, accurately describes the current state of affairs in the United States: "the real meaning of the American system," Calhoun pointed out, "is that system of plunder which the strongest interest has ever waged, and will ever wage, against the weaker, where the latter is not armed with some efficient and constitutional check to arrest its action."[22]

That Calhoun was defending a sectional interest in his argument he candidly admitted. "It had pleased Providence, said Mr. Calhoun, to cast his lot in the slaveholding States. There were his hopes, and all that was near and dear to him. His first duty was to them, and he held every other, even his obligation to this Government and the Union, as sacred as he regarded them, subordinate to their safety."[23] Privately, Calhoun well knew that his definition of America was not shared by many of his fellow citizens, perhaps not even by a majority of his fellow Southerners. "Certain it is," he sadly noted in 1847, "that the preservation of our institutions and liberty occupy but little the attention of our Government, Federal or State, or that of the people. Wealth and power engross the attention of all. We act as if good institutions and liberty belonged to us of right, and that neither neglect nor folly can deprive us of their blessing. I almost stand alone, in taking a different view, and soon I fear shall be entirely out of

☆

[22] "A Speech on the Force Bill," Crallé (ed.), *op. cit.,* vol. II, pp. 246–247, 251–252, 253.

[23] "Remarks Made During the Debate on His Resolutions, In Respect to the Rights of the States and the Abolition of Slavery," December 27, 1837, Crallé (ed.), *op. cit.,* vol. III, p. 178.

fashion."[24] Feeling to some degree isolated, and understanding that he was the South's principal sentinel against a hostile North, Calhoun could not himself engage in that most important of constitutional practices, the art of compromise.

As early as 1836 he could describe relations between North and South as those of nations involved in what today we would call a cold war. A year later he reviewed the Missouri Compromise with utter regret, saw it as an act whose products could only be described as vicious and dangerous. By 1849 he was willing to risk everything rather than modify demands: "Now is the time to vindicate our rights. We ought rather than to yield an inch, take any alternative, even if it should be disunion, and I trust that such will be the determination of the South." Proponents of future compromise threw him into a total frenzy. "Expediency, concession, compromise!" he thundered in the Senate, "Away with such weakness and folly! Right, justice, plighted faith, and the constitution: these only, can be relied on to avert the conflict. These have been surrendered for 'inexpediency.'"[25] Calhoun's inability to entertain compromise in the political arena is analagous to his inability to justify compromise adequately in his political theory, and as a consequence his usual position was seriously damaged in both spheres. There had been a time, however, when Calhoun's political principles, both practical and theoretical, needed little in the way of logical justification, for his earliest arguments found him propounding a very different set of political doctrines.

The "Other" Calhoun

Whereas in the *Disquisition* Calhoun advanced a theory of representation that pictured legislators, when acting properly, as faithful and immediate agents of their constituents' interests,[26] as a member of the House in 1811 he held a much more Burkean view. "I am not here to represent my own State alone," he declared. "I renounce the idea. And I will shew by my vote that I contend for the interests of the whole people of this community."[27] If this concept of representation

☆

[24] "To Mrs. T. G. Clemson," June 10, 1847, J. Franklin Jameson (ed.), *Correspondence of John C. Calhoun*, Annual Report of the American Historical Association for 1899, United States Government Printing Office, Washington, D.C., 1900, p. 731.

[25] "On the Abolition Petitions," March 9, 1836, Crallé (ed.), *op. cit.*, vol. II, pp. 483-484. "Remarks of December 27, 1837," *ibid.*, vol. III, pp. 185-190. "To James Hammond," February 14, 1839, Jameson (ed.), *op. cit.*, p. 763.

[26] "Disquisition," Crallé (ed.), *op. cit.*, vol. I, p. 14.

[27] "Speech on the Apportionment Bill," December 5, 1811, Robert L. Meriwether (ed.), *Papers of John C. Calhoun*, University of South Carolina Press, Columbia, S. C., 1959, vol. I, p. 72.

meant that sectional interests might be given short shrift or totally ignored in the process, then this was the price one must pay in a nation of such size and diversity. "To legislate for our country," Calhoun contended, "requires not only the most enlarged views, but a species of self-devotion, not exacted in any other. In a country so extensive, and so various in its interests, what is necessary for the common good, may apparently be opposed to the interest of particular sections. It must be submitted to as the condition of our greatness. But were we a smaller republic; were we confined to ten miles square, the selfish interests of our nature might in most cases be relied on in the management of public affairs." But remoteness itself must somehow be overcome and in a speech in support of federal internal improvements (a program resisted by early states righters) Calhoun held that "those who understand the human heart best, know how powerfully distance tends to break the sympathies of our nature. No thing . . . tends more to estrange man from man. Let us . . . bind the Republic together with a perfect system of roads and canals. Let us conquer space."[28] Such a victory would make it easier to heed the kind of advice proffered by men like Adams and Hamilton.

At this early point Calhoun grasped perfectly the Hamiltonian argument for feats of national greatness. But where Hamilton would tie national achievement to interest, Calhoun would go even further and find in glorification of nation that sentiment which could *overcome* interest. "Our Union cannot safely stand on the cold calculation of interest alone," he informed the House in 1812. "It is too weak to withstand political convulsions. We cannot without hazard neglect that which makes man love to be a member of an extensive community — the love of greatness — the consciousness of strength. So long as an American is a proud name, we are safe; but that day we are ashamed of it, the Union is more than half destroyed." Although Calhoun agreed with Hamilton that warfare was a very useful device in securing loyalty and unification,[29] he stood for the most part with Adams in believing that public virtue, along with patriotism, provided the best hope for a free society. In a prose that was common to all writers of the day he observed that the evil of party conflict "is deeply rooted in the constitution of all free governments, and is the principal cause of their weakness and destruction." The "one remedy," as Adams for one never tired of pointing out, is "the virtue and intelligence of the people." Freedom requires the enlightened participation of the popu-

☆

[28] "Speech on Internal Improvements," February 4, 1817, Meriwether (ed.), *op. cit.*, vol. I, pp. 401, 402.

[29] "Speech on Merchants' Bonds," December 8, 1812, *ibid.*, vol. I, p. 145. "Speech on Suspension of Non-Importation," June 24, 1812, *ibid.*, pp. 131-132.

lace: "it presupposes mental and moral qualities of a high order . . . It mainly stands on the faithful discharge of two great duties which every citizen of proper age owes the republic; a wise and virtuous exercise of the right of suffrage, and a prompt and brave defence of the country in the hour of danger."[30]

Institutionally speaking, the government would have to wield considerable power in such a system, even to the point of occasionally controlling business ventures in the latters' own interests. The executive branch in particular, because of its obligations to the whole society and because of its patronage prerogatives, is necessarily and constitutionally very powerful. If this power suggests a possible danger, the only neutralizing factor is a strong and sagacious House of Representatives.[31] But surveillance by the House should not be thought of in the usual terms of separation of powers, for in the structure of American government "the prevailing principle is not so much a balance of power, as a well connected chain of responsibility. That responsibility commenced here, and this House is the centre of its operation . . . This, then, is the essence of our liberty: Congress is responsible to the people immediately, and the other branches of government are responsible to it."[32] The reason this chain of responsibility can be expected to hold is that both the people and their elected representatives will have the largest interests of the nation intelligently before them and will seek to effect policies which ensure that these interests are advanced.

This entire effort has a universal significance, for the American mission has relevance far beyond its national boundaries. Later Calhoun would wish that American and European institutions could be frozen for another one hundred years so that human capacities could catch up with political innovations,[33] but at this stage he could equal the most ardent follower of Paine in optimism for the future. "We are charged by Providence," he declared, "not only with the happiness of this great and rising people, but in a considerable degree with that of the human race. We have a government of a new order, perfectly distinct from all which has ever preceded it. A government founded on the rights of man, resting not on authority, not on prejudice, not on superstition, but reason. If it succeeds, as fondly hoped by

☆

[30] "Speech on the Bill for an Additional Military Force," January 14, 1813, *ibid.*, vol. I, p. 160. "Speech on the Revenue Bill," January 31, 1816, in *ibid.*, p. 325.

[31] "Speech on the Albany Petition for Repeal of the Embargo," May 6, 1813, *ibid.*, p. 104. "Speech on Compensation of Members," March 8, 1816, *ibid.*, pp. 343-344.

[32] "First Speech on Amendments to Compensation Law," January 17, 1817, *ibid.*, vol. I, pp. 383-384.

[33] "To Mrs. T. G. Clemson," November 21, 1846, Jameson (ed.), *op. cit.*, pp. 711-712.

its founders, it will be the commencement of a new era in human affairs. All civilized governments must in the course of time conform to its principles."[34] Calhoun would never repeat this enthusiastic forecast, and when he came to write his more formal political theory in a later period he would offer remedial suggestions for a system that, in his eyes, had gone desperately wrong.[35]

Liberty, Equality, and Power

It was mentioned earlier that evidence for Calhoun's ideological position could be found within the *Disquisition* as well as in his earlier Senate speeches. This evidence lies in a "digression" (to use Calhoun's own word) that is comprised of remarks about properly interpreting and relating the concepts of liberty, power, equality, and the state of nature.[36] Calhoun was correct in labeling this discussion a digression, for given the way in which the remarks are formulated they seem out of place and not at all vital to the development of what appears to be Calhoun's main point; except for the state of nature, which ought logically to have been considered in the earlier argument about the naturalness of society. In fact, however, this "digression" is crucial, for it makes clear that Calhoun's constitutionalism had a purpose other than the protection of American pluralism and the realization of a sense of community.

Calhoun began by arguing at some length that society can last only if a proper balance is struck between liberty as exercised by the citizenry and power as wielded by government. To extend the former too far "would be to weaken the government and to render it incompetent to fulfill its primary end—the protection of society against dangers, internal and external." This balance will, moreover, vary from country to country, depending on the peculiar institutions, history, and geography of each. But, however much liberty is permissible in a particular society, its excess must in all cases be prevented, for liberty in superabundance invariably leads to anarchy. Consequently, should liberty

☆

[34]"Speech on the Revenue Bill," January 31, 1816, Meriwether (ed.), *op. cit.*, vol. I, p. 325.

[35]One can mark the beginning of a shift in Calhoun's thinking in 1824, even before he took office as Vice-President. He informed a correspondent that "if there is one portion of the Constitution . . . I most admire, it is the distribution of power between the States and general Government. It is the only portion that is novel and peculiar. The rest has been more or less compiled. This is our invention and is altogether our own, and I consider it to be the greatest improvement which has been made in the science of government, after the division of power into the legislative, executive, and judicial." ("To Robert S. Garnett," July 3, 1824, Jameson [ed.], *op. cit.*, p. 219.)

[36]This section of the *Disquisition* runs from pp. 51-59 of Crallé (ed.), *op. cit.*, vol. I; the quoted material is taken from these pages.

and internal security come into conflict, the former must always give
way, since the government cannot morally be expected to relinquish
its power to preserve the society. Furthermore, it is folly to assume
that all people are equally entitled to liberty. "It is a reward to be
earned, not a blessing to be gratuitously lavished on all alike — a reward
reserved for the intelligent, the patriotic, the virtuous and deserving —
and not a boon to be bestowed on a people too ignorant, degraded, and
vicious to be capable either of appreciating or of enjoying it."

It is also a grave error to tie liberty closely to equality and to make
the latter a prerequisite for the former. The natural side of man is, in
fact, *in*equality, for "as individuals differ greatly from each other, in
intelligence, sagacity, energy, perseverance, skill, habits of industry
and economy, physical power, *position and opportunity* — the necessary effect of leaving all free to exert themselves to better their condition must be a corresponding inequality between those who may
possess these qualities and advantages in a high degree, and those who
may be deficient in them." [Emphasis added.] Indeed, inequality of
condition is that which gives progress its greatest impulse by engendering a strong incentive to those in the back ranks to press forward
and an equally strong motivation to those in front to maintain their
position. "To force the front rank back to the rear, or attempt to push
forward the rear into line with the front, by the interposition of government, would put an end to the impulse, and effectually arrest the
march of progress." The only reason men adhere to an egalitarian doctrine in the first place is because they have been indoctrinated by the
promulgators of the fallacious state-of-nature thesis. If such a state had
ever existed, men would surely have been free and equal within it; but
there never was such a state. Man's "natural state is, the social and
political — the one for which his Creator made him, and the only one in
which he can preserve and perfect his race . . . it follows, that men
. . . instead of being born free and equal, are born subject, not only
to parental authority, but to the laws and institutions of the country
where born, and under whose protection they draw their first breath."

What is to be made of this "parenthesis"? It appears not just discontinuous with the rest of the *Disquisition,* but in many ways contradictory to it. How is it that, after railing at governmental tyranny and
arguing the case for liberty, Calhoun can suddenly speak of liberty
"in excess" and justify governmental action against libertarian incli-
nations? How can he, moreover, declare government off limits in
advancing equality when it is through political means that he would
bring equality to the various interests of society? If we were to take
him seriously on this point, the "rights" of interests would presumably
carry more weight than the rights of persons. Such an interpretation
would not be far from the mark, for Calhoun's extended discussion of

liberty, power, and so forth, represents in reality the recitation of his Southern catechism. It validates an unequal society where slavery can be regarded as natural and therefore moral.

The existence of *society*, and not liberty, is basic and the givens of particular societies must as a result be accepted without question, even, as in the South, where they openly work to repress libertarian convictions. If in fact it can be shown that liberty and especially equality threaten society, then their virtual eradication can be morally countenanced. Calhoun's parenthetical analysis is offered despite the logic of concurrent majorities being clearly both libertarian and equalitarian in direction. In this connection it was appropriate to save the treatment of the state-of-nature thesis until last, because with equality and liberty already discredited on more or less "natural" grounds, it was a simple matter to destroy the theoretical foundation that had traditionally supported these concepts.

It must be concluded that Calhoun's argument for the institutional reification of pluralism and community was, consciously or not, disingenuous. What makes his position so dolorous is that in its Madisonian formulation it totally failed to reach the actual principles involved —those which, as Fitzhugh candidly acknowledged, were quasi-Aristotelian and antidemocratic. Perhaps Calhoun himself was incapable of admitting that his basic beliefs ran counter to liberal constitutionalism. At any rate, his statement was fully in keeping with states rights advocates from his day to the present, men who despite appearances have had no particular brief *against* federal authority or *for* state sovereignty, *except* where such a question as slavery or white supremacy is at issue. When one understands this, Calhoun's theoretical attempt to establish positive government[37] and national community through Madisonian means is seen to be twice removed from the reality he desired. Had Calhoun's efforts been more direct, one might have found a touching quality about them, for, at bottom, he sought to raise political principles in a system designed only to deal with interests. As Calhoun's final intransigence indicated, beyond a certain point compromise became impossible for him and for the South in general. If it had been purely an economic dispute, as some have

☆

[37] Despite its "naturalness," government, in Calhoun's typical view, fit very much into the mold cast by the national purpose. "Leave the resources of individuals under their own direction, to be employed in advancing their own and their country's wealth and prosperity, with the extraction of the least amount required for the expenditure of Government," Calhoun recommended in 1836, "and draw off not a single laborer from his present productive pursuits to the unproductive employment of the Government, excepting such as the public service may render indispensable." ("On the Bill to Regulate the Deposits of the Public Money," May 28, 1836, *ibid.*, vol. II, pp. 546-547.)

argued it was, the North-South conflict might have been settled over time through a process that saw each side get at least something of what it wanted. But when, for whatever reasons, the issue reached the level of principle, the political system had no meaningful way of dealing with it, just as today there is no resolution to the civil rights question, despite a plethora of federal and state legislation aimed at its diminution. In this respect the Abolitionists surely won the forensic battle by being typically able to keep their arguments on a high plane of principle (whether they were always committed to liberty in *practice* is perhaps another question). Calhoun, on the other hand, was entirely warranted in claiming Madison as his theoretical antecedent, but in adopting Madisonian trappings he rendered his Southern apology complete with very serious flaws.

Calhoun as Conservative Theorist

There remains one other assessment of Calhoun that deserves comment here, and that is the viewpoint which sees in Calhoun a genuine spokesman of American conservatism, a political thinker rooted in the Burkean tradition.[38] Calhoun himself was openly enamored of Burke, whom he alluded to as the "wisest of modern statesmen, and who had the keenest and deepest glance into futurity." He was, moreover, fond of pronouncing Burkean postulates. "It ought never be forgotten," he wrote in 1848, "that *the past is the parent of the present.*"[39] But although, like Burke, Calhoun was conservative in wishing to preserve a status quo, his political theory, quite unlike Burke's, barely addressed itself to what he really wanted to save. In fact, it sought to expand American pluralism in a way that logically would disrupt the status quo. What Calhoun wanted was the protection of Southern institutions, and it ultimately matters little whether these institutions were constituted merely of hybrid liberalism glossed by a veneer of ersatz traditionalism—as Hartz and, in a slightly different vein, William R. Taylor have argued[40] —or whether there was something after all to Calhoun's bucolic picture of stable Southern communities living in

☆

[38]See, for example, Gunnar Heckscher, "Calhoun's Idea of 'Concurrent Majority' and the Constitutional Theory of Hegel," *American Political Science Review*, vol. 33, pp. 585-590, August, 1939.

[39]"In Reply to the Speeches of Mr. Webster and Mr. Clay, on Mr. Crittenden's Amendment to Distribute the Revenue from the Public Lands Among the States," January 30, 1841, Crallé (ed.), *op. cit.*, vol. III, p. 591. "To Mrs. T. G. Clemson," April 28, 1848, Jameson (ed.), *op. cit.*, p. 753.

[40]William R. Taylor, *Cavalier and Yankee*, George Braziller, New York, 1961; note in particular p. 335.

harmony and avoiding the degenerate class warfare of the North.[41]
The important point is that in either case Calhoun's complicated correctives were not going to remedy the situation. His theory was fundamentally irrelevant to the problem, and one wonders whether in his most sober moments he really believed in it himself.

George Fitzhugh

The same doubts cannot be raised about George Fitzhugh, who stands in relation to Calhoun somewhat in the same manner as Brownson to Ralph Waldo Emerson. Although Fitzhugh was not the most systematic political theorist, one finds in his writings a remarkably straightforward statement of the Southern viewpoint carried to its most extreme conclusion. Fitzhugh looked the Abolitionist squarely in the eye and insisted that, far from being in need of remedial change, Southern institutions actually embodied man's highest aspirations, and that the corrupt and interest-riddled North would do well to regenerate itself by emulating Southern ways. In his two main works, *Sociology for the South, or the Failure of Free Society* (1854) and *Cannibals All! or Slaves Without Masters* (1857), Fitzhugh dissected the American purpose and showed why its component parts were conducive to the worst sort of social evils.

The Foibles of Liberalism

Fitzhugh began by tracing the problem back to theoretical premises that he found to be tragically unsound. Hobbes, Locke, Adam Smith, Benjamin Franklin, the philosophers of free society—the "political economists," as Fitzhugh called them—all in one way or another contributed to the Northern malaise. The ideas of Smith were especially pernicious. "Smith's philosophy," according to Fitzhugh, "is simple and comprehensive . . . Its leading and almost its only doctrine is, that individual well-being and social and national wealth and prosperity will be best promoted by each man's eagerly pursuing his own

☆

[41] "Remarks made During the Debate on His Resolutions, In Respect to the Rights of the States and the Abolition of Slavery," December 27, 1837, Crallé (ed.), *op. cit.*, vol. III, p. 180. It is plain, however, that peace and love were not always present on the Southern plantation, even within Calhoun's own ken. When he learned that family slaves were behaving in an unruly fashion, he informed his son that he hoped "the negroes . . . have been brought into entire subjection; but I must ask it as a favour for you to see that all is right, and if not most decided measures be adopted to bring them to a sense of duty." ("To John Ewing Calhoun," January 15, 1827, Jameson [ed.], *op. cit.*, p. 240.)

selfish welfare unfettered and unrestricted by legal regulations, or governmental prohibitions, farther than such regulations may be necessary to prevent positive crime." Indeed, Smith's position may be summed up in one sentence: "'Every man for himself, and Devil take the hindmost.' This saying comprehends the whole philosophy, moral and economic, of the *Wealth of Nations.*"[42]

Another of the main precepts of political economy was the notion of the social contract, and on this concept Fitzhugh was particularly adamant. As far as he was concerned there never existed a brutal state of nature out of which society grew through the agency of a social contract. Hobbes probably invented the state-of-nature thesis because he had been conditioned by the vicious free competition he saw about him.[43] In carrying the social contract doctrine into his liberal ideology, Locke served to inculcate a belief in individualism that has subsequently proven socially self-destructive. As Fitzhugh saw it, "man isolated and individualized is the most helpless of animals . . . Some animals are by nature gregarious and associative. Of this class are men, ants, and bees . . . Man is born a member of society, and does not form society. Nature, as in the case of bees and ants, has it ready formed for him. He and society are congenital. Society is the being—he one of the members of that being. He has no rights whatever, as opposed to the interests of society; and that society may very properly make any use of him that will redound to the public good. Whatever rights he has are subordinate to the good of the whole; and he has never ceded rights to it, for he was born its slave, and had no rights to cede."[44]

When Fitzhugh granted society "being" he meant it seriously. As he explained in *Cannibals All!,* "men . . . have a community of thought, of motions, instincts, and intuitions. The social body is of itself a thinking, acting, sentient being." And while it is true that government is the creature of society and therefore may theoretically be said to derive its powers from the consent of the governed, this has nothing to do with the rights and freedoms of *individuals,* since "society does not owe its sovereign power to the separate consent, volition or agreement of its members." In actuality, governmental authority always depends on force, not on consent, although citizens may come to act as if the force is not present. Moreover, constitutions aimed at restricting governmental action are inexpedient as well as ill-

☆

[42] George Fitzhugh, *Sociology for the South, or the Failure of Free Society* (1854), Burt Franklin, New York, 1965, p. 10.

[43] *Ibid.,* pp. 32-33.

[44] *Ibid.,* pp. 25-26.

founded, for one can never foresee the exigencies of a changing world and the possible uses of political power.[45]

Despite their obvious iniquity, contract, constitutionalism, individualism, and consent are part and parcel of the teachings of political economy, or the free society, and it is therefore no accident that free society's highest level of achievement is embodied in a man like Benjamin Franklin, a man who, as an individual "and as a philosopher, is the best exponent of the working of the system. His sentiments and his philosophy are low, selfish, atheistic and material."[46] As with Franklin, so with the whole of free society, in which Fitzhugh was hard put to find a single institution of redeeming value.

Individualism in the "Free" Society

To look closely at the free polity was to see a bleak picture indeed; it was to find a society where selfishness transcended all other values, where bitter differences bordered constantly on open conflict. Fitzhugh claimed that in "free society the sentiments, principles, feelings and affections of high and low, rich and poor, are equally blunted and debased by the continual war of competition. It begets rivalries, jealousies and hatreds on all hands. The poor can neither love nor respect the rich, who, instead of aiding and protecting them, are endeavoring to cheapen their labor and take away their means of subsistence. The rich can hardly respect themselves, when they reflect that wealth is the result of avarice, caution, circumspection and hard dealing."[47] The society is divided into four equally malignant parts: the rich, who live well but do no labor; professionals, who receive disproportionately high wages for little work; workers, who support everyone but starve in the process; and swindlers, who live on the labor of others. Being on the bottom of this stratified order, the laborer is particularly disadvantaged, or "exploitated," as Fitzhugh described him. In a phrase which he may have borrowed directly from Brownson, Fitzhugh argued that the masses "labor under all the disadvantages of slavery, and have none of the rights of slaves."[48] The immediate causes of the laborer's sorry plight are political and economic, and both categories are derivative of the theoretical propositions that underlay free society.

☆

[45] Fitzhugh, *Cannibals All! or Slaves Without Masters*, C. Vann Woodward (ed.), The Belknap Press, Harvard University Press, Cambridge, Mass., 1960, pp. 132, 244, 249. Fitzhugh, *Sociology for the South*, p. 26.

[46] *Ibid.*, p. 90.

[47] *Ibid.*, pp. 38-39.

[48] Fitzhugh, *Cannibals All!*, pp. 12, 16.

On economic grounds, the belief that the public good is achieved when each citizen seeks to advance his own pecuniary interests inevitably leads to corruption, for those who espouse this view "forget that men eager in the pursuit of wealth are never satisfied with the fair earnings of their own bodily labor, but find wits and cunning employed in over-reaching others much more profitable than their hands." The unavoidable result of this process in societies of long standing is the division of the population into two basic classes: the haves and the have-nots. "A few individuals possessed of capital and cunning acquire a power to employ the laboring class on such terms as they please," and it was Fitzhugh's conviction that they "seldom fail to use that power. Hence the numbers and destitution of the poor in free society are daily increasing, the numbers of the middle or independent class diminishing, and the few rich men growing hourly richer." This inequity is the natural product of the fact that in all old countries the laboring population far exceeds the number of available jobs. "Yet," Fitzhugh remarked, "all the laborers must live by the wages they receive from the capitalists. The capitalist cheapens their wages; they compete with and underbid each other, for employed they must be on any terms. This war of the rich with the poor and the poor with one another, is the morality which political economy inculcates."[49]

In explaining why the North had not quite reached this state of economic barbarism, Fitzhugh introduced his own frontier thesis long before Turner's version came to dominate American historiography. "Society need not fail in the Northeast," he noted, "until the whole West is settled, and a refluent population . . . overstocks permanently the labor market on the Atlantic board. Till then, the despotism of skill and capital, in forcing emigration to the West, makes proprietors of those emigrants, benefits them, peoples the West, and by their return trade, enriches the East."[50] Despite this temporary respite, however, the North's day of doom would surely come, for all free societies are fated ultimately to the same end.

The Decline of Civilization

Although very far indeed from the American mainstream, Fitzhugh's critique to this point has a rather familiar ring to it, for in its moral indictment of capitalism it resembles the position of Brownson and other non-Marxian socialist writers of the day. But when Fitzhugh turns from

☆

[49] Fitzhugh, *Sociology for the South*, pp. 18, 21, 22-23.
[50] Fitzhugh, *Cannibals All!*, p. 11.

economic to political explanations, his analysis becomes completely his own. When he argued that free society was corrupt, he meant that the extent of its corruption was in vital ways directly a function of the amount of its freedom. Not only was individualism found wanting but liberty itself was to be regarded as generative of the worst kind of evil. Fitzhugh believed that liberty and society were mutually antagonistic. From his perspective "the love of personal liberty and freedom from all restraint are distinguishing traits of wild men and beasts."[51] Not just society, but *democratic* society is incompatible with liberty; "for liberty permits and encourages the weak to oppress the strong, whilst democracy proposes, so far as possible, to equalize advantages, by fairly dividing the burdens of life and rigidly enforcing the performance of every social duty by every member of society, according to his capacity and ability."[52] Moreover, if one wished to chart a history of civilization's progress, one would find that it was a history of liberty's decline. "As civilization advances," Fitzhugh argued, "liberty recedes, and it is fortunate for man that he loses his love of liberty just as fast as he becomes more moral and intellectual. The wealthy, virtuous and religious citizens of large towns enjoy less of liberty than any other persons whatever, and yet they are the most useful and rationally happy of mankind. The best governed countries, and those which have prospered most, have always been distinguished for the number and stringency of their laws. Good men obey superior authority, the laws of God, of morality, and of their country; bad men love liberty and violate them." Indeed, the equation of bad men and liberty allowed Fitzhugh to indulge in a bit of rhetorical hyperbole. "It is remarkable," he wrote, "that sin began by the desire for liberty and the attempt to attain it in the person of Satan and his fallen angels."[53]

More to the historic point, however, Fitzhugh could trace a direct line from the Reformation through the right of private judgment, human individualism, the social contract, *laissez-faire* economics, egalitarianism, the freedom of religion, speech, and press to the sovereignty of the individual, and the abnegation of government.[54] Since civilization can only advance as liberty declines, the post-Reformation era must be regarded as a period of increasing retrogression. Although all of these libertarian innovations are unfortunate, the abnegation of government is particularly detrimental, for, according to Fitzhugh, there can be "little danger of too much government. The danger and evil with us is of too little."[55]

☆

[51] Fitzhugh, *Sociology for the South*, p. 29.

[52] Fitzhugh, *Cannibals All!*, p. 82.

[53] Fitzhugh, *Sociology for the South*, p. 30.

[54] Fitzhugh, *Cannibals All!*, p. 53.

[55] Fitzhugh, *Sociology for the South*, p. 31.

Fitzhugh was prepared to argue that even those who preferred individualism did not really understand what they wanted, or at least how best to achieve it. "In ancient times," he wrote, "the individual was considered nothing, the State every thing. And yet under this system, the noblest individuality was evolved that the world has ever seen."[56] Fitzhugh was scarcely interested in promoting individualism, however, and his most important area of reform was more social and economic than governmental—although with his organic conception of society, changes in the social structure would of course lead directly to changes in the political sphere as well.

Man as Property

Fitzhugh was an abolitionist in reverse. In the face of attacks upon the South, he took the offensive and called for abolition in the North, the abolition of free society and its replacement by the institutions of slavery. As with his critique of the North, his argument in support of slavery was made on economic and social as well as philosophical grounds. The economic rejoinder was perhaps the most cogent, since it spoke directly to the serious problems created by capitalism. Somehow the interests of the rival classes must be joined and, according to Fitzhugh, "it is impossible to place labor and capital in harmonious or friendly relations, except by the means of slavery, which identifies their interests." Slavery brings together "the interests of rich and poor, master and slave, and begets domestic affection on the one side, and loyalty and respect on the other."[57] The reason that this can happen is that, as their interests coalesce, the two classes are drawn closely together in a way unimaginable in free society. For his part, the master, through sheer economic self-interest, looks to the happiness and well-being of his slaves. To do otherwise would be virtually impossible, for negligence, as the master well knows, would in the end cost him dearly, and he would therefore never act so irrationally. By the same token, the slave, freed from the tortuous pressures of economic individualism, thrives under this benign rule and furthermore he works hard, for he knows that good fortune for his master will redound to his benefit. What happens, in effect, is that each develops a vested interest in the other, or, to use Fitzhugh's phrase, they evolve "property rights" in each other.

"'Property in man' is," Fitzhugh maintained, "what all are struggling to obtain." Property in man already exists in the South and ought to exist in the North where property owners should "be obliged to take

[56] *Ibid.*, pp. 26-27.

[57] Fitzhugh, *Cannibals All!*, p. 31. Fitzhugh, *Sociology for the South*, p. 43.

care of man, their property, as they do of their horses and their hounds, their cattle and their sheep."[58] As this concept is applied in the South it carries that society to the highest level of community. If only those outside the South could understand that "god makes masters and gives them affections, feelings and interests that secure kindness to the sick, aged and dying slave. Man can never inspire his rickety institutions with those feelings, interests and affections. Say the Abolitionists — 'Man ought not to have property in man.' What a dreary, cold, bleak, inhospitable world this would be with such a doctrine carried into practice. Men living to themselves, like owls and wolves and lions and birds and beasts of prey? No: 'Love thy neighbor as thyself.' And this can't be alone till he has a property in your services as well as a place in your heart." Even free society obliquely recognizes this principle, as the diffusion of voluntary associations in the North indicates.[59]

The principle of property in man, moreover, works both ways. It is crucial to notice, although few outsiders do, that slaves also have a valuable property in their masters. Thus, the master feels obliged to care for infant, aged, and infirm Negroes even though they have no present value for him and may never have. "He is bound to support them, to supply all their wants, and relieve them of all care for the present or future. And well, and feelingly and faithfully does he discharge his duty."[60]

With such a system firmly placed, the whole understanding of property's social role undergoes a radical transformation. The proper view of property is attenuated in the North where "wealthy men, who are patterns of virtue in the discharge of their domestic duties, value themselves on never intermeddling in public matters. They forget that property is a mere creature of law and society, and are willing to make no return for that property to the public."[61] With property in man as a fixed doctrine in the South, wealth automatically carries with it duties in the form of taxation obligations. "Capital is not taxed in free society," Fitzhugh contended, "but *is taxed* in slave society, because, in such society, labor is capital. The capitalist and the professional can, and do, by increased profits and fees, throw the whole burden of taxation on the laboring class. Slaveholders cannot do so; for diminished allowance to their slaves would impair their value and lessen their own capital."[62] Consequently, the interests of the whole society and those

☆

[58] Fitzhugh, *Cannibals All!*, p. 20
[59] Fitzhugh, *Sociology for the South*, pp. 68-69.
[60] *Ibid.*, p. 68.
[61] *Ibid.*, p. 27.
[62] Fitzhugh, *Cannibals All!*, p. 34.

of the slave master are amalgamated in a system that brings maximum well-being to all concerned. It must not be forgotten, however, that it is the worker who benefits most by being saved from the destitution visited upon him by free society. "The association of labor properly carried out under a common head or ruler, would render labor more efficient, relieve the laborer of many of the cares of household affairs, and protect and support him in sickness and old age, besides preventing the too great reduction of wages by redundancy of labor and free competition. "Slavery," Fitzhugh insisted, "attains all these results. What else will?"[63]

Slavery and Socialism

American followers of Robert Owen or Charles Fourier might have replied that socialism of one kind or another would achieve these results and retain freedom in the bargain. For this answer Fitzhugh was totally prepared. As far as he was concerned there was no logical dispute between slavery and socialism; their interests and aims were in fact identical. Socialists were entirely correct in their critique of capitalism. Indeed, Fitzhugh was happy to admit that he had gleaned many of his most important insights into free society from socialist writings.

The problem with socialism was that it did not comprehend the force of its own argument. "Our only quarrel with Socialism," Fitzhugh stated, "is, that it will not honestly admit that it owes its recent revival to the failure of universal liberty, and is seeking to bring about slavery again in some form."[64] All socialist theories demand that the individual to some extent give up part of his personal freedom to an organization that acts for the collectivity. To Fitzhugh it seemed only reasonable to carry this principle to its logical conclusion. He felt, moreover, that, although they refused to admit it, this is what the socialists also wished to do. "We believe," he wrote, "there is not an intelligent reformist in the world who does not see the necessity of slavery—who does not advocate its reinstitution in all save the name." "No association, no efficient combination of labor can be effected till men give up their liberty of action and subject themselves to a common despotic head or ruler. This is slavery, and towards this socialism is moving . . . *free trade or political economy is the science of free society,* and *socialism the science of slavery.*[65] [Emphasis added.]

☆

[63] Fitzhugh, *Sociology for the South*, p. 28.
[64] *Ibid.*, p. 70.
[65] *Ibid.*, pp. 66, 61.

With socialism posited as the "science of slavery," it was an easy task for Fitzhugh to describe the plantation in Fourierist language. "A Southern farm," he indicated, "is a sort of joint stock concern, or social phalanstery, in which the master furnishes the capital and skill, and the slaves the labor, and divide the profits not according to each one's input, but according to each one's wants and necessities." The culmination of such organization is nothing less than the realization of socialism's ultimate desire. Unlike the situation in free society where the "wages of the poor diminish and their wants and families increase," in the South the wages of the slaves "invariably increase with their wants. The master increases the provision for the family as the family increases in number and helplessness. It is a beautiful example of communism, where each one receives not according to his labor, but according to his wants."[66] The obvious model for the radical transformation of civilization, according to Fitzhugh, thus resides in the everyday activity of Southern society.

The "Naturalness" of Slavery and White Supremacy

There were, however, justifications for slavery even more fundamental than the need for reform. Given the character of mankind, it follows that slavery is the only natural organizing principle for the structuring of society. Fitzhugh could agree with Jefferson that there are such things as natural rights and that it would be against the design of Providence to violate such rights. An examination of nature, however, reveals precisely what these rights are and how they ought to operate.

> The order and subordination observable in the physical, animal, and human world show that some are formed for higher, others for lower stations — the few to command, the many to obey. We conclude that about nineteen out of every twenty individuals have "a natural and inalienable right" to be taken care of and protected, to have guardians, trustees, husbands, or masters; in other words they have a natural and inalienable right to be slaves. The one in twenty are as clearly born or educated or some way fitted for command and liberty. Not to make them rulers or masters is as great a violation of natural right as not to make slaves of the mass. The American Revolution did nothing to alter this natural organization of society, for the Revolution was an act of a people asserting its independence and had nothing to do with manufacturing individual rights and liberties.[67]

The natural right of rulership deserves special attention because without this principle in effect the wrong men seek and inevitably gain

☆

[66] *Ibid.*, pp. 29, 48.
[67] Fitzhugh, *Cannibals All!*, pp. 69, 133.

power. At the same time, one should not fear the ambition of natural rulers: "the actively good," Fitzhugh pointed out, "are always ambitious, and desire to possess power, in order that they may control, in some measure, the conduct of those whom they desire to benefit."[68] This has been the order of things in the most civilized of societies, and its perfect manifestation is, as it always had been, the institution of slavery. Nothing short of this will do, for a "less degree of subjection is inadequate for the government and protection of great numbers of human beings."[69] The stress on civilized societies is crucial since orderly institutions and the rule of law, in other words civilization itself, are indigenous to one race above all. "There never was yet found a nation of white savages," Fitzhugh contended. Their wants and their wits combine to elevate them above the savage state. Nature, that imposed more wants on them, has kindly endowed them with superior intelligence to supply those wants."[70] With the connection between civilization and white superiority established, Fitzhugh could meet head-on the most strenuous attack from the North.

Just as no analysis of the nineteenth or twentieth century South would be complete without a treatment of the white supremacy doctrine, so too with the writings of Fitzhugh. If all his other arguments failed to convince, Fitzhugh could, at the conclusion of *Sociology for the South*, calmly assert that the Negro was simply unfit for freedom. The Negro is, after all, a child who finds in his master a life-long parent or guardian. Childlike, he is therefore improvident, and given his liberty he would prove an "insufferable burden to society." Since he is inferior to whites, he would quickly be exterminated in open society. From Fitzhugh's point of view, Harriet Beecher Stowe had a wildly irrational understanding of Negro capability. "We presume," he wrote, "the maddest abolitionist does not think the negro's providence of habits and money-making capacity at all to compare to those of the whites. This defect of character would alone justify enslaving him."[71] Slavery in America not only saves the Negro from his own destruction, but has the added advantage of bringing to the Negro the teachings of Christianity and the refinements of civilized life. Those who would abolish slavery and transport the slaves back to their native Africa are guilty of great inhumaneness, for returning the Negro to Africa would not only abandon him to pagan idolatry but would condemn this newly civilized soul to instant extinction. He is unused to

☆

[68] *Ibid.*, p. 188.
[69] Fitzhugh, *Sociology for the South*, p. 33.
[70] *Ibid.*, p. 20.
[71] *Ibid.*, p. 84.

the brutal ways of the bushmen, and if "he went to Africa," Fitzhugh vividly explained, "the savages would cook him and eat him."[72] On all the grounds that matter, then, Southern slavery is necessary and beneficial to mankind, to slave and master alike, and those who would stand in its way simultaneously place themselves in the way of human progress.

The Status of Fitzhugh's Critique

It is impossible to imagine a position further removed from the American consensus than was Fitzhugh's. Whether he was entirely right or not, Fitzhugh understood the Southern social system to be absolutely opposed to everything the North stood for. If there were similarities between the two, he failed to see them: the thought that the cotton economy, for example, was deeply capitalistic seems never to have occurred to him. On theoretical ground his views departed even from those of his leading compatriots. C. Vann Woodward argues that "when compared with Fitzhugh, even John Taylor of Caroline, John Randolph of Roanoke, and John C. Calhoun blend inconspicuously into the great American consensus, since they were all apostles in some degree of John Locke."[73] The contrast with Calhoun might be regarded as questionable by some, for it could be argued that beneath his Madisonian facade, Calhoun agreed with Fitzhugh's every contention. But Fitzhugh himself saw that he and Calhoun followed different paths. In a letter to George Frederick Holmes, his friend and ideological consort, he drew clear boundary lines. "I find," he wrote, "that although Locke, Rousseau, Adam Smith, Jefferson, Macaulay, and Calhoun are against me, Aristotle, Carlyle, you and all the leading minds of the day are with me."[74] For Fitzhugh, then, Calhoun was not only neither a true defender of slavery nor a leading mind of the day, he could actually be associated with those responsible for civilization's deterioration. Measured by his own radical philosophy, no other conclusion about Calhoun was possible.

The irony of Fitzhugh's effort was that it contained many telling insights into the weaknesses of economic individualism. Although exaggerated, his picture of labor "exploitated" in the newly industrialized North had enough attribution to real life to make it readily believable. But the attack on liberty and the defense of slavery doomed his critique to the propaganda heap, for even the most nonpartisan

☆

[72] *Ibid.*, p. 88.

[73] Fitzhugh, *Cannibals All!*, Introduction, p. viii.

[74] Quoted by Harvey Wish, *George Fitzhugh, Propagandist of the Old South*, Peter Smith, Baton Rouge, La., 1943, p. 119; Fitzhugh, *Cannibals All!*, Introduction, p. xxxii.

American was unwilling to listen seriously to such cant, even though, like Lincoln, many fully accepted the wholly unproved dissertation on racial inferiority. And the argument about mutual obligation and democratic responsibility, based as it was on the slavery system, did little good to the theory of community. It could, in fact, allow the Northern victory in the Civil War to seem a vindication of economic individualism: since economic individualism stood opposed to the cause of slavery, it must therefore stand also as a primary expression of human liberty. Thus Fitzhugh's critical argument could paradoxically serve to entrench further the very dogma he wished to uproot. With Fitzhugh's position rendered irrelevant (by its own questionable logic and by the fact that the other side won) the connection between economic individualism and liberty emerged from the Civil War tighter than ever and would not be forcefully challenged again until the end of the century.

7

IN DEFENSE OF
THE NATIONAL PURPOSE
WILLIAM GRAHAM SUMNER

During the last third of the nineteenth century the national purpose
began to lose its hold on America, for, despite glowing promises to the
contrary, deprivation and often penury seemed the permanent expectation of certain classes of citizens. Voices of protest were now heard
from various sectors of society, some challenging the very principles
upon which the national ideology was based. Confronted by mounting
criticisms, defenders of economic individualism were forced to expand
their arguments in an effort to recapture the mass support of previous
generations. Of these attempts at reintegration, most influential by far
were the doctrines of Social Darwinism and the tales of Horatio Alger.

Although only the former merit detailed discussion in this book, it
is important for the larger argument to notice that Darwinism and the
Alger myth were very closely related. They arose simultaneously to
justify a social environment that could no longer satisfy the universal
demands of the American purpose. In one sense, the Alger myth
could be accepted because there were just enough cases of sudden
success abroad to make success itself seem a real possibility for all.
On the other hand, the myth provided its own brand of Darwinism for
popular consumption. A process akin to "natural selection"—one of
Darwinism's main precepts—ran through each of Alger's stories as his

ragamuffin heroes triumphed in a bitter world, aided usually by a rewarding capitalist, nature's agent. And as unprecedented millions devoured these tales, each could identify with the rags-to-riches prodigy and hope that he, or at least his children, would be among those selected. If Social Darwinism said that only the fittest would survive, the Alger myth held out the promise that with sufficient pluck and a dash of "Luke's Luck," even the most humble could eventually join the ranks of the fit.

As promulgated by its leading American exponent, William Graham Sumner, Social Darwinism was far more complex than the simple message of Horatio Alger. Sumner's interests ranged over a very wide expanse, and his views underwent subtle shifts as his focus or his subject matter changed. Although first and last an intellectual dedicated to the work of the academy, Sumner was deeply concerned with matters of public policy, and he continually sought to influence popular opinion through publication and from the public lecture stand. He would reach the average man through such magazines as *Cosmopolitan, Collier's,* and *Popular Science,* as well as through articles in Providence, New Haven, and Chicago newspapers. The business community would read Sumner in Rand McNally's *Banker's Monthly.* He would find a general intellectual audience through the pages of the *North American Review* and the *Yale Review,* and more specialized students in readers of the *Yale Law Journal* and the *American Sociological Review.* While Sumner's public would never rival Alger's in quantity—no writer's could—it is still accurate to say that from his audience the teachings of Social Darwinism received a very wide hearing, far wider than that traditionally afforded to social instruction emanating from the halls of higher learning.

Survival and Adaption

The Doctrine of Laissez Faire

On its simplest level Sumner's lesson was easily grasped, for it followed Herbert Spencer in taking certain Darwinian concepts and applying them directly to society in support of a conservative political philosophy. Thus, in Sumner, men are likened to animals in the wilderness who must combat nature in a constant effort to stay alive. "Man," Sumner believed, "is born under the necessity of sustaining the existence he has received by an onerous struggle against nature, both to win what is essential to his life and to ward off what is prejudicial to it. He is born under a burden and a necessity."[1] He can,

☆

[1] "The Challenge of Facts," A. G. Keller (ed.), *The Challenge of Facts and Other Essays* (hereafter referred to as *Challenge of Facts*), Yale University Press, New Haven, Conn., 1914, p. 17.

moreover, expect no help from his protagonist, for nature's existence is in no way connected with the well-being of man. Indeed, there "is no need for man and no demand for man, in nature; it is complete without him." And just as "nature's forces know no pity," so it is in society whose forces likewise "know no pity."[2] In such a state those succeed in their battle for longevity who are best suited to the task.

It is not only wrong but actually harmful to attempt to create conditions favorable to all contestants. "The law of the survival of the fittest," Sumner pointed out, "was not made by man and cannot be abrogated by man. We can only, by interfering with it, produce the survival of the unfittest."[3] We must leave to nature the necessary correctives, even when they strike us as unduly harsh. We must not, for example, seek to ameliorate the environment to prevent the occurrence of social vices. "Vice," Sumner reported, "is its own curse. If we let nature alone, she cures vice by the most frightful penalties. It may shock you to hear me say it, but when you get over the shock, it will do you good to think of it: a drunkard in the gutter is just where he ought to be. Nature is working away at him to get him out of the way, just as she sets up her processes of dissolution to remove whatever is a failure in its line . . . Nine-tenths of our measures for preventing vice are really protective towards it, because they ward off the penalty."[4] The moral of such instruction is plain: "Every man and woman in society has one big duty. That is, to take care of his or her own self." Politically speaking, this is nothing more than the doctrine of *laissez faire* which, if translated "into blunt English . . . will read, Mind your own business."[5] This done, the law of survival of the fittest will be followed to a measure.

In Defense of Wealth

Correlative to the survival of the fittest axiom in Darwinian thought was the notion of natural selection. Sumner reserved this concept for a special individual, the man of wealth, upon whose shoulders rested a heavy responsibility. When Sumner remarked that nature had no intrinsic need of man, he also noted "that the men in all history who

☆

[2] "The Demand for Men," *ibid.*, p. 113. William Graham Sumner, *What Social Classes Owe to Each Other* (hereafter referred to as *Social Classes*), Harper & Brothers, New York, 1883, p. 154.

[3] "Sociology," A. G. Keller (ed.), *War and Other Essays* (hereafter referred to as *War*), Yale University Press, New Haven, Conn., 1911, p. 177.

[4] "The Forgotten Man," A. G. Keller (ed.), *The Forgotten Man and Other Essays* (hereafter referred to as *Forgotten Man*), Yale University Press, New Haven, Conn., 1919, p. 480.

[5] Sumner, *Social Classes*, pp. 113, 120.

have proved by their life and works that the world did need them and could illy have spared them, are not more than a score or two." These rare men have had various occupations throughout history. In the late nineteenth century they are the wealthy industrialists whose services to civilization far exceed the monetary recompense they receive in return. It would be the height of folly to legislate against their interest, for "the millionaires are a product of natural selection, acting on the whole body of man to pick out those who can meet the requirement of certain work to be done. In this respect they are just like the great statesmen, or scientific men, or military men. It is because they are thus selected that wealth — both their own and that intrusted to them — aggregates under their hands . . . They get high wages and live in luxury, but the bargain is a good one for society." Placed as they are above the multitude, the wealthy stand as models worthy of general emulation. It is true that they escape many difficulties of normal living, but, Sumner argued, we must see that "those who to-day enjoy the most complete emancipation from the hardships of human life, and the greatest command over the conditions of existence, simply show us the best that man has yet been able to do."[6] We would pull such men down at our own peril, for then society would be without proper examples to follow.

Sumner's theoretical defense of wealth was frequently mixed with a more utilitarian understanding of the problem. "Capital," he wrote, "is only formed by self-denial, and if the possession of it did not secure advantages and superiorities of a high order men would never submit to what is necessary to get it."[7] Although it cannot be argued that those who inherit their wealth have to delay self-gratification and thereby improve their character as their ancestors did, the institution of inheritance must nevertheless be protected from the assaults of socialists and other reformers. Being crucial, the amassment of capital must be supported in every way. "The right of bequest rests on no other grounds than those of expediency. The love of children is the strongest motive to frugality and to the accumulation of capital. The state guarantees the power of bequest only because it thereby encourages the accumulation of capital on which the welfare of society depends." And for Sumner this prudent social policy had even broader implications. He believed that "hereditary wealth transmitted from generation to generation is the strongest instrument by which we keep up a steadily advancing civilization."[8]

☆

[6] "The Concentration of Wealth: Its Economic Justification," Keller (ed.), *Challenge of Facts*, p. 90. Sumner, *Social Classes*, p. 70.

[7] *Ibid.*, pp. 76-77.

[8] "The Challenge of Facts," Keller (ed.), *Challenge of Facts*, pp. 42, 43.

This point was all the more important now that civilization had entered into the era of machines. In such an age of complexity and delicate economic arrangements, the capitalist has become the indispensable man. "The more the machines do," wrote Sumner, "the more the rational animal, man, needs to bring brains to bear to rise above the machines . . . The man who has won most of all from the progress is the man who possesses executive power and organizing ability. We get together vast masses of capital and hundreds of laborers, and the happiness or misery of thousands comes to depend on the man whose judgment and knowledge decide what shall be done, and how. We cannot break out of this intense and exacting social organization without sacrificing our means of comfort and throwing thousands into distress; hence we pay the man who can manage organization a monopoly price for his rare and indispensable abilities."[9] For Sumner, this role could have very specific application. After traveling the railroads of the German Empire, for example, he was moved to comment that the Germans would make a handsome bargain by turning their lines over to a Vanderbilt for twenty-five years of reorganizing at a fee of one million dollars a year. If civilization as a whole would place itself more in such hands the result could only be beneficial to all concerned. Sumner seemed to understand that riches and power went together, and he argued that the "concentration of power (wealth), more dominant control, intenser discipline, and stricter methods are but modes of securing more perfect integration. When we perceive this we see that the concentration of wealth is but one feature of a grand step in societal evolution."[10] Since they occupy the forefront of this movement, Americans in particular ought to comprehend this reality.

Self-Interest and the Survival of the Fit

Americans especially ought to realize that the pursuit of economic individualism is perfectly in keeping with the direction of social evolution, for "fortunately," Sumner announced, "the matter stands so that the duty of making the best of one's self individually is not a separate thing from the duty of filling one's place in society, but the two are one, and the latter is accomplished when the former is done."[11] This has always been the case, and in fact the measure of social progress is nothing more than the amount by which individual interest

☆

[9] "Who Win by Progress?" *ibid.*, p. 173.

[10] "The Absurd Effort to Make the World Over," Keller (ed.), *War*, p. 201. "The Concentration of Wealth: Its Economic Justification," Keller (ed.), *Challenge of Facts*, p. 82.

[11] Sumner, *Social Classes*, p. 113.

is enhanced. That this is a "narrow" view of the matter Sumner would not deny. He insisted, however, that it was the only realistic view: "the motive to all immediate efforts," he argued, "is either self-interest or the desire to gratify one's tastes and natural tendencies. I say that all the grand results which make up what we call social progress are the results of millions of efforts on the part of millions of people, and that the motive to each effort . . . was the gratification of a need or a tendency of his nature. I know that some may consider this a selfish doctrine . . . but to me it is a pleasure to observe that we are not at war with ourselves, and that the intelligent pursuit of our best good as individuals is the surest means to the good of society." To engage in "war with ourselves," to attempt, especially through political means, to work for the "good" of all citizens, or of all men, is to court disaster. "I promise you," Sumner declared, "that if you pursue what is good for yourself, you need not take care for the good of society." To heed contrary advice was to go against the principles of social evolution. "If we do not like the survival of the fittest," Sumner never tired of pointing out, "we have only one alternative and that is the survival of the unfittest." [12] Sumner was very specific in indicating the kinds of activities that would operate against the survival principle. These activities involved government and would be concerned with questions of property, liberty, and equality.

Sumner posited survival of the fit and survival of the unfit as mutually exclusive possibilities because he believed that action in behalf of the latter could only be taken at a severe cost to the former. Unlike the situation in the free marketplace where individual capital accretion redounded to the benefit of countless citizens by creating new economic opportunities — "The wealth which [the capitalist] wins," Sumner wrote in *What Social Classes Owe to Each Other*, "would not be but for him" [13] — *political* programs aimed at raising the lowest economic classes could only be realized by simultaneously reducing the hard-earned capital of those who stood at higher levels and who worked to advance social progress. Time and again Sumner tried to hit this lesson home. "The notion is accepted," he wrote, ". . . that if you help the inefficient and vicious you may gain something for society or you may not, but that you lose nothing. This is a complete mistake. Whatever capital you divert to the support of a shiftless and good-for-nothing person is so much diverted from some other employment, and that means from somebody else. I would spend any conceivable amount of zeal and eloquence if I possessed it to try to make

☆

[12] "Discipline," Keller (ed.), *Forgotten Man*, pp. 428, 429. "The Predicament of Sociological Study," Keller (ed.), *Challenge of Facts*, p. 423.

[13] Sumner, *Social Classes*, p. 54.

people grasp this idea. Capital is force. If it goes one way it cannot go another." Sumner possessed considerable eloquence and he could use analogies from natural science to reinforce his point: "if you undertake to lift anybody," he wrote, "you must have a fulcrum or point of resistance. All the elevation you give to one must be gained by an equivalent depression on some one else." "In Society," he wrote elsewhere, ". . . to lift one man up we push another down."[14] If we permit such practices, we violate a cardinal tenet of natural law, that of free competition. Nature, we must remember, is entirely neutral to this competition; "she submits to him who most energetically and resolutely assails her." If we do not like this arrangement, "if we try to amend it, there is only one way in which we can do it. We can take from the better and give to the worse. We can deflect the penalties of those who have done ill and throw them on those who have done better."[15]

The Forgotten Man

And who will suffer from wrong-headed attempts at social amelioration? The capitalist somewhat, since his opportunities for enlarging his fortune would be greatly limited. But since the capitalist's economic assets would likely protect him from personal deprivation, society as a whole would lose even more by being deprived of the advantage gained from the capitalist's energy and resourcefulness. But the real loser would be a particular kind of citizen whom Sumner symbolically labeled the "Forgotten Man," the man who quietly and efficiently, with honesty and integrity, does his work, cares for his family, casts his vote, and pays his taxes.

It is this man, who goes about his business essentially unseen and unheard, who will pay the price of social reform. To exact such a levy of him is grossly unfair, for it is to reverse completely the natural system of penalties and rewards. It is to elevate men who exert no energy or effort in their own behalf. Although it is the interference of the political arm that typically produces this iniquity, Sumner was sufficiently disturbed by its potential for general harm that he warned with almost equal ardor against similar practices by private agencies. "The next time that you are tempted to subscribe a dollar to a charity," he informed his audience as Emerson had nearly a half-century earlier, "I do not tell you not to do it, because after you have fairly

☆

[14]"The Forgotten Man," Keller (ed.), *Forgotten Man*, pp. 475-476, 478. Sumner, *Social Classes*, p. 128.

[15]"The Challenge of Facts," Keller (ed.), *Challenge of Facts*, p. 25.

considered the matter, you may think it right to do it, but I do ask you to stop and remember the Forgotten Man and understand that if you put your dollar in the savings bank it will go to swell the capital of the country which is available for division amongst those who, while they earn it, will reproduce it with increase."[16] But more important, and far more dangerous, than private philanthropy were programs of public improvement enacted and administered by the deadening hand of government.

The Heavy Hand of Government

In Sumner's view, there was every reason to be fearful of governmental intrusion into economic areas that ought to be free from political influence. Because certain classes possessed less power than they desired, conditions were ripe for a wholesale display of schemes for radical change. "Of course, in such a state of things," Sumner noted, "political mountebanks come forward and propose fierce measures which can be paraded for social effect. Such measures would be hostile to all our institutions, would destroy capital, overthrow credit, and impair the most essential interests of society. On the side of political machinery there is no grounds for hope, but only for fear." Viewed historically, Sumner found little reason to be surprised at this propensity, for most of the evils that encumber contemporary social progress are the effects of precisely such political interloping. He contended that "we have inherited a vast number of social ills which never came from Nature. They are the complicated products of all the tinkering, muddling, and blundering of social doctors in the past . . . The greatest reforms which could now be accomplished would consist in undoing the work of statesmen in the past, and the greatest difficulty in the way of reform is to find out how to undo their work without injury to what is natural and sound." For his own time Sumner would adopt the motto of the old *Congressional Globe:* " 'The world is governed too much.' "[17]

The reason government has been able to perpetrate its evils is that people, historically and contemporaneously, have been in the habit of expecting too much from it. This characteristic appeared in America with the rise of the Republican party, a party that exceeded natural political boundaries by moving into the realm of morality. "It enlisted unselfish and moral and religious motives. It reached outside the

☆

[16] "The Forgotten Man," Keller (ed.), *Forgotten Man*, p. 477.

[17] Sumner, *Social Classes*, pp. 110-111, 118. "Separation of State and Market," A. G. Keller (ed.), *Earth-Hunger and Other Essays* (hereafter referred to as *Earth-Hunger*), Yale University Press, New Haven, Conn., 1913, p. 307.

proper domain of politics—the expedient measures to be adopted for ends recognized as desirable—and involved justice and right in regard to the ends.[18] While justice and right have relevant procedural dimensions, they are not in themselves legitimate political ends. To view them in this way is to carry political institutions even farther from their appropriate setting, for from the search for absolute justice it is but a short step to seeing government as an agency instituted to bring about human happiness.

As far as Sumner was concerned, no conviction could be more erroneous. "It is not at all the function of the State to make men happy," he wrote. "They must make themselves happy in their own way." The correct political economy would render this category totally irrelevant. "We never supposed that *laissez faire* would give us perfect happiness," Sumner argued. "We have left perfect happiness entirely out of our account."[19] If this is not done, the governmental structure takes on far too much importance and becomes involved in a baleful profusion of deliberating and decision-making procedures. The result is that from the citizen's viewpoint, government grows remote and becomes clouded in mystery. Sumner remarked that people "are always prone to believe there is something metaphysical and sentimental about civil affairs, but there is not. Civil institutions are constructed to protect, either directly or indirectly, the property of men and the honor of women against the vices and passions of human nature."[20] The honor of women was apparently not a very grave problem in Sumner's eyes, for he devoted precious little space to its solution. The protection of property, however, was perhaps the most serious issue related to the question of governmental trespass, and to this matter Sumner gave considerable attention.

Misguided Reformers

The Attack on Property

Sumner was enormously distressed by proposals from socialists and other reformers for redistributing property throughout society in a more equalitarian manner. Writing in the 1880's he believed that these proposals were gaining the support of the majority, and he despaired lest ways not be found to protect property against majoritarian sentiments. He argued that such protection constituted "the first and greatest function of government and element in civil liberty." Those

☆

[18] "Politics in America, 1776-1876," Keller (ed.), *Forgotten Man*, p. 323.

[19] Sumner, *Social Classes*, pp. 35, 121.

[20] "The Forgotten Man," Keller (ed.), *Forgotten Man*, p. 487.

who challenge property rights challenge an attribute of man that comes very close to being part of his natural character. "Property," Sumner suggested, "is the first interest of man in time and in importance. We can conceive of no time when property was not, and we can conceive of no social growth in which property was not the prime condition. The property interest is also the one which moves all men, including the socialists, more quickly and deeply than any other."[21] A threat to property rights is, in fact, a threat to man's security, for security is, after all, nothing more than "the assurance that one's own will shall dispose of one's own person and property. For men it applies to the holding and employment of capital without the danger of its being transferred to some one else."[22] Since we cannot foretell the distant future, Sumner would admit that the day may possibly come when private ownership of land will be discarded; "but the grounds for private property in land are easily perceived, and it is safe to say that no *a priori* scheme of state ownership or other tenure invented *en bloc* by any philosopher and adopted by legislative act will ever supplant it."

Legislators and philosophers who seek to undermine the status of property should understand that they are doing nothing less than jeopardizing the existence of civilization. Laws that are inimical to property interest "contain the radical vice of socialism. They demand correction," Sumner asserted, ". . . in the direction of greater purity and security of the right of property."[23] For property "is dear to men, not only for the sensual pleasure which it can afford, but also because it is the bulwark of all which they hold dearest on earth — above all else because it is the safeguard of those they love most against misery and all physical distress."

To Sumner, the thought of securing property immediately called to mind the need to protect the assets of the very rich. "The reason why I defend the millions of the millionaire," he wrote, "is not that I love the millionaire, but that I love my own wife and children, and that I know no way in which to get the defense of society for my hundreds except to give my help, as a member of society, to protect his millions."[24] To those who would not join him in this defense, Sumner promised the gravest of consequences. Whatever assails the

☆

[21] "The Challenge of Facts," Keller (ed.), *Challenge of Facts*, p. 50. "Reply to a Socialist," *ibid.*, p. 61.

[22] "The Theory and Practice of Elections," *Collected Essays in Political and Social Science* (hereafter referred to as *Essays*), Henry Holt and Company, Inc., New York, 1885, pp. 99-100.

[23] "Sociology," Keller (ed.), *War*, pp. 179-180. "The Challenge of Facts," Keller (ed.), *Challenge of Facts*, p. 51.

[24] "The Family and Property," Keller (ed.), *Earth-Hunger*, pp. 268-269.

right of property, he wrote, "or goes in the direction of making it still more uncertain whether the industrious man can dispose of the fruits of his industry for his own interests exclusively, tends directly towards violence, bloodshed, poverty, and misery." "A redistribution of property means universal war . . . Property is the opposite of poverty; it is our bulwark against want and distress, but also against disease and all other ills . . . If we weaken the security of property or deprive people of it, we plunge into distress those who are now above it. Property," Sumner concluded, "is the condition of civilization."[25] And unless this condition is satisfied, all talk about liberty, democracy, and civil rights is essentially meaningless.

Liberty and Equality

Liberty in particular stood in great peril, for if the state succeeded in invading the sanctity of private property, liberty would be the first principle of modern life to be extinguished. Broadly speaking, this would be true because liberty is itself a product of civilization and not, as many believe, vice versa. Theories of presocial inalienable rights were for Sumner simply idle fancies. "I reject any theory of natural rights which has ever been propounded," he stated. "Men are born without any endowment of either physical or metaphysical goods. A man is born to struggle, work, and endure, as long as he can, by the expenditure of his energies." Or, to put the matter a little differently, Sumner insisted that civil "liberty is not a scientific fact. It is not in the order of nature. It is not positive and objective . . . It is historical and institutional." Indeed, it would be "far wiser to think of rights as rules of the game of social competition which are current now and here. They are not absolute. They are not antecedent to civilization."[26] The true definition of liberty makes clear why liberty could not precede the establishment of civilization.

Sumner dealt with the meaning of liberty in many of his works, but perhaps his most complete definition appeared in "Liberty and Responsibility," an essay written sometime between 1887 and 1889. Personal liberty, he explained, as distinct from civil liberty, meant "the chance to fight and struggle for existence for one's self, to the best of one's will and ability, within the bounds of one's personal circumstances, for which other men are not responsible, without any risk of being compelled to fight the struggle for anybody else, and without

☆

[25] "The Challenge of Facts," Keller (ed.), *Challenge of Facts*, p. 51. "Reply to a Socialist," *ibid.*, pp. 60-61.

[26] "The Theory and Practice of Elections," *Essays*, p. 98. "What is Civil Liberty?," Keller (ed.), *Earth-Hunger*, pp. 128-129. "Rights," *ibid.*, p. 83.

any claim to the assistance of anybody else in one's own."[27] *Civil liberty* meant simply an arrangement of legal and political institutions in such a way that an individual is secured the right to keep that which he extracts from nature, or, as Sumner stated elsewhere: "Civil liberty is the status of the man who is guaranteed by law and civil institutions the exclusive employment of all his own powers for his own welfare."[28] This elevated condition was reached long after civilization had been established; prior to civilized life men blindly struggled against nature's forces and seldom lifted themselves above the animal level — let alone to the level of freedom. Liberty, moreover, is a fairly recent product of civilization, occurring only within the last three centuries and dependent upon specified institutional dispositions within society. "Liberty, therefore, is entirely political, and has nothing to do with such hindrances to human effort after happiness as come from nature or lie in the conditions of human life."[29] Being a political "rule of the game," liberty could therefore be contracted or lost by an improper exercise of political power.

It was this imminent possibility that perpetually exercised Sumner. He felt that all of the reform policies, all attempts to right economic imbalances, to curb the rights of property, to legislate in behalf of the lower classes and against the middle and upper classes, would strike a death blow to liberty and thereby eradicate in one unwise moment the progress of civilization that had been slowly and painfully achieved in recent centuries. He wrote: "If we have been wrong for the last three hundred years in aiming at a fuller realization of individual liberty, as a condition of general and widely-diffused happiness, then we must turn back to paternalism, discipline, and authority; but to have a combination of liberty and dependence is impossible." Sumner could see no alternative to liberty, with its attendant risks and adversities, save its total opposite. "If any one thinks that there are or ought to be somewhere in society guarantees that no man shall suffer hardship," he declared, "let him understand that there can be no such guarantees, unless other men give them — that is, unless we go back to slavery, and make one man's effort conduce to another man's welfare."[30]

Implicit in this whole perspective is the rejection of equality, for Sumner sought to legitimize an order that took basic inequality as one

☆

[27] *Ibid.*, p. 198. This definition also fits what Sumner meant by equality before the law, which, he said, "leaves each man to run the race of life for himself as best he can." ("The Challenge of Facts," Keller [ed.], *Challenge of Facts*, p. 45.)

[28] "The Forgotten Man," Keller (ed.), *Forgotten Man*, p. 472.

[29] "The Theory and Practice of Elections," *Essays*, p. 99.

[30] Sumner, *Social Classes*, pp. 98, 65-66.

of its starting points. He could be more than merely implicit on this point. "If there is any place where men are equal," he remarked, "it is not the cradle but the grave." Indeed, equality, at least as the American typically understood it, had no standing in logic or in legal philosophy. Sumner held that political "justice does not include political equality, i.e. equality of political power, much less socialistic equality, i.e. equality of possession and enjoyment in life, for all men; much less for all members of society." Justice merely dictates the enforcement of equality before the law and that rights and obligations fall equally upon those "who are in the same status."[31] The enactment of policies that seek to "remedy" social and economic inequality will end in disaster for everyone. By such policies, Sumner maintained, we "shall favor the survival of the unfittest, and we shall accomplish this by destroying liberty." Sumner insisted that only two choices lay before society. "Let it be understood," he said, "that we cannot go outside of this alternative: liberty, inequality, survival of the fittest; not-liberty, equality, survival of the unfittest. The former carries society forward and favors all its best members; the latter carries society downwards and favors all its worst members."[32]

It would be suicidal for any society to choose the latter course. For America to select this alternative would, in Sumner's eyes, be unutterably tragic. He believed that America, above all nations, exemplified that which a people dedicated to liberty might achieve. "It is the glory of the United States," he wrote, "and its calling in history, that it shows what the power of personal liberty is—what self-reliance, energy, enterprise, hard sense men can develop when they have room and liberty and when they are emancipated from the burden of traditions and faiths which are nothing but the accumulated follies and blunders of a hundred generations of 'statesmen.'"[33] It was, in other words, America's obligation to maintain its national purpose—and consequently its greatness—and to resist those who would offer novel purposes in the name of necessary reform.

Lessons of the Past

Sumner said all of these things and he meant them, and he hoped, moreover, that his words might have some impact on his audience. It would, nevertheless, be unfair to allow Sumner's Darwinian endorsement of economic individualism to stand as the sum and substance of his philosophy. Sumner's views seemed to vary with his distance from

☆

[31] "The Theory and Practice of Elections," *Essays*, pp. 102, 101.

[32] "The Challenge of Facts," Keller (ed.), *Challenge of Facts*, p. 25.

[33] "State Interference," Keller (ed.), *War*, p. 219.

his subject matter. Absorbed in an immediate question of policy his remarks tended to be pronounced and somewhat strident. Slightly removed from the subject at hand, he tended to expound the views of a traditional conservatism that had obvious roots in the ideas of Burke. At his furthest remove, Sumner's conservatism took on universal proportions as he reflected on the past and future of all civilization in categories that were frequently transcendental, if not cosmic, in their application.

These three perspectives formed a continuum along which Sumner's ideas moved. The only problem in terms of understanding his philosophy is that he sometimes went from one end of the continuum to the other within the confines of a single essay. We have already seen small indications of this in Sumner's espousal of the national ideology and his simultaneous repudiation of majoritarian and equalitarian principles, principles that had become — at least on the rhetorical level — fixed ingredients in the national purpose since the days of Jackson. Notwithstanding this difficulty, we will follow Sumner to his higher levels of abstraction in the attempt to understand his largest view of politics and the progress of civilization.

History and Democracy

Like Emerson, Sumner sometimes felt that his readers did not grasp his main position, and in this he was probably correct. This difficulty arose because Sumner's starting point and that of his audience were for the most part radically different. The American thought of himself as a member of a young society, and his historical sense scarcely comprehended that which preceded the American Revolution. Oriented to such an immediate and affluent past, he took his nation's political ideals and material success for granted and, at the same time, he could display keen disappointment when that success was not forthcoming to him personally; when this happened he felt somehow that the political ideals were being dishonored.

Sumner, on the other hand, avidly studied the history of man dating back to precivilized epochs, and he extracted from this study the distressing but unavoidable knowledge that man's tenure on earth had comprised little more than a record of incessant exertion simply to keep the human species going. He therefore regarded the existence of *any* social life beyond the subsistence level as a wonderful achievement. "The real marvel," he wrote, "is that civilization has triumphed so far that, in three or four great civilized nations, a few million people can so far control the condition of existence that they can live their lives out in peace and security."[34] Sumner took it as one of his respon-

☆

[34]"The Predicament of Sociological Study," Keller (ed.), *Challenge of Facts*, p. 421.

sibilities to make people understand this fact. Everyone must come to realize that the "institutions which we possess have cost something. Few people," he lamented, "seem to know how much — it is one of the great defects of our education that we are not in a position to teach the history of civilization in such a way as to train even educated men to know the cost at which everything which to-day separates us from the brutes has been bought by the generations which have preceded us."[35] The American accomplishment in particular is a product neither of ideals nor, in the first instance, of institutions. Both ideals and institutions derived from preexisting natural factors that in the end dictated their form and much of their content.

In reviewing the post-revolutionary history of the nation, Sumner offered an explanation of American democracy that presaged by over half a century the similar analysis that would be made by Daniel Boorstin and other contemporary historians. "Democracy," he contended, ". . . was, and still is . . . deeply rooted in the physical and economic circumstances of the United States." Sumner's rendering of the evolution of this phenomenon deserves lengthy quotation.

> The great mass of the population found themselves steadily gaining in property and comfort. Their independence and self-reliance expanded . . . They had full confidence in their own powers, feared no difficulties, made light of experience, were ready to deal offhand with any problems, laughed at their own mistakes, despised science and study, overestimated the practical man, and overesteemed material good. To such a class the doctrines of democracy seemed axiomatic, and they ascribed to democracy the benefits which accrued to them as the first-comers in a new country. They generally believed that the political system created their prosperity; and they never perceived that the very bountifulness of the new country, the simplicity of life, and the general looseness of the social organism, allowed their blunders to pass without evil results which would have followed in an older and denser community. The same causes have produced similar results ever since.

For those who spoke of the triumph of democracy or of the historical wisdom of the people, Sumner had a quick and simple reply. "We have not made America," he said, "America has made us."[36] And as with America, so it was everywhere in the world.

The Impact of Nature

The Darwinian perception made a belief in environmentalism mandatory, since it held that all species, man included, change by adapting

---

☆

[35] "The New Social Issue," Keller (ed.), *Challenge of Facts*, p. 208.

[36] "Politics in America, 1776-1876," Keller (ed.), *Forgotten Man*, pp. 291, 306-307. "Advancing Social and Political Organization in the United States," Keller (ed.), *Challenge of Facts*, p. 304.

(or failing to adapt) to changes that occur in the external world. As far as the movement of civilization is concerned, the single most important cause of change derives from the relation between population numbers and the amount of land and resources available at a given moment in time. When "the actual number present is very much less than the number who might be supported, the condition of all must be ample and easy. Freedom and facility mark all social relations under such a state of things."[37] The tendency in this situation is for society to be organized along democratic lines.

On the theoretical level, many of the concepts of liberal democratic thought, which Sumner placed under the general heading of "humanitarianism," originate in the favorable balance between men and their environment. "The ultimate explanation of the rise of humanitarianism," Sumner noted, "is the increased power of man over nature by the acquisition of new land, and by advance in the arts. When men ceased to crowd on each other, they were all willing to adopt ideas and institutions which made the competition of life easy and kindly."[38] As advances become increasingly worldwide in compass they generate a felicity of outlook that permeates all levels of thought. "The human race," Sumner indicated, "is going through a period of enlargement with ease and comfort; accordingly a philosophy of optimism prevails, and the world-beatifiers reign in philosophy. Since, as a fact, the struggle for existence and competition of life are not severe, the philosophy prevails that so they always ought to be. An ethical ideal is carried into nature."[39]

To project this ideal onto nature was wrong for many reasons. Sumner argued that social progress is a function of the contest *against* nature, when her resources are in relatively short supply: "It is when the social pressure due to an unfavorable ratio of population to land becomes intense that the social forces develop increased activity. Division of labor, exchange, higher social organization, emigration, advance in the arts, spring from the necessity of contending against the harsher conditions of existence which are continually reproduced as the population surpasses the means of existence on any given status."[40] There appears, however, to be a point beyond which an unfavorable ratio operated directly to the disadvantage of social progress. Indeed, it is under this condition that the "struggle for existence" degenerates into the "competition of life." "It is," according to Sumner, "when two men are striving side by side . . . to extort from nature the supplies they need, that they come into rivalry and a collision of

☆

[37] "Sociology," Keller (ed.), *War*, p. 174.

[38] Sumner, *Folkways*, Ginn and Company, Boston, 1906, p. 39.

[39] "The Mores of the Present and the Future," Keller (ed.), *War*, p. 159.

[40] "Sociology," *ibid.*, p. 174.

interest with each other takes place."[41] Society at this point is dreadful to behold. "The finer sentiments decline; selfishness comes out again from the repression under which culture binds it; the social tie is loosened . . . Men are habituated to see distorted bodies, harsh and frightful diseases, famine and pestilence; they find out what depths of debasement humanity is capable of. Hideous crimes are perpetrated; monstrous superstitions are embraced even by the most cultivated members of society; vices otherwise inconceivable become common, and fester in the mass of society; culture is lost, education dies out; the arts and sciences decline."[42] It is, in short, a time when civilization itself stands on the brink of annihilation. Moreover, despite the current superabundance, it is also a time that could quickly reappear on the face of the globe.

The benign aspect of contemporary arrangements allows ephemeral illusion to pass for ultimate reality. "The new status," wrote Sumner, "makes us believe in all kinds of rosy doctrines about human welfare, and about the struggle for existence and the competition of life; it also gives us all our contempt for old-fashioned kings and nobles, creates democracies, and brings forth new social classes and gives them power. For the time being things are so turned about that numbers are a source of power . . . Why then should we not join in dithyrambic oratory, and set all our mores to optimism? The reason is because the existing status is temporary and the conditions in it are evanescent." When things change, as they must, democracy will become a thing of the past, for democracy cannot thrive when times are hard. When population pressures breed increased inequality, a social aristocracy will arise and eventually grow into a political aristocracy. "The United States," Sumner felt, "are far from having reached any such state as yet,"[43] but a word of caution was certainly in order.

Sumner was not clear as to whether the desperate life of overpopulation appeared coterminously with the advent of aristocratic rule, or whether aristocracy might characterize that period of pronounced progress engendered by *moderate* insufficiency. He frequently seemed to indicate that progress could be supervised by an enlightened elite. In fact, he appeared far more concerned that the democratic masses would condense time and plunge society directly into the abyss of dire scarcity. It is in this context that we must understand his strictures against anticapital legislation. Civilization is at

☆

[41] "War," *ibid.*, p. 9.

[42] "The Significance of the Demand for Men," Keller (ed.), *Challenge of Facts*, pp. 120-121.

[43] Sumner, *Folkways*, p. 163. "Politics in America, 1776-1876," Keller (ed.), *Forgotten Man*, p. 292. See also Sumner, *Folkways*, pp. 50, 53.

best a fragile creation and a series of wrong moves could virtually destroy it. It is particularly the case that laws or institutions that work against capital tend "to produce a large population, sunk in misery. All poor laws and all eleemosynary institutions and expenditures have this tendency. On the contrary, all laws and institutions that give security to capital against the interests of other persons than its owners, restrict numbers while preserving the means of subsistence. Hence every such law or institution tends to produce a small society on a high stage of comfort and well-being."[44] Ministers of reform, in other words, totally misapprehend the realities of social evolution and, if followed completely, their preachment can only lead civilization to decay and ruin.

The Conservative Viewpoint

The Case for the Status Quo

Noting Sumner's pessimism, it is not surprising to find that he took the conservative side on most important issues. Generally speaking, he believed that the presumption is always in favor of that which exists for the very reason of its existence. Echoing Burke, he stated that the "institutions whose growth constitutes the advance of civilization have their guarantee in the very fact that they grew and became established. They suited men's purpose better than what went before. They are all imperfect, and all carry with them incidental ills, but each came to be because it was better than what went before, and each of which has perished, perished because a better one supplanted it." Since this is the case it is foolish and almost unnatural to attempt to unseat time-honored institutions by means of radical schemes for political change. Society must not be tampered with on impulse. By way of analogy Sumner suggested that it "may pay to experiment with an individual, because he cannot wait for medical science to be perfected; it cannot pay to experiment with a society, because the society does not die and can afford to wait."[45]

   Sumner continually counseled patience and self-restraint to those who felt provoked to move for dramatic alterations. "Wait for the occasion," he cautioned. "Do not attempt to generalize those interferences or to plan for them *a priori*. We have a body of laws and institutions which have grown up as occasion has occurred for adjusting rights. Let the same process go on . . . and by no means seize occasion for interfering with natural adjustments."[46] The reference to

☆

[44] "The Challenge of Facts," Keller (ed.), *Challenge of Facts*, pp. 27-28.

[45] "Sociology," Keller (ed.), *War*, pp. 179, 172.

[46] Sumner, *Social Classes*, pp. 120-121.

a priori judgments was particularly crucial, for Sumner, believing his own views to be the product of experience and deductive reasoning, could not tolerate suggestions for reform that he felt stemmed from preconceived ideas. "Any legislation which does not proceed out of antecedants, but is invented in order to attain to ideals," he argued, "is necessarily speculative; it deals with unverified and unverifiable propositions and lacks all guarantees of its practicability or of the nature of its results." The most notable example of speculative legislation that Sumner could think of was the passage of the Interstate Commerce Act. The establishment of the Interstate Commerce Commission, America's first independent regulatory agency, embodied everything that could be wrong in public policy: it did not emerge as a result of growth, "i.e. by movement which is guided from behind, which springs from antecedent facts, which advances by imperceptible stages, and which builds and unbuilds at the same time by infinitesimal small degrees."[47]

The fact is that attempts to induce basic social changes through political channels must always founder, since they will never penetrate beneath the surface of society. This is the case, according to Sumner, because "all the life of human beings, in all ages and stages of culture, is primarily controlled by a vast mass of folkways handed down from the earliest existence of the race . . . only the topmost layers of which are subject to change and control, and have been somewhat modified by human philosophy, ethics, and religion, or by other acts of intelligent reflection."[48] Stated in such uncompromising terms, this proposition, which appears innumerable times in Sumner, raises problems with respect to his antireformist argument, for if it were true that the folkways exercise such encompassing dominance over social trends, then it would seem logical simply to dismiss radical reformers either as crackpots who must eventually see the light and adapt to natural ways, or as misfits who will ultimately find themselves cast into the backwash of historical progress. Sumner, however, was simply inconsistent in this regard, and he vacillated between outright derogation of social uplift advocates and strenuous argumentation against their malicious proposals.

Conservative Action and the Demos

This problem is made still more complex by the fact that it was not always the extreme minority that aggravated Sumner, but occasionally the practices of society as a whole evoked his scorn. Sumner was

☆

[47] "Speculative Legislation," Keller (ed.), *Challenge of Facts*, p. 215. "The Theory and Practice of Elections," *Essays*, p. 102.

[48] Sumner, *Folkways*, p. 4.

considerably attracted by the constitutional republicanism of the Founding Fathers, and he believed that much of its wisdom had been adulterated over the generations by the incursions of the majority. Ironically, he placed the burden of remedying excessive majoritarianism — certainly a stupendous task in light of its deep infusion into the American system — on the shoulders of conservatives, those who presumably would otherwise be concerned with resisting change. We "have need," Sumner told them, "of the same sense of duty which has animated all the heroes of constitutional government and civil liberty, and I am not sure but we need some of their courage also, for it demands at least as much moral courage to beard King Majority as it ever did to beard King Caesar. Nothing less than the experiment of self-government is at stake . . . Such . . . I conceive to be the calling of the conservative class of this country, at least for this generation . . . We have got to face the problems like men, animated by patriotism, acting with business-like energy, standing together for the common weal. Whenever we do that we cannot fail of success in getting what we want." [49] Sumner's only defense of what seems a plea for conservative action was a rather weak qualification of conservatism itself. While the inability of man to comprehend the vast workings of the universe made conservatism the only position, he insisted that we do not "need to resist all change or discussion — that is not conservatism. We may, however, be sure that the only possible good for society must come of evolution not of revolution." [50] But the concept of active conservatism scarcely eliminates the inconsistencies, for Sumner inextricably linked the majority rule principle to the democratic system, and his attack was ultimately directed against democracy itself.

Inconsistent or not, Sumner did not hesitate to launch this attack. Democracy, he repeated time and again, was simply the by-product of economic development, and at best it provided a certain "looseness and simplicity" that gave social competition room in which to operate. Paradoxically, this looseness has had the unintended virtue of producing inequality because it allows merit to seek its natural level in all domains, save the political; "in other words, liberty has tended to destroy equality in other spheres, and since the doctrine of equality prevailed in politics, the contradictions between political and social development are readily explained." [51] But the stress on equality in the political realm was critically important, since political equalitarianism could vitiate the gains made in other areas.

In reading Sumner, however, it is difficult to be certain about the amount of damage he thought the majority could actually inflict. A

☆

[49] "The Administration of Andrew Jackson," Keller (ed.), *Forgotten Man*, pp. 366-367.

[50] "The New Social Issue," Keller (ed.), *Challenge of Facts*, p. 207.

[51] "Democracy and Responsible Government," *ibid.*, p. 274.

certain ambivalence is revealed in the following quotation in which Sumner states that democracy is conducive to social disintegration, and therefore to manipulation by interests, for no sooner does he make this case than he appears to retract it. He begins by arguing that "democracy is atomistic. It breaks the society up into individuals who are political units. The peril of such a system is that it is at the mercy of any organization formed inside of it which gives coherence and order to its disintegrated elements. Such an organization will begin to move the whole . . . If individualism destroys institutions, and if democracy, with its dream of equality, simply works disintegration, the society is at the sport of the new elements which combine and organize on new centers, for," Sumner concludes curiously, "*actual disintegration and atomization is impossible.*"[52] The difference between "disintegration" and "*actual* disintegration" is not made clear, but suggests a similar difference between Sumner's levels of thought, one of which could view democracy as the agent of social destruction, while the other would see society as fundamentally indestructible despite a profusion of dangerous elements.[53] The latter view dominates when Sumner is at his most abstract.

In his discussion of the masses in *Folkways*, it is hard to understand how in its languid state the masses could ever be moved to destructive action, let alone become disintegrated. "The masses," Sumner wrote, "are not large classes at the base of a social pyramid; they are the core of the society. They are conservative. They accept life as they find it and live on by tradition and habit. In other words, the great mass of any society lives a purely instinctive life just like animals . . . The conservatism of the masses . . . is not produced by interests, but it is instinctive." The mass, Sumner added a few pages later, is "a great body which is neutral in all the policy of society . . . It is not brutal, but it is shallow, narrow-minded, and prejudiced. Nevertheless it is harmless. It lacks initiative and cannot give an impulse for good or bad . . . It can sometimes be moved by appeals to its fixed ideas and prejudices. It is affected in its mores by contagion from the classes above it. The work of popularization consists in bringing about this contagion."[54] Mass mores can never be engineered and the best that great leaders and reformers have ever done is to take hold of "new currents in the mores," tendencies of which the society is

☆

[52] "Separation of State and Market," Keller (ed.), *Earth-Hunger*, pp. 308-309.

[53] In a like vein, see Sumner's distinction between "political machinery" and "political will," a distinction which allows him to conclude that because of the purity of the latter, American society is not degenerating, although there is pronounced deterioration in its political machinery. ("Politics in America, 1776-1876," Keller [ed.], *Forgotten Man*, p. 333.)

[54] Sumner, *Folkways*, pp. 12, 16, 43.

becoming aware, and help carry them into complete consciousness. We will examine in a moment the nature of "class contagion from above," which Sumner alludes to, but first it must be noted that despite its innate lethargy and conservatism, the masses, in Sumner's narrower view, could, at least in a democracy, be seen as dangerous in the extreme.

To begin, citizens in a democratic society are totally devoid of historical perspective. "Democracy," Sumner noted, also in *Folkways*, "is . . . indifferent to history, and the dogmas of democracy make history unimportant. If 'the people' [the masses?] always know what is right and wise," Sumner added acidly, "then we have the supreme oracle always with us and always up to date."[55] The very fact that democracy operates on the basis of dogma is cause for alarm. The great achievement of early American constitutionalism was that it evolved a method, a "system of rule," as opposed to a political theory, by which conflicting interests could be handled in an impartial manner. But in its commitment to the majority principle, democracy has abandoned this system and has become the embodiment of a doctrinal political theory. Of the two main principles of this theory—that man should be esteemed for what he is worth and that all men ought to be equal in possession—only the former, to the limited extent it is attainable, is socially productive.[56] The attempt to realize the latter can only carry society to a most unfortunate end.

The Perils of Plutocracy

If one were to ask Sumner what terrible destiny awaited a democracy that misunderstood history and acted on the basis of mindless dogma, his answer would, perhaps unexpectedly, be: the rise of plutocracy. Although Sumner believed wholeheartedly in giving capital its due, he also believed that the power of capital ought to be kept exclusively within the economic and commercial spheres, and not be allowed to exert inordinate influence on the political realm. Although he knew that political power and wealth frequently coalesced, Sumner did not feel that this combination always reached dangerous proportions. "A great capitalist," he argued, "is no more necessarily a plutocrat than a great general is a tyrant. A plutocrat is a man who, having the possession of capital, and having the power of it at his disposal, uses it, not industrially, but politically; instead of employing laborers, he enlists lobbyists. Instead of applying capital to land, he operates upon the

☆

[55] *Ibid.*, p. 637.

[56] "Politics in America, 1776-1876," Keller (ed.), *Forgotten Man*, pp. 290 et seq.

market by legislation, by artificial monopoly, by legislative privileges."[57] Sumner could scarcely imagine a more sinister turn of events than one that transformed the capitalist into a plutocrat. "I regard plutocracy," he said, ". . . as the most sordid and debasing form of political energy known to us. In its motive, its processes, its code, and its sanctions it is infinitely corrupting to all the institutions which ought to preserve and protect society." It seemed to Sumner that democracy did little but encourage this depressing transformation. "There is no form of political power which is so ill-fitted to cope with plutocracy as democracy," he contended. In atomizing society, democracy permits interests to develop as power centers that seek to influence public policy in order to maximize their own pecuniary gain. "Here," Sumner noted, "is where the plutocratic element finds entrance into the democratic system, and here lies the weakness of democracy."[58]

It is difficult to be certain of Sumner's conception of this weakness. Recalling his remark about the contagion of the masses from above, one can imagine that he had in mind a majority that could be bought and sold by an aristocracy of wealth. This appears to be his position in at least one essay where he described at length a class of citizens that has come to be perpetually on the make because it accepts the popular belief that everyone ought to enjoy comfort and luxury. "The principle of plutocracy," Sumner continued, "is that money buys whatever the owner of money wants, and the class just described are made to be its instruments."[59] But elsewhere he seemed to indicate that it is more than just their base habits that make the masses vulnerable to exploitation, that more important is the fact that they attempt to gratify their desires through political means at the expense of the wealthy.

In other words, it is the invasion of politics by the economically oriented masses that causes the men of wealth to retaliate in kind, thus corrupting the whole system. For this reason Sumner warned the reformists that their remedies would engender problems far greater than those they thought now existed. Be aware of what you are changing, he told them. "We may find that instead of democratizing capitalism we have capitalized democracy—that is have brought in plutocracy."[60] As things stand, the power of wealth is chiefly industrial and social, and only slightly political. Political radicalism, how-

☆

[57] "Definitions of Democracy and Plutocracy," Keller (ed.), *Earth-Hunger*, p. 298.

[58] *Ibid.*, pp. 295, 299. "Separation of State and Market," *ibid.*, p. 309.

[59] "Definitions of Democracy and Plutocracy," *ibid.*, p. 294.

[60] "The Absurd Effort to Make the World Over," Keller (ed.), *War*, pp. 206-207.

ever, will bring capital totally into the political sphere, and it was the possibility of this total commitment that Sumner feared. "This," he wrote, "is the thing which seems to me to be really new and really threatening; there have been states in which there have been large plutocratic elements, but none in which wealth seemed to have such absorbing and controlling power as it threatens us."[61] Of course, whether it was more or less natural or in retaliation that wealth began to penetrate politics, its plutocratic tendencies could only come into play if wealth itself were overly valued by the masses, for even powerful influences from above could never do more than take advantage of preexisting majoritarian propensities. This, according to Sumner, exactly described contemporary conditions where the "thirst for luxury," as he called it, had become all-pervasive.

Theoretical Complexities

The difficulty in Sumner's call for a conservative corrective is that the lust for riches had come to dominate all social classes, high as well as low. Sumner believed that men of means could, if they tried, divorce their economic interests from their interest in the political affairs of the nation and, furthermore, that rich men had an obligation to concern themselves in an objective way with questions of public policy. In America, however, this had not occurred, and Sumner could only see plutocratic rule as the unhappy consequence. He argued that "men of true culture, high character, and correct training can abandon public political effort only by the surrender of some of the best interests of themselves and their posterity. The pursuit of wealth, which is the natural alternative, has always absorbed far too much of the ambition of the nation, and under such circumstances there could be no other result than that a wealthy class should arise, to whom wealth offers no honorable social power, in whom it awakens no intellectual or political ambition, to whom it brings no sense of responsibility, but for whom it means simply the ability to buy what they want, men or measures, and to enjoy sensual luxury."[62] This formulation makes one wonder about Sumner's hope for improvement. His suggestion about minding one's own business and advancing one's self-interest apparently had serious qualifications attached to it. The pursuit of wealth was apparently a very healthy activity as long as it did not become all-consuming for all classes. Sumner placed himself in the logically

☆

[61] "Definitions of Democracy and Plutocracy," Keller (ed.), *Earth-Hunger*, p. 293.
[62] "Politics in America, 1776-1876," Keller (ed.), *Forgotten Man*, p. 295.

difficult position of simultaneously advocating self-aggrandizement and self-restraint.

Even more difficult would be the task of the conservative, for he would have to "beard the minority," as well as the majority, since both were engrossed in the desire for wealth. What this attempt would look like in practice is hard to say. Presumably the conservative would have to call for self-abnegation on the part of upper classes (the conservatives?) in the hope that they would rise above social mores and influence the majority, insofar as possible, to follow other directions. But this possibility seems especially remote when one considers the status occupied by the mores. They stand on faith. "They are not affected by scientific facts or demonstration," wrote Sumner. "We 'believe in' democracy, as we have been brought up in it, or we do not. If we do, we accept its mythology . . . Argument would not touch this faith." The conclusion to be drawn from this condition is obvious and, in his darker moments, Sumner drew it.

Generally he seemed to feel that there was still time for effective action. In *Folkways* he wrote: "modern financiers, masters of industry, merchants, and transporters now hold control of movable capital. They hold social and political power. They have not yet formed a caste of nobles, but they may do so."[63] In much of his other writing, however, the possibility of plutocracy moved to a very high degree of probability. "We have no democracy now," Sumner wrote in a 1904 essay; "all the institutions are broken down; they are turned into oligarchies. The captains of industry and other great leaders in industrial enterprise do not mind this, for it gives them something which they can deal with better."[64] With the capitalist thus discredited, there could be little hope for the rest of society.

Rights and Duties

The Rights of Labor

Like many conservatives before him, Sumner hoped that a higher class could distinguish its private interests from those of the nation and could thereby emerge in a position of social and political leadership. Also in keeping with the traditional conservative perspective was Sumner's understanding of the plight of the lower classes. While social critics were filling the air with protests against the inhumane treatment of working men, Sumner informed the proletariat that their

☆

[63] Sumner, *Folkways*, pp. 98, 162.

[64] "Economics and Politics," Keller (ed.), *Earth-Hunger*, pp. 329-330.

condition was far better than they realized. The protests themselves indicated this. "I maintain," he said, "that the progress of the arts and sciences in the last hundred years has inured most of all to the benefit of the non-capitalists and that the social agitation which we are now witnessing is a proof of the strength, not of the weakness, of that class. If any one wants to see how weak classes have been treated in all ages of the world, let him note how landlords are treated now."

Indeed, as history has unfolded it can be seen that *all* classes have benefited from social progress. "There is not a person in a civilized state," Sumner asserted, "who does not share in the inheritance of institutions, knowledge, ideas, doctrines, etc., which come down as fruits of civilization; we take these things in by habit and routine, and suppose that they come of themselves or are innate."[65] The claim that workers are badly off is simply untrue, and therefore their appeal for special protection is without merit. "The wage-class is not a pauper class," Sumner stated. "It is not a petitioner for bounty nor a social burden. The problem of how that part of society is to earn its living is not a public question . . . The question how to earn one's living, or the best living possible in one's circumstances, is the most distinctly individual question that can be raised." And the context in which this question is asked is conducive to the most optimistic expectations, for it "is a fact that the great masses of the human race get on very well with a minimum of education, for the conditions favor most, proportionately, those who are worst off—the unskilled laborers."[66] The work of the common man suits him very well, and from his rather lofty position in the academy Sumner permitted himself to comment on the nature of that work. "Labor does not brutalize," he remarked. "The people who are accustomed to factory work are not conscious of the hardships which a literary man may easily imagine they must feel in it, any more than other men are conscious of hardship in the confinement of the editorial sanctum or the laboratory. It is only in literature or in the semi-loafer class that we find people actually reflecting and moralizing and complaining about whether the way in which they get their living is irksome."[67]

The solution advocated by such moralizers warranted caricature and Sumner amused himself in the 1870's and 1880's by imagining the state of things in a socialist system. He did this by conjuring up, in rather heavy-handed satire, the contents of a socialist newspaper, the *New Era*, July 4, 1950 edition. By way of depicting the new society,

☆

[65] "Who Win By Progress?" Keller (ed.), *Challenge of Facts*, pp. 170-171. "Sociological Fallacies," Keller (ed.), *Earth-Hunger*, p. 358.

[66] "Industrial War," Keller (ed.), *Challenge of Facts*, p. 95.

[67] "Liberty and Responsibility," Keller (ed.), *Earth-Hunger*, p. 193.

one of the reports quotes from the inaugural address of the former socialist chief-of-state, the Grand Past Master Cooperator. *"Of old ye were enslaved by those who said: Work! Save! Study! We emancipate you by saying: Enjoy! Enjoy! Enjoy!"*[68] Sumner was not necessarily against enjoyment itself; he simply felt that the workers had to achieve their own rewards by their own hands. "The laborers about whom we are talking," he said, "are free men in a free state. If they want to be protected they must protect themselves." Part of their failure to organize for protection is due to the individual worker being so strong and so mobile.[69]

On moral grounds the worker owes it to himself to remain in this position, to retain his freedom and independence. This requires that he avoid certain involvements. He must not, for example, be beholden to anyone, for, Sumner argued, one "who takes a favor or submits to patronage demeans himself. He falls under obligation. He cannot be free and he cannot assert a station of equality with the man who confers the favor on him . . . Therefore, in a country which is a free democracy, all propositions to do something for the working classes have an air of patronage and superiority which is impertinent and out of place."[70] If this idea recalls a similar expression by Emerson, Sumner could carry the argument even further and find, like Emerson, compensatory factors in the nature of things that suggest a general condition of balance. He observed that there is "a certain law of compensation [which] runs through human life, by virtue of which, when all things are taken into account—health, wealth, talent, fame, power, domestic relations, and all other elements of human happiness—the lot of men on earth, at least within the same political body, is far more equal than the sentimentalists, the agitators, and the discontented are willing to admit."[71]

Sumner's conclusion from all of this was that the lower classes should leave well enough alone. Relatively speaking, they occupy an exceptionally favorable status, a status, however, that could be easily lost should the complex connections of modern civilization be broken at their hand. "If the society does not keep up its power," Sumner warned them, "if it lowers its organization or wastes its capital, it falls back toward the natural state of barbarism from which it rose, and in so doing it must sacrifice thousands of its weakest members. Hence human society lives at a constant strain forward and upward, and those who have most interest that this strain be successfully kept up, that

☆

[68] "The Cooperative Commonwealth," Keller (ed.), *Forgotten Man*, p. 443.

[69] Sumner, *Social Classes*, pp. 95, 96.

[70] "The Forgotten Man," Keller (ed.), *Forgotten Man*, p. 477.

[71] "The Theory and Practice of Elections," *Essays*, p. 102.

the social organization be perfected, and that capital be increased, are those at the bottom."[72] In other words, if men found that the "strain forward and upward" created serious stresses in their daily lives, they should learn to live with these burdens, for they are nothing compared to what they would be if the strain were removed.

But this was not Sumner's last word on the problem of the worker. While hardly sensitive to the abuses of labor that scores of contemporary writers were daily bringing before the nation, Sumner was not unmindful of what he took to be the *rights* of labor. As in the case of the rich, Sumner had little objection to labor's use of power, so long as it kept within its proper sphere, and he devoted substantial space to justifying labor's power in *What Social Classes Owe to Each Other.*[73]

Sumner thought it perfectly legitimate for workers to seek improvements in safety, sanitation, hours for women and children, length of the work week, and so forth, and he even felt that, as an absolutely last resort, the strike constituted a justifiable use of power. He believed fully in the obligations of contract—a contract once agreed to "binds the liberty" of the workman—and he believed that contracts in practice most benefitted the laborer by freeing him of economic responsibility. Despite this conviction Sumner realistically understood that the employer held the upper hand and that certain factors were common to all workers. "Those," he wrote, "who have neither capital nor land unquestionably have a closer class interest than landlords or capitalists." The way to effectuate that class interest, Sumner was frank to acknowledge, was to organize. He argued that the idea "that a true adjustment . . . follows from the free play of interests [cannot] be construed to mean that an interest which is neglected will get its rights. The employes have no means of information which is as good and legitimate as association, and it is fair and necessary that their action should be united on behalf of their interests. They are not in a position for the unrestricted development of individualism in respect to many of their interests." Sumner's endorsement of unionism was not without reservation, however. "Unquestionably," he continued, "the better ones lose by this, and the development of individualism is to be looked forward to and hoped for as a great gain. In the mean time the labor market, in which wages are fixed, cannot reach fair adjustments unless the interest of the laborers is fairly defended, and that cannot, perhaps, yet be done without association of laborers." While not exactly a ringing declaration in behalf of the trade union movement, this qualified support of temporary unionism apparently served to extend the perimeters of Sumner's philosophy.

☆

[72] Sumner, *Social Classes*, pp. 67-68.

[73] The materials quoted in the following discussion are taken from pages 79-163.

Voluntary Associations and Equality of Opportunity

Although it might be unreasonable to expect individualism to evolve out of association—"All organization," Sumner wrote elsewhere, "implies a restriction of liberty. The gain of power is won by narrowing individual range"[74]—the central message of *What Social Classes Owe to Each Other* seems to be that all such associations should be encouraged; the work, in other words, expounds the doctrine of social, but not *political*, pluralism. "The chief need," Sumner suggested, "seems to be more power of voluntary combination and co-operation among those who are aggrieved. Such co-operation is a constant necessity under free self-government; and when, in any community, men lose the power of voluntary co-operation in furtherance or defence of their own interests, they deserve to suffer." Whether on logical grounds this argument fits into Sumner's overall schema, Sumner himself found that it squared entirely with his explication of civil liberty. Thus, if one were to ask, what *do* social classes owe each other, Sumner was prepared with an immediate answer: the *chance* to help themselves.

He held that whenever "a law or social arrangement acts so as to injure any one, and that one the humblest, then there is a duty on those who are stronger, or who know better, to demand and fight for redress and correction. When generalized this means that it is the duty of All-of-us (that is, the State) to establish justice for all, from the least to the greatest, and in all matters. This, however, is no new doctrine. It is only the old, true, and indisputable function of the State . . ." So it would not be misunderstood, Sumner explained further what is meant by this duty. "We each owe it to the other," he continued, "to guarantee rights. Rights do not pertain to *results,* but only to *chances.* They pertain to the *conditions* of the struggle for existence, not to any of the results of it; to the *pursuit* of happiness, not to the possession of happiness." In short, Sumner wished, like Madison, to see interests completely secure in their right to associate and in their right to take action in their own behest; and, also like Madison, he believed the interests of the nation would best be served if these associations, especially when they comprised a majority, kept their demands primarily social and economic, and outside of the political arena.

Pluralism and the Organic State

If Sumner followed Madison in this desire, he could follow the Madisonian conception of political structure only with difficulty and only to a degree, for his own view of the nature of society made complete ac-

☆

[74]"The Absurd Effort to Make the World Over," Keller (ed.), *War*, pp. 197-198.

ceptance of the Madisonian formulation impossible. Like Madison, and perhaps more clearly than Madison, Sumner placed government in a proper pluralistic perspective. "The state," he said, "exists to provide justice, but the state is only one among a number of social organizations. It is parallel with the others, and has its own functions. To confuse the state with society is to produce a variety of errors, not the least of which is to smuggle statecraft into political economy."[75] With respect to statecraft alone, Sumner, operating purely on his conservative level, was forced to admit that the Madisonian model had much to be said for it. Since in all societies there exists a ruling class that, once in authority, can be expected to abuse its power, Sumner held that the "task of constitutional government is to devise institutions which shall come into play at the critical periods to prevent the abusive control of the powers of a state by the controlling classes in it . . . In honor of the bourgeoisie it must be said that they have invented institutions of civil liberty which secure to all safety of person and property."[76] But when Sumner thought more narrowly about contemporary abuses of power, or when he began to fill in the content of his conservatism—considered those institutions which *in fact* merited conservation—his tribute to the bourgeoisie would be quickly retracted in favor of an overriding concern for the safety of person and property, especially of property.

In its fullest statement of balanced power, Madisonianism was for Sumner an unacceptable form of government, for, strictly speaking, it led to total political inaction. "The old writers," Sumner noted, "thought that good government could be secured by a division of departments and a system of checks and balances. But the division of departments—if it means that we need only make them sufficiently independent of one another and then that they will be sure to go right—is an empty dogma; and the system of checks and balances, if it were perfect, would bring equilibrium—that is, no movement at all. The more difficult task," Sumner felt, "is to secure harmonious action, in due proportion, without friction—in other words, to give to political organs an organic instead of a mechanical activity."[77] Mechanistic controls would naturally be out of place in society conceived of as an organism; but the introduction of the organic metaphor causes problems in interpreting Sumner similar to those encountered in analyzing Calhoun.

Before turning to this difficulty, however, it is worth noting that the organic conception, especially with its Darwinian attributes of

☆

[75] "Sociological Fallacies," Keller (ed.), *Earth-Hunger*, p. 364.

[76] Sumner, *Folkways*, p. 169.

[77] "Democracy and Responsible Government," Keller (ed.), *Challenge of Facts*, p. 283.

growth and progress, made it a foregone conclusion that Sumner would reject an equilibrium model. Again the factor of Sumner's levels of analysis is relevant. In his most contracted view, which we have already seen, Sumner reproached government for its illegitimate intervention in society. In this frame of mind Sumner concluded that "the way to minimize the dangers to democracy, and from it, is to reduce to the utmost its functions, the number of its officials, the range of its taxing power, the variety of its modes of impinging on the individual, the amount and range of its expenditures, and, in short, its total weight."[78] However salutary such reforms might normally be, Sumner, from an organicist point of view, could bestow upon government a full complement of political authority.

If constitutionalism were to be truly realized, politics could *not* be irrelevant to the lives of citizens, and in his treatment of this issue we find in Sumner echoes of John Adams. Sumner believed that a genuine constitutional republic "assumes and imperatively requires high intelligence, great political sense, self-sacrificing activity, moderation, and self-control on the part of the citizens. It is emphatically a system for sober-minded men. It demands a manliness and breadth of view which consider all the factors in a question . . . and, above all, which can measure a present advantage against a future loss, and individual interest against the common good."[79] Once such "sober-minded men"—who, it goes without saying, are also law-abiding and civic-minded—establish political rule, government will legitimately have unchallengeable powers within its prescribed jurisdiction. "Those who pay taxes," commented Sumner, "do jury duty, or are otherwise liable to bear the burdens of carrying out what the nation may attempt, are those who may claim the right to have a voice in determining what it shall attempt. They therefore make the national will, and out of the nation they form a state. The nation is an organism like a man; the state is like the man clothed and in armor, with tools and weapons in his hand. When, therefore, the will of the state is formed, the state must act with authority in the line of its determination and must control absolutely the powers at its disposal." Sumner made it clear, moreover, that the "tools and weapons" of the trade would be placed directly into the hands of political craftsmen. "In our own society," he wrote, "the legislator is needed to give to customs and usages definite form and sanction. He becomes the guardian of public or common interests, especially in regard to franchises, privileges, and compulsory powers. Here the delicacy of his function becomes appar-

☆

[78] "Democracy and Modern Problems," Keller (ed.), *Earth-Hunger*, p. 304.
[79] "Politics in America, 1776-1876," Keller (ed.), *Forgotten Man*, p. 331.

ent, for he creates and grants privileges and overrides private rights and individual will in the name of a public interest. It is necessary that he should do so—we do not see how the public necessity and convenience can be served without giving this power to the legislature."[80] However delicately handled, endowed with these powers, government seems a far cry from the pared down version that Sumner typically proposed. The organic society required, so it would appear, considerably more of the political realm than did a society atomized by economic individualism.

Organicism and Mechanism

Indeed, Sumner's full description of a nation conceived in organic terms could have been taken straight out of Burke. Like Burke, Sumner could distinguish between the sovereignty of a people and the sovereignty of the majority. The two concepts must always be kept clear; the former "is the nation as a great community of men, women, and children, knit together by a thousand bonds, having diverse interests, various abilities, manifold diversities of circumstance, but yet held to one common movement by the great laws which govern human life. In this sense the nation, as a whole, has wishes, power, will, passions, motives, and purposes, just like a man." "A nation," Sumner told a Memorial Day audience in 1872, "is not a certain extent of territory on the earth's surface; nor is it the mere aggregate of the persons who may live within a certain territory. A nation . . . is a unit which has organic life. It is enduring in its existence, spanning over individual lives and generations . . . It is, therefore, in the strictest sense, a common-wealth, in which each participates in the prosperity of the whole and all suffer through the misfortune of one." With this conception Sumner could speak of a nation's need for a homogeneous population with shared convictions and common aims. "The institutions of a country," he concluded, "are only an embodiment and expression of the national faiths."[81] But from a totally opposite frame of reference Sumner depicted society as moving in a radically different direction.

What is the "national faith" that is expressed in American institutions? Sumner's usual ground left him ill-prepared to answer this question, for he understood fully the enormous social alterations that had taken place in the transition from older ways to modernity, and that these alterations had been characterized by a dramatic *loss* of

☆

[80] "Republican Government," Keller (ed.), *Challenge of Facts*, p. 239. "Economics and Politics," Keller (ed.), *Earth-Hunger,* p. 319.

[81] "Democracy and Responsible Government," Keller (ed.), *Challenge of Facts,* p. 264. "Memorial Day Address," *ibid.*, pp. 353, 354-357.

such faith. "In our modern state," he remarked, "and in the United States more than anywhere else, the social structure is based on contract, and status is of the last importance. Contract, however, is rational—even rationalistic. It is also realistic, cold, and matter of fact . . . In a state based on contract sentiment is out of place in any public or common affairs." In spite of the absence of public sentiment, Sumner was ready to celebrate the new order as well worth the price. "A society based on contract," he asserted, "is a society of free and independent men, who form ties without favor or obligation, and cooperate without cringing or intrigue." "The free man in a free democracy, when he cut off all the ties which might pull him down, severed all the ties by which he might have made others pull him up. He must take all the consequences of his new status. He is, in a certain sense, an isolated man . . . A free man in a free democracy has no duty whatever toward other men of the same rank and standing, except respect, courtesy, and good-will." [82]

Although he was completely ready to confront the demands of modernity, Sumner occasionally displayed a certain wistfulness for the human bonds that modern man had discarded. He knew that individualism was possible "only in a society where the ties of kinship have lost nearly all the intensity of poetry and romance which once characterized them. The ties of sentiment and sympathy have faded out." Feeble remnants of the old connections may be seen only in rare instances, in a few academic societies, for example, and, Sumner reported, "it is unquestionably a great privilege and advantage for any man in our society to win an experience of the sentiments which belong to a strong and close association." With prescription and fixed status overturned, society is left with liberty and equality before the law, and in such a condition, argued Sumner, "there is no place for sentiment in trade or politics as public interests." [83] Nostalgic sentiments aside, the important thing to notice here is that Sumner's commitment to modernity went so far that it left scant room for the development of a common rational faith, and one is hard put to imagine the exact content of "the great laws governing human life" that would cohere the nation into a unified whole.

The fact is that Sumner tried to have it both ways. His conservative perspective dictated on the one hand an organic view of society, while his social Darwinism made it logical to stress the unsentimental, mechanical relationships of contractualism. His ambivalence appears clearly in his variegated use of metaphor. At times his organ-

☆

[82] Sumner, *Social Classes*, pp. 24-25, 26, 39.
[83] "The Forgotten Man," Keller (ed.), *Forgotten Man*, pp. 474-475.

icism was full-bloom and biological. "The analogy from individual disease to social disease is," Sumner contended, "one of the safest that can be drawn . . ."[84] He instructed his fellow social scientists that, as in the human body, "every action inside of the social organism is attended by a reaction, and that . . . reaction may be spread far through the organism, affecting organs and modifying functions which are, at the first view of the matter, apparently so remote that they could not be affected at all." The parts of a society must therefore not be seen as in a condition of mechanical friction, nor as pieces in an orchestra, nor as units of an army. Rather they are delicate cellular structures; they are "elastic and they are plastic. They suffer both temporary and permanent modifications in form and function by their interaction on each other, and by the arbitrary interferences to which they are subjected by legislation or artifice of any kind."[85] Notwithstanding the explicit rejection of mechanistic imagery and the earlier repudiation of Madisonian mechanisms, Sumner himself found occasion to employ notions which, if not palpably mechanistic, came very close to so being. Elsewhere, for example, he referred to social laws as "precisely analogous to those of the physical order,"[86] and, more narrowly, as identical to the "laws of physics."

In the following quotation Sumner employs both metaphors as he seems to envision society as an "organic machine." "The modern industrial system is a great social cooperation. It is automatic and instinctive in its operation. The adjustment of the organs takes place naturally. The parties are held together by impersonal force—supply and demand. They may never see each other; they may be separated by half the circumference of the globe. Their co-operation in the social effort is combined and distributed again by financial machinery, and the rights and interests are measured and satisfied without any special treaty or convention."[87] Now it may be argued that one could conceive of an organic physics, of the entire physical order, as an enormous organism, and that therefore Sumner did not in fact mix his metaphors. But this argument falls on Sumner's own words, for his organic view of "co-operation in the social effort" required a conscious commitment to common values, to the public interest, while, to the contrary, his individualism necessitated that "rights and interests are measured" by contracts and constitutions of a very specific nature. Perhaps some notion of an "organic contract," running along Rousseauian lines,

☆

[84] "The State and Monopoly," Keller (ed.), *Earth-Hunger*, p. 275.

[85] "Democracy and Plutocracy," Keller (ed.), *Earth-Hunger*, pp. 283, 284-285.

[86] "The Challenge of Facts," Keller (ed.), *Challenge of Facts*, p. 37.

[87] Sumner, *Social Classes*, p. 66.

could have combined the two perspectives. Sumner, however, would listen to no social contract theories. "Human society," he said, "exists because it is, and has come to be on earth because forces which were present must produce it."[88] Since these forces were beyond apprehension, the matter was entirely closed.

The Public Interest

There was, however, at least a partial way out of this dilemma and, although Sumner never quite realized that he possessed it, the way is contained in sections of his own writings. His occasional willingness to allow the legislator to work for the public interest could only have importance if the concept of public interest itself had significant political meaning. Although Sumner usually advocated privatism, arguing that the public interest could and would take care of itself, in an 1877 essay he departed somewhat from this position.

"The public interest," he informed the readers of the *Providence Evening Press*, ". . . is the thing for which government exists. It is not the sum of private interests, nor a compromise between them, but a distinct conception by itself; and it is the true object of the statesman. It is neutral and impartial to all private interests; it simply creates equal conditions under which private interests may develop."[89] But real equality of conditions is extremely difficult even to approximate, and Sumner knew that governments could institute policies aimed at this end merely as a cover for the aggrandizement of certain special interests. "The interests of the society or nation furnish an easy phrase, but such phrases," Sumner believed, "are to be regarded with suspicion. Such interests are apt to be the interests of a ruling clique which the rest are to be compelled to serve." The only solution to this problem, Sumner indicated, lay in the development of a vital and cogent national purpose. He argued that "a really great and intelligent group purpose, founded on correct knowledge and really sound judgment, can infuse into the mores a vigor and consistent character which will reach every individual with educative effect . . . The interests must be real, and they must be interests of the whole."[90] The protection of liberty is doubly guaranteed when a part of the national purpose, when a central component of the mores themselves, is the habitual recognition of the need for such protection, for, in the final analysis, liberty is only safe when its pursuit as a national inter-

☆

[88] "Sociological Fallacies," Keller (ed.), *Earth-Hunger*, p. 364.
[89] "Democracy and Responsible Government," Keller (ed.), *Challenge of Facts*, p. 261.
[90] Sumner, *Folkways*, p. 64.

est becomes an instinctual activity on the part of all citizens. Fortunately, wrote Sumner, we "have inherited the love of civil liberty . . . from family life and from the whole social and political life of the nation. Civil liberty has thus become a popular instinct. Let us guard well these prejudices and these instincts, for we may be well assured that in them lies the only real guarantee of civil liberty. Whenever they become so blunted that an infringement of one of the old traditions of civil liberty is viewed with neglect and indifference then we must take the alarm for civil liberty."[91] With the appropriate tradition deeply entrenched, Sumner could rest content that the principle of liberty was firmly intact.

If this had been Sumner's usual approach he might have resolved some of his conceptual problems, for, on these grounds, civil liberty and personal freedom on the one hand, and governmental operations in the public interest on the other, could have been "organicized" and made part of those "great laws of humanity" that maintain civilized society. With this formulation Sumner could have dropped contractualism, with its mechanistic overtones, while his notion of organic folkways would at the same time have lost much of its quality of absoluteness. But Sumner's particular rejection of democratic and majoritarian traditions frequently caused him to inveigh against traditionalism itself, and his commitment to Darwinian precepts made his typical emphasis on struggle so strong that it virtually excluded thoughts of general social cooperation for commonly shared goals. Sumner's political thought is thus left bifurcated at one point and tenuously balanced between contradictory propositions at another.

The Tragic View of Life

Individual Morality

From a wholly different standpoint, however, consistency of thought on the political and social level is not the most important consideration in treating Sumner's ideas, for his range of interests carried him both below this level to an analysis of the individual, and beyond it to a contemplation of transcendental principles. The individual in particular occupied much of his attention as he repeatedly felt it necessary to instruct the citizenry in the proper ways of getting along in the world. "The true system of self-government for a nation," Sumner wrote, "comes nearest to self-government in a man; the man who governs himself must find the resources for reform, resolution, and self-

☆

[91] "Republican Government," Keller (ed.), *Challenge of Facts*, p. 239.

control in himself."[92] The identification of personal and political self-government was for Sumner more than just rhetorical for, as he understood it, weaknesses of human character were causally related to maleficent political practices.

Thus in his most famous essay, "The Forgotten Man," he argued that "cupidity, selfishness, envy, malice, lust, vindictiveness, are constant vices of human nature. They are not confined to classes or to nations or particular ages of the world . . . All history is only one long story to this effect: men have struggled for power over their fellow-men in order that they might win the joys of earth at the expense of others and might shift the burdens of life from their own shoulders upon those of others."[93] Those who thought of themselves as above these proclivities—and Sumner had reformers especially in mind—were badly deluded. "Let us not . . . make the mistake of assuming that some of us are good and strong and others bad and weak, for that would be to misconceive the whole case," Sumner told them. "All of us are only more or less idle, vicious, and weak. We all have to fight the same temptations, and each one has enough to do to fight his own battle; that is just the reason why it is unjust and socially ruinous to reward one for having done his duty, simply by making him go on to do other people's duty."[94] One does one's own duty simply by being a virtuous citizen.

The properties of virtue, Sumner indicated time and again, are temperance, prudence, industry, energy, frugality, and foresight. Continued and undeviating fealty to their practice would assure success, if success were to be had. No other path lay open. The idea of quick and easy achievement is a myth. "Let us put down now the cold, hard fact," Sumner declared, "and look at it just as it is. There is no device whatever to be invented for securing happiness without industry, economy, and virtue."[95] To follow these dictates in the modern world might be a burdensome task, for Sumner pointed out that tensions between the individual and social institutions had become an inevitable source of difficulty for contemporary man. "The individual," Sumner maintained, "has an interest to develop all the personal elements there are in him . . . He does not want to be planed down to a type or pattern. It is the interest of society that all original powers it contains should be brought out to their full value. But the

☆

[92] "Responsible Government," *ibid.*, p. 285.

[93] "The Forgotten Man," Keller (ed.), *Forgotten Man*, p. 470.

[94] "The First Steps Toward a Millennium," Keller (ed.), *Earth-Hunger*, p. 97.

[95] "The Forgotten Man," Keller (ed.), *Forgotten Man*, p. 468.

social movement is coercive and uniformitarian. Organization and discipline are essential to effective common action, and they crush out individual enterprise and personal variety."[96] Moreover, as society becomes more complex and more refined, personal stakes, both positively and negatively, become increasingly greater. "At every step of civilization," Sumner noted, "the rewards of right living, and the penalties of wrong living, both become far heavier; every chance for accomplishing something better brings with it a chance of equivalent loss by neglect or incapacity."[97] And whereas a lack of comfort might have been predicted for one who succumbed to folly, error, or vice in the past, modern man will find himself thrown directly into pauperism, prostitution, and crime by failing to overcome these weaknesses. And as if the trials of modernity were not enough, Sumner at one point went so far as to intimate that society, past or present, is inimical to individual development. "The first task of men," he wrote, "is self-maintenance, or nutrition; the second is maintenance of the race. The two tasks are in antagonism with each other, for they are both demands on one source of power, *viz.,* the productive power of the individual."[98] Given the claims made on his energy and resourcefulness, then, it goes without saying that the individual could seldom deviate from the straight and narrow if he hoped to gain the upper hand on his competitors.

In the final computation, however, even diligence and perseverance might prove insufficient, for although Sumner tirelessly preached his syllabus of virtues, at one point he had to admit that while virtuous behavior provided the only means to rising in the world, without another necessary ingredient, virtue might sometimes have to be its own reward. "The industrial virtues," Sumner wrote, "are industry, frugality, prudence, and temperance. We cannot, however, deny the presence of another element which is powerful in determining our success—the element of good or ill fortune . . . This element, however, is irrational; there is an element in it of which we are ignorant. Therefore, it is beyond our command and we have to submit to it and make the best of it."[99] With the addition of Dame Fortune, Sumner followed exactly the line of Alger's stories where virtue only payed off when in addition a benign capitalist fortuitously lent an unexpected helping hand. Thus, in a kind of refashion-

☆

[96] "State Interference," Keller (ed.), *War,* p. 218.
[97] "The Abolition of Poverty," Keller (ed.), *Earth-Hunger,* p. 229.
[98] "What the 'Social Question' Is," Keller (ed.), *Challenge of Facts,* pp. 127-128.
[99] "The Power and Beneficence of Capital," Keller (ed.), *Earth-Hunger,* pp. 345-346.

ing of the old Calvinist distinction between divine grace and good works, both Alger and Sumner found a device that attempted to explain why the good do not always receive their just deserts. Needless to say, this qualification was not dwelt upon by their avid readers.

Ultimate Reality

More important, at least for our understanding of his writings, the admission that one's destiny may ultimately be outside of one's control forced Sumner onto a more abstract level of analysis where factors external to man seemed to be in command. While Sumner often remarked that the "progress of society is nothing but the slow and far remote result of steady, laborious, painstaking growth of individuals,"[100] the emphasis on this higher level was far more on the remoteness than on individual effort. Men are products of their society, and as such have nothing to do with really significant changes. Their folkways, for example, "are not creations of human purpose and wit. They are like products of natural forces which men unconsciously set in operation, or they are like the instinctive ways of animals, which are developed out of experience . . . which are handed down by tradition and admit of no exception or variation, yet change to meet new conditions, still within the same limited methods, and without rational reflection or purpose." This being the case, "social improvement is not to be won by direct effort. It is secondary, and results from physical or economic improvements."[101] Indeed, from the broadest possible perspective, even men's secondary efforts seem lost in the unfathomable ebb and flow of cosmic forces.

Sumner suggests this possibility in the essay appropriately entitled, "The Absurd Effort to Make the World Over," from which the following is taken.

> If this poor old world is as bad as they say, one more reflection may check the zeal of the headlong reformer. It is at any rate a tough old world. It has taken its trend and curvative and all its twists and tangles from a long course of formation . . . If we puny men by our arts can do anything at all to straighten them, it will only be by modifying the tendencies of some of the forces at work, so that, after a sufficient time, their action may be changed a little — and slowly the lines of movement may be modified. This effort, however, can only be slight, and it will take a long time. In the meantime spontaneous forces will be at work, compared with which our efforts are like those of a man trying to deflect a river, and those forces will have changed the whole problem before our interferences have time

☆

[100] "Discipline," Keller (ed.), *Forgotten Man*, p. 427.

[101] Sumner, *Folkways*. p. 4. Sumner, *Social Classes*, p. 160.

to make themselves felt. The great stream of time and earthly things will sweep on just the same in spite of us. It bears with it now all the errors and follies of the past, the wreckage of all the philosophies, the fragments of all the civilizations, the wisdom of all the abandoned ethical systems, the debris of all the institutions, and the penalties of all the mistakes. It is only in imagination that we stand by and look at and criticize it and plan to change it. Every one of us is a child of his age and cannot get out of it. He is in the stream and is swept along with it . . . The things which will change are the great discoveries and inventions, the new reactions inside the social organism, and the changes in the earth itself on account of changes in the cosmical forces."[102]

Thus, Sumner advised man, weak before the power of the universe, and essentially ignorant of its ways, to eschew radicalism and to adopt an outlook of patience and forbearance. And while it is possible to detect a slight note of optimism in Sumner because things seem to move up an ascending scale to higher plateaus of civilization, Sumner is so vague about what these plateaus might look like that there is hardly reason for any particular society to feel optimistic, and still less reason for an individual to hope for significant improvement.

Darwinism postulated an unceasing process of change, and the increments of upward movement could be so exceedingly small as to defy recognition.[103] Since the process never ends, neither should man's attempts to adapt to his environment and elevate his species. Sumner foresaw only a continuation of the expenditure of human energy, with steps backward as well as forward. "How then is it possible to imagine that the human race will ever get its work done?" he asked. "If it ever stops to rest it will retrograde. It will then have its work to begin all over again. Poverty, if ever conquered and banished, will come again through the vices engendered in a world without poverty, and so the conflict with it must begin again."[104] The logic of this position dictates a tragic view of life and a tragic note is naturally sounded near the conclusion of *What Social Classes Owe to Each Other.* "The truest and deepest pathos in this world," Sumner wrote, "is not that of suffering but that of brave struggling. The truest sympathy is not compassion, but a fellow-feeling with courage and fortitude in the midst of noble effort." Earlier in the same work Sumner

☆

[102] Keller (ed.), *War*, pp. 208-210.

[103] Even the word "upward" may be inappropriate. Albert G. Keller, Sumner's disciple, biographer, and posthumous editor, notes that Sumner (wrongly as far as Keller is concerned) did not clearly describe the process of evolution in the mores, that he confused the idea of progress with the concept of evolution in this context. (Sumner and Keller, *The Science of Society*, Yale University Press, New Haven, Conn., 1927, p. xxv.) Whether Keller is correct or not, it is clear that there is reason to be cautious about imputing a positive direction to the movement of society in Sumner.

[104] "Power and Progress," Keller (ed.), *Challenge of Facts*, p. 146.

said that men "owe to men, in the chances and perils of this life, aid and sympathy, on account of the common participation in human frailty and folly."[105] Pathos and sympathy are indeed relevant to this struggle, for in the end the struggle might amount to neither more nor less than the "noble effort" of a Sisyphus.

But while Sumner was capable of tragedy, and irony as well, like Emerson, his teaching was diffuse and ecumenical, and it is difficult to know whether his audience understood him on more than one dimension. One thing is certain, and that is that Social Darwinism, in its plainest statement of adaptation, natural selection, and survival of the fittest, would fit readily into the conservative side of the national purpose. This was the age of sweat shops and robber barons and although Sumner endorsed the liberal side as well by arguing for equal opportunity and the rights of labor and against political class domination, his intractable defense of property and his adulation of the great capitalist—property and capitalism being natural products of man's adaptation to nature—could only play into conservative hands. Above all, Sumner's deprecation of political action as a means for remedying social injustice meant a logical reaffirmation of the status quo, because from the situation of the dispossessed, no other avenues for institutional change appeared available. Sumner's inapposite support of governmental authority and political involvement by conservatives not only caused problems internal to his theory, but may also be understood as typifying the American experience that has seen a demand for positive political programs even as politics has been blamed for all social deficiencies. Sumner and the American masses might differ on certain points, but on many of the questions that really mattered they were probably closer than they appeared, closer, at any rate, than Sumner ever imagined.

☆

[105] Sumner, *Social Classes*, pp. 165, 159.

IDEOLOGICAL revOLT

eDwarD BeLLamy

Although many of Sumner's ideas were exemplary of the American consensus, his considerable apprehension was by no means unfounded, for serious critiques of American society abounded in the last decades of the nineteenth century. In the writings of publicists like Henry George, Lawrence Gronlund, Edward Bellamy, and Henery Demerest Lloyd, in the growing protest of the rising labor movement, in the political programs of radical Populists, in the remonstrations of such academics as Lester Ward and Richard T. Ely, there emerged an attack upon the national purpose that ranged in perspective from mild revisionism to advocacy of revolution. The attack was lent salience because the nation had to live through a series of panics, depressions, and recessions from 1873 to the turn of the century. For the first time a really significant number of Americans began to question whether they in fact occupied the best of all possible worlds. In their search for reliable answers they frequently turned to ideas of the sort that filled Sumner with great anxiety, ideas, for example, like those propounded by the utopian novelist, Edward Bellamy.

Of the many theorists of this period Bellamy commands the closest attention. In the first place, he was the most widely read social critic of his day. At the very peak of its popularity, *Looking Backward* sometimes sold over 1,000 copies a day, and Houghton, Mifflin & Company, its second publisher, announced in 1890 that 300,000 copies of its issue had been printed within two years of publication, a feat theretofore equaled in American literary history only by *Uncle Tom's Cabin*.[1] Bellamy, in short, was probably the only writer who from a radical standpoint could begin to compete with Horatio Alger for the ear of the American citizen. It is equally important for our purposes, however, that Bellamy's thought has a completeness seldom encountered in American political theory. While the diverse writings of George and Gronlund contain a very thorough analysis of American society and recommendations for reform, the works of neither match the argument found in *Looking Backward* (1888) and its sequel, *Equality* (1897), for its rare combination of conciseness and amplitude.[2]

The completeness of Bellamy's thought was perhaps not accidental. His own account of the workings of his mind is very similar to what I have suggested is the creative process of the best political theorists. "My mind," Bellamy wrote in one of his notebooks, "is not stratified as that of a practical man's should be, I mean, is not divided by horizontal floors; the floors of practice and of theory, of phenomena and nomena . . . The strata with me are like those disjointed commingled strata of rock that puzzle the geologists. *I start on the practical plane but it is the will of God how long I stay there.*"[3] [Emphasis added.] For reasons of both significance and intrinsic merit we shall use Bellamy as our representative spokesman of late nineteenth century American disaffection.

The vantage point of the year 2000, the fictional date of his two utopian novels, allowed Bellamy to treat American society from a unique point of departure, as if he were a visitor from a strange land who had to question the moral and institutional underpinnings of the whole nation in order to understand how any particular part was made to work. The manipulation of time, however, was merely an artistic device aimed at enticing the reader for, as his political essays of the period amply demonstrate, Bellamy was quite prepared to make

☆

[1] Everett W. MacNair, *Edward Bellamy and the Nationalist Movement, 1889-1894*, The Fitzgerald Company, Milwaukee, 1957, p. 7. Robert L. Shurter, Introduction to *Looking Backward, 2000-1887* (Modern Library edition), Random House, Inc., New York, 1951, p. xiv.

[2] For the works of Henry George, see in particular *Progress and Poverty* (1879); *Social Problems* (1883); *A Perplexed Philosopher* (1892); and *The Science of Politics* (published posthumously in incomplete form in 1898). *Progress and Poverty*, George's most influential book, was primarily economic and only incidentally political in focus. For Lawrence Gronlund, see *The Cooperative Commonwealth* (1884), his most important work; *Our Destiny; The Influence of Socialism on Morals and Religion* (1891); and *The New Economy* (1898).

[3] Arthur E. Morgan, *The Philosophy of Edward Bellamy*, King's Crown Press, New York, 1945, p. 28.

identical arguments from the perspective of a contemporary critic advocating immediate change. In his own mind his proposals were not "utopian," in the pejorative sense of the term. Bellamy believed that he was working for changes within reach of his society, changes that would address major problems susceptible to correction. One must, therefore, make use of his numerous political articles in addition to his two major treatises in order to gain a complete understanding of his position. This is especially true with respect to Bellamy's critique of mainstream American life, in which the author systematically examines the traditional ways of his countrymen and finds them almost without exception repugnant to the principles of a good society.

The Myth of Success

The Alger myth, despite its built-in selectivism, could convince many that opportunity abounded and that Americans enjoyed a singular advantage over the rest of the world. For Bellamy, all such myths had to be shown for precisely what they were, since an exposure to the conditions of real life revealed a very different picture. Even those who were theoretically most aware of public problems were in need of the lessons of reality. Bellamy noted that while "the economists have been wisely debating whether we could dispense with the principle of individual initiative in business, that principle has passed away and now belongs to history." From his advanced point in time, Dr. Leete, historical expositor in both novels, could state categorically that "in the United States there was not, after the beginning of the last quarter of the century, any opportunity whatever for individual enterprise in any important field of industry, unless backed by a great capital."[4]

Rich and Poor

So far from being a country in which chances for individual success were plentiful, America faced a future where opportunities would continue to decrease. "What this means," Bellamy stated in December 1889, "is that we are rapidly approaching a time when there will be no class between the very rich, living on their capital, and a vast mass

☆

[4]Edward Bellamy, "Plutocracy or Nationalism—Which?" Address at Tremont Temple, Boston, May 31, 1889, *Edward Bellamy Speaks Again*, The Peerage Press, Kansas City, 1937 (hereafter referred to as *Bellamy Speaks Again*). Edward Bellamy, *Looking Backward, 2000-1887*, Houghton Mifflin Company, Boston, 1889 (hereafter referred to as *Looking Backward*), p. 53.

of wage and salary receivers absolutely dependent upon the former class for their livelihood."[5] Indeed, it was perhaps logically unnecessary to project into the future, for Bellamy adduced various census data showing that as things currently stood, ten to twelve per cent of the population owned somewhere between seventy-five and ninety per cent of the nation's wealth.[6]

The impact of such egregious disparity upon the country as a whole was devastating. "In this old nation," Bellamy observed, "a million strong men are even now vainly crying out for work to do . . . though . . . there is plenty always for the little children, who flock, in piteous armies, through the chilling mists of winter dawns into the factories . . . In this old nation, year by year, the natural wealth of the land, the heritage of the people, is being wasted by the recklessness of individual greed . . . under a vain form of free political institutions, the inequalities of wealth and the irresistible influence of money upon a people devoured by want, are making nominally republican institutions a machine more convenient even than despotism for the purposes of plutocracy and plunder."[7] Comparisons of conditions in the United States to those in Europe are, despite the contrary belief of many, scarcely favorable to America. America, moreover, has had far less time to prepare itself for disadvantage and impoverishment. "History," Bellamy wrote, "records no expropriation of a nation so complete as this, effected within so short a time, since the ages when military conquest meant wholesale confiscation of the goods and persons of the conquered people. The population of Europe, indeed, groan under similar conditions, but with them they are the heritage of past ages, not, as in America the result of an economic revolution effected within one lifetime."[8] In short, people must confront the fact that the American Dream has served to conceal a vale of tears and that, as inappropriate as the dream is today, it will be even less relevant in the future.

Americans had not come to understand the economic facts of life much earlier because the institutions of acculturation were dominated by the dollar, had become dependent upon capitalists for financial support, and had therefore promoted a faith in economic individualism and the notion that well enough should be left alone. If it had

☆

[5] "Nationalism — Principles, Purposes," Address at Tremont Temple, Boston, December 19, 1889, *Bellamy Speaks Again*, p. 57.

[6] Edward Bellamy, *Equality*, D. Appleton & Company, Inc., New York, 1897, pp. 321-322. "The Programme of the Nationalists," *The Forum*, March, 1894, *Bellamy Speaks Again*, p. 154.

[7] "Why a New Nation?" *The New Nation*, January 1894, *Bellamy Speaks Again*, pp. 24-25.

[8] "The Programme of the Nationalists," *ibid.*, p. 154.

been otherwise, Bellamy believed, "if the reformers had been put in possession of press, pulpit, and university, which the capitalists controlled, whereby to set home their doctrine to the heart and mind and conscience of the nation, they would have converted and carried the country in a month."[9] Although never mentioned by name, the teachings of one university mentor in particular needed to be dislodged: namely, those of William Graham Sumner.

A Critique of Darwinism

One by one, Bellamy found the conservative principles of Social Darwinism either inadequate as bases for social organization or entirely antisocial in character. On Sumner's fundamental point that every individual is essentially on his own in his battle against nature, Bellamy turned the concept of the organic society in order to argue precisely the reverse. "There is," Bellamy insisted, "no such thing in a civilized society as self-support . . . from the moment that men begin to live together, and constitute even the rudest sort of society, self-support becomes impossible. As men grow more civilized, and the subdivision of occupations and services is carried out, a complex mutual dependence becomes the rule. Every man, however solitary may seem his occupation, is a member of a vast industrial partnership, as large as the nation, as large as humanity. The necessity of mutual dependence should imply the duty and guarantee of mutual support."[10] Mutual support would of course impose on society a collective responsibility for the well-being of particular individuals, and with this in mind Bellamy had his transplanted nineteenth century capitalist raise the typical Darwinian question.

Having listened to Dr. Leete criticize the old order for honoring contracts made under duress—all contracts are so attacked—Julian West, emigré from the nineteenth century, objects: "But the compulsion of want," he declares, "meaning hunger and cold, is a compulsion of Nature. In that sense we are all under compulsory servitude to Nature." "Yes," replies Leete, "but not to one another. That is the whole difference between slavery and freedom . . . Under your system the compulsion of Nature through the appropriation by the rich of the means of supplying Nature's demands was turned into a club by which the rich made the poor pay Nature's debt of labor not only for themselves but for the rich also, with a vast overcharge besides for the needless waste of the system."[11] Even if the moral sentiments of

☆

[9] *Equality*, p. 336.

[10] *Looking Backward*, p. 132.

[11] *Equality*, p. 82.

capitalism had been favorable toward mutual responsibility, its appalling economic waste would have made this noble goal impossible to realize. There was waste as the result of mistaken ventures for which no necessary correlation between supply and demand existed. Waste was also the product of bitter competition between entrepreneurs vying for the same customers. Julian West returns in a dream from the twenty-first century to discover the pitiful deceits engendered by this competition in the form of pleading, mendacious advertising. "Wretched men," he cries, ". . . who, because they will not learn to be helpers of one another, are doomed to be beggers of one another from the least to the greatest!"[12]

The most debasing beggary occurred in periods of economic crisis, when wastage was most ironic, for it took place at precisely the moment when the market was glutted with consumer goods – goods, however, that no one could afford to purchase. Such times were characterized by enormous additional waste because vast numbers of men and huge quantities of capital lay idle while the economy stagnated. Furthermore, the latter condition was not restricted to times of crisis; it was more or less natural to all periods under capitalism. Indeed, so wasteful, unorganized, and antagonistic was the old system that Leete could sum it up by asserting that it "was as absurd economically as it was morally abominable. Selfishness was their only science, and in industrial production, selfishness is suicide. Competition, which is the instinct of selfishness, is another word for dissipation of energy."[13] As bad as this was, it was the phenomenon of social irresponsibility induced by capitalism that drew Bellamy's most heated fire.

The old concept which held that individuals strove for their own stake in society could, as far as Bellamy was able to see, only lead to perverse behavior on the part of all citizens, especially that class most adulated by Sumner, the very rich. "Such a separate stake," Bellamy believed, "or the ambition to obtain it, far from making its owner or seeker a citizen devoted to the common weal, was quite likely to make him a dangerous one, for his selfish interest was to aggrandize his separate stake at the expense of his fellow-citizens and of the public interest. Your millionaires . . . appear to have been the most dangerous class of citizens . . . and that is just what might be expected from their having . . . a stake in the country. Wealth owned in that way could only be a divisive and anti-social influence." The competitive system, so warmly endorsed by Sumner, is in fact counter-productive for, instead of advancing the race, it does quite the opposite. It tends, according to Bellamy, "to the survival of the unfittest. Not that the

☆

[12] *Looking Backward*, p. 313.
[13] *Ibid.*, p. 244.

rich are worse than the poor, but that the competitive system tends to develop what is worst in the character of all, whether rich or poor. The qualities which it discourages are the noblest and most generous that men have, and the qualities which it rewards are those selfish and sordid instincts which humanity can only hope to rise above by out-growing."[14] Outgrowing such tendencies, however, would mean completely reversing current ideas about evolution and progress in America.

Bellamy was convinced that the present system worked against the forces of progress. Just as Sumner had, he attributed America's good fortune, such as there was, to environmental factors rather than to any genius intrinsic to the people or their institutions. Where America had succeeded it was because "the wonderful economic opportunities of a new country had given them a vast though temporary advantage over other nations." The bountifulness of America had been so great, Bellamy contended, "that the individualistic, every-man-for-himself-and-the-devil-for-the-hindmost way of getting a living — crude, wasteful, brutal as it was — nevertheless sufficed to secure a good degree of general comfort and an approximate equality of fortunes."[15] However great the comparative advantage might have been, consultation with the people, rather than with the professional sociologists, revealed that by the end of the nineteenth century all advantages had been virtually lost and the masses were "in danger of sinking into the degraded condition of the proletariat and peasantry of the ancient and contemporary European world."[16] This, unless drastic changes were introduced, was what the future held in store, and not the unending progress promised by the nation's financial giants. Capitalism bred individualism and was therefore "not only . . . fatal to any vital sentiment of brotherhood and common interest among living men, but equally to any realization of the responsibility of the living for the generation to follow."

The Extent of the Problem

How deep social changes would have to run in order to improve things for coming generations could be calculated by looking at the size of current impediments to renovation. Bellamy asked his readers to "consider what a tremendous, almost insurmountable, obstacle to human progress was presented by the fact that intellectual leaders of

☆

[14]*Equality*, p. 27. "Plutocracy or Nationalism — Which?" *Bellamy Speaks Again*, p. 35.
[15]*Equality*, p. 233. "Introduction to 'The Fabian Essays,'" American edition, 1894, *Bellamy Speaks Again*, p. 233.
[16]*Equality*, p. 234.

the nations and the molders of the people's thoughts, by their economic dependence upon vested economic interests in established ideas, were biased against progress by the strongest motives of self-interest. When we give due thought to the significance of this fact, we shall find ourselves wondering no longer at the slow rate of human advance in the past, but rather there should have been any advance at all."[17] In fact, Bellamy's typical description of things made the increments of forward social progress almost imperceptible.

On the political side of the ledger he felt that, despite the conservative legalism of the Founding Fathers, democratic institutions had been established and had for a time worked well in America. The problem, however, was that democracy had never been extended to the economic sphere and for this reason the political protections afforded by democratic rule had largely become counterfeit. Bellamy argued, for example, that without a prior condition of economic equality, equality before the law was simply unworkable and the poor inevitably received short shrift from the hand of justice.[18] Under the ongoing routine of economic exploitation, liberty was also an unreachable objective. By "liberty" Bellamy meant "the right not only to live, but to live in personal independence of one's fellows, owning only those common social obligations resting on all alike." For Bellamy, those who saw the dangers to liberty emanating primarily from political sources missed the crucial point entirely. Threats to liberty were chiefly economic, and only the blindest of governments could misperceive this. Such blindness, however, seemed characteristic of the times. "Because the state absolutely ignored this side," Bellamy argued, ". . . its pretense of defending the liberties of citizens was as gross a mockery as that of guaranteeing their lives. Nay, it was a yet more absolute mockery and on a far vaster scale. For . . . the main practical effect of the system was not to deprive the masses of mankind of life outright, but to force them, through want, to buy their lives by the surrender of their liberties. That is to say, they accepted servitude to the possessing class and became their serfs on condition of receiving the means of subsistence."[19] Bellamy, moreover, meant the talk about slavery quite literally, and in this connection he drew comparisons similar to those found in Brownson, Fitzhugh, and Sumner.

Acknowledged slavery, he believed, had in some ways been superior to the plight of the wage-earner under capitalism. Not only did self-interest force the slave-owner to maintain minimal living standards

☆

[17] *Looking Backward*, p. 268. *Equality*, p. 229.

[18] *Ibid.*, p. 78.

[19] *Ibid.*, pp. 79-80.

for his slaves — "There were never any slave quarters," Bellamy wrote, "so vile as the tenement houses of the city slums where the wage-earners were housed" — but it also caused him to attend to their health, unlike the capitalist who allows working conditions to cripple and maim thousands annually.[20] Even more important was the totality of the worker's subservience to his masters. "It was possible," Bellamy remarked, "for the slave to rise in soul above his circumstances and be a philosopher in bondage like Epictetus, but the hireling could not scorn the bonds he sought. The abjectness of his position was not merely physical but mental. In selling himself he had necessarily sold his independence of mind also."[21] The reason that this complete bondage was allowed to take place was that Americans refused to recognize the enormous public impact of what they chose to call private enterprise. As far as Bellamy was concerned "no business is [as] essentially the public business as the industry and commerce on which the people's livelihood depends, and that to entrust it to private persons to be managed for private profit is a folly similar in kind, though vastly greater in magnitude, to that of surrendering the functions of modern government to kings and nobles to be conducted for their personal glorification."[22]

Although not exactly identical, a similar misconception existed with respect to property, for Americans commonly thought of property relations as existing between men and things, and as such in no need whatever of external controls. But a view that permitted unlimited accumulation, as this one did, "ignored," Bellamy asserted, "the social consequences which result from an unequal distribution of material things in a world where everybody absolutely depends for life and all its uses on their share of those things. That is to say, the old so-called ethics of property absolutely overlooked the whole ethical side of the subject — namely, its bearing on human relations."[23] The only true ethics in this regard is one in which equality of rights and dignity are derived from a prior equality of property ownership.

The Evils of Capitalism

Bellamy employed elaborate metaphor to capture the essence of a nation run by the force of capitalism. In the opening pages of *Looking Backward,* he likened society to an enormous coach, viciously driven by hunger, harnessed to the masses who dragged the coach agonizingly

☆

[20] *Ibid.,* pp. 83, 85.
[21] *Ibid.,* p. 101.
[22] *Looking Backward,* pp. 56-57.
[23] *Equality,* p. 87.

along a difficult and frequently miasmal terrain. Seated precariously at the top were members of the leisure class who spent their time jealously guarding their positions and commenting on the abilities of those who pulled the coach. At every jolt of the wagon a number of those on or near the top would fall from their seats, be compelled to join the straining team, and be immediately replaced by some from that body which was constantly competing for higher positions on the coach. Bellamy's description of the dynamics of this situation is worth quoting. Was there no sympathy, he asked, from those who rode above and whose weight increased the toil of their brothers and sisters in harness?

> Oh, yes; commiseration was frequently expressed by those who rode for those who had to pull the coach, especially when the vehicle came to a bad place in the road, as it was constantly doing, or to a particularly steep hill. At such times, the desperate straining of the team, their agonized leaping and plunging under the pitiless lashing of hunger, the many who fainted at the rope and were trampled in the mire, made a very distressing spectacle, which often called forth highly creditable displays of feeling on the top of the coach. At such times the passengers would call down encouragingly to the toilers of the rope, exhorting them to patience, and holding out hopes of possible compensation in another world for the hardness of their lot, while others contributed to buy salves and liniments for the crippled and injured. It was agreed that it was a great pity that the coach should be so hard to pull, and there was a sense of general relief when the specially bad piece of road was gotten over. This relief was not, indeed, wholly on account of the team, for there was always some danger at these bad places of a general overturn in which all would lose their seats.[24]

An equally bleak picture is drawn in *Equality,* where the "Parable of the Water Tank" is constructed in order to show how in the old society massive poverty could exist amidst obvious plentitude. Water stands simultaneously for the productivity of the people and the nourishment of the body without which no man can live. Things were so arranged that the tank which contained the water was controlled by a small class of capitalists. Periodically the tank became full and at such times the capitalists refused to pay the masses for carrying water to the tank, thus depriving the people of the pennies which were their only means of purchasing water from the capitalists. "And the people," wrote Bellamy, "murmured against the capitalists and said: 'Behold the tank runneth over, and we die of thirst. Give us, therefore, of the water, that we perish not.' But the capitalists answered: 'Not so. The water is ours. Ye shall not drink thereof unless ye buy it of us with

☆

[24] *Looking Backward,* pp. 11-12.

pennies.' And they confirmed it with an oath, saying, after their manner, 'Business is business.'"[25] It was this recollection of business as usual that caused the people of the year 2000 to look back upon the old society with utter derision. "Our generous race," Bellamy has Dr. Leete report to Julian West, "has remembered without rancor all the oppressions it has endured save only the rule of the rich. The dominion of the money power had always been devoid of moral basis or dignity, and from the moment its material supports were destroyed, it not only perished, but seemed to sink away at once into a state of putrescence that made the world hurry to bury it forever out of sight and memory."[26]

And with the death of plutocracy went the multitudinous array of political institutions that no longer had reason to exist. Such institutions never performed useful functions in the first place; they served only to keep the peace. Why was this the case? Because, Bellamy argued, "of the inequality of conditions which prevailed. The strife for wealth and desperation of want kept in quenchless blaze a hell of greed and envy, fear, lust, hate, revenge, and ever foul passion of the pit. To keep this general frenzy in some restraint, so that the entire social system should not resolve itself into a general massacre, required an army of soldiers, police, judges, and jailers, and endless law-making to settle the quarrels. Add to these elements of discord a horde of outcasts degraded and desperate, made enemies of society by their sufferings and requiring to be kept in check." The lesson of the old order for the builders of the new was consequently crystal clear: "whatever the previous governments had done, the people as rulers ought not to do, and whatever the previous governments had not done, it would be presumably for the interest of the people to do."[27] Considerable portions of *Looking Backward* and *Equality* were devoted to delineating as plainly as possible precisely what it is that government properly conceived could and could not do.

A New Society

If the old society had been so myopic as to leave control of the economic realm in private hands, then this condition would be exactly turned round by the new order. Industry, productivity, distribution, and exchange would all become public functions not merely controlled but actually run by the federal government. After the peaceful revolution, which Bellamy saw beginning in his own day and culminating a

☆

[25] *Equality*, pp. 197-198.
[26] *Ibid.*, p. 116.
[27] *Ibid.*, pp. 10, 20.

decade or two into the twentieth century, private profit would be permanently banished and, as a consequence, the profit motive itself would disappear. With private profit would go that most ancient pinion of the masses, economic inequality. All citizens, male and female, would now stand on equal footing. All would receive a free, well-rounded education until the age of twenty-one and thereafter would be required to serve the nation, and thus their fellow-citizens, by laboring in the national work force: the first three years in common labor, the next twenty-one in a self-chosen occupation, with additional schooling provided where necessary. The citizen would be retired at age forty-five, at which time he would be free to pursue his special interest as he saw it.

Job allocation, distribution, and working conditions would be varied so that, consistent with individual preferences, sufficient workers would be available where and as needed. The "pay" for each position, regardless of its ease or difficulty, would be identical and after retirement all workers would be equally remunerated with funds sufficient to provide a good standard of living plus a surplus to be spent as the individual desired. Money per se would be abolished and replaced by credit cards, the value of which would be computed by dividing the estimated productive wealth for the forthcoming year by the number of people in the country. All goods would be purchased directly from government stores. Merchandizing by individuals, aside from being unprofitable, would be unbecoming to the free and equal citizen: "buying and selling," Dr. Leete reported, "is considered absolutely inconsistent with the mutual benevolence and disinterestedness which should prevail between citizens and the sense of community of interest which supports our social system. According to our ideas, buying and selling is essentially antisocial in all its tendencies. It is an education in self-seeking at the expense of others, and no society whose citizens are trained in such a school can possibly rise above a very low grade of civilization."[28] This failing, if allowed to occur, would be tragic indeed, since the new order aspired to the very highest degree of civilized life.

Public Life and Competition

It would not, however, seek to change human nature. It fully understood that competitive instincts and differential rewards were necessarily connected to human motivation and an active existence. The work force, or industrial army, as Bellamy called it, would be systematically graded and ranked in terms of responsibility and decision-

☆

[28] *Looking Backward*, pp. 88, 89.

making power, these being scientifically correlated with the abilities of the individuals involved. With the highest rankings would go preferences in choosing an area of specialization within one's industry, as well as minor privileges and immunities respecting discipline. With all ranks would go a badge indicating by its metallic content the level of its wearer; the highest demarcation would be a ribbon bestowed by the people upon the greatest authors, engineers, artists, physicians, and inventors of each generation. Exact records would be kept of everyone's work and excellence of performance would never go unrewarded. Additionally, numerous prizes and awards would be given for improvements, special accomplishments, etc.

In looking at the capitalist mentality that believed only in the stimulus of financial emolument, Bellamy argued: "the assumption that there would be no incentives to impel individuals to excel one another in industry merely because these incentives would not take a money form was absurd. Every one is as directly and far more certainly the beneficiary of his own merits as in your day, save only that the reward is not in what you called 'cash' . . . Compared with the emulation aroused by this system of nobility by merit, the incentives to effort offered under the old order of things must have been slight indeed."[29] Even the nineteenth century unconsciously understood that when the call was sufficiently noble men would exert themselves greatly for reasons other than fear of want and love of luxury; such was the call of patriotism when the nation encountered hostility abroad. Given a *conscious* appreciation of this fact, the new system would ensure that invidious distinctions would never be drawn between ranks even though it would inevitably be the case that some men would fail to rise very far in the industrial army. Whatever their rank, all would participate in the common effort and work to the best of their ability. "The worker," Dr. Leete indicated, "is not a citizen because he works, but works because he is a citizen."[30]

The Nationalist Order

The economic and political systems would coalesce in the new order or, more accurately, since the entire society would center around the necessities of industrial organization, the political realm as previously understood would no longer exist. As far as governmental authority was concerned, the industrial army would constitute the nation. The work force would be hierarchically structured, with rankings analogous to those of the military, ranging from lieutenants in

☆

[29] *Equality*, pp. 389-390.
[30] *Looking Backward*, pp. 96, 134-135.

charge of small units at the bottom, to generals of guilds responsible for entire trades, culminating in pyramidal fashion at the top in the general-in-chief, or President of the nation. All promotions in rank are to be made from above until the level of general is reached. Generals are to be elected to office by a vote of the honorary members of the guild; that is, those men who had passed the age of forty-five and had been mustered out into "retirement"—a retirement in which they would form a very active alumni group maintaining a keen interest in the developments of their former professions. The workers would have no vote whatever, thus the new Nationalist order would avoid the usual kinds of political intrigue characteristic of nineteenth century electioneering.

The President would be chosen for a five-year term by a vote of all members of the industrial army and would be selected from among a number of guild generals who had been out of office for at least five years. At the end of his term, the President would report to a national Congress which, if approving of his report, would reelect him for another five years. Congress would be called exclusively for this purpose and would dissolve immediately after taking action. There would be no national legislature for, with the abolition of capitalism, there would be no need of the endless parade of law-making characteristic of earlier times. Similarly, there would be no state legislatures or administrations, which could only form divisive influences, nor would there be prodigious bureaus, duplicative agencies, and military organizations. All that would remain reminiscent of the older ways would be the legal system: a small number of citizen-judges, appointed by the President; and a minute police force needed in order to deal with the few cases of "ativistic" behavior that occasionally appear among an otherwise law-abiding citizenry. Law schools would no longer exist, since the simplicity of a noncapitalist society would render legal training obsolete.

Bellamy felt that an uncomplicated bureaucracy could manage most affairs because the new society, freed of the degradations of capitalist inequity, would partake fully of a sense of community. He called his philosophy "Nationalism," and those who followed its tenets were perforce members of the "Nationalist party." Nationalist, according to Bellamy, was the only accurate description of his party, "for its purpose was to realize the idea of the nation with a grandeur and completeness never before conceived, not as an association of men for certain merely political ends . . . but as a family, a vital union, a common life, a mighty heaven-touching tree whose leaves are its people, fed from its veins, and feeding it in return. The most patriotic of all possible parties, it sought to justify patriotism and raise it from an instinct of rational devotion, by making the native land truly a father who kept the people alive and was not merely an idol for which they were expected to die."[31]

Bellamy insisted that nationalism was not to be confused with that mindless brand of chauvinism that sets one state off as superior to all others. National solidarity need not be placed in opposition to human solidarity. "Too often what was called love of country might better have been described as hate and jealousy of other countries, for no better reason than that there was other, and bigoted prejudices against foreign ideas and institutions — often far better than domestic ones — for no other reason than that they were foreign."[32] Bellamy knew that many progressive critics posited universal and particular, humanitarian and patriotic categories as mutually exclusive. "There are," he observed, "social reformers who believe, the less one's devotion to his own country and countrymen, the better he will love other countries and humanity at large, as if a man were usually found to be a better neighbor in proportion as he neglects his own family. This is a belief which Nationalists utterly repudiate. The very word Nationalism is an appeal to love of country. Patriotism, though so often misdirected, is the grandest and most potent form under which the enthusiasm of humanity has yet shown itself capable of moving great masses, and in its spirit is contained the promise and potency of the world-embracing love in which it shall some day merge."[33]

But love of nation was only justified when national institutions were based on equalitarian principles. The national idea — "which is that of the union of a people to use collective strength for the common protection and welfare" — was logically inconceivable without the correlative of equality, for the idea of a community of unequals would constitute a contradiction in terms. "Those," said Bellamy, "who believe that all men are brothers . . . must believe in the equality of man, for equals only can be brothers. Even brothers by blood do but hate each other the more bitterly for the tie when the inheritance is unequally parted between them, while strangers are presently made to feel like brothers by equality of interest and community of loss and gain. Therefore we look to the establishment of equality among men as the physical basis necessary to realize that brotherhood of humanity regarded by the good and wise of all ages as the ideal state of society."[34]

A truly equalitarian society would be organic in a sense that meant far more than the functional division of labor that many organicist theorists had spoken of in the past. Bellamy stated that society must be

☆

[31] *Ibid.*, pp. 253-254.

[32] *Equality*, pp. 278-279.

[33] "Looking Forward," *The Nationalist*, December, 1889, *Bellamy Speaks Again*, pp. 176-177.

[34] "Nationalism — Principles, Purposes," *ibid.*, p. 60.

contemplated "not as an accidental conglomeration of mutually independent and unconnected molecules, but as an organism." The individual must not be seen "as standing alone, or as living or working to or for himself alone." He must be regarded "as an inseparable member of humanity, with an allegiance and a duty to his fellows which he could not, if he would, cast off, and with claims upon his fellows which are equally obligatory upon them . . . every one is born into the world a debtor to society for all he can do, a creditor to society for all he needs."[35] But while there would be mutual dependence and obligation between the individual and society, this relationship would never take the form of economic dependence between any two particular individuals. "That any person should be dependent for the means of support upon another would," Bellamy felt, "be shocking to the moral sense as well as indefensible on any rational social theory. What," he asked, "would become of personal liberty and dignity under such an arrangement?"[36]

Dignity and liberty would be difficult to preserve unless a cooperative community were established, and a communal society could persevere only if the people were dedicated to communalism with a religious kind of commitment. It was to precisely such a commitment that Bellamy meant to call his fellow Americans. "The sentiment of human brotherhood," he told them, ". . . is a religion in itself, and to understand it in its full significance implies a sense of consecration on the part of those who devote themselves to it. Nationalism is indeed based also upon the soundest of economic laws; the principle of fraternal cooperation is as certainly the only true science of wealth-production, as it is the only moral basis for society; but the latter is so much more the important consideration that even if a brotherly relation with our fellow-men could only be attained by the sacrifice of wealth, not the less would the true Nationalist seek it."[37] Such a dedication would, moreover, revivify the political life of the country. A system of popular referenda would automatically go into effect when decisions of any importance were made, and citizens would maintain a perpetual interest in public questions. "We could," Dr. Leete explained, "safely turn over to a selected body of citizens the management of the public affairs for their lifetime. The reason we do not is that we enjoy the exhilaration of conducting the government of affairs directly."[38] More importantly, with society dedicated to community, Bellamy, at his most exultant, could foresee entirely new horizons for mankind.

☆

[35] "'Looking Backward' Again," *North American Review*, March, 1890, *Bellamy Speaks Again*, pp. 193-194.

[36] *Looking Backward*, p. 263.

[37] "Looking Forward," *Bellamy Speaks Again*, p. 174.

[38] *Equality*, p. 275.

Community and Solidarity

Mr. Barton, a twenty-first century clergyman, informs Julian West that the literature of the new era has a "total lack of the tragic note. This has very naturally followed from a conception of our real life, as having an inaccessible security, 'hid in God,' as Paul said, whereby the accidents and vicissitudes of the personality are reduced to relative triviality." Freed from necessity, from tragedy, a new man, man in his true identity, emerges. "Through boundless love man becomes a god, for thereby is he made conscious of his oneness with God, and all things are put under his feet. It has been only since the great Revolution brought in the era of human brotherhood that mankind has been able to eat abundantly of this fruit of the true tree of knowledge, and thereby grow more and more into the consciousness of the divine soul as the essential self and the true hiding of our lives. Yes, indeed, we shall be gods. The motto of the modern civilization is *'Eritis sicut Deus.'*" [39] It was appropriate that this speech should be delivered by a moral sage of the new world, for these sentiments represented more than excessive euphoria on Bellamy's part.

In an essay entitled "The Religion of Solidarity," Bellamy, at the age of twenty-four, had advanced a philosophy which demonstrated the very high possibilities he held out for mankind. [40] In a clear echo of transcendentalism he spoke of an important dualism in man's nature. On the one hand was cosmic unity and coalescence: "The instinct of universal solidarity," he wrote, "of the identity of our lives with all life, is the centripetal force which binds together in certain orbits all orders of beings. In fine, the instinct of solidarity in the moral universe correlates with the attraction of gravitation in the particular world." On the other hand was discreteness and separation: "The fact of individuality with its tendency to particularizations is the centrifugal force which hinders the universal fusion, and preserves the variety in unity which seems the destined condition of being." A complete acceptance of universal identity would reveal a very different variety of life, a variety fully in keeping with the conceptualizations of Emerson and Thoreau.

In such an existence the usual categories of both the secular domain and religious tradition lose their significance. "For this life of solidarity," Bellamy stated, "there is neither past nor present, morality nor immortality, but life ever present, which dons and doffs the countless and varied guises of individuality as one puts on and takes off his garments." Viewed from this perspective the intense selfness of indi-

☆

[39] *Ibid.*, pp. 266, 267.

[40] This essay appears in Arthur E. Morgan, *The Philosophy of Edward Bellamy*, pp. 5-22; all quoted material is taken from these pages.

viduality is as ridiculous as it is wrong-headed. "Our lives," Bellamy suggested, "are comedy. In the universal there is no tragedy, and in the realm of the individual the experiences are too trifling for the dignity of tragedy . . . Justly regarded, human life is a delightful game of passions and calculating, superior in interest to chess on account of the sense of partial identity with the personalities which serve us as puppets." Bellamy did not, however, preach a life of escape from the world.

Neither extreme — neither the disregard of the ascetic nor the self-seeking of individualism — is in the end a source of satisfaction. The ideal man is one who combines his worldly acts with a comprehension of the infinite, one "whose spirit dwells in the stars and in all time, but whose hands are as deft with the most menial as with the mightiest tasks through which the promptings of the soul of solidarity can find expression." The problem is that this happy combination is not only infrequently achieved but it is scarcely ever pursued as most men encapsulate themselves in their individuality, attempt to crowd universal life into personal experience. Unlike Emerson, Bellamy believed that even men of extraordinary conquest were imperfectly developed human beings. He declared that "given great powers, of such men are made Napoleons and Caesars. Yet such as these are great in the individual plane only. He who has but glimmering visions of the universal stands on a plane infinitely above them . . . Alexander, thus seeking to fill the void within him, must needs eternally weep for new worlds to conquer, although forever conquering . . . Poor Alexander had his problem by the wrong end. As individuals we are indeed limited to a narrow spot in today, but as universalists we inherit all time and space." Beyond this point of disagreement, Bellamy drew lessons from their common Weltanschauung that deviated even more from the conclusions of Emerson.

Emerson had difficulty reconciling the secular and spiritual levels. The self-aggrandizing of the former often seemed as natural to him as the contemplativeness of the latter. This was not the case for Bellamy. He stated unequivocally that "unselfishness, self-sacrifice, is the essence of morality. On the theory of ultimate individualities, unselfishness is madness; but on the theory of the dual life, of which the life of solidarity is abiding and that of the individual transitory, unselfishness is but the sacrifice of the lesser self to the greater self, an eminently rational and philosophical proceeding *per se*." Emancipated from individualism, man soars to great heights. "The half-conscious god that is man is called to recognize his divine parts. The soul then is what it would be. It has," Bellamy concluded, "the infinity it craves."

And whereas Emerson sometimes suggested that disconnection and resignation were the only roads to the infinite, Bellamy saw a clear line running from solidarity to acts of public involvement. Solidarity, the instinct of oneness, he explained, "in the organic world we may imagine . . . as the attraction of cohesion. In the various orders of animated nature it appears in the shape of varied laws of mutual independence and attractions. Manifested in men it takes the form of loyalty or patriotism, philanthropy or sympathy." Since solidarity could find expression in patriotism it would be the case that changes in the meaning and significance of patriotism would have dramatic impact on the attitudes and activities of the citizenry. Given this philosophical position it was only natural that Bellamy could in his political writings argue that the radical transformation of society would effect an even more radical transformation in the behavior of man. This argument provided the *sine qua non* of *Looking Backward* and *Equality*.

Bellamy's Radicalism

The extent of Bellamy's radicalism is easily perceived when his ideas are placed against those which preceded him in the history of American political theory. But just how radical was Bellamy when measured against his own times? More radical certainly than Henry George whose advocacy of a repressive tax on property ownership Bellamy endorsed but found far too modest a means of total social reform.[41] Socialism, at least as Bellamy saw it, also fell short of Nationalism in that it did not insist on absolute economic equality and did not necessarily call for industrial organization established on a national basis.[42] Perhaps the best way to assess Bellamy's position is to compare his ideas with the doctrines of Marxism, by far the most radical of the period.

Bellamy and Marx

Points of similarity are not difficult to fix. On the broadest level Bellamy, like Marx, believed that economic arrangements exerted a formative influence on the way that people act in society. Consequently, Dr. Leete could report from the year 2000 that the "conditions of human life have changed, and with them the motives of human

☆

[41] *Equality*, p. 91. "Nationalism — Principles, Purposes," *Bellamy Speaks Again*, pp. 69-70.

[42] "The Programme of the Nationalists," *ibid.*, p. 157. "Introduction to 'The Fabian Essays,'" *ibid.*, p. 237.

action."[43] Moreover, in a chapter in *Equality* entitled "Economic Suicide of the Profit System," Bellamy advanced a theory of capitalism that fully affirmed Marx's idea of surplus value. Capitalism's self-destructive tendencies, described by Bellamy in the "Parable of the Water Tank," could easily be seen on those numerous occasions when the market became glutted. The citizenry grew increasingly impoverished because it received insufficient wages to purchase necessary goods whose prices had been inflated by the excess demands of profit return.[44]

The prolonged effects of this system are described in words that could have been taken from a Marxist tract. "It is not difficult," Bellamy wrote, "to forecast the ultimate issue of the concentration of industry if carried out on the lines at present indicated. Eventually, and at no very remote period, society must be divided into a few hundred families of prodigious wealth on the one hand, a professional class dependent upon their favor but excluded from equality with them and reduced to the state of lackeys; and underneath a vast population of working men and women, absolutely without hope of bettering a condition which would year by year sink them more and more hopelessly into serfdom."[45] In fact, Bellamy's understanding of plutocracy, which has the rich in virtual control of all political machinery despite the outward form of democracy, closely resembled the Marxian argument that the state and legal system constitute a superstructure which conceals behind a facade of legitimacy the surreptitious holders of power.

Not only did Bellamy agree with Marx about the economic-political power nexus, but one also finds in his writings a comprehension of historical necessity that is not unlike the traditional Marxist position. Dr. Leete thus suggests that although the deprivations of the nineteenth century were terrible misfortunes, tragic for their recipients, they were nonetheless vital parts of an inexorable process. "Therefore not one outrage, not one act of oppression, not one exhibition of conscienceless rapacity, not one prostitution of power on the part of the Executive, Legislature, or judiciary, not one tear of patriotic shame over the degradation of the national name, not one blow of the policeman's bludgeon, not a single bullet or bayonet thrust of the soldiery,

☆

[43] *Looking Backward*, p. 61.

[44] In yet another metaphor, Bellamy likened the economic system to a person with dyspepsia: "With abundance of dainties at hand he wasted away from lack of power to absorb nutriment. Although unable to eat enough to support life, he was constantly suffering the pangs of indigestion, and while actually starving for want of nourishment, was tormented by the sensation of an overloaded stomach." (*Equality*, p. 167.)

[45] "Plutocracy or Nationalism—Which?" *Bellamy Speaks Again*, p. 41.

could have been spared. Nothing but just this discipline of failure, disappointment, and defeat on the part of earlier reformers could have educated the people to the necessity of attacking the system of private capitalism in its existence instead of merely in its particular manifestation."[46] And just as the movement of history paved the way for benefitting from past calamities, so it also provided an opportunity to make use of current institutions.

Bellamy's argument in this regard was similar to one that Lenin would make a short time later. Like Lenin, Bellamy was impressed by the efficiency and organizational techniques of the large corporation and, just as Lenin would argue in *State and Revolution,* he felt that the new society could exploit this organization to its own advantage simply by divesting it of its profit-making orientation and then using its apparatus to run the new industrial order. This organizational transformation was seen by both Bellamy and Lenin almost as part of a natural process of evolution. Organizational rationality carried to its logical end was of course the military, and Bellamy's vision of an industrial army essentially devoid of political conflict calls to mind Lenin's (and Engels') idea that society would shift from the "government of men" to the "administration of things." While Lenin was never entirely clear about the meaning of this phrase, one suspects that he must have had in mind something similar to Bellamy's detailed picture of the national army of cooperative workers.

Revolution and the American Tradition

While the similarities with Marxism are apparent, there was one crucial Marxian proposition that Bellamy refused to adopt: the act of revolution. History was on the side of change. "We believe," Bellamy wrote, "that a wonderful confluence, at the present epoch, of material and moral tendencies throughout the world, but especially in America, has made a great step in the evolution of humanity, not only possible, but necessary for the salvation of the race." With the times propitious, a gradual process of change was altogether feasible. "We seek the final answer to the social question," Bellamy stated, "not in revolution, but in evolution; not in destruction, but in fulfillment—the fulfillment of the hitherto stunted development of the nation according to its logical intent."[47]

Evolutionary change was possible because the class antagonism that Bellamy foretold had apparently not yet reached the point of

☆

[46]*Equality*, p. 330.

[47]"Nationalism—Principles, Purposes," *Bellamy Speaks Again*, p. 60. "Plutocracy or Nationalism—Which?" *ibid.*, p. 48.

irrevocability. The growth of class hatred "was indeed beginning to proceed at an alarming rate, but the process had not yet gone far or deep" enough to resist the movement of peaceful revolution.[48] This being the case, Bellamy's plea was not the Marxist call to *class* consciousness, but a general call to *social* consciousness. "National-ism," he insisted, "is not a class movement." Being a citizens' move-ment, Nationalism had no violent designs on the rich or bourgeoise classes. "We make no war upon individualism," Bellamy asserted; "we do not censure those who have accumulated immense fortunes simply by carrying to a logical end the false principle on which busi-ness is now based."[49] For this reason Bellamy could side with the English Fabians against those who accused Fabianism of being overly academic and inadequate as a revolutionary force.

Similarly, he could argue that Nationalism was actually a conserva-tive doctrine aimed at returning America to its proper path. "We are the true conservative party," he wrote, "because we are devoted to the maintenance of republican institutions against the revolution, but that the people shall resist a revolution . . . Let no mistake be made here. We are not revolutionists, but counter revolutionists."[50] With this point in mind, the revolution might be seen, not as destroying private property, but as establishing property on equitable grounds, actually affirming it "in an incomparably more positive, beneficial, permanent, and general form than had ever been known before."[51] The revolution, in sum, would simply carry the *positive* propensities of the period and the logic of the Declaration of Independence to their natural conclu-sions and thereby restore the nation's rightful heritage.

Despite Bellamy's qualification, his goals were clearly not easily extracted from the American past and, while it is true that he eschewed violent change, the speed with which he expected the revolution to take place makes the argument for gradualism very questionable. By the same token, his descriptions of class exploitation were so severe that a reconciliation of classes short of violence seems highly improb-able. While it was not unreasonable for Bellamy to invoke a tradition of shared beliefs that could both mitigate class hatred and recall all citizens to common liberal ideals, his few remarks about the legacy of the Declaration of Independence scarcely provided for the existence

☆

[48] *Equality*, p. 346.

[49] "Looking Forward," *Bellamy Speaks Again*, p. 176. "Declaration of Principles," *The Nationalist*, May 1889, *ibid.*, p. 31.

[50] "Introduction to 'The Fabian Essays,'" *ibid.*, p. 236. "Nationalism — Principles, Purposes," *ibid.*, p. 59.

[51] *Equality*, p. 120.

of such a tradition. Few indeed would be the Americans, for example, who would find in the Declaration a definition of private property that fits Bellamy's specifications. Bellamy's national ideology, while logically deducible perhaps from the American tradition, was not part of that tradition; it constituted in fact a radical departure from tradition and created something new.

While not in themselves indices of his novelty, there are further differences between Bellamy's work and Marxism that are important to an understanding of his philosophy. As Bellamy himself indicated, for example, the insistence on economic equality would make inapplicable the Marxian axiom, "to each according to his needs, from each according to his abilities."[52] Perhaps of more interest was that Bellamy did not look upon work as a therapeutic means of healing man's alienation from nature. Many Marxists suggested that once the capitalist imperatives were removed from human labor, a man's work could prove a source of creativity and satisfaction that would help make him at one with his world. For Bellamy, however, alienation was strictly a function of excessive individualism, and consequently, while work might exemplify solidarity with the universe, solidarity itself was in no way dependent upon a particular mode of labor. The important thing was that equality displaced individuality in the new order and Bellamy could therefore contemplate new opportunities for human divinity. Work itself, through participation in the industrial army, would be done willingly but for the most part would be regarded as an obligation that had to be fulfilled before a man could devote himself to his more personal interests.[53]

But while valuable in terms of understanding Bellamy, these distinctions are not essential in determining his radicalism. Suffice it to say that Bellamy carried his argument very far beyond the usual limits of American political discourse, and only his reservations about the use of force kept him from moving completely into the most radical position of the period. These reservations were enormously important, however, for they allowed Bellamy to make connections with elements whose political credos were slightly nearer the general consensus. Before we examine the relationship of Bellamy's ideas to other contemporary doctrines let us look briefly at a few of the criticisms levelled against him by some of his more thoughtful readers, and in this way obtain a fuller understanding of his views.

☆

[52] "Some Misconceptions of Nationalism," *The Christian Union,* November 13, 1890, *Bellamy Speaks Again,* p. 121.
[53] *Looking Backward,* pp. 195-196.

Militarism and Democracy

In the March 1890 number of the *North American Review*, Bellamy wrote an essay entitled "'Looking Backward' Again," in which he attempted to respond to his critics, particularly to General Francis A. Walker, who had reviewed *Looking Backward* in the *Atlantic Monthly* thirty days earlier. Walker devoted special attention to Bellamy's industrial organization, which he found to be excessively militaristic in character. He argued that for Bellamy the modern military system was "not merely a rhetorical analogy for a national industrial service, but its prototype."[54] The regimentation and discipline so efficacious in the destructive processes of war are not applicable to the creation of industry. Not only are their purposes different, but men will simply not submit to wartime regimentation in their everyday lives.

Bellamy responded by claiming that Walker had misinterpreted him, that the military terminology was simply metaphorical and not to be taken literally. He pointed to the thousands of governmental clerks in Washington as examples of what he had in mind. The Post Office was as good an illustration as any. "There is, indeed," Bellamy asserted, "nothing in the National plan which does not already exist as a germ or vigorous shoot in the present order, and this is so simply because Nationalism is evolution."[55] Nothing is changed with respect to forcing men to work. In the current system a man must work or starve; he works, that is, if he can find employment, and if he should want to change jobs he can do so only if he finds an alternative. In the National plan he is guaranteed work, will be assisted in shifting employment, and will even be permitted to remain in leisure past the age of 33 providing that he is willing to accept one-half of the common stipend.

The main principle borrowed from military thinking is that under Nationalism all able-bodied citizens must work for the nation just as they are presently required to fight in its defense. Such work would in fact constitute a defining characteristic of citizenship. Also taken from the military perspective is the notion that honor and authority are the chief rewards for service. These traits distinguish a captain from a lieutenant, not the fact that the former makes more money; and for valorous action a man prizes the decorations of glory and not an increase in salary. In reply to the general charge of militarism in his system Bellamy confessed to "an admiration for the soldier's business as the only one in which, from the start, men throw away the purse and

☆

[54]*Atlantic Monthly*, vol. 65, pp. 256-267, February, 1890.

[55]"'Looking Backward' Again," *Bellamy Speaks Again*, p. 184.

reject every sordid standard and achievement. The very conditions which Nationalism promises — that is to say, as motives — are the actual conditions of military life. Is it a wonder that war has glamour? That glamour we would give to the peaceful pursuits of industry by making them, like the duty of the soldier, public service."[56]

Not only was Bellamy's equation of Army life with high-minded public service slightly romanticized, particularly at a time when mercenary armies were still abroad, it may have been the case that his over-all esteem of the military was due to factors which ran even deeper. It is apparent from some of his remarks in *Looking Backward* that he found the sheer rationality of the army's division of labor and functional distribution of authority enormously compelling. The sight of the military marching in cadence moved him immensely. In a dream Julian West returns to nineteenth century Boston where, after a series of melancholy experiences, he unexpectedly encounters a parade of soldiers. "A regiment was passing," he recounts. "It was the first sight in that dreary day which had inspired me with any other emotions than wondering pity and amazement. Here at last were order and reason, an exhibition of what intelligent cooperation can accomplish. The people who stood looking on with kindling faces — could it be that the sight had for them no more than but a spectacular interest? Could they fail to see that it was their perfect concert of action, their organization under one control, which made these men the tremendous engine they were, able to vanquish a mob ten times as numerous."[57] Excessive enthusiasm aside, and Julian West's exuberance certainly opened Bellamy to a charge of excessiveness, Bellamy was convinced that on practical grounds alone, industrial routinization based on the military model could be easily fitted into a democratic, libertarian mold.

Consequently, he was completely prepared to address the rebukes of those who thought a system based on this model too constricting with respect to the individual. The last chapter of *Equality* is entitled "The Book of the Blind," the "book" being a work written by a post-revolutionary author that both catalogues and criticizes the arguments of those who defended the old system. This chapter seems to be something of an appendage and was probably written as a defense against the attacks which had appeared in the decade between *Looking Backward* and its sequel. The principal of these took issue with Bellamy's conception of equality. Some said that his kind of equality would work to make everyone alike. Bellamy found in such arguments a perfect illustration of the perversity of capitalist thinking. "This objection," he wrote, "is beautifully typical of an age when everything and every-

☆

[56] *Ibid.*, pp. 188-189.

[57] *Looking Backward*, pp. 318, 322.

body has been reduced to money valuation. It having been proposed to equalize everybody's supply of money, it was at once assumed, as a matter of course, that there would be left no points of difference between individuals that would be worth considering. How perfectly does this conclusion express the philosophy of life held by a generation in which it was the custom to sum up men as respectively 'worth' so many thousands, hundred thousands, of millions of dollars!" Bellamy suggested that if we really want to discover natural differences between individuals, we must first give them common ground to stand on by equalizing their incomes.[58]

That equality would end the competitive system Bellamy was quick to acknowledge. This he felt was precisely what ought to happen; the old method was not worth saving. "For what was the competitive system," he asked, "but a pitiless, all-involving combat for the means of life, the whole zest of which depended on the fact that there was not enough to go round, and the losers must perish or purchase bare existence by becoming the bondsmen of the successful? Between a fight for the necessary means of life like this and a fight for life itself with sword and gun, it is impossible to make any real distinction." In the equalitarian community even the losers are winners, for their interests are better served by those who perform outstanding work for the whole of society.[59]

Perhaps the most serious charge against Bellamy was that his system would threaten liberty and encourage paternalism in government. The former accusation was, according to Bellamy, the result of an inability to think beyond current circumstances. Tyranny, he suggested, was a function of class warfare; therefore without class differentiation the reason for despotism vanishes: "What usurper," Bellamy inquired, ". . . ever essayed a task so hopeless as the subversion of a state in which there were no classes or interests to set against one another . . . a state the stability of which represented the equal and entire stake in life of every human being in it?"[60] As with tyranny, so with paternalism: a society that was not divided into superior and inferior parts could not practice paternalistic rule. To say that the people would be paternalistic towards themselves has no meaning. To find classic paternalism one need only look at the current treatment of the laborer by the owners of large corporations. The new administration would in fact be far removed from the usual blight of overbearing authority, would be greatly simplified as the result of dispensing with

☆

[58]*Equality*, pp. 391, 392.

[59]*Ibid.*, pp. 394, 398.

[60]*Ibid.*, p. 407.

the multiplicity of governmental parts and pieces, each of which goes its own way and is a law unto itself.[61] The economic and political machinery would be collected and assimilated into one homogeneous, streamlined institution, the whole of which would be energized and kept upright by a nationwide unanimity of purpose.

Nationalism and Political Action

Bellamy's conception of an amalgamated work force would reappear in variant form in the ensuing decade expressed in the call of the Industrial Workers of the World for "One Big Industrial Union." Bellamy's ideas did not, however, have to wait a decade to influence the political thinking of his contemporaries. Simply by writing *Looking Backward* he generated a popular political movement. Readers of his book spontaneously formed themselves into Nationalist clubs, of which over 150 were founded across the nation by 1890. Composed mostly of members of the middle and upper classes, never very large, and possessed of no real nationwide organization, the Nationalist clubs seldom lasted more than a year and did not in themselves constitute an important political force. Their members, however, deeply committed to Bellamy's views, were frequently influential in other reform circles, particularly those of the Populists.

Socialists and Populists

For obvious ideological reasons, and because of personality conflicts as well, Bellamy and his followers avoided an alliance with the Socialist Labor party and turned instead to the People's parties in the attempt to find a practical political vehicle for their ideas. The radicalism of many Populist groups, particularly in their earlier years, and the fact that Populism, at least in principle, sought support across class lines, made the liaison between the two movements almost natural. Bellamy personally seems to have been influential in formulating the platform of the May 1892 Populist convention of St. Louis. He took pride in the convention's call for nationalization of the issue of money, of banking, of the telegraph and telephone services, and of the railroads, and he fully concurred with the statement that land and natural resources should be regarded as the heritage of the nation.[62] Bellamy was

☆

[61] "Some Misconceptions of Nationalism," *Bellamy Speaks Again*, p. 128.

[62] "Progress of Nationalism in the United States," *North American Review*, June, 1892, *Bellamy Speaks Again*, p. 143.

particularly pleased that the platform no longer bore the exclusive stamp of the Farmer's Alliance, progenitor of the People's parties. "This," he said, "is a platform evidently constructed for artisan, merchant, and professional men as well as for farmers, a platform not for a class or classes, but for the masses."[63] And so constructed it marked a signal advance for the cause of Nationalism.

While a certain number of Nationalist clubs lasted beyond 1890, and although Bellamy did not begin the Nationalist journal, *The New Nation*, until 1891, it is safe to say that as effective political activists, most Nationalists had been absorbed into the Populist party by 1893. The history of Nationalism consequently becomes thereafter the history of Populism and, unfortunately for the Nationalist objective, it is a history of the decreasing influence of Bellamy's ideas.

From Nationalism to Populism

There has been some debate among scholars recently about the actual content of Populist society. Richard Hofstadter has pointed to the "hard" side of American agrarianism, to that part of the "agrarian myth" that served to cover an essentially commercial spirit with a veneer of simplicity and Jeffersonian ruralism. While Hofstadter draws a distinction between early and late Populism with respect to its radicalism, his emphasis on its conservative bent allows him to conclude that "populism can best be understood . . . not as a product of the frontier inheritance, but as another episode in the well-established tradition of American entrepreneurial radicalism, which goes back at least to the Jacksonian era."[64] In a similar vein, Bernard Crick has commented that "populism showed that the individualistic capitalist-farmer was beginning to realize that in times of tight credit he needed considerable help to remain a doctrinaire individualist."[65] Norman Pollack, on the other hand, has amassed an impressive amount of evidence showing that, at least in its midwestern variety, Populism was a profoundly radical movement entirely antagonistic to the doctrines of economic individualism.[66]

There seems, in balance, good reason for holding both positions. The very fact that Bellamy could feel enthusiastic about Populist intentions indicates that the People's party was more than another

☆

[63] Everett W. MacNair, *op. cit.*, p. 186.

[64] *The Age of Reform*, Alfred A. Knopf, Inc., New York, 1955, p. 58.

[65] *The American Science of Politics*, University of California Press, Berkeley, 1959, p. 54.

[66] Norman Pollack, *The Populist Response to Industrial America*, W. W. Norton & Company, Inc., New York, 1962.

example of discontented factionalism. And yet by 1895 the dramatic appeals of previous platforms had been virtually discarded in favor of the campaign for free silver. The Populist Manifesto of February 22, 1895, concluded by stating that the party should "extend the hand of fellowship to all who agree . . . on the money question, which is certainly the mightiest and most fundamental controversy evolved during the present century." From this it might have been easy to predict that Populism would fuse with the Democratic party the following year in support of William Jennings Bryan.

Pollack argues that Populism never really lost its radical edge, that fusion was a product of many factors: turmoil over strategy within the party, a feeling that Bryan Democrats were already or could be radicalized, a fear of continued and accelerated exploitation by the Republicans, a concern that the moment to assume power was at hand and should be seized even at the price of narrowing to the silver issue, and the seemingly well-founded conviction of many that Bryan was more sympathetic to their position than in fact he was. All of these causes combined under the imperatives of a still larger cause: Populism had no where else to go, its demise ultimately resulted from the fact that third parties in the American political system have no real chance of gaining power; they must ultimately coalesce or lose relevance. Populism, in other words, fused with the Democratic party because, in the end, it had no other choice.

Whether Pollack's analysis is entirely correct is not essential to our study. It is clear, however, that leadership within Populist ranks had grown increasingly conservative from 1890 to 1896. There is considerable difference between a Governor Teats remarking in Seattle in 1892 that "we populists . . . are the simon-pure socialists. Our ideals are socialistic," and the views of an 1895 editorial in the *National Watchman*. "What we want now," ran the editorial, "is a clean cut, aggressive, intelligent propaganda upon financial reform. Let us be honest and truthful in order to attract the good and just. Let us be conservative in order to secure the support of business men, the professional men, the well to do. These are elements we must use if ever success comes to our party. For every loud-voiced socialist who declares war upon us, we will get a hundred of the conservative element of the society. What we want is success now; a change of conditions in the immediate future. What will happen fifty or one hundred years from now is giving us no particular worry."[67] Pollack contends that sentiments like the latter were merely the expression of a dominant minority that did not represent mass feeling, and that Henry Demarest

☆

[67] MacNair, *op. cit.*, p. 181. Frank L. McVey, "The Populist Movement," *Economic Studies*, vol. 1, p. 200, August, 1896.

Lloyd was extravagent in claiming finally that the whole movement had sold out. Pollack could very well be correct in this view, but it should be noted that the same argument about representativeness could be raised about the radical party leadership of four years earlier.

At any rate it is not difficult to understand how Bryan could have captivated Populist enthusiasm despite his reluctance to accept their support. It is easier still to see, in retrospect, why Bryan was not really their man. His famous "Cross of Gold" speech, which inspired so many, censured the forces of big-city commercialism in stinging prose —but not before Bryan had established common ground by accusing the city manipulators of defining the term "businessman" too narrowly. The wage-earner, the country attorney, the farmer, the miner, all, declared Bryan, must be understood as businessmen and treated accordingly. This was hardly a doctrine of social revolution.

The end of the People's party marked the conclusion of a process that saw Bellamy's Nationalism absorbed into Populism and Populism in turn assimilated into the Democratic party. The death of Populism, therefore, marked the simultaneous death of Nationalism and with it a great reduction in the influence of Bellamy's ideas. But from the perspective of the national purpose, both Nationalism and Populism had an enormous, indeed a revolutionary, *negative* impact, for through their attack on conventional ideology, and through the fact that a few of their reforms were adopted, they effectively destroyed the descriptive reality of the national purpose. Economic individualism, whatever else it did, provided the nineteenth century with a set of ideals and objectives which could vivify an entire nation. But its ideological ties were always rather tenuous, since they caught the individual's imagination and desire but required nothing in return save that he look out for his own interest. Thus to tamper with the system only slightly was to tear out its underpinnings. Economic individualism tended to lose its hold as soon as large numbers of people began seriously to doubt its truthfulness, and neither the preachment of Darwinism nor the promise of Algerism could be substituted for material possession, at least not indefinitely, particularly when the Populist critics were almost daily pointing up the hypocrisies and inadequacies of the present system. Unable to withstand the storm of protest, the ideological base began to crumble. The tenets of economic individualism no longer accurately summarized the dominant activity of most citizens or the primary role of government.

But, whether for reasons endemic to the movement, as Hofstadter asserts, or as the result of forces intrinsic to American politics, as Pollack argues, Populism lost in the political arena, and this defeat meant that the positive and creative side of the Populist-Nationalist ideology lost also. After the endorsement of Bryan, Populism vanished with astonishing speed, and in so doing it left the nation at the turn of the century with no new purpose to replace the old. Effectively speaking, economic individualism would never regain its hold on America and, although its rhetoric remained amidst changed conditions, the nineteenth century *raison d'etre* no longer applied. Because this was the case, because there was no new set of beliefs that all citizens could share (the principles of socialism per se, as announced by Debs, de Leon, and others, were never able to command a significantly wide audience), Americans had, as it were, to pretend that their world had not been transformed, that government was still a peripheral institution, and that the business of the nation could still be business itself. Before the Nationalist-Populist revolution America had been essentially noncommunal but with a shared purpose which embodied and rationalized an individualistic way of life. Because the revolution had only negative success, it failed to alter the ideological consciousness of the country, and the result of this was to leave America thereafter still without a sense of community, and now without a national purpose as well. It was such an America—with neither community nor purpose—that twentieth century Progressives would seek to reform.

9

aTTenuaTeD vision
HerBerT CroLY

Progressive Moderation

At the conclusion of the last chapter I indicated that twentieth century American Progressives would confront a society whose purpose had been rendered essentially obsolete; this would be the case despite the fact that the old rhetoric of economic individualism might linger on and receive reflex-action pronouncement from men who either could not or did not wish to perceive the new realities. Whether Progressivism in its most public expression ever *consciously* engaged in a confrontation of these realities is doubtful. While Theodore Roosevelt could advance a concept of political power that permitted the Chief Executive to act in response to necessity in all cases except where the Constitution explicitly instructed to the contrary, and although he fought, at least forensically, against the growing amalgamation of financial trusts, his fundamental convictions appear to have deviated only slightly from traditional beliefs and his New Nationalism was more an attempt at social restoration than an effort to engage in basic renovation. It did not provide the population with a national purpose which could either promote unity of action or encourage common participation.

262

Still less creative in this respect were reforms on the electoral and local government levels advocated by middle-class urban Progressives whose position for the most part was avowedly based on the idea that throwing the rascals out and bringing the principles of better business and direct democracy in would return the nation to its rightful ways. Thus, while the various pieces of economic legislation relating to railroad regulation, taxation, wage and labor policies, and public utilities were sometimes radical in propensity and reminiscent of earlier Populist agitation, the introduction of initiative, referendum, recall, and direct primary devices, along with the restructuring of municipal government, were, however salutary in themselves, hardly potent enough to speak to an issue that in one way or another had a negative effect upon the character of the whole country. Although there were exceptions, especially later in the century, most Progressives in the first decades after 1900 failed to recognize the generic nature of the problem which faced them. Partly for this reason and partly because of their intrinsic recalcitrance, they settled for, indeed often insisted upon, fairly modest alterations in a democratic system that seemed to them otherwise estimable. In fact, however, the transposition of values of business efficiency to governmental processes could, if Sumner was right, in many ways serve purposes that would ultimately prove *un*democratic, for now the ability to meet a payroll would be a standard of political expertise as well as a mark of personal success. With this equation Sumner's worst fears of plutocracy might prove justified.

Standing distinctly apart from Progressivism's more conventional understanding was Herbert Croly, philosopher, political counsellor, and along with Walter Weyl and Walter Lippmann, co-founder of *The New Republic* in 1914. Through a radical interpretation of American history Croly was brought to a position which was unique in his own day. The analysis of the American past found in *The Promise of American Life* (1909) and *Progressive Democracy* (1914) was not only fresh and original in its time, but so cogent and incisive that historical interpretations published in subsequent years have frequently had the appearance of restating many of Croly's more penetrating insights. As a political *thinker*, able to comprehend and delineate the vital forces that energized and directed his society, Croly has few equals in American intellectual annals. It remains for our investigation to measure Croly's accomplishment as a political *philosopher*, to see not only whether he was able to grasp the historical meaning of contemporary institutions, but also whether he could respond in a way that transcended the narrowest demands of his own period. We shall look first at Croly's assessment of his nation's evolution, of events and ideas that bore a causal connection to the inadequacies and inequities that he saw about him.

America Past and Present

Croly's historical critique, made first in *The Promise of American Life*, then expanded and given structure in *Progressive Democracy*, was totally inconoclastic. He began by rejecting completely the dominant legacy of his forebears. He informed his readers that to persist in the current popular conviction characterized by a "mixture of optimism, fatalism, and conservatism," conceiving of the "American future as a consummation which will take care of itself," is to persist in a conviction that "is admirably designed to deprive American life of any promise at all."[1] The components of this passive mixture are in various ways products of the past. Optimism, perhaps the most accentuated of the three in the prevalent ideology, is the result of traditional beliefs in economic individualism, beliefs which existed even before the nation was settled. "America," Croly pointed out, "has been peopled by Europeans primarily because they expected in that country to make more money more easily. To the European immigrant . . . the Promise of America has consisted largely in the opportunity which it offered of economic independence and prosperity."[2] If these were the expectations prior to the nation's establishment, American political thinkers did little to alter these expectations thereafter. And, because of his enormous influence, Thomas Jefferson, despite his espousal of democratic egalitarianism, stands particularly guilty of maintaining his country on a misbegotten path.

The Jeffersonian Tradition

Croly was prepared to label as Jeffersonian a perverse national tradition which had held that economic improvement and democratic institutions could "be obtained merely by liberating the enlightened self-interest of the American people." The problem, according to Croly, was that on both political and economic grounds, Jefferson had advanced an inappropriate conception of democracy. "In Jefferson's mind," Croly wrote, "democracy was tantamount to extreme individualism . . . the motto of a democratic government should simply be 'Hands off.' " The operational effect of a system in which government kept its hands perpetually to itself could only be detrimental as far as the society as a whole was concerned. "The test of American national success," Croly argued, "was the comfort and prosperity of the individual; and the means to that end — a system of unrestricted individual aggrandizement and collective irresponsibility."[3] In order to effect

☆

[1] Herbert Croly, *The Promise of American Life*, Capricorn Books, New York, 1964, p. 5.
[2] *Ibid.*, p. 9.
[3] *Ibid.*, pp. 22, 43, 49-50.

the principle of individualism, Americans would have to follow separate competitive directions and, while he wrongly attributed the idea to Jeffersonianism, Croly fully understood the connection between a competitive, fragmented society and a compartmentalized government that Madison had so clearly delineated in his *Federalist* essays. He noted that "if the people are to be divided against themselves in order that righteousness may rule, still more must the government be divided against itself. It must be separated into departments each one of which must act independently of the others."

The consequence of such dispersion was twofold: it made unavoidable a system of political inaction, and it promoted rule by minority factions. Croly acknowledged that through the use of Jeffersonian controls the "government was prevented from doing harm, but," he contended, "in order that it might not do harm it was deliberately and effectively weakened. The people were protected from the government; but quite as much was the government protected from the people. In dividing the government against itself by such high and rigid barriers, an equally substantial barrier was raised against the exercise by the people of any easy and sufficient control over their government. It was only a very strong and persistent popular majority that could make its will prevail, and if the rule of a majority was discouraged, the rule of a minority was equally encouraged."[4]

So dubious was Croly of the merits of such arrangements that he seemed to feel that if there had been genuine alternatives at the crucible period, the Hamiltonian philosophy might have been the more appropriate choice. As far as Croly was concerned only Hamilton's economic elitism marred an otherwise praiseworthy theory. "In effect," he maintained, "the nationalism of Hamilton, with all its aristocratic leaning, was more democratic, because more constructively social, than the indiscriminate individualism of Jefferson."[5] For Croly the Jeffersonian tradition meant a nation that lacked cohesion and purpose, and for this reason he repudiated the tradition in toto.

American Constitutionalism and Economic Interest

While Croly reproached Jefferson for promulgating individualist doctrines (many of which could more accurately be ascribed to Madison), his arguments, particularly in *Progressive Democracy*, made it abundantly clear that in his mind the Jeffersonians were not singularly at fault; eighteenth century American constitutionalists could equally be called to account for the historical misfortunes troubling America

☆

[4] Herbert Croly, *Progressive Democracy*, The Macmillan Company, New York, 1914, p. 40.

[5] *Ibid.*, pp. 54-55.

in the following century. Indeed, the fact that the nation had for a time prospered under their constitutional institutions explained in part some of the apathetic conservatism existing in the beginning of the twentieth century.

Croly found the ideology built into the Constitution — an ideology which he labeled "the kingdom of the Law," or briefly "legalism" — quite frankly undemocratic. The Founding Fathers he likened to a man who leaves his estate to a son only after he has placed that estate within a strict system of rules, regulations, and procedures that are to be administered not by the son but by a set of powerful trustees.[6] The concept of government of laws was introduced not merely in order to delineate areas of legitimate political action but to circumscribe and inhibit political action itself. "The domination of the Law," Croly argued, "came to mean in practice a system in which the discretionary discriminating purposive action of the human will in politics, whether collective or individual, was suspect and should be reduced to the lowest practicable terms." The means employed to effect this end were of course to deprive the public realm of political power. "The active government was divided, weakened, confined and deprived of integrity and effective responsibility, in order that a preestablished and authoritative Law might be exalted, confirmed and placed beyond the reach of danger."[7]

That the constitutional system was fundamentally conservative, particularly in its solid support of property rights, could easily be shown when examined in an historical context. "In Great Britain," for example, "the association between the rigid protection of the right to property and comparative freedom from legal interference in the task of accumulating it had been and continued to be unfavorable to democracy, in that it resulted in the concentration of wealth in comparatively few hands."[8] If this was the case, why, Croly wondered, was the American public, demonstrably democratic in its sympathies, prepared to allow the structures of legalism to be imposed upon it? The answer to this question lay in a combination of the common economic aspirations of Americans and the surfeit of resources to be found in their environment.

Croly pointed out that the "peculiar economic conditions which obtained on a rich undeveloped continent enabled the American democracy to accept and employ a legal system which in the old country had been anti-democratic in its origin, its meaning and its effects. The new American system . . . was intended above all to strengthen

☆

[6] *Ibid.*, pp. 154-155.

[7] *Ibid.*, p. 41.

[8] *Ibid.*, p. 57.

the association between personal liberty and the security of private property . . . The democracy consented, because it expected on the whole to benefit from the association."[9] Moreover, one should not be deluded by the early factional differences over the issue of property, for while these differences were genuine, they were mostly superficial. "The truth," Croly suggested, "is that the American democracy rallied to an undemocratic Constitution, and have until recently remained loyal to it, because of the nature of their own economic interests. In certain respects the interests of the farmers were opposed to those of the capitalists; but in still more fundamental respects they were capable of adjustment. Both parties were seeking the satisfaction of individual economic purposes." And since all important factions tended to share this goal, even differences in political ideology that might otherwise produce serious divisions within society could be readily adjusted: "deeper than any division," Croly wrote, ". . . lay the common interest of all classes of America in rapid economic development." Consequently, an "essentially individualistic democracy had no difficulty in arranging a working compromise with a constitutional nationalism, which, although possessed of a higher sense of collective responsibility, still considered social and political organization chiefly as an instrument for the promotion of individual interests."[10] So it was at the founding of the nation and so, Croly asserted, it continued throughout the nineteenth century.

In considering the Jacksonian period, for example, Croly came to conclusions identical in many respects to those reached by Tocqueville. The meaning of Jacksonian democracy should be clearly understood. "When," Croly contended, "orators of the Jacksonian Democratic tradition begin to glorify the superlative individuals developed by the freedom of American life, what they mean by individuality is an unusual amount of individual energy successfully spent in popular and remunerative occupations. Of the individuality which may reside in the gallant and exclusive devotion to some disinterested, and perhaps unpopular moral, intellectual, or technical purpose, they have not the remotest conception; and yet it is this kind of individuality which is indispensible to the fullness and intensity of American national life."[11] And with the exception of such a rare specimen as Abraham Lincoln, few examples of this higher individualism can be found in the years between Jackson and the first decade of the twentieth century.

It was not that Croly was entirely unable to discover historical

☆

9 *Ibid.*, p. 57.

10 *Ibid.*, pp. 51, 58-59.

11 *The Promise of American Life*, p. 65.

indications of social progress or individual advancement. Nor was it that he wished to reject American history and return to preconstitutional times. Quite the contrary. "Legalism," he observed, "was an enormous improvement on the official tyranny of a class or an individual." The real problem was that legalism had brought with it class troubles of its own making. "It introduced into political and social organization the rule of live-and-let-live and some of the spirit of that rule. But in practice the rule of live-and-let-live has never successfully expressed its underlying spirit of fair play. Its usefulness has been impaired by an unfair division of labor. Upon the rich have been conferred the opportunity and the obligation of living; upon the poor, the opportunity and obligation of let-living."[12] And to document this contention Croly offered a partial description of the economic conditions which obtained in contemporary society.

Contemporary Divisiveness

If the fruit of individualistic legalism was the plight of the twentieth century workingman then it was a bitter fruit indeed. Much had been written to portray the freedom and independence, unique in the modern world, of the American laborer. The true situation of wage earners was very different. "Their employer," Croly remarked, "is literally their master. He supplies the opportunity of work, determines its conditions to a large extent, and is responsible for its successes or failure. They are often free to change their employer, but a new employer is only a new master." If the worker is not free, neither is he independent. Moreover, he has but two means of seeking independence, one of which is doomed to failure, both of which are ultimately divisive. The laborer may, according to Croly, "seek independence either by becoming a favored worker or by becoming himself a property owner. The first of these alternatives is denied by the very necessities of the case to the vast majority of wage-earners. The second costs more in human satisfaction than it is worth as a discipline of independence. Both of them divide the interest of the individual worker from that of the mass of his fellow-workers."[13] Divisiveness among the working classes, however, is simply a manifestation of the much larger divisions characteristic of a society that fails to attract the energetic interest and participation of its citizens.

There is nothing in such a society to prevent a proliferation of interest-oriented acts on the part of public functionaries. "The present

☆

[12] *Progressive Democracy*, pp. 418-419.

[13] *Ibid.*, pp. 383, 384.

system," wrote Croly, "is supposed to embody reason, and is intended to subordinate the collective will to rules which will prevent it from going astray. In practice its reasonableness is tantamount to automatic operation in the interest of existing property owners. It arouses luke-warm interest in its behavior, except on the part of those who benefit from its operation."[14] Clearly what is needed in such circumstances is a cohesive force that will unify the nation and provide the collective will with appropriate meaning and direction. And while Croly deni-grated the major thrust of the American past, he could look to a minor motif in that same past for sources of social cohesiveness.

It was not democracy but *Jeffersonian, constitutionalist* democ-racy that Croly found wanting. There was, however, more to the Amer-ican democratic tradition than its most conspicuous formulation. And more was certainly needed, for while it was perfectly clear that the Constitution had been successful in implementing the separation of powers principle, the real task, as Croly saw it, was to "graft on the Constitution some regular method of giving back to the government sufficient integrity of organization and action. In the end this integ-rity must be derived not from constitutionalism, but from the ability of the people to achieve some underlying unity of purpose."[15]

Such a unity of purpose could in fact be extracted from the Amer-ican people, from the highest expression of their democratic ideals, in everything that a commitment to equalitarianism implied. This ideal was possible despite the traditional domination of economic individualism. Croly argued that even "if Americans have neglected these ideal implications, even if they have conceived the better future as containing chiefly a larger portion of familiar benefits, the ideal demand, nevertheless, has always been palpably present." One can trace the growth of this ideal demand throughout the nineteenth cen-tury. "The more consciously democratic Americans became," Croly suggested, ". . . the less they were satisfied with a conception of the Promised Land, which went no farther than a pervasive economic prosperity guaranteed by free institutions." So true was this that, on a comparative basis, a deeper sense of national coherence can be said to have obtained in America than anywhere else in the civilized world. Croly could conclude that "the American nation, in spite of its parade of individualism and in spite of its individualist legal and economic methods, was fundamentally more socialized in purpose than were the European countries."[16]

☆

[14] *Ibid.*, p. 314.
[15] *Ibid.*, p. 227.
[16] *The Promise of American Life*, pp. 6, 12. *Progressive Democracy*, p. 205.

There was, furthermore, some evidence — less perhaps than in the case of national purpose — of a sense of community also present in the American tradition. Expositors of American ideals were correct in defining equality in terms of a general bestowal of benefits and responsibility upon the entire community and they were also correct in suggesting that equality so understood "is the one means whereby a community can be supplied with an ultimate and sufficient bond of union." The trouble with community, as with purpose, in America is that communal ties have always taken second place to the artificial connections of legalism, that is, to a *constitutional* as opposed to a *social* conception of equality. "The American democracy has attempted to manufacture a sufficient bond out of the equalization of rights: but such a bond," Croly wrote, "is . . . either a rope of sand or a link of chains."[17] The great task which lies before America in the twentieth century is that of extricating the national creed from its incrustation of legalism and individualism and of carrying the nation forward to the goals that in reality it has always sought, goals that transcend the dictates of the immediate past. The "American nation," Croly proclaimed, "is committed to a purpose which is not merely of historical manufacture. It is committed to the realization of the democratic ideal; and if its Promise is to be fulfilled, it must be prepared to follow withersoever that ideal may lead."[18] The nation, in other words, must create a unity of purpose that neither washes away like sand nor imprisons its citizens in chains of economic bondage.

Misguided Attempts at Reform

With these elevated ends in mind Croly looked at the various reform movements about him and found them largely inadequate. Since they did not perceive all dimensions of the problem their proposed solutions were either hopelessly inappropriate or positively reactionary. "The plain fact," said Croly, "is that the traditional American political system, which so many good reformers wish to restore by some sort of reforming revivalism, is just as much responsible for the existing political and economic abuses as the Constitution was responsible for the evil of slavery." Such reform constituted, in Croly's words, merely a "higher conservatism," higher, that is, than the programs of acknowledged conservatives, and this higher conservatism characterized much of what passed for doctrines of fundamental change. Woodrow Wilson's New Freedom, for example, looked to Croly "like a revival of

☆

[17] *The Promise of American Life*, pp. 194-195.
[18] *Ibid.*, p. 6.

Jeffersonian individualism."[19] Similarly, Insurgent Democracy, in some ways the radical edge of Progressivism, tried to eliminate special privilege and liberate the masses but did little more than replicate the approach of Jacksonianism. This approach, Croly believed, did "not constitute a sufficiently radical revision of the old national economic system." Indeed, because the ideology of Insurgency and the dogma of the old order are at one on the principle of individualism, the "controversy between them really turns upon a choice between two methods of promoting the free, fair and full exercise of the right to acquire and to hold property." If, in fact, we are simply to witness a conflict between traditional Republicanism and the proponents of Insurgency and the New Freedom, then, Croly insisted, "the conflict is merely one between two classes of property owners and capitalist productive agencies."[20]

The token offerings of these two classes would hardly reach the heart of the current difficulty. "Modern civilization," Croly remarked, "in dealing with the class of wage-earners is dealing with an ultimate economic condition, the undesirable aspects of which cannot be evaded by promoting one wage-earner out of every thousand into a semi-capitalist or a semi-employer. If wage-earners are to become free men, the condition of freedom must somehow be introduced in the wage-system itself."[21] As we shall see, Croly's own remedial suggestions attempted to deal directly with this "ultimate economic condition."

Roosevelt as Progressive

Generally speaking, Croly felt that only one political position of his day was germane to the needs of the nation, and that could be found in the program put forward by Theodore Roosevelt. If *The Promise of American Life* contained a contemporary heroic figure that figure was Roosevelt. And to show that Roosevelt still captured his imagination five years later, Croly noted in the introduction to *Progressive Democracy* that Roosevelt's brand of Progressivism was "committed to a drastic reorganization of the American political and economic system, to the substitution of a frank social policy for the individualism of the past, and to the realization of this policy, if necessary, by the use of efficient governmental instruments."[22] Despite this statement of

☆

[19] *Ibid.*, p. 147. *Progressive Democracy*, p. 16.
[20] *Ibid.*, pp. 108-109.
[21] *Ibid.*, p. 384.
[22] *Ibid.*, p. 15.

concordance, however, it is clear from Croly's own qualifications about Roosevelt in the first volume that he was reaching somewhat in order to embrace the renegade Republican.

Though he praised Roosevelt's efforts he also saw their shortcomings. "If," he wrote, "in one respect, he has been emancipating American democracy from the Jeffersonian bondage, he has in another respect been tightening the bonds, because he has continued to identify democracy with the legal constitution of a system of insurgent, ambiguous, and indiscriminate individual rights."[23] Croly felt that in actuality Roosevelt's program was far more radical than Roosevelt himself would admit; given the fact that Roosevelt was a man driven more by his will than by his intellect, perhaps even more radical than he understood. But if this were the case Roosevelt did "little to encourage candid and consistent thinking." And since such thought was essential to effectuating genuine change, Roosevelt could be taken at best as a mixed blessing. "Mr. Roosevelt and his hammer," Croly concluded, "must be accepted gratefully, as the best available type of national reformer; but the day may and should come when a national reformer will appear who can be figured more in the guise of St. Michael, armed with a flaming sword and winged for flight."[24] With no such paladin immediately in sight, Croly took it as his own task to point out the proper road which radical reform should follow.

A Theory of Purpose

Croly's response to the American malaise was made on two levels: one very general and philosophical in character, the other more specific and placed in the context of more immediate considerations. Seen from the broadest perspective the obvious objective was to introduce into the American polity that which it most seriously lacked: namely, a sense of national purpose. Croly clearly meant the word "purpose" to describe something more than the popular belief that America was inevitably destined for great accomplishment. In this connection he quoted H. G. Wells, who had noticed that when "'one talks to an American of his national purpose, he seems a little at a loss; if one speaks of his national destiny, he responds with alacrity.'" A nation devoid of purpose was for Croly something that bordered on

☆

[23] *The Promise of American Life*, p. 172.
[24] *Ibid.*, pp. 173, 174, 175.

the immoral. If the promise of a nation "is anything more than a vision of power and success," he wrote, "that addition must derive its value from a purpose; because in the moral world the future exists only as a workshop in which a purpose is to be realized."[25]

The Proper Uses of Nationalism

Since it was a *national* purpose that interested Croly, it was natural for him, like Bellamy, to adapt the categories of nationalism to his own uses. Thus he was quite prepared to turn first to Bismarck for an accurate definition of the nation — "'The true people is an indivisible multitude of spirits. It is the living nation — the nation organized for its historical mission — the nation of yesterday and of to-morrow'" — and then to translate Bismarck's continental notion into his own language: "A nation, that is, is a people in so far as they are united by traditions and purposes."[26] Nation and purpose are, in other words, interdependent variables; to speak of America as devoid of purpose was to view its people as a mere agglomeration of human beings which, in lacking true feelings of nationality, in no way comprised a real nation.

Croly's lexicon was varied and his definition of nationalism could at the same time denote the meaning of community. A people that shared a belief — or a faith, as he usually termed it — in a common purpose was for Croly a people that collectively could be referred to either as a community or a nation. The terms "nation," "purpose," "community," and "faith," are so closely related in Croly's vocabulary that ultimately they become almost interchangeable. A true nation is one that has a purpose, and a people with a common faith in a shared purpose may be said to constitute a community.

Croly best captured the connectedness among these concepts when he likened national citizens to voyagers journeying to the same destination. "Travellers who are united by a common and steadfast faith," he wrote, "come to feel peculiarly responsible one to another. The common faith sanctifies those who share it. All the brethren become objects of mutual solicitude. A fellow-feeling is born, which helps and promotes the pilgrims to reach a better mutual understanding. Thus faith in the unique value of the pilgrimage becomes a profoundly socializing influence."[27] As an historical expression of what

☆

[25] *Ibid.*, pp. 4, 6.
[26] *Ibid.*, pp. 265-266.
[27] *Progressive Democracy*, p. 191.

he was talking about Croly offered democratic nationalism as advanced by Guiseppe Mazzini. Mazzini, he asserted, gave voice to the "most luminous and the most soaring expression which the progressive democratic faith has ever received . . . but the Italians of his generation," he added, "were not prepared to live by it."[28]

As the following quotation indicates, Croly's own conception of democratic faith could also be described as soaring and luminous, and not unexpectedly, for as he saw the matter, the inherent limitations imposed upon the human condition since the beginning of time might be met, and perhaps even overcome, through the use of such faith.

> Admitting that human nature is in some measure socially rebellious, admitting that the ambitions of different classes and communities are dangerously conflicting, admitting and proclaiming the inability of society to attain cohesion by obedience to any natural law or moral and social code, democracy has still no reason for discouragement. What the situation calls for is faith. Faith is the primary virtue demanded by the social education of a democracy — the virtue which will prove to be salutary — in case human nature is capable of salvation. Only by faith can be established the invincible *interdependence* between individual and social fulfilment upon the increasing realization of which the future of democracy depends. It consecrates the will to the recognition of the most fundamental and exacting of personal and collective responsibilities. It constitutes the spiritual version of the indomitable instinct which has kept the human race on the road during all the discouragements and the burdens of its past, and which must not be the less indomitable because it becomes the more conscious.[29] [Emphasis added.]

Not only could Croly equal Mazzini in elegance of prose on this point, but he felt that his own situation provided more promising possibilities than did Mazzini's nineteenth century Italy. The subordinate themes of the American past made it entirely logical to anticipate fundamental changes for the better in the future. "The national experience of the American people," Croly suggested, "has prepared them to live by faith. Their political and economic education has reached a stage which necessitates, as a condition of any further national advance, the emancipation of the national will from specific tutelage, and the frank reliance for the building up of the national life upon the good faith with which, collectively and individually, they seek to realize the national or, if you prefer, the social purpose."[30] The great American purpose, then — the promise of American life — was not only a dream of enormous significance but, more importantly, a dream which might some day come true.

☆

[28] *Ibid.*, p. 202.
[29] *Ibid.*, pp. 424-425.
[30] *Ibid* , pp. 201-203.

Democratic Faith

Croly was aware that his talk about faith and purpose had a vagueness to it which some might find objectionable. He insisted, however, on the reality of his principles, and he labored arduously to make himself understood. He informed his readers that the kind of faith he had in mind "becomes effective through the agency of a social ideal which differs from and is independent of any collection of individual ideals." And social ideals were, in Croly's view, no less genuine because they could not always be attached to particular institutions. "The existence of an effective social ideal," he wrote, "is none the less real because it has no specific habitation as concrete and as visible as the individual body. A habitation it has in the whole group of political and social institutions which have been wrought as the instruments of its purposes; but in spite of this residence, it always requires an effort of the imagination to conceive the social mind and will as possessed of just as much reality as individual minds and wills. The social will is creating an increasing and an ascendant society out of the material afforded by human nature, just as the individual will creates individuals out of similar material."[31] The important thing to notice about the social will is its collective character. Its realization, contrary to the doctrines of Social Darwinism, is impossible without the combined efforts of all citizens. "Individuals," Croly pointed out, "can be 'uplifted' without 'uplifting' the nation, because the nation has an individuality of its own, which cannot be increased without the consciousness of collective responsibilities and the collective official attempt to redeem them."[32] If this point were correct, then clearly Progressivism could be successful only if these collective imperatives were taken directly to heart.

This was precisely Croly's argument. He instructed his fellow Progressives that they "must be prepared to replace the old order with a new social bond . . . The new system must provide . . . not merely a new method . . . but a new faith, upon the rock of which may be built a better structure of individual and social life."[33] And in order to be truly novel, the new system must advance values exactly opposite to those of the old. To indicate what he meant, Croly borrowed from the sociologist Albion Small a distinction between antithetical rules of life. Prevalent at the time, Croly stated, was the rule of live-and-let-live. This being the case, "the progressive democratic faith finds its consummation . . . in the rule of live-and-help-live. The underlying

☆

[31] *Ibid.*, p. 200.

[32] *The Promise of American Life*, p. 407.

[33] *Progressive Democracy*, p. 25.

assumption of live-and-let-live is an ultimate individualism, which limits the power of one human being to help another, and which binds different human beings together by allegiance to an external authority. The underlying assumption of live-and-help-live is an ultimate collectivism, which conceives different human beings as part of the same striving conscious material, and which makes individual fulfilment depend upon the fulfilment of other lives and upon that of society as a whole. The obligation of mutual assistance is fundamental."[34] Not only would such a philosophy provide a faith that was radically new, it would, Croly believed, require institutional rearranging of equally radical proportions. To make the faith operational, a totally new role for government would have to be constructed.

Governmental Authority and Political Obligation

Croly was particularly anxious to overcome the traditional suspicion of governmental action, a suspicion that over the years had grown into a mistrust of political power in all of its forms. If the nation was to be democratic it must, he declared, "learn, above all, that the state, and the individuals who are temporarily responsible for the action of the state, must be granted all the power necessary to redeem that responsibility. Individual opportunity and social welfare both depend upon the learning of this lesson."[35] Croly was so concerned that this lesson be understood that he called upon preceptors for whom he usually had only words of reproach in support of his position. "Popular political authority," he contended, "must be made effective and it must be made righteous. The degree of success which the American democracy may obtain will depend on its ability to make popular political authority practically effective without any ultimate sacrifice of righteousness, and sufficiently righteous without any sacrifice of ultimate effectiveness. In this sense the American democracy must always derive its vitality from the ideals of the fathers of the Republic—undemocratic in spirit though many of them were."[36] Croly's contemporary readers must have found it difficult to accept a democratic argument based on ideals that were at their inception undemocratic in intention.

This citation of the Founding Fathers, the positive references to Hamilton, the concept of governmental individuality, and the eulogy to Mazzini serve even more to arouse the suspicion of readers today, especially those who are acquainted with the similarity be-

☆

[34] *Ibid.*, pp. 426-427.
[35] *The Promise of American Life*, p. 201.
[36] *Progressive Democracy*, p. 39.

tween much of Mazzini's language and that later used by Italian fascist spokesmen. Croly's constant endorsement of enhanced and efficient political power—"Popular sovereignty," he wrote, ". . . brings with it a necessary distribution of power; but the power is distributed not for the purpose of its emasculation, but for the purpose of its moralization"[37]—laid him open to charges of statism; but Croly was prepared to be even more outspoken in this respect. One's tie to one's country was for Croly a bond that was enormously compelling, so compelling in fact that Croly, with a slight twist to the meaning of faith, could advance a concept of political obligation that *absolutely* ruled out the possibility of civil disobedience.

Protests against public policy were certainly desirable and in a healthy democracy are to be encouraged. But, Croly stipulated, such protests "must conform to certain conditions. They must not be carried to the point of refusing obedience to the law." Under no conditions could civil disobedience be tolerated. "Even if the national policy should betray indifference to the fundamental interests of a democratic nation . . . the obligation of patient good faith on the part of the protestants is not diminished . . . No effort should be spared to secure the adopting of a more genuinely national policy. But beyond all this there remains a still deeper responsibility—that of dealing towards one's fellow-countrymen in good faith, so that differences of interest, of conviction, and of moral purpose can be made the agency of a better understanding and a firmer loyalty."[38] While respect for the law had not been a concept inimical to traditional liberalism, Croly's argument went so far that even in the worst of circumstances, it excluded the right to rebel, a cardinal principle of liberal thought. It may be that to an America only two generations removed from its Civil War, theoretical reaffirmations of this right seemed less than crucial, and Croly's injunctions may therefore have passed unnoticed. It is highly unlikely, however, that the same thing would have occurred when Croly expressed his views on the question of democratic authority, a question closely related to the problem of political obligation.

He addressed himself to this issue in a section of *The Promise of American Life* entitled "Constructive Discrimination." "A democracy," he wrote, "should encourage the political leadership of experienced, educated, and well-trained men, but only on the express condition that their power is delegated and is to be used, under severe penalties, for the benefit of the people as a whole." Not only was Croly somewhat vague as to the institutional means of testing such

☆

[37] *Ibid.*, p. 229.
[38] *The Promise of American Life*, p. 286.

a delegation of power, but just a few paragraphs earlier he had seemingly suggested an arrangement which must have sounded distinctly *anti*democratic to at least some of his readers. "A democracy," he argued, "no less than a monarchy or an aristocracy, must recognize political, economic, and social discriminations, but it must also manage to withdraw its consent whenever these discriminations show any tendency to excessive endurance. The essential wholeness of the community depends absolutely on the ceaseless creation of a political, economic, and social aristocracy and their equally incessant replacement."[39] This sounds very much like the "circulation of elites" theory utilized by Pareto, Mosca, and other nineteenth century European political sociologists.

This theory held that conventional beliefs in popular sovereignty are myth-laden, that in actuality elites always control political power in all nations, whatever their governmental form, and that democracy may be said to exist when the content of the ruling elite changes periodically, allowing more than one class at least a minimal opportunity to be represented. As theory alone (aside from the question of its descriptive validity), this idea was anathema to Jeffersonianism, which believed that elites, once in power, always seek to perpetuate themselves, always tend to draw their replacements from their own class, and always try to exercise political power exclusively in their own interest. Moreover, the means used by such elites to protect themselves strike at the heart of free society, for inevitably they will be paternalistic and will consequently have the effect of restricting political pluralism and individual liberty. Croly was aware of these objections, and he spent considerable effort in the attempt to meet and eliminate them.

Nationalism and Democratic Pluralism

He frankly admitted that nationalism and democracy were not necessarily coterminous. His point was that neither principle was acceptable without an infusion of the other. But the infusion of democracy into nationalism had, from Croly's viewpoint, realistic limits: "the extent to which this infusion can go and the forms which it takes are determined by a logic and a necessity very different from that of an absolute democratic theory."[40] Democratic theory, pushed to its furthest extreme in practice, produces a stagnant society, a sterile and ineffective

☆

[39] *Ibid.*, pp. 199, 196.
[40] *Ibid.*, p. 255.

politics. The state, like the nation, is not a fixed entity but a process moving toward specific goals and purposes. "The state," Croly asserted, "lives and grows by what it does rather than what it is. Its integrity must be a creation rather than a permanent possession; and the work of building up the integrity of its own life is becoming more onerous and more immediately necessary"—more necessary because problems of the day are in urgent need of political solutions, more onerous because as government wields more power in the attempt to reach solutions, critics label every move paternalistic. It was Croly's conviction that such charges were unfounded. "A government," he argued, "does not become undesirably paternal merely as a consequence of the scope of its social program. The policy or the impolicy of its fatherly interest in the welfare of its citizens depends less upon the extent of its active solicitude for them than upon the extent to which this active solicitude is the result of a free and real choice of the popular will."[41] Strong only as long as it has popular support, government would not, logically speaking could not, force unwanted policies upon the nation. By the same token neither would a forceful display of governmental authority unduly harm the multiplicity of interest groups existing in the society.

To the extent that groups and associations have worked exclusively for their own ends they have actually been, Croly believed, undemocratic, for to ignore the needs of the people as a whole is to operate against the principles of democracy. Progressivism must offer an alternative: "the dominant purpose and effort of progressive democracy must," he contended, "be to bring into existence a genuine democratic community. It is the outcome of a far deeper sense of common responsibilities and policies, of the *interdependence* of individuals and local groups, of the necessity and fruitfulness of cooperation, and of the intimate relation between democracy and nationality. This sense . . . cannot be instructively and significantly realized, unless a dominant popular purpose can be expressed without unnecessary delay and without excessive effort."[42] [Emphasis added.] The dominant purpose would not be imposed upon the various groups from above. In a society that practices freedom of association a national purpose might be expected to arise naturally from the political interchange among all groups. In discussing this issue Croly offered a picture of society very similar to that which Arthur E. Bentley was painting at approximately the same time, a picture that has come to be known as the "group theory of politics."

☆

[41] *Progressive Democracy*, pp. 122, 214-215.
[42] *Ibid.*, pp. 238-239.

Croly argued that the primary units of society are not individuals but groups, each of which can be seen as comprising in itself a smaller society "whose reality is determined by the tenacity and the scope of the purposes which have prompted the association." Analytically speaking, such societies are ubiquitous and are variously constituted as churches, clubs, military and political organizations, trade unions, and even as families. Croly was prepared to carry the description still further: thus, "even every temporary social gathering constitutes a society of a kind." To this point Croly's position is quite in keeping with the group theory approach, but precisely at this point Croly and the group theorists part company. Where the latter tend to leave associations as distinct political forces whose autonomy is tempered only by factors of overlapping membership and common agreement on "rules of the game," that is, on democratic procedures and on the necessity of compromise, Croly sees a process of fusion and amalgamation developing. "As the work of socialization progresses," he writes, "these centres of association tend to become more numerous, more various and more significant, but socialization none the less does not consist merely in multiplying the objects and enlarging the machinery of association. The societies necessarily seek some form of mutual accommodation and adjustment. They acquire joint responsibilities and seek the realization of common purposes. Out of these joint responsibilities and common purposes a social ideal gradually emerges. Society comes to be conceived as a whole, with certain permanent interests and needs, into which the different centres of association must be fitted."[43]

This view of society, which Croly called "the fundamental idea of society as a process," was in no way hostile to the interests of pluralism; indeed, it allowed a healthy mixture of pluralism and individualism to exist. "The conscious bond of a common faith," Croly wrote, "makes not for an indiscriminate fusion, but for a genuinely social union, constituted both by individuals and by those smaller social groups which give direction to so much of individual life. The bond stimulates mutual understanding and is itself strengthened thereby."[44]

Of course an important prior question would have to do with the nature of fusion itself: Why, in light of their many purposes, would the multifarious groups be expected to fuse in agreement on one particular national purpose? Croly nowhere responds to this question directly, and his failure to do so suggests the possibility of a tautology: basic agreement on a common purpose can exist because the elements

☆

[43] *Ibid.*, p. 197.
[44] *Ibid.*, p. 192.

of such a purpose, inculcated earlier as part of the socialization process, can be taken for granted. In other words, one reaches consensus on national purpose primarily because one begins with such a consensus already in hand. Croly's understanding of the influence of the American founding suggests the possibility of this tautology.

An even more important question, however, focuses on the role of the individual, for whether the individual was postulated as primary or not, his relationship to society and to government would need considerable elaboration in an American environment that took individual rights as the quintessential social issue. That Croly was sensitive to this problem is illustrated by the heavy emphasis in his works on the function and role of the individual.

The Individual and Society in Process

Time and again Croly maintained that he was not interested in seeking to extinguish individualism or to subsume the individual under the corporate state. "The antithesis," he insisted, "is not between nationalism and individualism, but between an individualism which is indiscriminate, and an individualism which is selective."[45] What in particular a selective individualism might involve we will take up later. It is important at this point to establish the connection between individualism and the processes of society.

For Croly this connection was logically fixed, and psychologically it provided the defining characteristics of both variables: in Croly's formulation the relation between society and individual approached that of symbiosis. As society emerges as a whole, he contended, "a different conception of individuality also comes to the surface. From the point of view of social psychology, the individual, merely in the sense of a man who inhabits a certain body and possesses a certain continuity of organic sensations, is largely an illusion." The nature of the primitive, for example, is indistinguishable from that of his immediate society. "Genuine individuality is also essentially an ideal which does not become of great value to men and women except in a society which has already begun to abstract and to cherish a social ideal. The sacred individual and the sacred community were born of a similar sentiment of loyalty to ideal values."[46] Thus the development of individuality and of "sociality" are firmly linked to the formulation of national values and purposes in a connection that is perhaps even more than symbiotic.

☆

[45] *The Promise of American Life*, p. 409.
[46] *Progressive Democracy*, pp. 197-198.

But it makes all the difference, according to Croly, how one views this set of relationships. If, for example, one conceives of either or both variables as finished products then "the result is a tendency either to sacrifice the individual to society or society to the individual." The proper perspective is to see both entities in process, in a stage of becoming: "if the individual and society are both conceived as formative ideals, which are creating centres of genuine individual and social life out of the materials offered by human nature, then a relation of *interdependence* can be established between the two, which does not involve the sacrifice either of the individual to society or of society to the individual."[47] [Emphasis added.] This is another way of restating Croly's collective journey metaphor, now with the added attention to individualism; and with the notion that individuality itself is a product of that journey, or is at least functionally related to the journey, one discovers just how potent Croly's formulation of the national faith could be.

Interdependence produced by a common striving for a national purpose would mean not only the possibility of communal association but, even more, the possibility of a community of authentic individuals. Individualism in its older form could now be abandoned. This would of course require a dramatic shift in emphasis. "The being of better men and women will," Croly argued, "involve . . . the subordination, to a very considerable extent, of individual interests and desires to the requirements of social welfare. In so far as the democracy succeeds in its intention of enabling society to do very much more for the individual, it will necessarily ask the individual to do very much more for society."[48] But the important point is that only if society reaches such democratic proportions will a more meaningful kind of individualism be possible. Croly stipulated that "just in so far as a people is sincerely seeking the fulfilment of its national Promise, individuals of all kinds will find their most edifying individual opportunities in serving their country. In aiding the accomplishment of the collective purpose by means of increasingly constructive experiments, they will be increasing the scope and power of their own individual action."[49] The ultimate effect of the national purpose, then, is the establishment of an ethos which allows citizens to become genuine individuals and which permits an otherwise indiscriminate mass of people to form a truly cohesive society.

☆

[47] *Ibid.*, pp. 198-199.
[48] *Ibid.*, p. 406.
[49] *The Promise of American Life*, p. 406.

Practical Applications

Croly argued not only for a revitalized national faith but for a revamping of social and political institutions as well, and to this end he believed that a proper understanding of America's purpose could provide lessons that had direct practical application. If the new view permitted a more positive exercise of political power, then it must also allow government to abandon its archaic role as neutral arbiter among competing interests, for if the national purpose is to be realized, government can never be merely a neutral umpire. "The state," Croly observed, "which proposes to draw a ring around the conflicting interests of its citizens and interfere only on behalf of a fair fight will be obliged to interfere constantly and will never accomplish its purpose. In economic warfare, the fighting can never be fair for long, and it is the business of the state to see that its own friends are victorious . . . While preserving at times an appearance of impartiality so that its citizens may enjoy for a while a sense of the reality of their private game, it must on the whole make the rules in its own interest. It must help those men to win who are the most capable of using their winnings for the benefit of society."[50] When this statement—and we will return later to its explicit call for political deception—is put together with Croly's earlier-quoted remarks about the need for radical revision of the wage-system, the side that should at the moment claim governmental support becomes evident.

Government and Labor

In *The Promise of American Life*, Croly was somewhat ambivalent on this point. On the one hand he was so convinced of the need for workers to organize in their own interest that he insisted upon the disallowance of nonunion labor as a matter of public policy: it "should be rejected," he said, "as emphatically, if not as ruthlessly, as the gardener rejects the weeds in his garden for the benefit of fruit- and flower-bearing plants." Government policy should be so constructed that it favors union organization to the serious disadvantage of the existing system. But while Croly was prepared to advance organized labor and collective bargaining at the expense of workers who wished to remain unorganized, he saw the conflict between trade unionism, once organized, and consolidated capital more as a standoff. The power of corporations was already enormous and in this respect trade union-

☆

[50] *Ibid.*, pp. 192-193.

ism with its huge membership potential was fast catching up. Both parties tended to exploit government for their own benefit but resisted all notions of governmental control. Neither seemed sufficiently concerned with promoting the interest of the larger public.[51]

By the time of *Progressive Democracy*, Croly had apparently come to shift his view, for in this work his advocacy of political action in behalf of labor did not include qualifications regarding the self-interested use of union power. Indeed, the institution of a new system and the direct advancement of the workingman now seemed to run hand in hand. "What the wage-earner needs," Croly advised, "is not the equalization of an existing system of privilege, but the construction of a new system which will repair the inadequacies and redress the grievances of the old. The aim of the whole program of modern social legislation is at bottom the creation of a new system of special privilege intended for the benefit of a wage-earning rather than a property-owning class." And a system which worked to the laborer's advantage would be far likelier to enhance the Progressive cause than would the present arrangement. "The democratic ideal," wrote Croly, "has a better chance of being sincerely accepted among people whose outlook is largely determined by the possession of accumulated property. A democracy of essential workers can be more quickly and thoroughly socialized than a democracy of essential property owners, because property owners can be emancipated without being socialized as a consequence of their emancipation."[52]

It is important to notice in these remarks that Croly is using the conventional conception of democracy rather than his own; this usage allows him to distinguish "democracy" from "socialized" or "Progressive" democracy, the latter carrying far beyond connotations of mere emancipation. "Essential workers" will be those whose participation in industrial organization allows them to become "enlightened, competent and loyal citizens of an industrial commonwealth." And these virtues are not the automatic products of traditional democratization. "I do not believe," said Croly, ". . . that a more democratic industrial organization will bring with it necessarily a more enlightened democratic political organization."[53] Thus, while government should clearly support organized labor and thereby strengthen the whole society, it should not expect that merely by organizing workingmen along customary democratic lines such new strength will be

☆

[51] *Ibid.*, pp. 387, 130-131.
[52] *Progressive Democracy*, pp. 118-119, 385.
[53] *Ibid.*, p. 379.

achieved. Progress in labor, if it is to come, will involve the consideration of a variety of issues, all of which are raised in the following paragraph.

> The further improvement of their position does not depend upon their acquisition of property. It depends upon the increasing productivity of the industry; and increasing production will depend upon the increasing excellence of individual work, upon the equally meritorious work of the cooperators, upon skilful and economical management, and, finally, upon the general increase in industrial and social efficiency. Thus the wage-earners will have won a kind of independence, in which devotion to work will individualize their lives without dividing them from their fellow-workers. The democracy will derive its education, both morally and socially, from the liberalizing, leavening and humanizing effect of its working activity and of the resulting responsibilities and discipline. [54]

To make sense of Croly's position here we shall have to explore in some depth his conceptions of property, production, excellence, efficiency, and education. We turn first to his treatment of property.

Property and Class

What the laborer requires at the outset is precisely that status which property ownership affords. The wage-earner, Croly believed, ought to have the same legal security, dignity, and control over his own destiny as the propertied man. Property ownership per se, however, provided a poor source of industrial motivation. Croly pointed out that the "wage-earner whose greatest stimulus to work is assumed to be the ultimate chance of becoming a property owner, may be a hard worker, but he will rarely be a good worker or a desirable citizen in an industrial democracy. As a worker his eye will be fixed rather on the goal than on the job. As a property owner he will be afraid of being unable to keep his property. In both aspects his motives will be interested and self-involved rather than disinterested and social." While Croly found revolutionary methods of syndicalism repugnant, the fundamental aim struck him as worth pursuing. "The older unionism," he felt, "was driven into the proclamation of a restricted and interested program, which converted work into a kind of class property, and which proposed to exchange a minimum of work for a maximum of cash . . . It was a distinct gain when syndicalism demanded of the old craft unionism that it cease to be a parasite upon a perverted economic system, and that it should fight and plan for the creation of a new system, based upon the dignity, the responsibility and the moral

☆

[54] *Ibid.*, pp. 395-396.

value of human work."[55] But while Croly could express sympathy with syndicalist goals—he went so far as to warn his nation that, should syndicalist ideals not be honored, labor's impatience might turn all workingmen to revolutionary violence—he was not prepared to carry his sympathies to a point that included endorsement of class struggle and the abolition of private property.

Class struggle he saw as aimless unless tempered by the influence of Progressive principles. The nationalist principle alone would of course strip struggle doctrines of their rationale for violence, since nationalism implied positive governmental action for all classes funneled through normal political channels. Private property, while it often led to unhappy consequences, must be accepted as an irremovable aspect of civilized life. Croly was quick to admit that economic privilege stemmed from the combination of ability and property, but he was equally quick to add that "the institution of private property, as we now have it, has its root buried so deep in the average human nature, that no partial alteration in economic mechanism can possibly eliminate privilege . . . Unquestionably the institution of private property stimulates human cupidity, particularly under the conditions prevailing since the industrial revolution. A modification of that institution will itself tend to socialize human nature. But to modify is not to eliminate; and so long as private property endures, as it must for a long time, it will carry with it a certain substantial measure of economic privilege." Indeed Croly was convinced that, while private property unavoidably led to inequality and injustice, recognizing that this institution could not and should not be undermined constituted the foundation of any valid program for Progressive change.[56]

Democracy and Education

More critical than his views on property was Croly's conception of education, a concept that runs to the core of his theory and brings most of his central ideas into focus. In *The Promise of American Life*, Croly speaks metaphorically of the formation of a national school. "The nation," he writes, "like the individual, must go to school; and the national school is not a lecture hall or a library. Its schooling consists chiefly in experimental collective action aimed at the realization of the collective purpose."[57] Though metaphor, inasmuch as the notion of a national school merely provided Croly with a useful way of describing a purposeful society, the continued mention of collective

☆

[55] *Ibid.*, pp. 385-386, 388-389.
[56] *Ibid.*, pp. 392, 112, 113.
[57] *The Promise of American Life*, p. 407.

education indicates clearly that the idea was for Croly more than just metaphor, that in his eyes citizen involvement in nationwide programs constituted a genuine learning process simultaneously benefitting both nation and individual. The nation would benefit simply through the existence of a process that brought citizens together for conjunctive action; the individual, all individuals, could reap advantages by experiencing the ways of social involvement and, from this experience, by learning an individualism possessed of higher and more creative qualities.

Croly was prepared to rest his case on the doctrine of man's perfectibility. "Democracy," he said, "must stand or fall on a platform of possible human perfectibility. If human nature cannot be improved by institutions, democracy is at best a more than usually safe form of political organization; and the only interesting inquiry about its future would be: How long will it continue to work? But if it is to work better as well as merely longer, it must have some leavening effect of human nature; and the sincere democrat is obliged to assume the power of the leaven."[58] Since education is the intermediary through which democratic institutions operate on the individual, the concept of education becomes crucially important.

The exact nature of the national school is not easily perceived. Functionally speaking, Croly expressed the highest of hopes. He stressed that "the social education appropriate to a democracy must be, above all, a liberal education. It must accomplish for the mass of the people a work of intellectual and moral emancipation similar to that which the traditional system of humane culture has been supposed to accomplish for a minority."[59] While the enthusiasm of this expression goes beyond Jefferson, and in its cultural optimism even beyond Matthew Arnold, the meaning of a "liberal" education is still left somewhat in doubt. In the following quotation we begin perhaps to get a feeling for what Croly had in mind. He argued that "the creation of an adequate system of educating men and women for *disinterested* service is a necessary condition both of social amelioration and social conservation—once this underlying condition is fully and candidly accepted, then a fair chance exists of ultimately uniting *disinterested* and *aspiring* people upon a practicable method of accomplishing purpose."[60] [Emphasis added.]

On the most general level the combination of "disinterested" and "aspiring" behavior presents no logical difficulty for, remembering

☆

[58] *Ibid.*, p. 400.
[59] *Progressive Democracy*, p. 417.
[60] *Ibid.*, p. 408.

Croly's redefining of individualism into social terms, one can imagine a process of education through which individuals find identity in participation in such a way that disinterest in personal aggrandizement on the one hand and aspiring toward the realization of common goals on the other would develop as a matter of course. It is exactly this picture that Croly draws when he places the workingman in an educational context. He speaks of a "socially educative distribution of wealth." The former condition will not only yield the latter, but it will do so automatically, thereby rendering the syndicalist brand of reform irrelevant, while at the same time producing a much improved individual citizen. A "society which socializes labor," Croly contended, ". . . need not fear revolutionary agitation in favor of dispossession. A socializing system of labor constitutes an infallible and indispensable means of social education. It converts a worker into a good citizen, not by demanding of him the prostration of his own life before the idol of self-repression, but by encouraging him to renew his life through exhilarating activity for his own benefit and that of his fellow-citizens." [61] Thus, on this level, "disinterested" behavior can be equated with a self-actualization realized in concert with the realization of the national purpose. On narrower grounds, however, disinterestedness would seem to raise certain problems, particularly since Croly acknowledged that inequality of property and talent would continue to produce aggrandizement throughout society.

"Disinterested" Work and Progress

Very early in his first book Croly suggested the area in which these problems might reside. "The Promise of American life," he wrote, "is to be fulfilled—not merely by a maximum amount of economic freedom, but by a certain measure of discipline; not merely by the abundant satisfaction of individual desires, but by a large measure of individual subordination and self-denial." [62] At this point progress would seem to depend upon the very repression of self that in *Progressive Democracy* Croly would find reason to exclude. Although there is considerable discussion of self-realization through community, purpose, and faith in the intervening chapers, Croly reiterated this assertion at the conclusion of *The Promise of American Life*. In the final section, entitled "Constructive Individualism," he observed that the "men most possessed by intense brotherly feelings fall into an error . . . as to the way in which those feelings can be realized.

☆

[61] *Progressive Democracy*, p. 423.
[62] *The Promise of American Life*, p. 22.

Consumate faith itself is no substitute for good work. Back of any moral conversion must come a long and slow process of social reorganization and individual emancipation; and *not until the reorganization has been partially accomplished,* and the individual *released, disciplined* and *purified,* will the soil be prepared for the crowning work of some democratic Saint Francis."[63] [Emphasis added.] I have stressed certain words and phrases in this quotation because I think that, taken together with remarks quoted earlier, they indicate a slightly different side of Croly, a side cautious enough to project significant social change to a point in the fairly remote future and, more importantly, a side that constrains the exercise of democratic faith by necessitating a prior process of purification, disinterest, and discipline.

Thus, early in the last chapter of *The Promise,* Croly could note that, while asking individuals continually to sacrifice their private interests to the welfare of the whole society was to demand the impossible, just such sacrifices would be required. "The only entirely satisfactory solution," he wrote, ". . . is offered by the systematic authoritative transformation of the private interest of the individual into a disinterested devotion to a special object." As presented here, disinterestedness is clearly something very different from that mental state reached through social and political involvement. This difference is made clearer still when Croly writes: "The truth is that individuality cannot be dissociated from the pursuit of a disinterested object. It is a moral and intellectual quality, and it must be realized by moral and intellectual means."[64] The quality and the means must assuredly be intellectual but their moral content is questionable, for as illustrations of disinterestedness Croly offers the achievement of distinction in painting, railroad management, corporate leadership, indeed, in carrying to a level of excellence the exercise of any particular craft, trade, or profession. Disinterestedness, finally, is equated with discipline and repression only insofar as vocation or occupation are attached to the end of making money. Croly would thus reverse Sumner's position by positing for work goals far loftier than those of mere subsistence or the attainment of bourgeois comforts.

Croly, in fact, followed Marx in believing that man finds his essential meaning in his work and that pecuniary incentives serve only to alienate him from his source of identity. "A man's individuality," he wrote, "is projected into his work . . . He is identified with his job, and by means of that identification his individuality becomes constructive." Having said this, Croly then added a thought which Marx would never have accepted. "His achievement," he said, "just because of

☆

[63] *Ibid.,* p. 453.
[64] *Ibid.,* pp. 418, 411.

its excellence, has an inevitable and an unequivocal social value."[65] This statement allowed Croly to carry his idea to a completely un-Marxian conclusion.

> What the better American individual particularly needs, then, is a completer faith in his own individual purpose and power—a clearer understanding of his own individual opportunities. *He needs to do what he has been doing, only more so,* and with the conviction that thereby he is becoming not less but more of an American. His patriotism, instead of being something apart from his special work, should be absolutely identified therewith, because no matter how much the eminence of his personal achievement may temporarily divide him from his fellow-countrymen, he is, by attaining to such an eminence, helping in the most effectual possible way to build the only fitting habitation for a sincere democracy. He is to make his contribution to individual improvement primarily by making himself more of an individual. The individual as well as the nation must be educated and "uplifted" chiefly by what the individual can do for himself. Education, like charity, should begin at home.[66] [Emphasis added.]

The individual, in short, is exhorted to contribute to the national faith by shifting his focus from financial considerations to the intrinsic merit of his own work and, as that work improves, the Progressive renovation of society may be said to be underway.

The concept of disinterest, then, posited as a means to pave the way for a new national purpose, transports Croly finally to an idea of citizenship that is essentially devoid of public content and that focuses the individual's attention not upon national objectives or purposes but upon the ultimate perfection of his own capabilities. Precisely how this ties in with social amelioration is difficult to say. Presumably the common pursuit of excellence will yield collective action of a beneficial kind. Although Croly does not make an explicit connection, one can surmise how the two areas might be bridged.

Before examining this problem, however, it is fair to ask how Croly saw individuals being educated through democratic institutions to pursue vocational excellence rather than pecuniary gain. Croly is not entirely satisfying on this point. He knew that complete rejection of monetary incentives could only come through changing the whole basis of the competitive system. This he did not advocate, and short of this he could only suggest that government-induced economic reforms, the reorganization of labor, and the utilization of efficiency principles in business would at least minimize those instances where making money and excellence of work were unrelated,

☆

[65] *Ibid.,* p. 412.

[66] *Ibid.,* p. 431.

while state assistance to the disadvantaged would reduce class differences and thereby discourage class consciousness and make the accumulation of dollars less important. If these devices seemed insufficient Croly could only remind his readers that what mattered most was the goal and not the particular means used for its realization. [67]

Collective Action and Efficiency

The question of how individual and collective action are taken together is more difficult. Some general remarks on Croly's work are necessary in order to deal with this question. The argument in *The Promise of American Life* and the argument in *Progressive Democracy* follow roughly the same pattern. Croly begins with a critical evaluation of current political practice based on an interpretation of the American past; this is followed by a critique of contemporary institutions and of the movements for institutional reform. Both books conclude with some general observations on future possibilities and suggestions for immediate changes that might make these possibilities more conceivable.

As the logical movement of the argument is similar in both volumes so too are the changes in mood and tone that characterize each of its steps. Croly's stance at the outset is profoundly critical as he seeks to uncover the causes underlying the political and social evils of his day. But as he progresses his tone begins to soften, to become more moderate, until finally he concludes his argument on a note which, if not entirely cheerful and optimistic, is at least conciliatory and at some considerable remove from the radicalism that its earlier formulation implied. The call to individual excellence—to fashion oneself, in Croly's words, into a "moral instrument"—at the end of *The Promise of American Life* comes as a dramatic surprise in light of the heavy emphasis on common values and collective action that preceded it, and in simply recasting a norm already cherished by the society it very much reminds one of the similar position taken by Emerson a half-century earlier. A close reading of *Progressive Democracy*—with a focus on its language and logic rather than on its specific recommendations—is necessary in order to comprehend Croly's mixture of individual and social categories.

The methods advocated by Croly for generating high individual achievement could also be applied to society. "Societies," Croly felt, "will never be socialized out of scripts, speeches, exhortations

☆

[67] *Ibid.*, pp. 414-417.

and creeds, unless their interest has been aroused, their attention concentrated, and their will *disciplined* by loyal action on behalf of the
social ideal."[68] [Emphasis added.] The last requisite, a disciplined
will, was especially important, as critical for the forging of good institutions as it was in forming good individuals. The problem was in
finding a repository of institutional discipline similar to that which
the individual could find within himself. This problem was particularly acute with respect to the industrial realm, that area where basic
reform would hopefully begin.

In this quest Croly turned to the application of principles drawn
from a field that had been looming increasingly large in intellectual
circles—namely the discipline of science. America must, Croly believed, have decisive increases in industrial efficiency, and such
increases "can," he wrote, "ultimately be derived from only one
source—from the more comprehensive and more successful application to industry of scientific methods and of the results of essentially
scientific research. The use of scientific methods and results in industry
is the natural and inevitable accompaniment of its reorganization in
the interest of democratic fulfilment. Industrial democracy will never
accomplish its purpose, unless science can be brought increasingly
to its assistance; and the needed assistance will have to be rendered
in a most liberal measure."[69] Science, then, would provide the canons
of discipline for the economic sphere, and its use could probably be
defended more easily than could self-discipline as applied to the
individual, for whereas the individual would always have to struggle
to overcome a more or less natural tendency toward self-indulgence,
science in its very nature, at least as Croly understood it, was the very
measure of disinterestedness.

At the same time, science in its applied aspect, and this was the
side of science that Croly seemed usually to have in mind, could also
introduce disciplinary standards against which individuals could
assess their personal attempts at achieving excellence. A man whose
trade or craft was subject to technical standards would, Croly suggested, "be kept up to the level of his best work by a motive which had
almost become disinterested." And the model for such standards was
obvious. "The perfect type of authoritative technical methods are
those which prevail among scientific men in respect to scientific work
. . . There is only one standard for all scientific investigators—the
highest standard; and so far as a man falls below that standard his
inferiority is immediately reflected in his reputation." The man who
has mastered a body of "technically competent work . . . is," Croly

☆

[68] *Progressive Democracy*, p. 216.
[69] *Ibid.*, p. 397.

concluded, "by way of being the well-forged and well-tempered instrument." [70]

The ramifications of a "scientific" view would extend very far. In the first place science is a very severe taskmaster. The application of scientific techniques to industrial management, for example, would require a discipline on the part of workers which would logically necessitate a military kind of regimentation. For this reason Croly, while he believed that workers ought to submit to such a regimen, felt that they should do so democratically, of their own free choice. Industry restructured in this way would find the need to introduce new organizational methods on the managerial level as well. Continuing the military analogy, Croly observed that it "is better to depend on a well-equipped general staff, which will obey the orders of society and carry out an approved policy, than upon Napoleons, who convert the national economic resources into an instrument of personal aggrandizement . . . The Napoleons of business are being succeeded by the Von Moltkes." The lessons of scientific methodology are, furthermore, essential to all areas of society, and with their application older boundary distinctions tend to break down. "The successful conduct of both public and private business is becoming more and more a matter of expert administration, which demands the use of similar methods and is confronted by the solution of similar problems. Both are coming to meet on the same plane of scientific method and social responsibility. Private business of all kinds is becoming affected with a public function, and must be equipped for an increase in efficiency and for an increase in human responsibility." [71]

Efficiency, the hallmark of scientific administration, was more than a task of organizational excellence; it was ultimately at least a partial measure of democracy itself. Croly insisted that the dictates of science and efficiency must never be allowed to replace social fulfillment and national purpose as goals of the society. And yet so enamored was he of scientific procedures that he could not imagine the achievement of democratic ends without the use of such means. Society, he wrote, "is organized for efficiency chiefly because in the absence of efficiency no genuine formative popular political experience can be expected to accrue." [72] Scientific efficiency, then, becomes an absolute necessity if democratic Progressivism is to be realized and, because Croly is vague about specific *political* goals, it is difficult to see why scientific efficiency is not logically a Progressive end in itself.

☆

[70] *The Promise of American Life,* pp. 416, 434, 433.

[71] *Progressive Democracy,* pp. 398, 400.

[72] *Ibid.,* pp. 404-405, 378.

Progressive Expectations

The move from communalism to individual technique in *The Promise of American Life* and to scientific organization in *Progressive Democracy* is in many respects truly astonishing in light of Croly's radical starting points. On the other hand many hints are dropped en route so that by the time the reader reaches the concluding sections of both books he has begun to suspect that he may be in for an anticlimax. Time and again Croly tells us that he is distrustful of doctrinaire "intellectualism," that he prefers a pragmatic approach to all social problems. "The goal," he writes, "is sacred. The program is fluid."[73] But so fluid is the program and so distant is the goal that it is extremely difficult to know how, or indeed if, Croly's suggestions for immediate programs relate to the ultimate promise that his goals imply. For example, when the endorsement of government manipulation is added to the picture of the citizen as instrument, willingly submitting to organized scientific discipline, one begins to envisage a Hamiltonianism complete with the possibilities of elitist rule. Such a possibility in Croly's writings cries out for a full discussion of national leadership and its relation to democratic forms. Croly's adulation of Roosevelt and Lincoln — the latter he called "more than an American" — suggests what his views might be. But except for a few brief remarks to the effect that strong executive leadership would revitalize the American party system, he confined himself to a consideration of leadership on the state level.

There is no reason why an analysis of political leadership on this level could not be used to shed light on the larger problem. But Croly makes this extension difficult. In *Progressive Democracy* he spends an entire chapter outlining the reform plan advocated by the People's Power League of Oregon. This plan called for an enormous shift of power and responsibility to the governor's office through the following means: (1) unicameralism based on proportional representation to be introduced, with the governor and the legislature elected simultaneously for four-year terms; (2) the governor to appoint his own cabinet and *all* other state officials except local sheriffs and county attorneys; (3) the governor to have the right to sit in the legislature, cast a vote, and introduce bills and advocate their passage. Croly gave a reasoned justification for these changes and stipulated that the exercise of such power could judiciously be checked by the wise use of the recall petition and by not giving a veto to the governor.[74]

☆

[73] *Ibid.*, pp. 178, 217.

[74] *Ibid.*, pp. 284-302, 325.

The problem with this whole conception is that in the very next chapter Croly goes a fair distance towards nullifying it. He states that, while he finds "permanent value" in the underlying principles of the Power League plan, he is by no means wedded to it, that he presented it only by way of illustrating ideas worthy of attention: "a sincere progressive democracy must, in my opinion, ultimately consider them."[75] Left in this indeterminate state, the reader is still justified in worrying about the problem of democratic leadership degenerating into autocratic tyranny.

Theoretical Ambiguity

Similar uncertainty clouds many of Croly's other major recommendations. For example, while he alluded to the distant time when workers, after first educating themselves in the art of self-government, might gain control over the industrial sector, he did not treat this issue in depth but turned instead to an extended evaluation of the direct democracy procedures which operated on the local levels. Even more critical in producing this uncertainty was Croly's ultimate ambivalence about the very need for serious reform. In fairness Croly had to admit that the current system "with all its deficiencies has probably enabled a larger proportion of its beneficiaries to live bravely than any other political and economic system." Meaningful reform, moreover, must begin with the understanding that constitutionalism is here to stay and that its very existence makes democratic change possible. "Progressive democracy," Croly wrote, ". . . can afford to combine more democracy with more progressiveness than . . . in the past, partly because an attachment to legal methods has become deeply rooted in the national tradition."[76]

With these remarks in mind it is not surprising that Croly should find himself occasionally pulled in opposite directions. Thus, on the one hand his reliance on scientific administration naturally led him to defend the huge corporate monopolies as useful mechanisms performing invaluable technical services for the society. That the economic giants gain their prosperity at the expense of the small businessman is in fact in the public interest, for the latter are frequently wasteful and inefficient. "The competitive methods of nature," Croly noted, "have been, and still are, within limits indispensable." The men who run the mammouth organizations should be publicly controlled only in order that their margin of profit does not exceed a

☆

[75] *Ibid.*, pp. 327-328.
[76] *Ibid.*, pp. 225-226.

justifiable reward for their advancement of efficiency. Beyond this Croly could foresee the remote possibility of a corporation becoming so large and comprehensive that it "possessed" one of the nation's natural resources. "In all such cases," he suggested, "some system of public ownership and private operation should, if possible, be introduced." Short of this, monopolies and oligopolies should be tolerated, indeed encouraged, with government regulation consisting primarily of a gradually increased corporation tax.[77]

From his more critical perspective, however, Croly lashed out at institutionalized corporate giants. "If a localized economic system wishes to hold its own against a centralized economic system, it must," Croly declared, "take care to strip the agencies of big business of every shred of governmental favor. Nay, considering the favors which those agencies have enjoyed in the past, and the grip which they have obtained on the vitals of the American economic system, they must be discriminated against and reduced to comparative impotence. The American territorial democracy have awakened to the necessity of such a policy in their own class interest." Croly allowed, moreover, that a case could be made for such policies as operating in the public interest. Having said this, however, he immediately began to equivocate. He noted that recent economic changes have benefitted property owners as much as corporations, that anticorporation policies will not abolish privilege but will merely remove it from one sector and place it in another and, finally, that the whole idea of politically opposing corporations "may or may not be justifiable" on grounds of equity.[78] Croly's approach, in short, left him frequently in the curious position of finding no way of connecting specific proposals with his general philosophy, and this in turn caused him to feel at least cautious, and often ambivalent, about his very own recommendations.

The problem of relating practical proposals to a large political philosophy is not unique to Croly; it is a difficulty that has characterized the tradition of political theory at least since Aristotle. Thus one might sympathize with Croly caught in a painful dilemma. But such sentiment is inappropriate, for in delineating his own task Croly ruled the dilemma itself out of bounds. To show that he fully understood the issue Croly stipulated that a "radical theory does not demand in the interest of consistency an equally radical action. It only demands a sincere attempt to push the application of the theory as far as conditions will permit, and the employment of means sufficient probably to accomplish the immediate purpose." While one might wish for more

☆

[77] *The Promise of American Life*, pp. 115, 359, 204, 379, 367-376.
[78] *Progressive Democracy*, pp. 110-112.

elaboration on this point, this is not an unfair statement of the theorist's obligation.

Croly saw himself, however, as more than a political theorist; he perceived his role as that of public educator as well. In "the endeavor to establish and popularize his theory, a radical critic," he argued, "cannot afford any similar concessions. His own opinions can become established only by the displacement of the traditional opinions; and the way to displace a traditional error is not to be compromising and conciliatory, but to be as uncompromising and as irritating as one's abilities and one's vision of the truth will permit. The critic in his capacity as agitator is living in a state of war with his opponents; and the ethics of warfare are not the ethics of statesmanship."[79] If Croly's relation to the defenders of the system may be described as a state of war, one wonders what phrases would be appropriate to describing the condition in which men like Eugene Debs, Lawrence Gronlund, and Daniel DeLeon found themselves.

Croly's Insight

Croly's personal summation, on the other hand, is not without merit. Strictly as *critic* he attacked boldly and without reservation principles revered by generations of Americans. Anyone courageous enough to publicly denigrate Thomas Jefferson in Croly's day is justified in labeling himself radical. But as *constructive theorist* Croly failed to carry his insights to their logical conclusion, and his failure in this respect tends to dull the brilliance of his social criticism. His fear of ideology, particularly of Marxist derivative, caused him ultimately to devitalize the faith he had called for by submerging it beneath a sea of technical efficiency and scientific expertise. "Faith," wrote Croly in *Progressive Democracy*, "is necessary and constructive, precisely because the situation demands both risks and sacrifices, and because the readiness to incur the risk and make the sacrifices is an essential part of political character in a democracy."[80] But in the end Croly himself retreated from risk.

The exaltation of science was for the Progressive intellectual what the espousal of business methodology was for the Progressive layman. Both served to distract attention from the political and economic question and thereby to reaffirm the status quo. Moreover, in elevating corporate organizational principles Croly brought the realms of science and business into harmony and in so doing helped to bridge the gap

☆

[79] *The Promise of American Life*, p. 420.
[80] *Progressive Democracy*, p. 170.

between Progressivism of the civic improvement variety and that form which tended toward a more theoretical expression. When Croly argued that the immense wealth of the minority could not be distributed among the masses because this action would produce social lethargy in the latter,[81] he demonstrated just how close the two Progressive lines could come.

Croly's theoretical diffidence is striking precisely because his critical vision is so astounding. Progressivism in its typical form never perceived the fundamental nature of the question. By focusing on the idea of national purpose Croly reached the heart of the American problem and crystalized the issue as had no political writer before him. His irresolution was perhaps in some ways a function of his role as popular educator. Rather than placing him at war with society, as he believed, this role may, as it has to so many American thinkers, have forced him to tailor his theory to fit within the boundaries of conventional political action. There was no a priori reason why Croly should have constructed a theory along Marxist lines, unless, of course, the logic of his argument demanded such a construction. As the argument stands — with its accentuation of class differentiation, its association of power and property, and its initial call for a revolutionary transformation of society — a perfectly good case can be made for reaching conclusions entirely congruent with those of Marxism.

In this connection Croly's attenuated perception is genuinely disturbing, for the concept of *interdependence* that he frequently utilized[82] might have led him to a totally new response to the American condition. Interdependence is highly suggestive in that it offers the possibility of a conceptual middle ground between the isolation and competitiveness of complete independence and the subservience and paternalism characteristic of an excessively dependent society. The concept might have provided Croly with a starting point, one which at the very least could have forced him to deal more directly with problems of leadership, authority, and freedom in a society that possessed a sense of community and was dedicated to a national purpose.

But Croly did not follow his own lead, and it is therefore hardly surprising that the more compliant Progressive movement stopped considerably to the rear of his position. Largely reticent to begin with, the movement fixed even more firmly than Croly on the doctrine of pragmatic reform, and given this fixation, it is still less surprising that pragmatism itself would soon become the American substitute for national purpose.

☆

[81] *Ibid.*, p. 422.
[82] See pp. 274, 279, 282.

10

THE Great community
JOHn Dewey

Pragmatism and the New Deal

From a theoretical point of view it is a short step from Progressivism to the 1930's and the era of the New Deal. But it is a difficult step to take, for one is continually put off by a perpetuation of the older rhetoric. If economic individualism had begun to lose applicability in the 1880's and 1890's it surely was irrelevant to Franklin Roosevelt's far-flung system of public and private regulation. And yet, even after the New Deal and its proliferation of administrative agencies, the old purpose remained on the linguistic level, was clung to tenaciously by an America reluctant to give up, even symbolically—perhaps especially symbolically—the only national purpose it had ever known. The result of this reluctance was a kind of dialogue in tongues that was imperfectly understood by most participants; where, for example, people still spoke of success but usually meant the attainment of personal security; where business was still regarded as the independent source of national energy even as government, under the euphemism of "pump-priming," continued to enlarge its sphere of economic control.[1]

☆

[1] For an especially enlightening viewpoint on certain aspects of this problem, see Thurmond Arnold, *The Folklore of Capitalism*, Yale University Press, New Haven, Conn., 1937; Thurmond Arnold, *The Symbols of Government*, Yale University Press, New Haven, Conn., 1935.

Linguistic uncertainty among the public reflected an equivalent uncertainty on the political level. If Progressivism was unprepared finally to entertain significant and immediate innovation, the New Deal was, as Rexford Tugwell soon discovered, still less ready to embark upon avenues of fundamental change. While FDR's early speeches often struck radical notes, his reforms were primarily corrective and regenerative in intent, so much so that some commentators have depicted Roosevelt as a conservative whose great contribution was to shore up and thereby to perpetuate an archaic system that was amenable to total transformation. In important ways, however, Roosevelt seemed to be without ideology, a problem-solver who would try a little of everything in order to bring a semblance of economic stability to the nation.

This approach, eclectic in its willingness to borrow from a variety of ideologies, selective in its reluctance to utilize wholly the remedies of any one ideology, aimed always at alleviating immediate stress and eschewing goals of long-term effect, has come to be known as the "pragmatic approach," and the term "pragmatism" has frequently been used to summarize the entire New Deal philosophy. Thus it could be said that whatever the pronouncements of Roosevelt and his "brain trust," their political program was invariably pragmatic: described positively by those who admired an American tradition of employing the means at hand to meet specific, short-run problems; negatively by critics who felt that because pragmatism provided no general set of national ideals it would serve to maintain the basic inequities of the current system by curbing and controlling only its most obvious excesses.

To picture the New Deal in these terms seems not entirely unfair. As Tugwell has noted, "the nation was advancing into a future which was no more than half understood, which, psychologically, was resented, and yet which produced things and services people could no longer do without. A stage in intellectual history had been reached at which the New Deal would linger for years, unwilling to name the sacrifices of private privilege and of speculative hope necessary to a world in which security is achieved by management, rather than by nature's largesse or by good luck. This lingering between two worlds . . . would be evident in the cautious and half-hearted approaches we should make to any guarantees of security as well as to the overhead management of industry."[2] Whether, on the other hand, it is appro-

☆

[2] Rexford Tugwell, "The Progressive Orthodoxy of Franklin D. Roosevelt," *Ethics*, vol. 64, pp. 2-3, October, 1953. Tugwell's retrospective observations on the New Deal he knew so well are particularly illuminating from an ideological point of view. In addition to the quoted article see: "The Experimental Roosevelt," *Political Quarterly*,

priate to designate this approach as pragmatic is another question entirely.

The relevance of pragmatism to the New Deal as well as the intrinsic meaning of the term itself can only be discovered by examining the works of John Dewey, the twentieth century's most noted philosopher of pragmatism. Dewey may not have been quite the central figure that Commager makes of him — "he became," Commager writes, "the guide, the mentor, and the conscience of the American people: it is scarcely an exaggeration to say that for a generation no major issue was clarified until Dewey had spoken" — but he lived and wrote during both the Progressive and New Deal periods, and in his works he attempted, as has no other writer in American history, to bring genuine philosophical reasoning and the solution of important political problems into close association. It is safe to say that his influence was substantial, and that one cannot adequately understand American thought between the periods of the two Roosevelts without a careful consideration of his ideas. As late as 1960, Charles Frankel could state categorically that "to know where we stand toward Dewey's ideas is to find out, at least in part, where we stand with ourselves."[3] Frankel's remark may be just as applicable today as it was in 1960.

In Dewey's time, as in our own, pragmatism in its popular meaning suggested practicality, the ability to make do with available resources, an interest in quick and tangible results, and a corresponding avoidance of long range programs whose success might be regarded as somewhat dubious. To one who is interested in radical change it is easy to see how this view could serve the interests of those who control existing political and financial institutions. The equating of pragmatism and mere practicality, however, was not confined to the masses, and from its very inception sophisticated commentators could be found who decried the conservative bias of the philosophy. In the 1920's, for example, Lewis Mumford could look back to the late nineteenth century and accuse William James of using pragmatism as an apology for the status quo. It was James, Mumford contended, who gave the "attitude of compromise and acquiescence a name: he called it pragmatism." As Mumford saw it, pragmatism constituted a "blessed anaesthetic" which produced a "paralysis" of public policy. And no

---

vol. 21, pp. 239-270, July, 1950; "The Protagonists: Roosevelt and Hoover," *Antioch Review,* vol. 13, pp. 419-442, December, 1953; "Franklin D. Roosevelt on the Verge of the Presidency," *Antioch Review,* vol. 16, pp. 367-373, September, 1956; "The Fallow Years of Franklin D. Roosevelt," *Ethics,* vol. 66, pp. 98-116, January, 1956.

[3] Henry Steele Commager, *The American Mind, An Interpretation of American Thought and Character Since the 1880's,* Yale University Press, New Haven, Conn., 1950, p. 100. Charles Frankel, "John Dewey's Legacy," *American Scholar,* vol. 29, p. 314, Summer, 1960.

less a figure than Bertrand Russell, writing also in the 1920's, summed up pragmatism by labeling it the philosophical expression of American commercialism. And, although far from the positions of either Mumford or Russell, Arthur E. Murphy, writing as recently as 1960 in the *Journal of Philosophy*, argued that however laudable Dewey's personal commitments, his philosophy never went beyond the level of methodology—of charting general patterns of human conduct—and, by providing no objective standards of judgment, left the reformer "moralizing in a moral vacuum of his own making," powerless to engage in really serious programs of reform.[4] Whether viewed favorably by the popular mind, as it usually was, or criticized by professional scholars, pragmatism was typically identified as that philosophy which above all espoused expedience, availability, adaptation, utility, and convenience, especially as applied to matters of social or political policy. Since Dewey's name and pragmatism were virtually synonymous, we will test the accuracy of this view by looking closely at Dewey's political philosophy.

America Adrift

If a theorist is to escape the charge of political apologist, or the less serious charge of institutional tinkerer, his works must possess two basic ingredients: a thoroughgoing critique of society, and an understandable set of suggestions for meaningful change. On the first of these there is absolutely no doubt with respect to Dewey's writings. Dewey cast a critical eye upon his nation, and the result was an analysis of America that was cogent and profound and that called into question many of the conventional ideas and practices of his time.

The basic problem, Dewey felt, was that things—events, institutions, the future—had been allowed to run out of control. Mainly responsible for this phenomenon was the generally held belief in progress, a belief which saw progress as an objective force that moved toward higher levels of civilization independent of intelligent foresight and planning. Dewey found this conviction not only wrongheaded but exceedingly dangerous. "Progress," he maintained, "is not automatic; it depends upon human intent and aim and upon

☆

[4] Mumford's observations are quoted by Dewey in "Philosophy and the Social Order" (published originally in *The New Republic*, January 5, 1927, under the title "The Pragmatic Acquiescence"), Joseph Ratner (ed.), *Characters and Events: Popular Essays in Social and Political Philosophy*, Henry Holt and Company, Inc., New York, 1929, vol. II, p. 435. Russell's position is cited by Dewey in "Pragmatic America," *ibid.*, p. 542. Arthur E. Murphy, "John Dewey and American Liberalism," *Journal of Philosophy*, vol. 57, p. 436, June 23, 1960.

acceptance of responsibility for its production . . . I doubt if the whole history of mankind shows any more vicious and demoralizing ethic than the recent widespread belief that each of us, as individuals and as classes, might safely and complacently devote ourselves to increasing our own possessions, material, intellectual, and artistic, because progress is inevitable anyhow." This passive view of progress Dewey saw as directly connected with *laissez faire*, the dominant economic and political ideology of the day, "a philosophy which trusts the direction of human affairs to nature, or Providence, or evolution, or manifest destiny—that is to say, to accident."[5] Left in such empty hands, human affairs can only degenerate.

Citizens Without Purpose

Despite appearances the affairs of individuals are similarly affected. The personal corollary to *laissez faire* is economic individualism, and fealty to this principle eventually robs the individual of a purposeful life. For Dewey the public and private realms were organically related. "Assured and integrated individuality," he believed, "is the product of definite social relationships and publicly acknowledged functions. Judged by this standard, even those who seem to be in control and to carry the expression of their special individual abilities to a high pitch, are submerged. They may be captains of finance and industry, but until there is some consensus of belief as to the meaning of finance and industry in civilization as a whole, they cannot be captains of their own souls—their beliefs and aims." And the fact that modern society is characterized by increased organization and corporateness in no way alleviates the situation. The organizations are in one way or another related to pecuniary interests and they therefore cultivate aspirations on the part of their members that are primarily egoistic and private. The effect of such organizations can only be harmful. "An economic individualism of motives and aims," Dewey asserted, "underlies our present corporate mechanisms, and undoes the individual."[6]

Part of the reason that individuals are in such straits is that contemporary knowledge has not caught up with present circumstances. Men are prisoners of very old beliefs whose connection to reality has vanished. So far is this the case that even economic individualism, although an accurate summation of behavior and motivation, fails in its ideological formulation to provide valid explanations. "For the

☆

[5] "Progress," Ratner (ed.), *op. cit.*, vol. II, pp. 824, 827.
[6] John Dewey, *Individualism Old and New*, Capicorn Books, New York, 1929, pp. 53, 59.

most part," Dewey argued, "economic individualism interpreted as energy and enterprise devoted to private profit, has been an adjunct, often a parasitical one, to the movement of technical and scientific forces." This being the case, men are not only captives of a misconceived ideology, but one which is in fact at odds with actual conditions. "This profound split," Dewey observed, "is the cause of distraction and bewilderment."[7] Indeed, it might eventually cause large scale alienation, for if men should seek to change their institutions with ideas based on false knowledge or inadequate preparation they are certain to experience frustrations of the most serious kind. The "split," Dewey suggested, "may be more than an incident of a particular individual's experience. The social situation may be such as to throw the class given to articulate reflection back into their own thoughts and desires without providing the means by which these ideas and aspirations can be used to reorganize the environment. Under such conditions, men take revenge, as it were, upon the alien and hostile environment by cultivating contempt for it, by giving it a bad name. They seek refuge and consolation within their own states of mind, their own imaginings and wishes, which they compliment by calling both more real and more ideal than the despised outer world."[8] Such men are not only incapable of improving current conditions, they constitute a real threat to that which has already been achieved.

Legacies of the Past

Like Croly, Dewey was aware of the historical tradition that gave rise to America's faith in *laissez faire*, progress, and economic individualism. Unlike Croly, however, he traced the genealogy of these sentiments to ideas that predated those of either Jefferson or Hamilton. Their origin lay neither in the fortuitous growth of commerce, nor in conspiracies perpetrated by the trading class; they stemmed from the intrinsic meaning of the Enlightenment itself: "the belief in nature as a mighty force, and in reason as having only to cooperate with nature, instead of thwarting it with its own petty, voluntary devices, for it to usher in the era of unhindered progress." This philosophy, whose clearest political exponent was Locke, was radically individualistic "in the sense in which individualism is opposed to organized social action." The individual and society came to be understood as occupying entirely separate realms. These ideas, which found a congenial

☆

[7] *Ibid.*, pp. 91-92, 70.

[8] John Dewey, *Democracy and Education, An Introduction to the Philosophy of Education,* The Macmillan Company, New York, 1920 (hereafter referred to as *Democracy and Education*), p. 405.

home in the frontier conditions of America and which were promulgated in the Declaration of Independence, evolved ultimately into an absolute creed, which Dewey called the "dogma of natural rights of the individual." Dogma though it was, as a philosophy of daily life it went largely unexpressed. "The gospel of self-help and private initiative," wrote Dewey, "was practiced so spontaneously that it needed no special intellectual support." The ideology received silent but strict obedience in the form of American practice. And since there were few social institutions that demanded large scale reform, since the ideology proved successful for most citizens, competing ideas that might ultimately run counter to those of economic individualism seldom came to the fore.[9]

In other words, the inheritance of European ideas placed in an American context had more to do with the evolution of the national creed than did any specific notions of Jefferson or of the Founding Fathers. This was also true with respect to the creed's later evolution. Dewey noted that legal and political forces had gradually relocated the center of the dogma. In comparing the American and English experiences, he argued that "as this country changed from an agrarian one to an urban industrial one, the qualities of initiative, invention, vigor and intrinsic contribution to progress which British *laissez-faire* liberalism had associated with manufacturing pursuits were transferred by American Courts and by the political representatives of business and finance from Jeffersonian individuals and given to the entrepreneurs who were individuals in the British sense." For Dewey, Jefferson remained a noble figure, and he was persuaded that these historical permutations had distorted Jefferson's position. There was no reason to be surprised that interests once represented by Hamilton now enunciated Jefferson's ideals. "Jeffersonian principles of self-government, of the prime authority of the people, of general happiness or welfare as the end of government, can," he maintained, "be appealed to in support of policies that are opposite to those urged by Jefferson in his day."[10]

As far as the history of ideas in general was concerned, two additional concepts figured importantly in the development of the American dogma. The first was private property, which Locke dwelt upon, but whose institution long antedated Lockean liberalism. Freedom sifted through the filter of private property had always meant dis-

☆

[9]"Herbert Spencer" (originally published as "The Philosophical Work of Herbert Spencer," *The Philosophical Review*, March, 1904), Ratner (ed.), *op. cit.*, vol. I, p. 55. "Pragmatic America," *ibid.*, vol. II, p. 546. John Dewey, *Liberalism and Social Action*, G. P. Putnam's Sons, New York, 1935, pp. 5, 18.

[10]John Dewey, *Freedom and Culture*, G. P. Putnam's Sons, New York, 1939, pp. 26, 61-62.

proportionate benefits for the propertied class, and with the advent of industrialism, these benefits quickly accrued to the newer possessors of property, the mercantile class.[11] This situation still obtained in large measure in the United States despite the introduction of democratic procedures and measures aimed at establishing legal equality.

The second important historical idea was Social Darwinism, particularly in its formulation by Herbert Spencer. Spencer reached some of his extreme conclusions, Dewey felt, primarily because he accepted certain notions of eighteenth century liberals wholly and unquestioningly, without taking into account even their own reservations and qualifications. Dewey argued that in particular it "was this thoroughgoing unconscious absorption that gave him a confident, aggressive, dogmatic individualism."[12] And it was in this same unqualified, dogmatic form that many American intellectuals received and adopted Spencer's conception of individualism.

If Dewey was right about Spencer, then American individualism was twice removed from sources of modification. Initially it took hold of feudal institutions that might have had the effect either of lessening its overall force or of channeling its energies in other directions. Secondly, it was advanced and dogmatized by a theory that in its inception was without historical sources of restraint. Given that American individualism was already relatively unconstrained, it was perhaps natural that Spencer's ideas should receive a warmer reception in America than on their native soil.

The Absence of Democratic Goals

Natural or not, Spencerism, added to an already acute individualism, served to produce a system that, contrary to expectation, narrowed rather than expanded the area of human freedom. "The result," Dewey observed, "is the present scene of confusion, conflict and uncertainty. While decrying the principle of authority . . . the new philosophy in fact erected the wants and endeavors of private individuals seeking personal gain to the place of supreme authority in social life. In consequence, the new philosophy, in the very act of asserting that it stood completely and loyally for the principle of individual freedom, was really engaged in justifying the activities of a new form

☆

[11] John Dewey, *Liberalism and Social Action*, G. P. Putnam's Sons, New York, 1935, pp. 75-76.

[12] "Herbert Spencer," Ratner (ed.), *op. cit.*, vol. I, p. 52, Dewey, incidentally, also felt that Spencer's work had very little connection with that of Darwin and that the nearly simultaneous appearance of their theories was a "tremendous piece of luck" for both. (*Ibid.*, p. 57.)

of concentrated power—the economic, which . . . has consistently and persistently denied effective freedom to the economically under-powered and underprivileged."[13] Confusion, conflict, and uncer-tainty were the unavoidable by-products of this philosophy, since it ran directly counter to democratic ideals and threatened to obliterate them entirely. While this had not yet happened, it was on the verge of happening; the society's spasmodic accommodation to democratic forms did little to unify or inspire the country and were in fact re-garded as sheer hypocrisy by many segments of the population. There was a democratic, spiritual element to the American heritage but this was essentially without force. Certainly, Dewey insisted, "its promise of new moral and religious outlook has not been attained. It has not become the wellspring of a new intellectual consensus; it is not (even unconsciously) the vital source of any distinctive and shared philos-ophy."[14] The American birthright had, in short, produced no national sense of purpose.

On the one hand, the absence of purpose showed merely that America was still in thralldom to European ideas and had yet to achieve its own identity. Dewey remarked that "though we have be-come a single body . . . and are in possession of our senses, we have not yet found a national mind, a will as to what to be."[15] Concentra-tion on economic considerations, that which dominated in lieu of a national purpose, was not in and of itself deleterious since commerce per se served the useful quasi-public functions of intercourse, com-munication, and distribution of goods. When concentration turned to ideology, however, there was cause for concern. "Commercialism," wrote Dewey, "like all isms is evil. That we have not as yet released commerce from bondage to private interests is proof of the solidity and tenacity of our European heritage."[16] But the matter was far more serious than adherence to anomalous European doctrines.

As the predominant ideology, economic individualism had the effect of demoralizing the entire society, even those citizens who were largely public-minded and substantially free of pecuniary inter-ests. "It would be difficult," Dewey contended in 1918, "to bring any more severe indictment against anything that calls itself civilization, than the fact that it is not able to utilize the energy, physical, intel-

☆

[13] John Dewey, "Authority and Resistance to Social Change," *Problems of Men*, Philo-sophical Library, New York, 1946, p. 100.

[14] *Individualism Old and New*, p. 17.

[15] "The Emergence of a New World" (published originally in *The Seven Arts*, May, 1917, under the title "In a Time of National Hesitation"), Ratner (ed.), *op. cit.*, vol. II, p. 445.

[16] "Pragmatic America," *ibid.*, p. 546.

lectual and moral, of the members who are desirous and anxious of rendering some kind of service, of producing some kind of needed and useful commodity." Such collective efforts as do exist seek the usual goals, and consequently the participating individuals tend to perform their duties in a mechanical manner—"like that of the parts of a machine"—and are therefore politically sterile.[17] Events between the two world wars convinced Dewey that a nation whose citizenry was mechanistically devoted to private aggrandizement stood in real danger of losing freedom altogether. He argued that "economic competitive individualism, free from social control, had created a moral and social vacuum which recourse to dictatorship is filling."[18] That Dewey found conditions favorable to dictatorship characteristic of America gives some indication of how grave he felt the situation to be.

But it was far from hopeless. On the positive side was the fact that many individuals had consciously weaned themselves from the inherited social philosophy. And because it was initially inherited and not self-constructed, there was still a possibility for the nation to create its own philosophy. Dewey believed that a true contemporary national ideal would reflect the unconscious aspirations of the whole society, as economic individualism, a borrowed and now archaic ideology, could never do. A new ideal, one that took into account the full range of social needs, was entirely conceivable. The nation possessed the constituent elements of such an ideal and needed only to bring them to the level of consciousness.[19]

The Need for Radicalism

But consciousness of purpose, while entirely imaginable, was by no means necessarily likely. Dewey observed that liberals, upon whom change would depend, were in the habit of hoping and waiting for an administration that would advance their policies on its own incentive. "I know of nothing in history," he reported, "that justifies the belief and hope." Not only would liberals have to take direct action, they would have to adopt a program that differed drastically from current practice. "Humane liberalism," Dewey held, ". . . must cease to deal with symptoms and go to the causes of which inequalities and oppressions are but the symptoms. In order to endure under present conditions, liberalism must become radical in the sense that, instead of

☆

[17] "Elements of Social Reorganization" (published originally under the title "Internal Social Reorganization after the War," *The Journal of Race Development*, April, 1918), *ibid.*, p. 747. *Freedom and Culture*, p. 167.

[18] "Authority and Resistance to Social Change," *Problems of Men*, pp. 103-104.

[19] "Universal Service as Education," Ratner (ed.), *op. cit.*, vol. II, p. 471.

using social power to ameliorate the evil consequences of the existing system, it shall use social power to change the system." Time and again Dewey tried to drive this lesson home. With those who felt that liberalism meant experimentation, but that experimentation called for diffidence and caution, he had little patience. "Experimental method is not," he maintained, "just messing around nor doing a little of this and a little of that in the hope that things will improve . . . there is nothing in the nature of liberalism that makes it a milk-water doctrine, committed to compromise and minor 'reforms.' It is worth noting that the earlier liberals were regarded in their day as subversive radicals."[20] And if Dewey were not calling his fellow reformers to outright subversion, he was certainly asking them to entertain a very subversive brand of liberalism.

In *Liberalism and Social Action* Dewey attempted to spell out his comprehension of radicalism. Radical, he said, meant "perception of the necessity of thoroughgoing changes in the set-up of institutions and corresponding activity to bring the changes to pass . . . The process of producing the changes will be . . . a gradual one. But 'reforms' that deal now with this abuse and now with that without having a social goal based upon an inclusive plan, differ entirely from effort at re-forming, in its literal sense, the institutional scheme of things . . . If radicalism be defined as perception of need for radical change, then today any liberalism which is not also radicalism is irrelevant and doomed."[21] And while the contemplated changes might be gradual, they would also be dramatic, for they would be directed at altering the very foundation of the nation's economic system.

Dewey was convinced that economic forces were the real wielders of power. He argued that "the control of the means of production by the few in legal possession operates as a standing agency of coercion of the many . . . It is foolish to regard the political state as the only agency now endowed with coercive power. Its exercise of this power is pale in contrast with that exercised by concentrated and organized property interests."[22] And in case there were any doubt, Dewey made clear in many places the precise target for change. In the mid 1930's he wrote that "existing materialism, with the blight to which it subjects the cultural development of individuals, is the inevitable product of exaggeration of the economic liberty of the few at the expense of the all-around liberty of the many. And . . . this limitation upon genuine liberty is the inevitable product of the inequality that arises

☆

[20] *Liberalism and Social Action*, p. 15. "The Future of Liberalism," *Problems of Men*, pp. 132, 137-138.

[21] *Liberalism and Social Action*, p. 62.

[22] *Ibid.*, pp. 63-64.

and must arise under the operations of institutionally established and supported finance-capitalism." Three years later he put his position in even stronger language. "The idea of a pre-established harmony between the existing so-called capitalistic regime and democracy is as absurd a piece of metaphysical speculation as human history has ever evolved."[23] So disturbed was he at ongoing tendencies that he could even look with favor at the advent of the depression. "The intellectual function of trouble," he suggested, "is to lead men to think. The depression is a small price to pay if it induces us to think about the cause of the disorder, confusion, and insecurity which are the outstanding traits of our social lives."[24] If men could think creatively about new alternatives, then economic hardship would be a small price indeed.

Restoration and even regeneration would not do. "Cure," Dewey remarked, "is a negative idea; health a positive one." That so much attention is paid to cures and salvations demonstrates how sick society really is. Treating symptoms and effects will never get to the root causes of the difficulty and consequently will never achieve social health. As an example of retarded thinking arrested at the symptomatic level Dewey pointed to those who still approached things from the capitalist premise of perpetual scarcity. Trapped by this old view, men fail to realize that an age of potential plenty is at hand, that science and technology can end, perhaps forever, the ceaseless efforts to satisfy physical need. If this fact were to be comprehended, men would be free to drop permanently the concept of human insecurity, a concept that is the correlative of economic scarcity and that serves to lock men into accepting and patching up patently antilibertarian institutions and procedures. Thus liberated from insecurity, men can imagine and work for entirely new institutions.[25]

The realization of these ends will require not only new thought and new action, but new organization as well. Borrowing from Lenin, Dewey asserted that "the question of 'what is to be done' cannot be ignored. Ideas must be organized and this organization implies an organization of individuals who hold these ideas and whose faith is ready to translate itself into action . . . It is in organization for action that liberals are weak, and without this organization there is danger that democratic ideals may go by default."[26] For Dewey, radical liber-

☆

[23] "Liberty and Social Control," *Problems of Men*, p. 117. *Freedom and Culture*, p. 72.

[24] "Science and Society," John Dewey, *Philosophy and Civilization*, G. P. Putnam's Sons, New York, 1931, p. 330.

[25] "A Sick World," Ratner (ed.), *op. cit.*, vol. II, pp. 761-762. *Liberalism and Social Action*, pp. 59-60.

[26] *Ibid.*, p. 91.

alism thus meant not only a vision of a new society; it also meant that those who called themselves liberals must be prepared to adopt concrete policies and to engage in specific activities in order that the vision might become reality.

It is clear, then, that with respect to his critique of society and his assessment of the liberals' mission Dewey was, by any standard short of violent revolution, radical beyond dispute. By American standards his position verged on heresy. Pragmatism was the philosophy Dewey placed in opposition to "the American way" — "Legalism," he wrote, "along with feudalized commercialism, wedded to form modern commercialism, is the anti-pragmatic 'made' which hinders and perverts our pragmatic makings"[27] — and thus conceived, pragmatism could hardly fit the description of Mumford and Russell.

And yet we are justified in reserving final judgment, for the critical side of Dewey, or of any writer for that matter, by no means tells the whole story. Croly, for example, was nearly as sweeping in his condemnation of the status quo, but his solutions failed to go far beyond the point of modification. We can only get a reasonable picture of Dewey after we have examined the positive side of his political philosophy. In order to do this, one must reach an understanding of what Dewey generally had in mind when he spoke of philosophy and, in particular, what he meant by the notion of pragmatic philosophy.

Pragmatic Philosophy

One of Dewey's more concise treatments of the nature of philosophy occurs in an address entitled "Philosophy and Democracy," which he gave before the Philosophical Union of the University of California in 1918.[28] Dewey began by responding to those who thought of philosophy not only as a body of knowledge much like natural science, but as a distinctive form of knowledge whose truths were deeper and more comprehensive than those of any other discipline. Critics and admirers alike tended to see philosophy in this light and both, Dewey announced, were wrong. Philosophy, he asserted, "is a form of desire, of effort at action — a love, namely, of wisdom; but with the thorough

☆

[27] "Pragmatic America," Ratner (ed.), *op. cit.*, vol. II, p. 547.

[28] Ratner (ed.), *op. cit.*, vol. II, pp. 841-855; all quotations are taken from these pages. This speech is used because of its brevity and its typicality. For a fuller understanding of the more general aspects of pragmatism, see Dewey's *Reconstruction in Philosophy*, Henry Holt and Company, Inc., New York, 1920. On more technical questions, see *Essays in Experimental Logic*, University of Chicago Press, Chicago, 1916; *Experience and Nature*, Dover Publications, Inc., New York, 1958; *Quest for Certainty*, Minton, Balch and Co., New York, 1929; and *Logic, The Theory of Inquiry*, Henry Holt and Company, Inc., New York, 1938.

proviso . . . that wisdom, whatever it is, is not a mode of science, of knowledge . . ." A conscious philosophy is "an inspiration subjected to rational discriminations and tests, a social hope reduced to a working program of action, a prophecy of the future, but one disciplined by serious thought and knowledge." And wisdom does not, as Plato contended, have to do with systematic knowledge of fact and truth; rather it pertains to standards for choosing. "Wisdom," Dewey argued, "is a moral term, and like every moral term refers not to the constitution of things already in existence, not even if that constitution be magnified into eternity and absoluteness. As a moral term it refers to a choice about something to be done, a preference for living this sort of life rather than that. It refers . . . to a desired future which our desires, when translated into articulate conviction, may help bring into existence."

Philosophy in quest of such wisdom does not concern itself with conclusive answers to questions of existence, and the student of historic philosophies would do well to look for "intellectual formulations of men's habitual purposes and cultivated wants, not . . . insight into the ultimate nature of things or information about the make-up of reality . . . In philosophy, 'reality' is a term of value or choice." To say this, however, and to say that philosophy is not scientific knowledge, is not to relegate philosophy to the realm of arbitrary wish or vague discrimination. Philosophy seeks to persuade and must therefore utilize the findings of science and adhere to the canons of logical and reasonable discourse. "It is this dependence upon the method of logical presentation and upon scientific subject matter," Dewey felt, "which confers upon philosophy the garb, though not the form, of knowledge." Thus clothed—and the clothing is absolutely necessary if the philosopher is to translate his passion into reasoned persuasion —philosophy invariably finds itself in a state of delicate balance, in danger of over-dressing in scientific attire and thus becoming merely learned and dialectical, or of being undisciplined to the extent that its lack of clarity produces nothing more than exhortation, sentiment, or fantasy. Maintaining this balance is extremely difficult, and what makes it worthwhile "is precisely the fact that it assumes the responsibility for setting forth some ideal of a collective good life . . . with the use of the characteristic knowledge of its day."

This last point was particularly crucial, for Dewey believed that philosophy must explicate contemporary usage strictly in terms of future expectations. Philosophy attempts to channel the currents of knowledge "into a central stream of tendency, to inquire what more fundamental and general attitudes of response the trend of knowledge exacts of us, to what new fields of action it calls us. It is in this sense, a practical and moral sense, that philosophy can lay claim to the epithets of universal, basic and superior. Knowledge *is* partial and incomplete, any and all knowledge, til we have placed it in the context of a future which cannot be known, but only speculated about and resolved upon." Attempts at speculation and resolution are part and parcel of the philosophic enterprise.

At this point in his University of California address Dewey moved from philosophy in general to the relationship between philosophy and democracy. We will deal with this matter shortly, but first it will be useful to consult some of Dewey's other works in order to elaborate a few of his more essential propositions.

Philosophy and History

Dewey's historical orientation and his stress on connecting philosophical reasoning to "characteristic knowledge of the day" caused many of his readers to charge him with moral relativism. This appelation Dewey gladly accepted. In his introduction to *Problems of Men* he argued that the only sensible approach was one which saw that problems change as conditions change. Only by linking philosophical inquiry to "urgencies that impose themselves at times and in places" could real understanding take place. This sort of relativity is the kind "which marks all scientific inquiry," and science "also finds [that] its only workable 'standards' are provided by the actual connections of things; connections which, when they are generalized, are given the name of space-time." The idea of liberty, for example, can only be understood in a space-time context. While liberty has always to do with release from oppressive forces, its particular meaning is only revealed when the distribution of power and the social class that is oppressed at any given time are discovered. If a classless society should ever come about, liberty per se would be without significance, since "the *fact* for which it stands would have become an integral part of the established relations of human beings to one another."[29]

Placing liberty in relation to class and power calls to mind Marx's analysis of society and, even more pointedly, the whole question of historical determinism, which was central to Marxism and which Dewey's relativism implied. If an idea can only be understood relative to its historical setting does this mean that it is "determined" by this context? Dewey seemed to answer yes to this question. He reasoned that men's sentiments and ideas are "not the author and judge of social institutions, but the product and reflex of the latter. They are functions of social organization . . . The notion that it is possible to get bodies of men to act in accord with finer moral sentiments while

☆

[29] *Problems of Men*, pp. 12-13. *Liberalism and Social Action*, p. 48.

the general scheme of social organization remains the same is not only futile, it is a mark of the subtlest form of conceit, moral egoism." The obvious difference between Marx and Dewey here is that Dewey's determinism is not confined to economic arrangements but includes all social institutions. [30] Unlike many Marxists, however, Dewey was prepared to allow philosophy certain possibilities of transcending the imperatives of time and place.

No philosophy worthy of name, he believed, constituted mere apology. "Yet," he wrote, "there is probably also no historic philosophy which is not in some measure a reflection, an idealization, a justification of some of the tendencies of its own age. Yet what makes it a work of reflection and criticism is that the elements and values selected are set in opposition to other factors, and those perhaps the ones most in evidence, the most clamorous, the most insistent: which is to say that all serious thinking combines in some proportion and perspective the actual and the possible, where actuality supplies contact and solidity while possibility furnishes the ideal upon which criticism rests and from which creative effort springs." Philosophy, then, while a product of its environment, is not totally bound to the existing order of that environment, and the notion of "creative effort" returns us to Dewey's close association between philosophy and action. That this was association and not identity Dewey made clear in *Democracy and Education*. "Philosophy," he wrote, "is thinking what the known demands of us — what responsive attitude it exacts. It is an idea of what is possible, not a record of accomplished fact . . . It presents an assignment of something to be done — something to be tried. Its value lies not in furnishing solutions (which can be achieved only in action) but in defining difficulties and suggesting methods for dealing with them." [31] The difference between suggesting a method and recommending a solution is important, and we shall return to it later. Before we can deal with this problem, however, it will be helpful to compare some of Dewey's broadest views of his own philosophy with his discussion of philosophy in general. [32]

☆

[30] "Morals and Conduct of States," Ratner (ed.), *op. cit.*, vol. II, p. 647. Dewey's often quoted phrase: Economic determinism is now a fact, not a theory" (*Individualism Old and New*, p. 119), ought not to be taken generically. When he said this he was referring to current economic conditions being morally corrosive and in need of change if society were to be improved. Dewey gave economic factors considerable formative power, but did not impute to them the function of absolute determination.

[31] "Philosophy and the Social Order," Ratner (ed.), *op. cit.*, vol. II, p. 437. *Democracy and Education*, p. 381

[32] We shall use the term "pragmatism," although Dewey often referred to his own position as "instrumentalism" or, less frequently, as "experimentalism." Of necessity the analysis here will not be exhaustive.

Philosophy and Pragmatism

In its most inclusive sense, pragmatism may be distinguished from older theories on the basis of its world view. Whereas Dewey saw the older, rationalistic philosophies seeking a single or monistic explanation of reality, he identified the pragmatic approach with pluralism, a view that suggested "a universe which is not all closed and settled, which is still in some respects indeterminate and in the making, which is adventurous and which implicates all who share in it, whether by acting or believing." As a starting point pluralism has the singular advantage of flexibility: it "leaves room for contingence, liberty, novelty, and gives complete liberty of action to the empirical method . . . It accepts unity where it finds it, but it does not attempt to force the vast diversity of events and things into a single rational mold." [33] This openness and flexibility Dewey identified as the method employed by modern science and the dichotomy between the new science and the old paralleled exactly that between pragmatism and the earlier rationalism. "Just as *necessity* and search for a *single* all-comprehensive law was typical of the intellectual atmosphere of the forties of the last century, so," Dewey observed, "*probability* and *pluralism* are the characteristics of the present state of science." And the "scientific temperament" was precisely the temperament possessed by the pragmatic philosopher. It consisted of: a "willingness to hold belief in suspense, ability to doubt until evidence is attained; willingness to go where evidence points instead of putting first a personally preferred conclusion; ability to . . . use [ideas] as hypotheses to be tested instead of as dogmas to be asserted; and (possibly the most distinctive of all) enjoyment of new fields for inquiry and of new problems." [34] To follow these procedures, Dewey believed, was to transform in a startling way the nature of the philosophical endeavor.

Empiricism, for example, although a crucial aspect of pragmatic understanding, must now be seen as only the beginning and not the end of philosophical investigation. Experimental science has demonstrated how properly to treat the realm of experience. It has shown "the possibility of using past experiences as the servant, not the master, of mind. It means that reason operates within experience, not beyond it, to give it an intelligent or reasonable quality." This emphasis on intelligence and reason was crucial, and those who believed that science utilized experience alone and was based on mere inductive empiricism were entirely off the mark, from Dewey's point of

☆

[33] "Philosophy and the Social Order," Ratner (ed.), *op. cit.*, vol. II, p. 439. "The Development of American Pragmatism," *Philosophy and Civilization*, p. 20.

[34] *Freedom and Culture*, pp. 84, 145.

view. That many espoused this belief he found enormously distracting. "Oh," he exclaimed, "the remoteness of the doctrine as we learn more facts, the outline simplifies: the vague remoteness of the plea that as science learns more facts, the multitude of details dissolves into general laws! That is precisely, according to the work of every existing living science, what doesn't happen." This is not to deny that the empiricist's stress on reality, on facts, on concreteness was a significant advance on the wildly abstract quality of earlier thought; and pragmatism, in the temper of modern science, "presents itself as an extension of historical empiricism, but with this fundamental difference, that it does not insist upon antecedent phenomena but upon the possibilities of action."[35] Once established, this "fundamental difference" involved significant changes in all components of philosophical perception.

The most important of these changes had to do with the means of establishing validity and led to the famous pragmatic dictum on truth and verification. Following Pierce and James, Dewey argued that it is "in submitting conceptions to the control of experience, in the process of verifying them, that one finds examples of what is called truth." One need not be a pragmatist, moreover, to come to this conclusion. Any "philosopher," Dewey wrote, "who applies this empirical method without the least prejudice in favor of pragmatic doctrine, can be led to conclude that truth 'means' verification, or if one prefers, that verification, either actual or possible, is the definition of truth." Dewey spelled out in some detail the logic of this verification process.

> If a notion or a theory makes pretense of corresponding to reality or to the facts, this pretense cannot be put to the test and confirmed or refuted except by causing it to pass over into the realm of action and by noting the results which it yields in the form of the concrete observable facts to which this notion or theory leads. If, in acting upon this notion, we are brought to the fact which it implies or which it demands, then this notion is true. A theory corresponds to the facts when it leads to the facts which are its consequences, by the intermediary of experience. And from this consideration the pragmatic generalization is drawn that all knowledge is prospective in its results . . . Every proposition concerning truths is really in the last analysis hypothetical and provisional.[36]

The prospective quality of knowledge is directly related to the belief in an open, pluralistic world. "Pragmatism," Dewey readily confessed, ". . . has a metaphysical implication. The doctrine of the value of

☆

[35] *Democracy and Education*, p. 263. "Social Absolutism," Ratner (ed.), *op. cit.*, vol. II, p. 722. "The Development of American Pragmatism," *Philosophy and Civilization*, p. 24.

[36] "The Development of American Pragmatism," *Philosophy and Civilization*, pp. 23-24.

consequences leads us to take the future into consideration. And this taking into consideration of the future takes us to the conception of a universe whose evolution is not finished, of a universe which is still, in James' term, 'in the making,' 'in the process of becoming,' or a universe up to a certain point still plastic." Or, to put it a little differently, this is a view that, following Einstein's theory of relativity, "substitutes for the neat, smooth, well-ordered world of Newton a world which is full of puckers and skews."[37] This conviction had importance for all of civilized life and was not merely a point of departure for the technical study of epistemological or ontological questions.

Pragmatism and Action

Dewey was thoroughly convinced that a public adoption of pragmatic perspectives — of the scientific method — would have an enormous and constructive impact on the quality of society. "If," he argued, "we form general ideas and if we put them in action, consequences are produced which could not be produced otherwise. Under these conditions the world will be different from what it would have been if thought had not intervened." Pragmatism will do nothing less than provide logical reasons for our actions, for how we behave, for what we believe. "We are," Dewey noted, "always obliged to act in any case; our actions and with them their consequences actually change according to the beliefs which we have chosen. Moreover it may be that, in order to discover the proofs which will ultimately be the intellectual justification of certain beliefs — the belief in freedom, for example, or the belief in God — it is necessary to begin to act in accordance with this belief." It is possible, in short, to show that "the affirmation of certain beliefs [can] be justified by means of the nature of their consequences, or by the differences which these beliefs make in existence." The social benefits derived from this position are manifold. "A conviction that consequences in human welfare are a test of the worth of beliefs and thoughts . . . makes for a fusion of two superlatively important qualities, love of truth and love of neighbor. It discourages dogmatism and its child, intolerance. It arouses and heartens an experimental spirit . . . It militates against too sweeping and easy generalizations, even against those which would indict a nation."[38] Pragmatism, in other words, would do much to advance those characteristics that Dewey typically associated with democracy.

☆

[37] *Ibid.*, p. 25. "Social Absolutism," Ratner (ed.), *op. cit.*, vol. II, p. 723.
[38] "The Development of American Pragmatism," *Philosophy and Civilization*, pp. 22, 25. "Pragmatic America," Ratner (ed.), *op. cit.*, vol. II, p. 544.

With this suggestion we may return to his discussion of philosophy and democracy in the University of California lecture.

The digression from Dewey's analysis of philosophy to present material explicating pragmatism was made so that one main point might now be established: namely that, despite occasional statements to the contrary, Dewey's conception of the spirit of modern philosophy and his formulation of the pragmatic attitude were virtually identical. We have already seen that the realm of action is critical both to philosophy and to pragmatism. As he placed philosophy in a democratic context other similarities became apparent.

Pragmatism as the Philosophy of Democracy

The idea of an open-ended universe was especially salient. Dewey contended that a philosophy which is "animated . . . by the strivings of men to achieve democracy will construe liberty as meaning a universe in which there is real uncertainty and contingency, a world which is not all in, and never will be, a world which in some respects is incomplete and in the making." The older philosophies were not only monistic but, in their commitment to "supreme reality" or "ultimate and comprehensive truth," they were antidemocratic. Such philosophies inevitably attempt to justify the dominance of some existing authority and thereby to foreclose the possibility of creativity and freedom, two of the hallmarks of democratic life. Not only liberty but equality as well was contingent upon the new view, and for roughly the same reasons. "Now whatever the idea of equality means for democracy," Dewey explained, "it means . . . that the world is not to be construed as a fixed order of species, grades or degrees. It means that every existence deserving the name of existence has something unique and irreplaceable about it, that it does not exist to illustrate a principle, to realize a universal or to embody a kind or class." This variety of equality could only prosper in a pluralistic, open-ended society where the test of the equalitarian assertion would of course lie in its consequences, in the results produced by treating people in such a unique way. Equality, in other words, just as liberty, is possible only in a society that follows a pragmatic philosophy.

Dewey made his view clear in his concluding paragraph, which he began by disclaiming any sort of advocacy: "All this, he said, ". . . is but by way of intimation. In spite of its form it is not really a plea for a certain kind of philosophizing. For if democracy be a serious, important choice and predilection it must in time justify itself by generating its own . . . institutions of life." Having said this, however, Dewey immediately gave his hand away. "It is not so much a question as to whether there will be a philosophy of this kind as it is of just who will be the philosophers associated with it. And," he said in his final remark, "I cannot conclude without mentioning the name of one through whom this vision of a new mode of life has already spoken with beauty and power—William James." Since James had already announced the new vision it is difficult to imagine a democratic philosophy, or a *modern* philosophy for that matter, that did not square with most of James' pragmatic propositions. Pragmatism and democratic philosophy were essentially the same in Dewey's mind.

Since science and pragmatism were so closely related, it is natural to expect Dewey to link science and democracy together as well. This is precisely what he did. In *Freedom and Culture* he wrote: "freedom of inquiry, toleration of diverse views, freedom of communication, the distribution of what is found out to every individual as the ultimate intellectual consumer, are involved in the democratic as in the scientific method." When American democracy makes full use of the scientific method, that is, when it becomes more fully a democracy by recognizing "the existence of *problems* and the need for probing them *as* problems as its glory," it will have achieved its logical objective.[39] The scientific, pragmatic, and democratic methods, and the philosophical as well, are at the very least congruous in Dewey's formulation, and the close proximity of these concepts had an important bearing on his recommendations for solving America's problems; how important we shall shortly see.

The Pragmatic Answer

The nature of Dewey's solutions follows logically from his depiction of the shortcomings. Economic individualism, you will remember, was prominent in his delineation of pernicious causes. The whole concept of "the individual," Dewey felt, had been twisted by a long and mindless acceptance of the American creed. The term "individual" was to begin with not inherently clear. It could mean, he suggested, "anything from egoistically centered conduct to distinction and uniqueness. It is possible to say that excessive individualism is an outstanding curse of American civilization, and that absence of individualism is our marked deficiency." For the quality that America lacked Dewey preferred the term "individuality," which carried connotations of distinctiveness and intrinsic freedom.[40]

☆

[39]*Freedom and Culture*, p. 102.
[40]"Mediocrity and Individuality," Ratner (ed.), *op. cit.*, vol. II, p. 479.

Individualism and Society

Individual*ism*, as defined by the tradition, failed to provide these higher connotations, even though they were part of the vision of the Founding Fathers. "Instead of the development of individualities," Dewey contended, ". . . there is a perversion of the whole ideal of individualism to conform to the practices of pecuniary culture. But the perversion of the ideal did not detract from the fact of its existence and, for this reason, Dewey hoped that the ideal could be resurrected. "A stable recovery of individuality," he wrote, "waits upon an elimination of the older economic and political individualism, an elimination which will liberate imagination and endeavor for the task of making corporate society contribute to the free culture of its members." This possibility of recovery existed because the old conception still had at least minimal adherence. Dewey felt certain that the "idea of a society of [true] individuals is not foreign to American thought; it penetrates even our current individualism which is unreflective and brutal." [41] As far as he was concerned, only a set of bogus intellectual distinctions prevented most men from seeing this possibility.

Dewey was not interested in denying historical significance to individualism. "It is completely possible," he reported in 1936, ". . . to recognize the need and important social consequences of the individualistic movement and yet also see that in its past mode of operation it has already run its socially justified and justifiable course." The older individualism remained despite its anachronistic quality because it early became dogmatized and thereafter claimed the blind obeisance of all citizens. The impact of this dogma was to create in liberal rhetoric a totally spurious dichotomy, what Dewey termed, "the myth of 'The Individual' set over in dualistic separation against that which is called 'The Social.'" [42]

Seen from this perspective, the individual appears essentially isolated and invincibly ego-centered. Dewey argued that such a view was groundless. "Individuals," he observed, "are certainly interested, at times, in having their own way, and their own way may go contrary to the way of others. But they are also interested, and chiefly interested upon the whole, in entering into the activities of others and taking part in conjoint and cooperative doings." Indeed, it is only through the latter activity that selfhood fully emerges. "There is," Dewey insisted, "no inherent opposition between working with

☆

[41] *Individualism Old and New*, pp. 13, 72. "The Development of American Pragmatism," *Philosophy and Civilization*, p. 33.

[42] Introduction to *Problems of Men*, p. 18. "Authority and Resistance to Social Change," *ibid.*, p. 101.

others and working as an individual. On the contrary, certain capacities of an individual are not brought out except under the stimulus of association with others."[43] In fact, analytically speaking, it is impossible to conceive of the individual divorced from his social context; the term in this sense is without meaning. If this cannot be seen from an analysis of individuality, then it certainly can from an examination of society.

Dewey held that society consisted of nothing more or less than the collective relations among individuals. This being the case, social and individual attributes are two sides of the same coin. "A collective unity may," Dewey reasoned, "be taken *either* distributively *or* collectively, but when taken collectively it is the union of its distributive constituents, and when taken distributively, it is the distribution of and within the collectivity . . . An individual cannot be opposed to the association of which he is an integral part nor can the association be set up against its integrated members."[44] The key words here are "integral part," and it is apparent from Dewey's analysis that individual*ism* was largely a function of the fact that Americans were *not* integrally related to their society. He could remain optimistic, however, because he felt that American ideology grossly distorted reality: if Americans were as independent of each other as the ideology suggested the society itself could not exist. But it did exist, and therefore a wholly different view of social relations was possible.

Society as a Collectivity

The collective nature of society could be rich and profound. "I often wonder," wrote Dewey, "what meaning is given to the term 'society' by those who oppose it to the intimacies of personal intercourse, such as those of friendship. Presumably they have in their minds a picture of rigid institutions or some set and external organization. But an institution that is other than the structure of human contact and intercourse is a fossil of some past socity; organization, as in any living

☆

[43] *Democracy and Education*, pp. 28-29, 353.

[44] John Dewey, *The Public and Its Problems*, Henry Holt and Company, Inc., New York, 1927, p. 190. On this general point, Horace Kallen quotes from *Knowing and the Known*, which was authored jointly by Dewey and Arthur E. Bentley. "Transactionally viewed, a widening or narrowing of attention . . . is about all that remains indicated by such words as 'social' and 'individual' . . . If one insists on considering individual and social as different in character, then a derivation of the former from the latter would, in our judgment, be much simpler and more natural than an attempt to produce a social by joining or otherwise organizing presumptive individuals. In fact, most of the talk about the 'individual' is the very finest kind of an illustration of isolation from every

organism, is the cooperative consensus of multitudes of cells, each living in exchange with others." With this organic metaphor in mind, Dewey could advance "the conception of a social harmony of interests in which the achievement by each individual of his own freedom should contribute to a like perfecting of the powers of all, through a fraternally organized society."[45]

To say that in America there was little "social harmony of interests" because individualism drives different interests apart was correct. But this was only half of the story. Individualism reigned supreme largely because collective alternatives had not received the serious attention they deserved. And such inattention was intellectually inexcusable, since it was patently obvious that the nature of collective institutions had a formative influence on the character of the men who take part in them. "It is absurd," Dewey argued, "to suppose that the ties which hold them together are merely external and do not react into mentality and character, producing the framework of personal disposition. The tragedy of the 'lost individual' is due to the fact that while individuals are now caught up into a vast complex of associations, there is no harmonious and coherent reflection of the import of these connections into the imaginative and emotional outlook on life. This fact is of course due in turn to the absence of harmony within the state of society."[46] The goal for pragmatism consequently was crystal clear: the introduction of a social harmony that will engender true individuality.

Although Dewey would turn to collective solutions to the problem, he continually stressed individuality as the end. "Pragmatism and instrumental experimentalism," he wrote, "bring into prominence the importance of the individual. It is he who is the carrier of creative thought, the author of action, and of its application." It was plain, however, that as things stood the thought, imagination, and emotion of the individual were poisoned by the continuation of economic individualism. A response that failed to recognize this fact, that perpetuated the individualist ideology, would only make the situation worse. "The sick," Dewey remarked, "cannot heal themselves by

---

form of connection carried to an extreme absurdity that renders inquiry and intelligent statement impossible." Kallen reports that he and Dewey once began a book together, but that because Dewey posited the individual as part of associated life, and Kallen considered individuality as "ineffable as well as inexpugnable," he (Kallen) eventually had to write the book by himself. (Horace Kallen, "Individuality, Individualism, and John Dewey," *Antioch Review*, vol. 19, pp. 305, 312, Fall, 1959.)

[45] *Individualism Old and New*, p. 86. "Intelligence and Morals," John Dewey, *The Influence of Darwin on Philosophy, and Other Essays in Contemporary Thought*, Henry Holt and Company, Inc., New York, 1910, p. 60.

[46] *Individualism Old and New*, p. 82.

means of their disease, and disintegrated individuals can achieve unity only as the dominant energies of community life are incorporated to form their minds."[47] Unity was possible; the sickness could be cured when there came into existence a collective purpose strong enough to overcome the divisive pull of possessive individualism.

Purpose, Community, and Democracy

Dewey believed that such a purpose was attainable. He felt that the experience of World War I had already demonstrated this fact. And in the postwar period the necessity of having a transcendent purpose of this sort was especially great, since most of the older intellectual convictions had lost their hold. "The weaker our faith in Nature," Dewey noted, "in its laws and rights and its benevolent intentions for human welfare, the more urgent is the need for a faith based on ideas that are now intelectually credible and that are consonant with present economic conditions, which will inspire and direct action with something of the ardor once attached to things religious."

The reference to religious fervor was, from Dewey's viewpoint, entirely appropriate since he regarded the issue — "what *should* be" — as a moral one in all of its particulars. He was quite prepared to state, at least in broad outline, what those particulars should encompass in a democratic society. He asked "all who would maintain and advance the ideals of democracy to face the issue of the moral ground of political institutions and the moral principles by which men acting together may attain freedom of individuals which will amount to fraternal associations with one another."[48] He asked in short, that his country become an organic community.

To Dewey this request was identical to asking the nation to become a democracy. In *Freedom and Culture* he wrote that "cooperation — called fraternity in the classic French formula — is as much a part of the democratic ideal as is personal initiative." In *The Public and Its Problems* he went even further. He argued that when regarded "as an idea, democracy is not an alternative to other principles of associated life. It is the idea of community life itself."[49] Stated in this ideal fashion, community represents a tendency carried to an analytical extreme rather than a set of relations that correspond directly to reality. The

☆

[47] "The Development of American Pragmatism," *Philosophy and Civilization*, p. 33. *Individualism Old and New*, p. 65.

[48] "Elements of Social Reorganization," (first published as "Internal Social Reorganization After the War," *Journal of Race Development*, April 1918, Ratner (ed.), *op. cit.*, vol. II, p. 755. *Freedom and Culture*, pp. 124, 164-165.

[49] *Ibid.*, p. 22. *The Public and Its Problems*, p. 148.

ideal is nonetheless exceedingly important. It represents "actual phases of associated life as they are freed from restrictive and disturbing elements, and are contemplated as having attained their limit of development." The ideal, moreover, has genuine meaning. "Wherever," Dewey suggested, "there is conjoint activity whose consequences are appreciated as good by all singular persons who take part in it, and where the realization of the good is such as to effect an energetic desire and effort to sustain it in being just because it is a good shared by all, there is in so far a community. The clear consciousness of communal life, in all its implications, constitutes the idea of democracy."[50] And the idea of democracy, to repeat, constitutes society organized on communal terms.

Dewey elaborated his conception of communal democracy in nearly everything he wrote. In *Freedom and Culture* he stressed the component of shared ideals. "Without them," he argued, "any so-called social group, class, people, nation tends to fall apart into molecules having but mechanically enforced connections with one another."[51] Almost twenty years earlier, in *Democracy and Education,* he explained the concept in much greater detail.

He began, as he so often did, by arguing that democracy was more than the sum of its political forms.[52] It is, he said, "primarily a mode of associated living, of conjoint communicated experience." Such a mode of existence implied many things. "The extension in space of the number of individuals who participate in an interest so that each has to refer his own action to that of others, and to consider the action of others to give point and direction to his own, is equivalent to the breaking down of those barriers of class, race, and national territory which kept men from perceiving the full import of their activity. These more numerous and more varied points of contact denote a greater diversity of stimuli to which an individual has to respond; they consequently put a premium on variation in his action."[53] The point about diverse stimuli and variation in behavior raises some difficulty, since it suggests that diversity is a desirable end, when at the same time, Dewey stresses the necessity for commonality and identity.

☆

[50] *Ibid.,* pp. 148-149.

[51] *Freedom and Culture*, p. 12.

[52] In *The Public and Its Problems* Dewey maintained that there was "no sanctity in universal suffrage, frequent elections, majority rule, congressional and cabinet government. These things are devices evolved in the direction in which the current was moving, each wave of which involved at the time of its impulsion a minimum of departure from antecedent custom and law." (p. 145.)

[53] *Democracy and Education,* p. 101.

This point gains added importance when one notices Dewey's unwillingness to compromise on the issue of deep-seated communal feelings. Joint participation, for example, an otherwise essential phenomenon, is in and of itself no guarantee that communal sentiments will develop. "Individuals," Dewey wrote, "do not even compose a social group because they all work for a common end. The parts of a machine work with a maximum of cooperativeness for a common result, but they do not form a community." "What they must have in common in order to form a community or society are aims, beliefs, aspirations, knowledge—a common understanding." Knowledge and common understanding were particularly critical, since Dewey felt that cognitive affinity—what he called "intelligent sympathy"—was if anything more important than emotional consanguinity. Sympathy, he maintained, "as a desirable quality is something more than mere feelings; it is a cultivated imagination for what men have in common and a rebellion at whatever unnecessarily divides them."[54]

Without this attachment among individuals and between individuals and social institutions, the aspect of community will quickly be replaced by artifice, by a ready-made *consensus*. "The individual," Dewey believed, "cannot remain intellectually a vacuum. If his ideas and beliefs are not the spontaneous function of a communal life in which he shares, a seeming consensus will be secured as a substitute by artificial and mechanical means . . . by external agencies which obtain factitious agreement."[55] And because intelligent sympathy within the citizenry was the chief means of avoiding an ersatz consensus, Dewey concluded that, with all of the other communal prerequisites present, sympathetic understanding would require one more prime ingredient: the ability to communicate.

Community and Communication

Recall Dewey's description of democracy as "conjoint communicated experiences." He regarded the capacity to communicate shared experiences, consciously and understandably, as absolutely decisive. He agreed with Carlyle that the invention of the printing press, which forced governments to bring the public into the political sphere, had made some form of democracy inevitable. Full democracy, communal democracy, would depend on social communication carried much

☆

[54] *Ibid.*, pp. 5, 141.

[55] *Individualism Old and New*, pp. 83-84. A few pages later Dewey added: "Our sociability is largely an effort to find substitutes for that normal consciousness of connection and union that proceeds from being a sustained and sustaining member of a social whole." (p. 88.)

further. "There is more," Dewey explained, "than a verbal tie between the words common, community, and communication. Men live in a community in virtue of the things which they have in common; and communication is the way in which they come to possess things in common."[56] This is especially the case with respect to *common actions*, without which communal relationships will develop inadequately. "Interactions, transactions, occur *de facto* and the results of interdependence follow. But participation in activities and sharing in results are additive concerns. They demand," Dewey pointed out, "*communication* as a prerequisite." Indeed, this Dewey saw as "the only possible solution: the perfecting of the means and ways of communication of meanings so that genuinely shared interest in the consequences of interdependent activities may inform desire and effort and thereby direct action." In the light of this conviction, the lesson for public policy was clear. "The essential need," Dewey concluded, ". . . is the improvement of the methods and conditions of debate, discussion and persuasion. That is *the* problem of the public."[57]

Whether or not one agrees to the pivotal status of communication, one can see how the necessity to communicate over wide horizons might serve to resolve the problem of diversity versus commonality. The achievement of community, the reaching for democracy, consisted, just as did the quest for truth in pragmatic philosophy and science, of involvement in a process, a mode of social and political action. What was shared was not so much points of agreement on social "truths" as involvement in the process itself. Since men can only reach harmony and understanding through intercommunication, then only the widest possible exposure of all citizens to the most diverse opinions and beliefs can ensure that harmony will be approximated. Experience that falls significantly short of full exposure will result in attenuated communication and will therefore produce some kind of tyranny. Dewey insisted that "to have a large number of values in common, all the members of the group must have an equable opportunity to receive and to take from others. There must be a large variety of shared undertakings and experiences. Otherwise the influences which educate some into masters, educate others into slaves."[58] In a master-slave relationship there is obviously little or no communication, certainly no community and, it goes without saying, no possibility of democracy.

☆

[56] "Education as Politics," Ratner (ed.), *op. cit.*, vol. II, p. 777. *Democracy and Education*, p. 5.

[57] *The Public and Its Problems*, pp. 152, 155, 208.

[58] *Democracy and Education*, p. 97.

Communication, Science, and Intelligence

The *conscious* communication that typified democratic processes took more than the simple ability to verbalize ideas; it required the use of intelligence so that ideas could be genuinely and meaningfully exchanged. It was, in fact, the faculty of intelligence which bridged the gap between simple ideas and ideas put into action. Just as in the case of community, feelings played a critical but secondary role. "Of course," Dewey argued, "intelligence does not generate action except as it is enkindled by feeling. But the notion that there is some inherent opposition between emotion and intelligence is a relic . . . that grew up before the experimental method of science had emerged. For the latter method signifies the union of ideas with action, a union that is intimate; and action generates and supports emotion."

The connection between intelligence and science was very close. As a matter of fact, just as pragmatism and science replicated each other, the same was true of science and intelligence. Nonviolent change was at last possible because "mankind now has in its possession a new method, that of cooperative and experimental science which expresses the method of intelligence." And to complete the equation, Dewey made it clear that the new method of intelligence was also the operational equivalent of liberalism itself: "the mediating function of liberalism," he pointed out, "is all one with the work of inetlligence. This fact is the root, whether it be consciously realized or not, of the emphasis placed by liberalism upon the role of freed intelligence as the method of directing social action."[59] It was, moreover, this ability to direct social action that distinguished the adaptive capacities of man from those of lower animals.

Dewey accepted the Darwinian notion that species adapt to new conditions as the environment shifts, but he rejected the Social Darwinist proposition that the entire process was necessarily teleological. Nature, he reasoned, "is not an unchangeable order, unwinding itself majestically from the reel of law under the control of deified forces. It is an indefinite congeries of changes."[60] Man's reaction to change was not passive; it generated a conscious involvement, which was altogether natural. "Reflection," Dewey wrote, "is an indirect response to the environment, and the element of indirection can itself become great and very complicated. But it has its origin in biological adaptive behavior and the ultimate function of its cognitive aspect is a prospective control of the conditions of the environment." Pragmatism, there-

☆

[59] *Liberalism and Social Action*, pp. 50, 51, 83.

[60] "Intelligence and Morals," *The Influence of Darwin on Philosophy, and Other Essays in Contemporary Thought*, p. 72.

fore, "assigns a positive function to thought, that of *re*constituting the present stage of things instead of merely knowing it." Dewey could put it even more forcefully: "what we insist upon," he declared, "above all else is that intelligence be regarded as the only source and sole guarantor of a desirable and happy future." And since the American ideology grossly overstated its case, the desire for intelligence should not be regarded as hopelessly romantic. Dewey insisted that the "individual which American thought idealizes is not an individual *per se*, an individual fixed in isolation and set up for himself, but an individual who evolves and develops in a natural and human environment, an individual who can be educated."[61] The notion of individuals amenable to education provided a cornerstone for Dewey's theory.

The goal of intelligence is communication. Through education one gains the former and participates in the latter. Without this process society would surely degenerate. "What nutrition and reproduction are to physiological life," Dewey explained, "education is to social life. This education consists primarily in transmission through communication." Dewey never tired of demonstrating to his fellow-liberals that genuine reform must begin in the educational system. Education, he told them, invariably comes "back to the schools, to the teachers, the text-books, the courses of study, the school-room methods of teaching and discipline . . . and with education the larger part of the conscious direction of our social affairs."[62] As a formative influence on the public mind, nothing rivaled the impact of education. "The school," said Dewey, "is the essential distributing agency for whatever values and purposes any social group cherishes." Because some liberals held a fairly static view of human nature they argued that schools were of secondary importance. Dewey replied that while he recognized certain constant human needs and attributes, their manifestations in society, largely controlled by habit, were enormously maleable. "For the very meaning of education," he wrote, "is modification of native human nature in formation of those ways of thinking, of feeling, of desiring, and of believing that are foreign to raw human nature."[63] The school, in brief, offered an optimal area for social innovation.

☆

[61] "The Development of American Pragmatism," *Philosophy and Civilization*, pp. 30, 31, 33, 34.

[62] *Democracy and Education*, p. 11. "The Schools and Social Preparedness," Ratner (ed.), *op. cit.*, vol. II, p. 474.

[63] "Democracy and Education in the World of Today," *Problems of Men*, p. 37. "Does Human Nature Change?" *ibid.*, pp. 185, 190-191.

Education Democratized

What would reformed education look like? Dewey devoted a considerable portion of his lifetime to this subject and we can deal here with only a few of his suggestions that bear directly on our topic. Since democracy was the prime value, the educational system would, of course, be geared toward the realization of a democratic society. And since, as we have already noted, the methodology of science and that of democratic procedure were identical, it would be logical, indeed essential, to introduce the scientific approach into the curriculum.

Dewey believed that science as traditionally treated in the schools was not very productive. "If, " he argued, "it were treated as what it is, the method of intelligence itself in action, then the method of science would be incarnate in every branch of study and every detail of learning. Thought would be connected with the possibility of action, and every mode of action would be reviewed to see its bearing upon the habits and ideas from which it sprang."[64] If we recall that philosophy rightly understood is also equatable with the use of the scientific-democratic method, then, if Dewey's logic holds, an education committed to change through the use of scientific intelligence must simultaneously constitute an education in philosophy. This was precisely the case. "If," Dewey remarked, "we are willing to conceive education as the process of forming fundamental dispositions, intellectual and emotional, toward nature and fellow men, philosophy may even be defined *as the general theory of education*." Objective conditions being what they were, Dewey saw congruence among the various modes of intellectual response as entirely natural. The dramatic social, industrial, scientific, and ecological changes characteristic of recent generations demanded corresponding alterations in men's attitudes and ideas. "The reconstruction of philosophy, of education, and of social ideals and methods," he wrote, "thus go hand in hand."[65]

Dewey had the highest expectations for a reconstructed and reconstituted education. It would be able, he believed, to accomplish many things: it "will reconcile liberal nurture with training in social serviceableness, with ability to share efficiently and happily in occupations which are productive. And such an education will of itself tend to do away with the evils of the existing economic system." This would occur because men would learn to participate in public life and thereby control their own destinies. The schools themselves would constitute

☆

[64] *Liberalism and Social Action*, p. 46.
[65] *Democracy and Education*, pp. 383-386.

full communities whose learning processes would involve a direct interplay between classroom activities and the larger interests of society. Involvement would be active, directive, and by no means neutral when democratic values were at stake. "It is the aim of progressive education," Dewey commented, "to take part in correcting unfair privilege and unfair deprivation, not to perpetrate them." He felt that general participation in this kind of a learning process could only serve to bring Americans closer together. "An education which should unify the disposition of the members of society," he contended, "would do much to unify society itself." A scientific-democratic education would change the schools almost beyond recognition. "When this happens," Dewey asserted, "schools will be the dangerous outposts of a humane civilization. But they will also begin to be supremely interesting places. For it will then have come about that education and politics are one and the same thing because politics will have to be in fact what it now pretends to be, the intelligent management of social affairs."[66] Under intelligent management, politics *qua* education would depart emphatically from longstanding American norms.

New Understandings

Educated democratically, Americans could give new meaning to such concepts as authority and liberty, concepts that, due to the nation's intense individualism, had fallen either into disuse or into misconception. For example, freedom, especially freedom of speech, has had such a difficult time in America precisely because it has been tied to the practice of individualism. Exclusively as an individual assertion, liberty could be generously tolerated so long as it in no way threatened the status quo. But, Dewey noted, when a genuine threat to utilize power is recognized, "every effort is put forth to identify the established order with the public good. When this identification is established, it follows that any merely individual right must yield to the general welfare. As long as freedom of thought and speech is claimed as a merely individual right, it will give way, as do other merely personal claims, when it is . . . represented to be, in opposition to the general welfare."[67] Liberty, Dewey was convinced, is a social question, and the liberties that any one person possesses depend directly upon the way and to what extent the political, legal, and economic institu-

☆

[66] *Ibid.*, pp. 140, 304, 305. "Education as Politics," Ratner (ed.), *op. cit.*, vol. II, p. 781.

[67] *Liberalism and Social Action*, pp. 65-66.

tions permit power to be distributed. Based on this premise the traditional liberal distinction between liberty and equality completely breaks down.

Liberty and Equality

Although Dewey did not mention him by name, it was Tocqueville who provided the classic analysis of liberty and equality that many of his contemporaries still followed. Tocqueville had argued that liberty implied the right to idiocyncrasy, to be creative, to hold unorthodox views, whereas equality tended to insist that everyone be treated the same, a stipulation that led in America to uniformity of behavior, intolerance by the majority of unpopular opinions, and a society whose ethos was characterized by the lowest common denominator of all citizens. While not unmindful of American tendencies towards conformity and intolerance,[68] Dewey found that, when considered in terms of power available in society as a whole, this theoretical differentiation was totally indefensible.

He observed that "the common assertion of the mutual incompatibility of equality and liberty rests upon a highly formal and limited concept of liberty. It overlooks and rules out the fact that the *actual* liberties of one human being depend upon the powers of action that existing institutional arrangements accord to other individuals. It conceives of liberty in a completely abstract way." Those who still believed that equality before the law sufficiently exhausted the question were just as abstract. "The notion that men are equally free to act if only the same legal arrangements apply equally to all—irrespective of differences in education, in command of capital, and the control of the social environment which is furnished by the institution of property—is," Dewey proclaimed, "a pure absurdity." Democracy unites equality and liberty and recognizes that "actual and concrete liberty of opportunity and action is dependent upon equalization of the political and economic conditions under which individuals are alone free *in fact*, not *in some abstract metaphysical way.*" And since this equalization does not at present exist, "the attainment of freedom conceived as power to act in accord with choice depends upon positive and constructive changes in social arrangements."[69] And if positive changes would give rise to a new conception of liberty, it might do the same for the concept of authority as well.

☆

[68] See "The Emergence of a New World," Ratner (ed.), *op. cit.*, vol. II, p. 447.

[69] "Philosophies of Freedom," *Philosophy and Civilization*, pp. 281-282. "Liberty and Social Control," *Problems of Men*, p. 116.

Liberty and Authority

In point of fact, liberty and authority were in Dewey's view intimately related. This connection had been missed in America because as the nation came into being, authority for most citizens stood for the very social and political structures against which they were rebelling. "Finding the existing institutions oppressive, the new movement reacted against authority as such, and began to conceive of authority as inherently external to individuality, and inherently hostile to freedom." As Dewey saw it, this was still the common understanding of authority, popularly identified with stability, and of liberty, which tended to be associated with change. This understanding was absolutely devastating, for it deprived "individuals of the direction and support that are universally indispensable both for the organic freedom of individuals and for social stability." That older political institutions failed to manifest *genuine* authority only made the situation more poignant. "As far as the idea of organized authority is concerned," Dewey wrote, "the pathos of the collective life of mankind on this planet is its exhibition of the dire human need for some authority; while its ever-mounting tragedy is due to the fact that the need has been repeatedly betrayed by the very institutions which claimed to satisfy it."[70]

A society organized along democratic lines would reanimate legitimate authority by placing it in its proper location. Put plainly and simply, democracy requires that authority be derived from democratic activity. Every individual, Dewey proposed, "must be consulted in such a way, actively not passively, that he himself becomes a part of the process of authority, of the process of social control; that his needs and wants have a chance to be registered in a way where they count in determining social policy." With individuals immediately involved in public affairs, exercising power and thereby enhancing their freedom, the traditional hostility between liberty and authority would automatically disappear. Wielding political power and endowing legitimacy to authority would in fact be one and the same act. There was the problem, naturally, of devising mechanisms to make this process of legitimation operational, but, however these mechanisms were to become effective, Dewey had in mind his usual model for what they would look like. "What is pertinent," he said, "what is deeply significant to the theme of the *relation* between collective authority and freedom, is that the progress of intelligence—

☆

[70] "Authority and Resistance to Social Change," *ibid.*, pp. 94-95, 100, 103.

as exemplified in . . . scientific advance—exhibits their organic, effective union."[71] Education was, of course, the general vehicle for transmitting the scientific method.

Political Action and Group Plurality

In terms of direct political participation, however, means were needed over and above those of the educational process. Democracy, if it were to remain viable, must confront what was perhaps the most massive fact of the twentieth century: the rise of organization. Due to the complexities of industrialization all aspects of society had become increasingly organized. Particularly relevant were the large economic interests that had come to wield incomparable political power. "In a word" wrote Dewey, "the new forms of combined action due to the modern economic regime control present politics, much as dynastic interests controlled those of two centuries ago. They affect thinking and desire more than did the interests which formerly moved the state." In the face of this kind of control, which is usually remote and discontinuous with daily activities, the citizen is forced to reply in kind, in a way that drastically alters the structure of society. Dewey noticed that the "comparative helplessness of persons in their strictly singular capacities to influence the course of events expresses itself in formation of combinations in order to secure protection from too destructive impact of impersonal forces. That groups now occupy much the same place that was occupied earlier by individuals is almost a commonplace of writers on sociology."[72] Dewey regarded group formation not only as natural but as absolutely vital, a phenomenon whose presence meant the difference between a sick and a healthy democracy.

For Dewey, a society containing a large variety of active groups and associations was a society that cultivated the pragmatic value of pluralism. What he said of individual temperament would apply equally or perhaps more cogently to society at large. "If a man cherishes novelty, risk, opportunity and a variegated esthetic reality," he wrote in the 1920's, "he will certainly reject any belief in Monism . . . But if, from the very start, he is attracted by esthetic harmony, classic proportions, fixity even to the extent of absolute security, and logical coherence, it is quite natural that he should put his faith in

☆

[71] "Democracy and Education in the World Today," *ibid.*, pp. 35-36. "Authority and Resistance to Social Change," *ibid.*, p. 106.

[72] *The Public and Its Problems*, p. 108. *Freedom and Culture*, pp. 62-63.

Monism."[73] In collective terms "esthetic reality" corresponded to ideological conviction, and for Dewey monistic political doctrines represented the assertion of ideological dogma, an assertion that inevitably led to tyranny. America embodied democratic principles just insofar as it rejected monism and embraced its opposite. "An American democracy," Dewey felt, "can serve the world only as it demonstrates in the conduct of its own life the efficacy of plural, partial, and experimental methods in securing and maintaining an ever-increasing release of the powers of human nature, in service of a freedom which is co-operative and a co-operation which is voluntary."[74] The voluntary association would provide the social means for such experimentation.

So dedicated was he to the idea of experimentation that Dewey was even prepared to learn from the Soviet Union, despite its dogmatism and despite the fact that Bolshevism knew little of democracy's real meaning, "its essential pluralism, experimentalism, and consequent toleration." He believed that the Russians had the right to make their own experiments, to learn from their own mistakes, and he was confident that, if let alone, they would eventually repudiate Marxism while developing many novel institutions worthy of serious emulation. Far more than Soviet absolutism, Dewey feared that American opposition to the Soviet Union on ideological grounds would serve to encourage an intense capitalist absolutism at home.[75] If that were to happen the principle of pluralistic associations would stand in great peril.

Organizations, Associations, and Community

To some extent this was already the case. Americans belonged to a multitude of organizations and associations, but such membership failed somehow to overcome the pressure of the dominant ideology; citizens were left "in the grip of immense forces whose workings and consequences they have no power of affecting." They were clearly in need of face-to-face relationships and interaction that could offset the impersonal forces lying beyond their control. But their groups tended to be arrested at the level of association and tended never to reach the level of community. "There is a difference," Dewey explained, "between a society, in the sense of an association, and a

☆

[73] "The Development of American Pragmatism," *Philosophy and Civilization*, p. 21.
[74] *Freedom and Culture*, p. 176.
[75] "Social Absolutism," Ratner (ed.), *op. cit.*, vol. II, pp. 725 727.

community. Electrons, atoms and molecules are in association with one another . . . Natural associations are conditions for the existence of a community, but a community adds the function of communication in which emotions and ideas are shared as well as joint undertakings engaged in. Economic forces have immensely widened the scope of associational activities . . . largely at the expense of the intimacy and directness of communal group interests and activities. The American habit of 'joining' is a tribute to the reality of the problem but has not gone far in solving it." [76]

Groups remain associational in large measure because of the absence of a national purpose that would provide them with external goals and directions. Without this, every group makes claim to the public interest and identifies its own ends as those of the wider society. "There is too much public," Dewey exclaimed, "a public too diffused and scattered and too intricate in composition. And there are too many publics . . . and each one of them crosses the others and generates its own group of persons especially affected with little to hold these different publics together in an integrated whole." [77] A pluralist society informed and energized by a collective purpose — which Dewey in *The Public and Its Problems* called "The Great Society," or, on its highest plane, "The Great Community" — would strike a necessary balance between group affiliation and national identification.

Dewey was concerned both about the problem of remoteness and that of size. With respect to the latter he understood the organizational paradox that Robert Michels and others had recently pinpointed. If, analytically speaking, there were differences between *communities* and *associations*, there were equally important differences between *associations* and *organizations*. "Individuals," Dewey argued, "can find the security and protection that are prerequisites for freedom only in association with others — and then the organization these associations take on, as a measure of securing their efficiency, limits the freedom of those who have entered them." This situation has grown worse as organizations have increased in size while local associations and the individuals within them have tended to lose the democratic qualities they once possessed. The end product of this process has been "a kind of molluscan organization, soft individuals within and a hard constrictive shell without. Individuals voluntarily enter associations which have become practically nothing but organizations; and then

☆

[76] *Freedom and Culture,* pp. 159-160.
[77] *The Public and Its Problems,* p. 137.

conditions under which they act take control of what they do whether they want it or not."[78] As serious as this condition is, the nation transformed into a Great Community would be able to deal with it.

Local Communities and National Purpose

This would be the case, however, only if communal sentiments on the local level, in local associations, were restored and strengthened. Indeed, in the final analysis the whole reorganization and reformation of society depended upon overcoming the barriers of remoteness and distance. "The Great Community," Dewey emphasized, "in the sense of free and full inter-communication, is conceivable. But it can never possess all the qualities which mark a local community. It will do its final work in ordering the relations and enriching the experience of local associations." Within a purposeful society local experience provides the kind of intimacy that can only develop at close range. Neighborhood involvement breeds not only insight and intercourse but "love and understanding," emotions highly relevant to the formation of democratic relationships. Dewey felt that intense activity on the local level was absolutely crucial. "Whatever the future may have in store," he wrote, "one thing is certain. Unless local communal life can be restored, the public cannot adequately resolve its most urgent problem: to find and identify itself." "Democracy," he proclaimed, "must begin at home, and its home is the neighborly community."[79]

While not entirely clear on the subject, Dewey seemed to suggest that local activity would provide the means for political participation; but even more importantly, it would provide a mechanism for social acculturation. Dewey realized that it was impossible in modern times to confine organizational activity to immediate spheres. "But," he asserted, "the problem of harmonious adjustment between extensive activities, precluding direct contacts, and the intensive activities of community intercourse is a pressing one for democracy. It involves even more than apprenticeship in the practical processes of self-government, important as that is, which Jefferson had in mind. It involves development of local agencies of communication and cooperation, creating stable loyal attachments, to militate against the centrifugal forces of present culture, while at the same time they are of a kind to respond flexibly to the demands of the larger unseen and indefinite public."[80] On their highest level, then, local associations

☆

[78] *Freedom and Culture*, pp. 166-167.
[79] *The Public and Its Problems*, pp. 211-213, 216.
[80] *Freedom and Culture*, pp. 160-161.

would transmit the "message" of the national purpose to their members, who would engage in activities, not necessarily political in character, that were productive of communal relations.

Dewey's final picture appears to be one of a society whose communal sentiments are derived from three main sources: the collective national purpose, the educational process, and proliferated local associations. Participation in the latter two allows the individual, together with his fellow citizens, to take part in the former. "A community," Dewey remarked, "thus presents an order of energies transmuted into one of meanings which are appreciated and mutually referred by each to every other on the part of those engaged in combined action."[81] The Great Community, in short, requires an organic and harmonious relationship among all important social institutions. This will naturally occur when citizens are educated democratically, participate in local associations, and are motivated by a shared and meaningful national purpose.

The Science of Pragmatism

We began this chapter with the consideration of pragmatism as apologetics for the status quo — not an easy task. That Dewey could collapse many of his essential categories — democracy, pragmatism, philosophy, science, education, intelligence, community — into one all-encompassing notion makes it difficult to systematically criticize his work. Charles Frankel refers to Dewey's argument as "semantic mayhem," a prose that, because of its continuous and gratuitous redefining of terms, was shot full of ambiguities. Frank Knight also finds various parts of his philosophy vague, ambiguous, and generative of considerable obfuscation.[82] While Dewey's writing was often lucid, sometimes elegantly so, there is some justice to the remarks of Frankel and Knight. Perhaps Dewey's own observations in a 1917 essay had a general relevance to his work. "Were I a poet," he began, "this should be . . . an ode . . . I can but set down a blurred perception of immense masses stirring across great spaces. There is not even the assurance that the fogged outlines mark a thing beheld."[83]

☆

[81] *The Public and Its Problems*, p. 153.

[82] Charles Frankel, "John Dewey's Legacy," *American Scholar*, vol. 29, p. 315, Summer, 1960. Frank Knight, "Pragmatism and Social Action," *International Journal of Ethics*, vol. 46, p. 230, January, 1936.

[83] "Emergence of a New World," Ratner (ed.), *op. cit.*, vol. II, p. 443.

Philosophical Ambiguities

While it would be inaccurate to describe Dewey's views as "fogged" or "blurred," we encounter problems in interpreting his statements similar to those found earlier in dealing with Emerson. Ambiguity and uncertainty appear even as Dewey stresses the need for clarity, concreteness, and empirical verification. In this connection, perhaps it is significant that Dewey was moved to defend Emerson against critics who charged that transcendentalism, as promulgated by Emerson, was a discontinuous, illogical, and incoherent philosophy.[84] In many respects Dewey and Emerson may have been kindred spirits.

Dewey was conspicuously ambiguous in treating the question of philosophy as a mode of inquiry. He insisted that he was trying to make the case for philosophy, for philosophical reasoning, and not for his own particular philosophy. "Please do not imagine," he requested his readers in 1931, "that this is a plea in disguise for any particular type of philosophizing." "The moral," he wrote in *Freedom and Culture*, "is not unintelligent glorification of empirical, pluralistic, and pragmatic method. On the contrary, the lesson to be learned is the importance of ideas and of a plurality of ideas employed in experimental activity as working hypotheses."[85] The cynical reader might be forgiven for interpreting this last remark as saying the moral is: the *intelligent* glorification of the "empirical, pluralistic, and pragmatic method."

As we have seen before, pragmatism and philosophy were virtually identical in Dewey's mind. Indeed, he felt that pragmatism was a logical extension of American experience, a natural child conceived on American soil; consequently when he wrote, with respect to modern America, "it is the part of men to labour persistently and patiently for the clarification and development of the positive creed of life implicit in democracy and in science," we have every reason to take him at his word and to remember that the creed of science and democracy was none other than pragmatism itself.[86]

Science and Social Change

Dewey's emphasis on science raises further problems when one recalls that active participation is an integral part of the democratic creed. Although he repeatedly asserted that meaningful change and progress depended upon man's intelligent direction, Dewey urged

☆

[84] "Ralph Waldo Emerson," *ibid.*, vol. I, pp. 69-77.

[85] "Philosophy and Civilization," *Philosophy and Civilization*, p. 11. *Freedom and Culture*, p. 95.

[86] "Pragmatic America," Ratner (ed.), *op. cit.*, vol. II, p. 543. "Religion and Our Schools," *ibid.*, p. 507.

that to be intelligent such direction must follow the scientific method. He was so enamored of science that he sometimes spoke as if it were an independent entity, an autonomous and powerful historical force. By 1924 he could write that "science has won its freedom . . . the scientific revolution is . . . accomplished." This was important for two reasons. In the first place science could be seen as providing the material preconditions for democratic institutions. "The industrial revolution," Dewey wrote, "was born of the new science of nature. Any democracy which is more than an imitation of some archaic re-publican government must issue from the womb of our chaotic indus-trialism. Science makes democracy possible because it brings relief from depending upon massed human labor, because of the substitution it makes possible of inanimate forces for human muscular energy, and because of the resources for excess production and easy distribution which it effects." It was precisely this phenomenon that the early critics of democracy missed when they predicted the splintering and ultimate disintegration of democratic government: "they ignored the technological forces making for consolidation."[87] Seen in this light, consolidation was presumably not the result of, and perhaps not even related to, conscious political action on the part of the public.

If science accomplished much for society in the past, it promised even further benefits in the future. Science was to be no less than the guarantor of perpetual stability. "We now have a sure method," Dewey announced. "Wholesale permanent decays of civilization are impos-sible. As long as there exists a group of men who understand the meth-ods of physical science and are expert in their use, recovery, under the worst of circumstances, of the material basis of culture is sure and relatively speedy."[88] The mention in this context of men expert in the new methodology brings into consideration the contribution not just of science as a discipline, but of science personified, of the special-ists and technicians who were engaged directly in its work and who would be responsible for civilization's speedy recovery.

Despite their small number these men exerted a great influence upon society. Dewey believed that to some degree "science has already created a new morale—which is equivalent to the creation of new desires and new ends. The existence of the scientific attitude and spirit, even upon a limited scale, is proof that science is capable of developing a distinctive type of disposition and purpose." At one point Dewey seemed to equate the emergence of political intelligence with the development of just such a distinctive expertise. "Is not the problem at the present time," he asked, "that of securing experts to

☆

[87] "Science, Belief and the Public," *ibid.*, vol. II, p. 461. "American Education and Culture," *ibid.*, pp. 501-502. *The Public and Its Problems*, p. 116.
[88] "Progress," Ratner (ed.), *op. cit.*, vol. II, p. 823.

manage administrative matters, other than the framing of policies? It may be urged that the present confusion and apathy are due to the fact that the real energy of society is now directed in all non-political matters by trained specialists who manage things, while politics are carried on with a machinery and ideas formed in the past to deal with quite another sort of situation."[89] Dewey by no means advocated administration by technocracy, nor did he for the most part divorce scientific involvement from the needs and goals of society. But since in his own mind social goals were so closely associated with scientific procedures, his formulation at the very least begs the question.

And his penchant for ambiguity did little to clarify the issue. He concluded one of his essays on pragmatism with the following:

> The essential and immanent criticism of existing industrialism and of the dead weight of science is that instruments are made into ends, that they are deflected from their intrinsic quality and thereby corrupted. The implied idealization of science and technology is not by way of acquiescence. It is by way of appreciation that the ideal values which dignify and give meaning to human life have themselves in the past been precarious in possession, arbitrary, accidental and monopolized in distribution, because of lack of means of control; by lack, in other words, of those agencies and instrumentalities with which natural science through technologies equips mankind. Not all who say *Ideals, Ideals,* shall enter the kingdom of the ideal, but only those shall enter who know and who respect the roads that conduct to the kingdom.[90]

The line between idealization, acquiescence, and appreciation is surely very fine, and it seems possible to conclude from this paragraph that we will be led into the kingdom of the ideal by those who already respect the road and know it best—that is, by the students and practitioners of natural science.

There is, furthermore, a legitimate question as to the exact nature of this road. According to pragmatism its character and direction would of course depend to a large extent on the previous experience of its builders. A utopian route would clearly prove unusable. "We cannot," said Dewey, "set up, out of our heads, something we regard as an ideal society. We must base our conception upon societies which actually exist, in order to have any assurance that our idea is a practicable one. But . . . the ideal cannot simply repeat the traits which are actually found. The problem is to extract the desirable traits or forms of community life which actually exist, and employ them to criticize undesirable features and suggest improvements."[91] But the obvious

☆

[89] *Freedom and Culture*, p. 147. *The Public and Its Problems*, p. 123.

[90] "Philosophy and the Social Order," Ratner (ed.), *op. cit.*, vol. II, pp. 441-442.

[91] *Democracy and Education*, p. 96.

questions are not answered by this statement. How, for example, do we decide which are the "undesirable features" or the "desirable traits?" If change is to come in the form of scientific experimentation, who advances the working hypotheses and how do we decide whether one set of hypotheses is more appropriate than another? And what do we do in the event of competing hypotheses? The pragmatic test for truth is less than helpful here, for it makes it impossible to judge the merit of a proposition (save for those which might be rejected out of hand as "antidemocratic" and therefore "antiscientific — if such exist) before it stands the existential test of future experience. Social reform requires experimentation, and experimentation requires testable hypotheses, but pragmatism leaves untouched the question of who advances the hypotheses and who selects them for testing.

Dewey at one point seemed to imply that the social scientist would furnish hypothetical propositions. He believed that the social sciences could perform an invaluable service if they would cease to look at the *conclusions* of natural science, that is, information derived from the accumulation of specified data, and begin to adopt its *methods*. By this he meant the attachment of scholarly investigation to prospective courses of action. "Social and historical inquiry is," he wrote, "in fact a part of the social process itself, not something outside of it . . . When the conclusions of inquiries that deal with man are left outside the program of social action, social policies are necessarily left without the guidance that knowledge of man can provide, and that it must provide if social action is not to be directed either by mere precedent and custom or else by the happy intuition of individual minds."[92] Dewey did not elaborate this point, and one is troubled by the ambiguities noted before.

It is not clear, for example, if, in the actual construction of public policies, the social scientist would take the lead. Nor is it clear how one would deal with the likely situation in which the conclusions of social scientists differ, or that in which their findings demonstrate a society that is rigidly divided, badly confused, or totally apathetic on a given issue. In the case of counterclaims by social scientists Dewey's logic would suggest that, as in natural science, the proof of a scientific assertion would lie in the results of a crucial experiment. Although Dewey did not say so, it follows from this suggestion that, with society as their laboratory, social scientists must be free to engage in whatever kinds of social experimentation they deem necessary. Those which "work" would of course be the ones proven appropriate to the times. As to the case of a serious fragmentation of public opinion, Dewey's

☆

[92]*Liberalism and Social Action*, p. 45.

theory was silent. His method seemed to presuppose that society, precisely because it constitutes an extant society, would contain a consensus on present standards and future directions sufficient to allow the method to work.

Pragmatic Democracy

Dewey looked to the past, to the American tradition, for "desirable traits" that might prove useful in advancing the cause of democracy. But his appeal to the past, even to the immediate past, was clouded because he was of two minds about past experience, insofar as it embodied traditional beliefs and customary practices. On the one hand he fully understood the impossibility of breaking entirely with historical antecedents. "The old and the new," he wrote, "have forever to be integrated with each other, so that the values of old experience may become the servants and instruments of new desires and aims. We are always possessed by habits and customs, and this fact signifies that we are always influenced by inertia and the momentum of forces temporarily outgrown but nevertheless still present with us as a part of our being. Human life gets set in patterns, institutional and moral." Dewey was completely aware of the binding and cohering force that such patterns possessed. When "tradition and social custom are incorporated in the working constitution of an individual, they have authority as a matter of course over his beliefs and his activities. The forces that exert and exercise this authority are so much and so deep a part of individuals that there is no thought or feeling of their being external and oppressive . . . They support him and give him direction. They naturally compel his allegiance and arouse his devotion."[93] This statement was as true of America as it was of any society.

Tradition, Democracy, and Science

Dewey was, moreover, fully prepared to endorse and build on the traditional aspect of American culture. "I hope," he declared, "I yield to none in appreciation of the great American tradition, for tradition is something that is capable of being transmitted as an emotion and as an idea from generation to generation. We have a great and precious heritage from the past, but to be realized . . . this tradition has to be embodied by active effort in the social relations which we as human

☆

[93] *Ibid.*, p. 49. "Authority and Resistance to Social Change," *Problems of Men*, p. 97.

beings bear to each other under present conditions."[94] The emphasis
on active effort, however, was vital, for tradition alone was scarcely
enough. The fact was that democratic sentiments had become primarily
"a matter of tradition and habit—an excellent thing as far as it goes,
but when it becomes routine is easily undermined when change of
conditions changes other habits." Indeed, when Dewey defined democracy in his usual terms of creative, pragmatic intelligence, he
shifted his ground and pictured custom and tradition as positively
reactionary factors. Pragmatically speaking, the choices were entirely
clear-cut. "There are," Dewey indicated, "ultimately but three forces
that control society—habit, coercive and violent force, and action
directed by intelligence." It is apparent from this formulation that
while the American tradition might provide a source of experimentation—"We have the material," Dewey wrote in 1916, "for a genuinely
unified ideal, much as that material requires focusing and articulation"
—as far as pragmatism was concerned tradition was an obstacle to be
overcome.[95]

For conditions *had* changed and as a consequence habits had to be
changed as well. "Nothing is gained," Dewey observed, "by attempts
to minimize the novelty of the democratic order, nor the scope of the
change it requires in old and long cherished traditions." On one level
he viewed the fact that Americans had only a weak consciousness of
tradition with considerable optimism. "There are," he suggested,
"bad traditions as there are good ones: it is always important to distinguish. Our neglect of the traditions of the past, with whatever this
negligence implies in the way of spiritual impoverishment of our life,
has its compensation in the idea that the world is recommencing and
being remade under our eyes." The remaking of society involved the
scientific reconstruction of the citizen—"the inner man," Dewey
wrote, "is the jungle which can be subdued to order only as the forces
of organization at work in externals are reflected in corresponding
patterns of thought, imagination, and emotion"—and this process
seemed only to discover bad traditions requiring extirpation.[96]

For Dewey the problem was to find ways to extend "the scientific
morale till it is part of the ordinary equipment of the ordinary individ-

☆

[94] "Democracy and Education in the World of Today," *ibid.*, p. 40.

[95] *Freedom and Culture*, p. 124. "The Teacher and His World," *Problems of Men*,
p. 79. "Universal Service as Education," Ratner (ed.), *op. cit.*, vol. II, p. 471. Dewey
may have felt that even more than the American tradition needed to be overcome. Of
the scientific characteristics—tentativeness, empirical orientation, adherence to canons
of evidence, openness to novelty—he wrote: "Every one of these traits goes contrary to
some human impulse that is naturally strong." (*Freedom and Culture*, pp. 145-146.)

[96] *Ibid.*, p. 163. "The Development of American Pragmatism," *Philosophy and Civilization*, p. 33. *Individualism Old and New*, p. 65.

ual . . . It is individual persons who need to have this attitude substituted for pride and prejudice, for class and personal interest, for beliefs made dear by custom and early emotional associations."[97] Tradition, precisely because it was identified with antiscientific factors, would, whether or not it contained "material for a genuinely unified ideal," be an unsuitable wellspring for hypotheses of change. Logically speaking, Dewey's theory was left with only the future to provide sources of justification, and one can see from this why some critics were apt to identify Dewey's predications with that which would work: only ideas which work will last long enough into the future to be evaluated; put differently, only that which works can stand the test of time. It was the implication of this last idea that caused many to discover in Dewey a conservative bias.

Political Goals, Educational Means

Dewey was perhaps victimized by his own methodology. On political grounds his position was far to the left of the American center. Although criticized by intellectual radicals, especially during the 1920's, he shared many of their ideas and went considerably beyond them in others. One commentator has found at least nine major points of similarity between Dewey and Marx, and Sidney Hook, Dewey's biographer, believed that democratic Marxists and Dewey could easily have brought their views into harmony.[98]

Very broadly speaking, Dewey advocated a change to industrial democracy and to socialism. "We are in for some kind of socialism," he predicted in 1931, "call it by whatever name we please, and no matter what it will be called when it is realized." His version of socialism, which would guarantee as part of its normal operation the right of all citizens to productive work, was to be distinguished from those systems in which the state takes over and bureaucratizes the means of production and distribution. State control, Dewey felt, really amounted to state *capitalism*. Properly conceived, socialism would not lead to absolute state ownership and control; it would involve a mixed system in which supervision and regulation of industry was jointly administered by the government — representing the public interest in general and the interest of the consumer in particular — by management, and

☆

[97] *Freedom and Culture*, p. 151.

[98] Jim Cork, "John Dewey, Karl Marx, and Democratic Socialism," *Antioch Review*, vol. 9, pp. 441-443, December, 1949. Cork quotes from a letter he received from Dewey in which Dewey said: "I can be classed as a democratic socialist. If I were permitted to define 'socialism' and 'socialist' I would so classify myself today." (*Ibid.*, p. 450.) Sidney Hook, "John Dewey and His Critics," *The New Republic*, vol. 76, p. 74, June 3, 1931.

by the workers through their democratically elected trade unions. On the precise functions of government Dewey had little to say. He envisaged "a federation of self-governing industries with the *government acting as adjuster and arbiter* rather than as direct owner and manager, unless perhaps in case of industries occupying such a privileged position as fuel production and the railways. Taxation will be a chief governmental power through which to procure and maintain socialization of the services of the land and of industries." [99] [Emphasis added.] Indeed, Dewey used the term "socialization" more often than "socialism," and it is perhaps a more accurate name for his mixed proposals.

Pure socialism or not, political life clearly played less than a central role in Dewey's theory. When he focused the issue of community in the local sphere, it appeared that he had left the realization of a social purpose, which would give meaning and direction to all groups within the country, to the national political level—the federal government. It is difficult, however, to contemplate the government, which he projected into the future as "adjuster and arbiter," figuring importantly in the achievement of the national purpose. While Dewey insisted that true modern liberals welcomed extended federal action, [100] nowhere did his theory provide a basis for such action. In fact, Dewey often seemed to lean in the opposite direction. "Political action," he stated, "is not basic . . . Politics is a means, not an end. But *thought* of it as a means will lead to *thought* of the ends it should serve." [101] [Emphasis added.] Thought is clearly the critical activity here, and this idea should not be surprising, for it was thought after all that needed primary attention. "The fundamental defect," Dewey pointed out, "in the present state of democracy is the assumption that political and economic freedom can be achieved without first freeing the mind." [102] While he unceasingly called for ideas that would instigate action, the only action Dewey could contemplate in full detail was educational reform, action, that is, directly related to the process of thought.

When he asked himself how to attack the evils of America, Dewey's first response was almost always that which he gave in the essay aptly entitled "Education as Politics": "It seems almost hopeless," he remarked, "to name the remedy, for it is only a greater confidence

☆

[99] *Individualism Old and New*, p. 119. "Elements of Social Reorganization," Ratner (ed.), *op. cit.*, vol. II, pp. 756-758. "The Social Possibilities of War" (first published as "What Are We Fighting For?" in *The Independent*, June 22, 1918), *ibid.*, pp. 558-559.

[100] *Liberalism and Social Action*, pp. 26-27.

[101] *Individualism Old and New*, pp. 118-119.

[102] "Science, Belief and the Public," Ratner (ed.), *op. cit.*, vol. II, p. 464.

in intelligence, in scientific method . . . What will happen if teachers become sufficiently courageous and emancipated to insist that education means the creation of a discriminating mind, a mind that prefers not to dupe itself or to be the dupe of others?"[103] What would happen would be the revolution of society, and Dewey's real revolutionary was the courageous teacher inculcating the lessons of the scientific method. This is what he meant when he said that schools would be dangerous outposts and that "education and politics are one."

With politics as education, Dewey's pronouncements on politics as *politics* were sometimes vague and equivocal. Apparently arguing against direct government control of industry, for example, he managed to touch all sides of the question without clearly stating a position of his own:

> Even if we are obliged to abandon permanently the earlier belief that governmental action is by its own momentum hostile to free self-government, we are far from having refuted the evidence of history that officials who have political power will use it arbitrarily. Belief in what is sometimes called taking industry out of private hands is naïve until it is shown that the new private – or personal – hands to which it is confided are so controlled that they are reasonably sure to work in behalf of public ends. I am not saying the problem cannot be solved democratically nor that "socialization" of industry is bound to be followed by the regimentation so freely predicted by adherents of *laissez-faire* individualism. What I am saying is that the issue of democracy has taken a new form, where not much experience is available about the relation of economic factors, as they now operate, to democratic ends and methods.[104]

One might agree that experience was lacking in this area, but there still remained the question of whether at the very least it might be possible to offer hypothetical propositions that were both relevant to the issue and squared with the dictates of "democratic ends and methods." When the question was put in this way Dewey was inclined to employ generality. "If I am asked," he said, "what is the nature of the plan to which the nation might respond, I can only say that ability to answer the question would signify that one had already penetrated to the depths of our unconscious practical endeavors and perceived their direction."[105] Abstractly speaking, this was true enough, but one might hope that the use of intelligence would have yielded, at least in the form of testable hypotheses, some insight into the possible directions America might follow.

☆

103 *Ibid.*, p. 781.
104 *Freedom and Culture*, pp. 71-72.
105 "Universal Service as Education," Ratner (ed.), *op. cit.*, vol. II, pp. 472-473.

The Logic of Pragmatism

Strictly speaking, this insight was lacking because Dewey's method logically foreclosed the possibility, and the commitment to his methodology, far more than a consuming interest in education, kept him from stating his case more coherently and more completely. To announce fully worked out political ideas would have been tantamount to the promulgation of dogma, and from the perspective of pragmatism, dogmatic assertions of any kind ran the risk of encouraging philosophical and political monism, a condition that would eventually mean the end of pluralism and freedom. Consequently, with one exception, Dewey eschewed all ideas that might run easily to dogmatism. The exception, of course, was his own belief in the relative nature of all judgments, which cast the test of all propositions into future experience. This belief, *when applied rigorously to the political and social sectors*, became Dewey's own orthodoxy, so much so that he was sometimes forced, when methodological considerations demanded, to retreat from positions that he otherwise strongly supported.

Thus, while Dewey vigorously espoused community and industrial democratic socialism as necessary to the achievement of democracy, the relativist and pluralist aspects of his method prevented him from maintaining these positions with any degree of consistency. "The very idea of democracy," Dewey wrote in 1932, "the meaning of democracy, must be continually explored afresh; it has to be constantly discovered, and rediscovered, remade and reorganized." "Every generation," he added a year later, "has to accomplish democracy over again for itself; that its very nature, its essence, is something that cannot be handed on from one person or one generation to another, but has to be worked out in terms of needs, problems and conditions of the social life that is changing with extreme rapidity from year to year."[106] And since it was also true that "the content of the individual and freedom change with time," many of Dewey's assumptions about politics and society were open to reinterpretation. Even economic aggrandizement, that propensity which so vitiated the forces of community, could be viewed in a positive light. "Conditions," Dewey argued, "are set by tradition, by custom, by law, by the kind of public approvals and disapprovals; by all conditions constituting the environment. These conditions are so pluralized even in one and the same country at the same period that love of gain . . . may be both socially

☆

[106] "The Challenge of Democracy to Education," *Problems of Men*, p. 47. "Democracy and Education in the World of Today," *ibid.*, pp. 39-40.

useful and socially harmful."[107] If plurality of conditions meant that love of gain could prove socially useful, conversely it might mean that under certain circumstances community could be productive of social harm and therefore ought to be discouraged. The pluralist and relativist logic of pragmatism was inescapable, and this logic cast its shadow over Dewey's entire social theory.

It is important that we notice the logical transformation performed by Dewey. His attack on dogma, on absolutism, on a priori convictions, was invariably made on the same ground. He tirelessly insisted that the untutored adherence to particular ends, without specification of their necessary means, leads ineluctably to the monistic doctrine that the end justifies the means. Once this belief gains even minimal support, experimentalism, pluralism, and freedom itself stand in great peril, for the usual means employed by this doctrine are those which seek to eliminate the proffering of competing ends and directions. It was not accidental that the argument the ends justified the means was historically associated with intolerant monistic philosophies.

Pragmatism as Doctrine

But in countering this position Dewey tended to carry the argument just as far in the opposite direction. He stated that "the positive counterpart of opposition to doctrinal absolutism is experimentalism."[108] As counterpart to doctrine, experimentalism became doctrine itself and permitted Dewey to construct an *absolutism of means* — rather than the end justifying the means, the means now justified the ends; or, more precisely, the means now *became* the ends. The identification of intelligence with pragmatism, democracy, liberalism, etc., could be made so easily because intelligence per se, the scientific method itself, was Dewey's prime objective. By attacking the old ends-means problem he unwittingly stood the controversy on its head so that now the question was, not how does one connect means to ends already established, but how does one obtain ends to work toward once the means are agreed upon? And following Dewey's methodology closely, one must ask the further question: how are ends obtained, even when proposed in the form of hypotheses? This was a sharper question for Dewey than for either Pierce or James, since, much more than his predecessors, he wished to place pragmatism in the service of the nation to achieve a better society. But beyond the achievement of means — of free intelligence — there is little in the logic of his theory

☆

[107] "The Future of Liberalism," *ibid.*, p. 136. *Freedom and Culture*, p. 111.
[108] "The Future of Liberalism," *Problems of Men*, pp. 136-137.

to substantiate many of the specific ends that his own pragmatic analysis suggested. Industrial democracy, socialization, legitimized authority, even community, stand in the end as hypothetical formulations, neither more nor less credible, in *logical* terms, than any others that might be put to the test of time.

That Dewey painted himself into a logical corner was tragic in light of his hopes and expectations. An America committed to pragmatic procedures could, he felt, have a worldwide impact. "In working out to realization the ideas of federation and of the liberation of human interests from political combination," he informed the students of Smith College in 1918, "we have been as it were, a laboratory set aside from the rest of the world in which to make, for its benefit, a great social experiment . . . But we need to recover something of the militant faith of our forefathers that America is a great idea, and add to it an ardent faith in our capacity to lead the world to see what this idea means as a model for its own future well-being."[109] Faith in the ideas and men of the past, however, is precisely what strict observance of Dewey's logic prevented

On the other hand, underlying Dewey's whole philosophy was a faith more compelling and more demanding than a belief in national origins or worldwide mission. It was the faith in man's intelligence, the conviction that, if given access to education and freedom of choice, men would develop the mental capacity to design their own world in a way useful and beneficial to all. Pragmatism, Dewey continually emphasized, "is the formation of a faith in intelligence, as the one and indispensable belief necessary to moral and social life." Democracy, the political expression of the pragmatic temperament, required the same commitment. "The foundation of democracy," Dewey wrote in 1937, "is faith in the capacities of human nature; faith in human intelligence and in the power of pooled and cooperative experience. It is not belief that these things are complete but that, if given a show, they will grow and be able to generate progressively the knowledge and wisdom needed to guide collective action."[110] This was a faith as generous as Jefferson's and without Jefferson's many reservations. It was, in fact, faith in the potential of human freedom carried to its highest expression.

It was not, however, a blind faith. In a rare moment of depressed spirits Dewey demonstrated (what Jefferson could never forget) an awareness that the heavy demands made by democracy might en-

☆

[109] "America and the World," Ratner (ed.), *op. cit.*, vol. II, p. 644.

[110] "The Development of American Pragmatism," *Philosophy and Civilization*, p. 35. "Democracy and Educational Administration," *Problems of Men*, p. 59.

counter a human nature unprepared to meet the challenge. The instrumental attitude, he explained,

> is clearly a faith, not a demonstration. It too can be demonstrated only in *its* works, its fruits. Therefore it is not a facile thing. It commits us to a supremely difficult task. Perhaps the task is too hard for human nature. The faith may demonstrate its own falsity by failure. We may be arrested on the plane of commercial "success"; we may be diverted to search for consequences easier to achieve, and may noisily acclaim superficial and even disastrous "works" and fruits as proof of genuine success instead of evidence of failure. We not only may do so, but we actually are doing so. If the course of history be run, if our present estate be final, no honest soul can claim that success exceeds failure.[111]

Having announced this tragic view, however, Dewey immediately reasserted his basic principles and reaffirmed his faith that, in James' words, "the world is still making," that especially in America the future still offered ample opportunity for democratic experimentation.

But since his faith was ultimately "reduced" to the sphere of intelligence, and since intelligence was ultimately the property of individuals, Dewey's theory always ran the risk of substituting the consideration of individuality itself for the treatment of the larger social and political questions. At certain times his conclusions exactly reiterated those of Croly. In *Individualism Old and New* he argued that "interest in techniques is precisely the thing which is most promising in our civilization, the thing which in the end will break down devotion to external standardization and the mass-quantity ideal . . . In the end, technique can only signify emancipation of individuality, and emancipation on a broader scale than in the past." With technique in hand the essential focus of the problem becomes clear. "The first move in recovery of an integrated individual," Dewey concluded, "is accordingly with the individual himself. In whatever occupation he finds himself and whatever interest concerns him, he is himself and no other, and he lives in situations that are in some respect flexible and plastic."[112] With primary responsibility thrown upon the individual, concentration on the social question becomes far less imperative.

And considering the enormous variety of individual experiences, the application of pragmatic solutions to society as a whole becomes almost impossible to conceive. But even if it were granted that there existed a commonality to the experiences of masses of individuals, a larger common experience that was expressable and subject to modification, it must be said that the pragmatic method in its most precise

☆

[111] "Pragmatic America," Ratner (ed.), *op. cit.*, vol. II, pp. 545-546.

[112] *Individualism Old and New*, pp. 30, 166.

formulation could be applied only after the fact, after all or most of the evidence was in. For Dewey there were times when even hypotheses were *logically* or epistemologically questionable. "As a matter of fact," he wrote, "men do not begin thinking with premises. They begin with some complicated and confused case, apparently admitting of alternative modes of treatment and solution. Premises only gradually emerge from analysis of the total situation." Confronted by the endless complexities and differentiations that characterize modern social affairs, and devoid of initial premises, this mode of thinking might be driven to the expedient of fostering reconciliation and compromise among contesting interests. Dewey suggested at one point that this was in fact the desired end. "The very heart of political democracy," he wrote, "is adjudication of social differences by discussion and exchange of views. This method provides a rough approximation to the method of effecting change by means of experimental inquiry and test: the scientific method."[113] From this perspective the role of government as adjuster and arbiter naturally followed, a role that, since it adhered to the scientific method, could be defended as pragmatically sound.

But as far as public policy was concerned this mode of government was *not* the end Dewey sought; his comments on authority, education, purpose, and community show this to be the case. Indeed, his sophisticated understanding of America and his ability to address the critical issues with foresight and imagination are unrivalled in the history of American thought. Dewey's difficulty arose not because of a faulty logic or because of unconsidered remarks about social conditions, but because he felt compelled to bring his logical propositions, which were essentially linguistic and cognitive in character, to bear on his treatment of social conditions. Given his concern for his world, perhaps this was inevitable. Philosophy in his mind could not be separated from public affairs. The result, however, of this merger was to force his social and political insights, profound and thought-provoking on their own ground, as the products of a brilliant mind, into a framework of instrumentalism where they were ultimately attenuated or adulterated. This process was especially characteristic of his reflections on politics, in which the antidogmatic spirit of experimentalism grew into antidogma*tism* itself and thereby foreclosed the possibility of carrying the inquiry to its natural conclusion. Instead of taking Jefferson's positive side as far as it would go, Dewey was unable to elaborate his conception of democracy, unable to clarify the idea of

☆

[113] "Logical Method and Law," *Philosophy and Civilization*, p. 134, "Challenge to Liberal Thought," *Problems of Men*, p. 157.

local participation, and in the end settled for Jefferson the scientist, the precursor to pragmatism, rather than Jefferson the democratic theorist. He would support his pragmatic view of modern democracy by stating that "it is not irrelevant . . . that a score of passages could be cited in which Jefferson refers to the American Government as an experiment."[114]

The range of Dewey's interests and his faith in human intelligence distinguish him, however, from those who followed his collaborator, Arthur E. Bentley, into the "group theory of politics." For these writers, group interests constitute the *only* expression of public goals, and government has the sole function of simultaneously reflecting and arbitrating among competing factions. All is process, oscillating between conditions of relative stability and those of equilibrium, the process itself being regulated by agreement on "rules of the game" that allow all significant groups to participate and to satisfy at least part of their distinct interest.

Dewey was not content to leave the argument at this point, and his consideration of other factors and his insistence that the critical questions were moral in character gave his position a far greater impact. But, *logically* speaking, his devotion to pragmatic methodology continuously forced him to yield ground, and his concept of scientific adjudication constituted in practice, at least for many of his followers, a tacit acceptance of the group theory. It was this acceptance, this giving way to the pressure of interests which group theory implied, that Tugwell sensed in Roosevelt. Early in the New Deal, Tugwell realized that the view he personally represented had been discarded. "I felt," he wrote, "that I had lost. I was asking too much. It was not only N.R.A., it was the whole organic conception of the living nation, equipped with institutions for foresight, conjuncture and balance." Roosevelt would continue to lead, but mainly through "cleverness and personal manipulation. He would still be the quarterback of a team without any other direction . . . he would temporize, experiment, tentatively put forward . . ."[115] He would, in short, run the New Deal not to the prescriptions of Dewey's political theory, but to the imperatives ultimately dictated by Dewey's pragmatic logic.

☆

[114] *Freedom and Culture,* p. 158.

[115] "The Experimental Roosevelt," *Political Quarterly,* vol. 21, p. 265, July, 1950.

modernity and purpose
Herbert marcuse
robert Dahl

Postwar Perspectives:
Organization Theory and Pluralism

Dewey's logical parameters may have limited his consideration of community and purpose, but it is fair to say that his work constituted a major effort to think creatively about such problems in the context of political philosophy. No similar work has appeared in America since Dewey's time. As analytical precepts, community and purpose have been largely appropriated by scholars interested in the structure and dynamics of the modern organization. This shift in subject matter was evident even in Dewey's early days when the terminology of economic individualism was already being transposed to fit the functions of America's newest and fastest-growing institutions. Thus, where such words as "economy," "efficiency," and "productivity" were formerly to be found in the vocabulary of the old national purpose, they were now used to describe the way large agglomerations of people were institutionally organized. Similarly, where the aspirations of community could previously be posited as the concern of individuals, or groups of individuals, in their capacity as public citizens, such aspirations now became the goal of individuals (or groups of individuals) in their organizational capacity, in their private corporate existence. Thus employed, purpose and community no longer had meaning in the larger context of nation or society.[1]

But these concepts have not been narrowed to a subpolitical area simply because organization theory has seen fit to make use of them. In the period following World War II there have been few attempts to construct political theories of *any* kind, whatever the prime categories of analysis. In other words, not only have community and purpose been removed as objects of political speculation, but political theory itself has fallen into massive neglect. Organization theory has not so much preempted the field as it has moved in to fill a conceptual vacuum.

As far as American political science is concerned, the major attempt at theorizing has been made by those who see themselves within the tradition of political pluralism. The emphasis in this tradition has always been on the free play of interests and associations inside of the political system, with a corresponding de-emphasis on large-scale governmental action in behalf of the entire population. Pluralist writers have, for example, been deeply suspicious of arguments, like that advanced in Chapter 1, that suggest a central role for government in the attempt to institutionalize a national sense of community. They recall that the stress placed on such concepts as the "State" and the "Community" by totalitarian ideologies have lead in practice to the destruction of meaningful pluralism, along with political liberty, in the name of a larger, more inclusive set of national ideals.[2] As recent history can testify, this wariness on the part of political pluralists has been well founded. But, at the same time, the suspicion itself has often run to excess; it has given pluralist analyses of American politics an ideological cast of their own and has created serious barriers to the possibility that pluralism might evolve into a political philosophy capable of filling the theoretical void and lending meaning to the postwar era.

Pluralist studies have typically involved a description of American practice and a simultaneous defense of the pluralist position. Because they are free of ideological commitment, the great number of American interest groups can be described as pluralistic in form and content; since they stand as powerful manifestations of pluralism, these inter-

☆

[1] For a broad discussion of organization theory in this connection, see Sheldon S. Wolin, *Politics and Vision: Continuity and Innovation in Western Political Thought*, Little, Brown and Company, Boston, 1960, pp. 363 et seq.

[2] On this issue see Robert Nisbet, *Community and Power*, Oxford University Press, New York, 1962.

ests necessarily add up to a social edifice that is both democratic and supportive of freedom. In response to totalitarianism, which allows but one definition of political truth and permeates all of society with its monolithic dictum, pluralists, whose every postulate runs counter to this idea, have tended to suspect all isms, whatever their source or direction, of totalitarian proclivities. Pluralists have consequently seen their own philosophy as the only reasonable counter to the perils inherent in ideologically based action, in ideology per se. This reaction has had the result of equating pluralism with democracy itself, and a society that meets pluralist specifications becomes therefore inescapably democratic. For example, while he is a good deal more cautious in his pronouncements than many of his colleagues, Robert Dahl, perhaps the most sophisticated of contemporary pluralist writers, comes ultimately to this identical conclusion.

Robert Dahl

Dahl, at least in his more recent writings, reaches this position only after noting that the successful story of American pluralism must include a candid acknowledgement of some very serious and seemingly permanent debilitations. Far from inducing perpetual peace and harmony, our pluralistic system has experienced *"about once every generation* a conflict over national politics of *extreme severity."*[3] The Civil War is merely the most dramatic illustration of such inordinate conflict; the labor wars of the last quarter of the nineteenth century, for example, were bloodier and more ferocious than those of any other nation. The Civil War itself was a product of the practice of compromise, that facility which lies at the center of any pluralist system. The fact is that previous compromises allowed slavery to become so deeply entrenched that eventually it could be rooted out only by violent means.[4] Moreover, the special form taken by pluralism in America has meant that problems related to issues of civil rights have never been dealt with satisfactorily, for within the pluralist context

☆

[3] Robert A. Dahl, *Pluralist Democracy in the United States: Conflict and Consent,* Rand McNally & Company, Chicago, 1967 (hereafter referred to as *Pluralist Democracy*), p. 282. This book contains Dahl's most complete application of pluralist principles and will serve therefore as the focal point of our analysis. To analyze Dahl is not of course to analyze the totality of pluralist writings; there are pluralists who differ from Dahl in certain important respects. Dahl is used not only because his works are intrinsically interesting, but because his conclusions tend.to be shared by at least the majority of those political observers who avowedly operate within the framework of contemporary American pluralism.

[4] *Ibid.,* pp. 434, 318.

political leaders have frequently ignored the needs of marginal groups, especially those of the black minority. So dominating has this context been that it has discouraged a healthy interest both in fundamental criticism of the system and in the formulation of positive alternatives. More importantly, it has bred a kind of political irrationalism: dissenters have often been forced to choose between the futility of their own actions and the unacceptable compromise offered by the narrow two-party system; as a consequence they have found their level of frustration raised and their sense of alienation drastically increased.[5]

Pluralist America

Despite this awareness of extreme conflict characteristic of the history of American pluralism, Dahl manages to come to the customary conclusions. The case of the black minority is, he tells us, "an extreme one, and it is worth keeping that fact in mind." "Extreme polarization," he contends, "is rare in American politics, and it never persists over long periods. Most of the time political life displays the characteristics of moderate conflict." Indeed, the ability of many *stable* democracies in the twentieth century to absorb conflict and to carry out extensive, "one might almost say revolutionary," programs of ameliorative social change is, in Dahl's mind, truly "astonishing." And at least in the United States it is fair to say that "few groups . . . who are determined to influence the government — certainly few if any groups of citizens who are organized, active, and persistent — lack the capacity and opportunity to influence some officials somewhere in the political system in order to obtain at least some of their goals."[6] American society, in sum, is reasonably responsive to the needs of most citizens; it is generally able to meet the prerequisites of a libertarian, pluralistic, political system.

Dahl attempts a fairly explicit statement of the theory that lies behind this society, a statement of what he calls "the fundamental axiom" of American pluralism. "Instead of a single center of sovereign power there must," he contends, "be multiple centers of power, none of which is or can be wholly sovereign. Although the only legitimate sovereign is the people, in the perspective of American pluralism even the people ought never to be an absolute sovereign; consequently no part of the people, such as a majority, ought to be absolutely

☆

[5] Robert A. Dahl, "The American Oppositions: Affirmation and Denial," in Robert A. Dahl (ed.), *Political Oppositions in Western Democracies*, Yale University Press, New Haven, Conn., 1966, pp. 64-65.

[6] *Pluralist Democracy*, pp. 182, 370, 261, 386.

sovereign." For Dahl this axiom contains an inherent practical logic. He argues that "the theory and practice of American pluralism tend to assume . . . that the existence of multiple centers of power, none of which is wholly sovereign, will help (may indeed be necessary) to tame power, to secure the consent of all, and to settle conflicts peacefully." In operation, power is tamed because it is divided into separate centers that compete with and thereby offset each other; consent is derived from the existence of veto groups, which exercise their ability to prevent the enactment of policies they totally oppose; and peaceful conflict is assured through the need of all groups and power centers to compromise in order to obtain at least part of their desired objectives.[7] In America, then, theory and practice come together. The nation adheres to and embodies the essential attributes of pluralist theory — it is perhaps the living model of this theory — and it therefore can, with some slight reservation, be defined as democratic in all the ways that really matter.

Pluralism and Stability

Whatever the objective validity of this assessment, as a theoretical formulation it verges on solipsism, for it is never able to move outside of itself in order to make a truly objective judgment. The conclusion is foregone, and the standard of evaluation becomes the very fact that the nation has persisted through time. In a variety of ways Dahl states this position. While he acknowledges the continual strains and conflicts within the country, he finds that the United States must be regarded as a *"success"* since, with only one "major breakdown," it has enjoyed "two centuries of continuous developments in the arts of operating;" it has avoided "those poisonous hatreds and resentments that seep through a system until it collapses in paralysis or in violent paroxism." The avoidance of collapse, longevity itself, is the major criterion. Dahl admits "the fact that local democracy — like national democracy — is highly defective. "Yet," he remarks, "to right the balance, one needs to consider what democracy would be like in the United States if representative governments did not exist in the states and localities." When the final evaluation is to be made it is always a question of the consequences of a possible negative alternative rather than an appraisal of that which exists based upon a firm set of principles. From this perspective America, however serious its many weaknesses, however defective its democratic apparatus, must be regarded as a success. As Dahl repeatedly cautions: "If the price of this success is

☆

[7] *Ibid.*, p. 24.

high, the costs of failure could be even higher."[8] When put in these terms, the logical measure of success becomes in fact the mere absence of failure.

The position enunciated in *Pluralist Democracy* is entirely consistent with that taken by Dahl in his most famous work, *Who Governs? Democracy and Power in an American City.* Responding to critics who have equated democracy with disorder and instability, Dahl grants that New Haven, the object of his study, is far from perfect. Nevertheless he is able to conclude that "New Haven is an example of a democratic system, warts and all." In the very next sentence he suggests why this is the case: "For the past century it seems to have been a highly stable system." And similarly, when he analyzes the reasons behind New Haven's consensus on the "democratic creed," he moves directly to a consideration of the "five alternative ways . . . to account for the stability of the political system in New Haven." And, finally, just as in *Pluralist Democracy*, the contemplation of opposite conditions is used to substantiate a conservative view of the status quo. Thus Dahl argues that when all is said and done "we can be reasonably sure of this: even if universal belief in a democratic creed does not guarantee the stability of a democratic system, a substantial decline in the popular consensus would greatly increase the chance of serious instability."[9] This is probably true.

This same coalescence of theory and description is evident in Dahl's most philosophical work, *A Preface to Democratic Theory.* Dahl announces in his Introduction that, in keeping with the book's title, his analysis is indeed merely a preface to political theorizing, a raising of important questions as opposed to the rendering of specific judgments or conclusions. Near the very end he tells us that in his treatment of American politics he has "not attempted to determine in these pages whether it [comprises] a desirable system of government." In his closing paragraphs, however, he cannot resist noting the system's receptivity to "any active and legitimate group," its conspicuous efficiency in "reinforcing agreement, encouraging moderation, and maintaining social peace." "The normal American system," he concludes, "has evolved, and by evolving it has survived."[10]

The marriage of theory and practice deprives the pluralist of ultimate grounds for a critical determination. Even Dahl, who on one

☆

[8] *Ibid.,* pp. 4, 197. "The American Oppositions: Affirmation and Denial," in *Political Oppositions in Western Democracies*, p. 64.

[9] Robert A. Dahl, *Who Governs? Democracy and Power in an American City*, Yale University Press, New Haven, Conn., 1961, pp. 311, 312, 325.

[10] Robert A. Dahl, *A Preface to Democratic Theory*, University of Chicago Press, Chicago, 1956, pp. 1, 149, 150, 151.

level argues against a simplistic equation of democracy with stability and consensus,[11] and who is exceedingly sensitive to the system's intrinsic shortcomings, is forced in the end to describe American undemocratic practices as foibles, transient abberations in an otherwise healthy polity. The point is not that Dahl is necessarily wrong, but that his starting position makes such a conclusion inescapable.[12] Since at the outset American diversity and pluralism are coterminous, and since pluralism is the defining characteristic of democracy, theoretical as well as practical, then it follows that America, whose interests are manifestly variegated and competitive, must be a democratic society. Aside from the questionable logic of this viewpoint, the viewpoint itself carries its holder into some crucial confusions about American political history.

Consensus and Ideology

Like most pluralists, Dahl devotes considerable attention to the parameters of American politics, especially to the study of factors that provide some degree of social unity, factors that, in keeping the conflicts among interests within acceptable bounds, serve to hold the whole system together. While not explicit in this regard, he examines the problem from three different and, as far as his study is concerned, essentially unrelated points of view: the historical, the theoretical, and the ideological. Looking back through time he observes the remarkably unexplainable phenomenon of American nationalism. "With exceptional speed," he writes, "Americans . . . developed a sense of nationhood. If it is difficult to be sure what the content of American beliefs is or has been, it is even harder to determine the exact nature of American Nationalism. That such a nationalism exists is, however, beyond doubt, and evidently it came about surprisingly soon."[13] It may be that surprise about a coherent nationalism is a natural product of a perspective that begins by looking for differentiation and disagreement. Whether or not this is the case, the nature of American nationalism might seem less opaque if it were seen to be coterminous, in apposition, with "the content of American beliefs." On the ideological level Dahl seems to sense this connection.

☆

[11] *Pluralist Democracy*, p. 261.

[12] It is interesting to note that in order to criticize the compromises of 1820 and 1877 that adversely affected the rights of black Americans, Dahl must reach beyond pluralism to those "moral limits" established "by the standards of the contemporary civilized world." (*Ibid.*, p. 297.)

[13] *Ibid.*, p. 73.

Theoretically speaking, however, he posits the traditional distinction between ends and procedures as a way of explaining what appears to be a fundamental political consensus. "If people cannot always agree on specific policies," it is possible, he argues, "to gain their consent for a *process*. It is perfectly reasonable of me to say that I approve of the process by which certain kinds of decisions are made, even if I do not always like the specific results. Thus the consent of the governed may be interpreted to mean their approval of the processes by which decisions are arrived at and their willingness to abide by these decisions even when they seem wrong." [14] While this may be a permissible interpretation, Dahl is perhaps aware that it is scarcely adequate as a description of what actually takes place, that other contingencies are of more critical importance, for when he moves to the ideological level these contingencies form the center of his analysis.

Unlike many pluralists, Dahl rejects the idea that America's relative quiescence is a consequence of a nonideological temperament. "Americans," he tells us, "are a highly ideological people. It is only that one does not ordinarily notice their ideology because they are, to an astounding extent, all agreed on the same ideology." Even in times of great stress the social system is held intact by "the extraordinary consensus among Americans on a number of basic ideological issues." This consensus simultaneously supports and is supported by the nature of political parties in the United States. Dahl suggests that the "similarity of ideological perspectives among most Americans has insured the success of ideologically similar parties; and the domination of American politics by ideologically similar parties has in turn reinforced the similarity of ideological perspectives among the American people." [15] But questions having to do with what this ideology consists of, how intensely it is held, how or why it began ("How," Dahl wonders at one point, "did such an astonishing unity of views ever come about?"), and why it "tolerates" the episodic appearance of serious internal divisions, can be dealt with by Dahl only with the greatest of difficulty.

Ideology and Action

These questions are particularly vexing since, as far as political action is concerned, Dahl recognizes that ideological commitment

☆

[14] *Ibid.*, p. 17.

[15] *Ibid.*, pp. 357, 441, 225-226.

seems largely irrelevant. One sees this clearly in the case of *inaction*. Dahl notices that, despite their ideological background, "many— perhaps most—Americans who express disagreement do not . . . try to change the attitudes of others by discussion, or bring about changes by joining dissident political movements or trying to secure the nomination and election of candidates favorable to their views." Since most of these citizens also do not vote, they may be described as nonparticipators in political action. And, according to Dahl, the reasons for their inaction "include political apathy and indifference, lack of strong feeling, pessimism over the prospects of success, ignorance, and so on."[16] If this description applies to a large percentage of Americans, and, when the category of political leaders is excluded Dahl finds the percentage depressingly large, then we are left with an ideology the force of which is to produce, or at least to accept, apathy, indifference, lack of commitment, pessimism, "and so on," on the part of large numbers of citizens. One wonders how it is possible to know that individuals hold to an ideological position when their behavior gives no evidence to this effect. Ideology *at some point* must be related to action: if it cannot be shown to generate or guide political action, its existence must be regarded as dubious.

One might argue that the test of a national ideology cannot depend upon those citizens, whatever their number, who are dissatisfied or apathetic, and who therefore do not participate. And yet when Dahl turns to voting behavior, the most conspicuous form of political participation, his position remains subject to the same criticism. "What seems to happen," he suggests, ". . . is that as a voter moves from indecision to decision, he bypasses his ideology and takes a much more direct route. Somehow ideology is shortcircuited. In some cases it is shortcircuited by immediate considerations of self-interest or group interest that do not require ideological analysis and that may, in fact, lead to support for policies that a full-blown ideologue would oppose."[17] But this hypothesis, if it is correct, raises the obvious question: namely, does it make any sense to speak of a pervasive and powerful ideology when the act of voting, in Dahl's eyes the primary mode of political participation, does not derive its meaning from ideological determinants? To put it differently, is a shortcircuited ideology still an ideology?

Dahl cannot respond to these questions because he cannot fill in the content of the American ideology. Except for vague references to accepted "democratic procedures," "economic institutions," and

☆

[16] *Ibid.*, p. 333.
[17] *Ibid.*, pp. 367-368.

"legal processes," he cannot tell us what in fact Americans agree upon. It may be the case, for example, that when one acts on considerations of interest in America, far from shortcircuiting one's ideology, one is acting precisely in accordance with ideological imperatives. Only when he tries to explain the staying power of the consensus does Dahl suggest ideological ingredients other than those related to the democratic process. Then he speaks of the ideology as being "liberal democratic, privatistic," and "success-oriented," an ideology whose repeated victories have helped it to become "thoroughly intertwined with traditionalism" and therefore impervious to attack. The mere inclusion of privatism as a traditional American value opens different possible ways of interpreting political practice: for example, it makes the appearance of inaction or of action taken in behalf of personal interest entirely understandable, *and* consistent with ideological preconceptions.

The pluralist starting point itself probably makes ideological discernment extremely difficult. One may speak of an "astonishing" agreement on basic principles but, as long as the agreement is put in the most general terms and is not tied to specific types of action, it cannot be looked upon as a kind of ism and therefore as possibly antagonistic to pluralist ideals. At any rate, despite his concern for ideology and his appreciation of severe internal conflict, Dahl clearly is caught in the pluralist logic, a logic that begins and ends with pluralism itself as the key to political understanding. Thus, in the American situation, all variables become equally reinforcing and none is given analytical primacy. The result is a series of tautologies. The consensus is carried forward both because it is popularly held — a growing tradition — and because it gains strength through triumphing over its competitors. Evidence of unity is discovered by finding large areas of agreement in the society and large areas of agreement are taken as indexes of general unity.[18] Like-minded parties sustain consensus, and consensus generates like-minded parties. Dahl, in sum, advances a circular theory wherein historical, psychological, structural, and tactical factors revolve without causal relevance or logical priority argued for or established. In the end, moderateness of conflict, marginality of change, weakness of opposition dedicated to structural or revolutionary upheaval, proliferation of inherent bargaining techniques, convergence of attitudes, and the fact that social cleavages are mitigated by overlapping group membership are correlated to produce a society that may be described as simultaneously pluralistic in theory and democratically monistic in ideology.

☆

[18] *Ibid.*, pp. 334, 330-331.

Pluralism as Ideology

To look critically into the pluralist argument is not to deny the validity of its own criticism. It is altogether proper to be concerned about a combination of ideological dogmatism and massive political energy. Under such conditions the possible development of political intolerance in a nation of committed true believers must not be taken lightly. But it is one thing to understand this potential danger and quite another to regard all attempts at political community and national purpose as threatening to the very life of democracy. The fact is that pluralism can, on its own terms, be posited as the defender of democratic practice only if there is at least relative parity among the various groups and interests in society. In this respect, American pluralism does not emerge with very high marks: not only do some groups count for more than others, but many have for generations counted not at all. When the pluralist argues that things could be considerably worse, he is of course entirely correct. But this does not mean that the existing order is necessarily the paragon of either theoretical contemplation or practical achievement.

The mere proliferation of diverse groups, while perhaps an example of *social* pluralism, does not guarantee a vital and meaningful *political* pluralism. The latter requires that all or most groups are able either to share in or to influence the exercise of political power *to a significant degree*. A necessary level of significance, although impossible to fix with precision, is absolutely crucial, for without it apologists are able to maintain a fiction of pluralist democracy by alluding positively to the fact that "over time" most "organized" groups get at least some of what they seek,[19] or, negatively, to the complementary fact that the "countervailing" power of the three or four most powerful interests keeps one interest from dominating all others all of the time. Even if these configurations were defined as pluralistic they would hardly be definitive of democracy. One can imagine, and in fact point to, oligarchic systems complete with some degree of alternation among elites, with widely differentiated groups and associations, and with large interests that are able to countervail the effective power of each other at various times.

Perhaps the main weakness of pluralism is that, even as a descriptive theory, it is ideologically unreal. Whatever the popular understanding of democracy, it has *not* included convictions about the

☆

[19] In 1967 Arnold Rose wrote: "it would be hard to find a need for a specific social change that existed as long as hundred years ago in the United States and that still exists today substantially unsatisfied." (Arnold Rose, *The Power Structure, Political Process in American Society*, Oxford University Press, New York, 1967, p. 250.)

necessity of a plurality of competing interest, and without such a tradition of popular support the theory makes little sense. The ease with which the military, regarded until recent decades as one aggrandizing interest among many, has been able to tower above all other interests since World War II demonstrates pluralism's lack of theoretical significance. The military interest has in fact become coterminous with the country's conception of the national interest ("national security"), and if prewar boundaries are ever reestablished it will not be because the citizenry has decided to reinstitute a healthy contest among competing interest groups but because a new conception of the national interest has come to the fore.

As Tocqueville noted over a century ago, the connection between democratic governance and pluralistic institutions is both real and important. But if pluralism is to be used as a theoretical means of political inquiry it must be divested of its ideological presuppositions. It cannot be employed as an index of democracy in America when its very definition assumes the preexistence of such a democracy. Tocqueville could define America as democratic, even though he saw the United States as beset by severe tyrannical propensities and as fundamentally devoid of an appreciation of human liberty. Tocqueville may be forgiven possible contradictions in his views, for he was forced to extrapolate from the only existing example of the very category in question. Democracy would necessarily be whatever America made of it. Contemporary theorists can be granted no such latitude. If they replicate Tocqueville they do no more than carry the understanding of American democracy back to its nineteenth century starting point.

Even more important is the fact that pluralism fails to provide fresh starting points for political speculation. It is probably not accidental that the most creative of recent contributions to political thought in America have come not from native Americans but from transplanted Europeans, most notably from Hannah Arendt and Herbert Marcuse. Neither writer has felt constrained to follow the orthodox modes of American political analysis. Both have freely employed categories and formulations that go beyond the limits of the pluralist perspective. Of the two, Marcuse moves slightly further from conventional American understandings and, for this reason, we will concentrate our attention on his works, with only occasional references to those of Miss Arendt.[20]

☆

[20] For a full understanding of Arendt's theoretical views see *The Human Condition*, Doubleday and Company, Inc., Garden City, New York, 1959; *Between Past and Future*, The Viking Press, Inc., New York, 1961; *On Revolution*, The Viking Press, Inc., New York, 1963; and the essay on Lessing in *Men in Dark Times*, chap. 1, Harcourt, Brace & World, Inc., New York, 1968.

Herbert Marcuse

Drawing primarily on principles of Hegel, Marx, and Freud, Marcuse attempts to examine the relationship between historical change and the psychological propensities of modern civilization. While it has been common in America for European political emigrès to grow increasingly conservative about the desirability of ameliorative political action, Marcuse's analysis leads him to a position which is not only nonconservative in this respect, but totally revolutionary. Indeed, so revolutionary is his conception of change that, if effectuated, it would alter not only current institutions and practices but the understanding of contemporary reality as well, the very meaning we give to civilized existence. Marcuse's revolution would bring the human condition, as normally understood, to its denouement, and thereafter the idea of humanity would take on an entirely new aspect. In Marcuse's own words, there would be a civilization "based on a fundamentally different experience of being, a fundamentally different relation between man and nature."[21]

Theoretical foundations for the possibilities of a new civilization are provided in *Eros and Civilization, A Philosophical Inquiry into Freud*, published in 1955. Marcuse argues in this book that the history of civilized institutions has been a history of the increasing political, social, and psychological enslavement of mankind. Enslavement has largely been a function of the psychological repression of the individual; consequently the objective of those who would engage in reform must be a civilization freed of this phenomenon, a style of life characterized for the first time in history by a mentality and behavior patterns that are psychologically nonrepressive. Marcuse is prepared to defend the legitimacy of this goal despite the evidence of two powerful contradictory forces: (1) traditional Freudian doctrine, which holds that civilization and repression are inextricably connected, and that the price of civilization is man's continual ability to repress those instinctual drives that, if left uncontrolled, would threaten the order and security necessary to civilized life; and (2) modern technological institutions whose organization and "rationality" require more and more self-repressiveness on the part of the individual. It will be easier to deal first with Marcuse's treatment of the latter problem since in this area he sees change occurring more or less of its own accord, apart from human intention or involvement.

☆

[21] Herbert Marcuse, *Eros and Civilization, A Philosophical Inquiry into Freud*, Random House, Inc., New York, 1955, 1961 (hereafter cited as *Eros and Civilization*), p. 5.

Technology, Work, and Change

Marcuse believed that the very success of science and technology carries with it a potential liberating force. Even as technological imperatives increase their dominance and lead to a larger and deeper form of repression, the whole process begins to approach a point where opposite tendencies come into play. This is the point of large-scale automation, where there exists "the possibility of working time becoming marginal, and free time becoming full time. The result would be a radical transvaluation of values, and a mode of existence incompatible with the traditional culture."[22] Work, and the role that work plays in society, is crucial to the kind of civilization that obtains at any given period. A significant change in the role and function of work will therefore cause dramatic shifts in the direction and form of civilization as a whole.

While the possibility of work as a marginal endeavor is critical for Marcuse, he is not entirely clear as to whether the negative aspects of work are to be seriously curtailed or entirely eliminated. Certainly work will no longer dominate man as it now does and cause him to live a life of constant repression. The sheer reduction in the length of the working day under a generally automized system will induce positive change; such a reduction is in fact "the first prerequisite for freedom." At present automation continues to spread, and as it does the amount of alienation man feels with respect to his labor, already very high, increases as his work becomes still more impersonal and more meaningless. While this indicates that repression is likely to increase it also means that man is simultaneously brought nearer to the possibility of genuine transformation. Ironically, perhaps, "progressive alienation itself increases the potential of freedom: the more external to the individual the necessary labor becomes, the less does it involve him in the realm of necessity. Relieved from the requirements of domination, the quantitative reduction in labor time and energy leads to a qualitative change in the human existence: the free rather than the labor time determines its content."[23] While this is an important point, Marcuse seems also to indicate that qualitative change in the content of existence will likewise mean a qualitatively different notion of the meaning of work.

He simply disagrees with Freud on this issue. Although oversimplifying greatly, we may say that Freud had correlated instinctual repression with socially useful labor in the formation and stabilization of civilized life. Since there was no original instinct for work, the

☆

[22] *Ibid.*, preface to the 1961 edition, pp. vii-viii.

[23] *Ibid.*, pp. 138, 203-204.

energy required for work was derived from that which would otherwise go towards satisfying Eros, the pleasure principle. And since the impulses contained in Eros have aggressive as well as benign tendencies, harbor a potential for destruction as well as for stability, the necessity to repress, to control erotic drives — to a large degree through the institutions of man's labor — carries with it the necessity to repress the pleasure principle itself. Work and repression are therefore coterminous and quintessential to the perpetuation of civilized human existence.

Surplus-Repression, Labor, and Play

For his part, Marcuse suggests the possibility of correlating work with "instinctual liberation" in the service of civilization. Freud either misstated or overstated the case. "The irreconcilable conflict," according to Marcuse, "is not between work (reality principle) and Eros (pleasure principle), but between *alienated* labor (performance principle) and Eros."[24] Moreover, repression itself is historically grounded. Its required amount varies according to the demands of necessity. In societies of relative abundance, which operate beyond the level of subsistence, less repression is called for. It is *surplus-repression* that Marcuse seeks to eradicate, that repression over and above the "natural" amount produced by that quantity of unpleasurable (alienated) work necessary to maintain any functioning society.

To release man from the hold of surplus-repression would be to open the doors to a new realm. Marcuse contends that "the elimination of human potentialities from the world of (alienated) labor creates the preconditions for the elimination of labor from the world of human potentialities." Thus liberated, labor would take on an entirely new function. "The elimination of surplus-repression would per se tend to eliminate, not labor, but the organization of the human existence into an instrument of labor . . . the liberation of Eros could," Marcuse insists, "create new and durable work relations."[25]

Again, however, it is not clear whether work relations are to be newly created or whether work is simply to be reduced to such a point that "the inevitably repressive work-world" will become a small and insignificant part of civilized life. When conditions of abundance allow it Marcuse would introduce the principle of *play* into the order of things. Play, rather than work, may become the dominating characteristic of civilization. On the one hand it is suggested that play will

☆

[24] *Ibid.*, p 43n.
[25] *Ibid.*, pp. 95, 140.

take place outside the area of labor; play, Marcuse reasons, implies "not the transformation of labor but its complete subordination to the freely evolving potentialities of man and nature. The ideas of play and display now reveal their full distance from the values of productiveness and performance; play is *unproductive* and *useless* precisely because it cancels the repressive and exploitative traits of labor and leisure; it 'just plays' with the reality."[26] Play, in short, is unrelated to *any* sense we might have of what it means to labor.

On the other hand, having noted earlier that Freud was wrong to regard all work as unpleasurable,[27] Marcuse concludes that labor itself might be transformed into a kind of play. If work could be infused with a pregenital mode of eroticism, that is to say, with the generalized (polymorphous) erotic impulses experienced by the child prior to the period of sublimation, prior to the time when sexuality is concentrated at one point in the body, then "it would tend to become gratifying in itself without losing its *work* content." It is precisely this reactivation of polymorphous eroticism which can be expected once alienation and scarcity are overcome. Sublimation of instincts still occurs under such conditions, but it is a self-regulated and self-imposed sublimation and therefore nonrepressive in content and effect. As such it is free from the external pressures of routinization of procedure and rationalization of method. "Work as free play," Marcuse writes, "cannot be subject to administration; only alienated labor can be organized and administered by rational routine. It is beyond this sphere, but on its basis, that nonrepressive sublimation creates its own cultural order."[28]

Whatever its final position — whether reduced to a nondetermining function or transmogrified into a mode of play — work will no longer place repressiveness at the core of civil society. Once the level of abundance is reached man can entertain the idea of a future in which the pleasure principle may be pursued for its own sake, where Eros, released from the repressive chains of necessity, is no longer regarded as a threat to civilized order.

Civilization and the Reality Principle

As to the attack on the general Freudian correlation between civilization and repression, Marcuse sees himself on relatively safe ground. That psychoanalytic theory has chosen to emphasize the "conservative" side of Freud is entirely to be expected; it follows from the fact that, in their psychotherapy, neo-Freudians tend to stress uncritical

☆

[26] *Ibid.*, p. 178.
[27] *Ibid.*, p. 76.
[28] *Ibid.*, pp. 196-197, 199.

adjustment to social norms as the prime way of achieving mental health. But there is another side to Freud that demands attention. In the first few pages of *Eros and Civilization,* Marcuse announces that "Freud's own theory provides reasons for rejecting his identification of civilization and repression."[29] These reasons can be delineated by reexamining Freudian principles from perspectives other than those of the "psychoanalytic ideologues."

Marcuse notes that while Freud typically saw the process of sublimation serving the interests of a repressed civilized order, he also alluded to "other modes of sublimation," those having to do with what Freud called "social instincts": the love between parents and children, feelings of friendship, the emotional ties which develop in marriage. For Marcuse this kind of sublimation implies a radically different conception of social formation, the possibility of society "evolving from and sustained by free libidinal relations."[30] As in the case of unalienated work, the opportunity for the realization of this possibility depends first and foremost on the existence of favorable historical circumstances.

Marcuse states repeatedly that despite the conventional psychoanalytic interpretation, Freud's theory applies to civilization as a whole and that historical factors provide the means of understanding the connection between the individual psyche and the nature of civilization. "Freud's psychology," he tells us, "is per se psychology of the genus. And his generic psychology unfolds the vicissitudes of the instincts as historical vicissitudes: the recurrent dynamic of the . . . building and destruction of culture, of repression and the return of the repressed, is released and organized by the historical conditions under which mankind develops." A focus on the individual as such yields the same conclusion. While it is true that the individual appears to "integrate" a variety of inherited and acquired characteristics into a whole personality, and while it is also true that the personality develops by relating to a variegated human and material environment, in a more important sense "this personality and its development are preformed down to the deepest instinctual structure, and this preformation, the work of accumulated civilization, means that the diversities and the autonomy of individual 'growth' are secondary phenomena. How much reality there is behind individuality depends on the scope, form, and effectiveness of the repressive controls prevalent at the given stage of civilization."[31] The idea of a ratio between individuality and amount of repression returns us to

☆

[29] *Ibid.,* p. 4.

[30] *Ibid.,* p. 189.

[31] *Ibid.,* pp. 96-97, 230.

Marcuse's most fundamental concept, that of surplus-repression.

While slightly ambiguous on this point, Marcuse for the most part acknowledges that necessity, however slight, inevitably dictates the use of a reality principle and therefore requires at least a modicum of psychological repression. It is not repression per se but the examples of its excessiveness—the monogamic-patriarchal family, the hierarchal division of labor, the public control over private affairs—that have caused so much misery. What is wanting is resistance to this excess, what Marcuse calls the "Great Refusal": "this Great Refusal is the protest against unnecessary repression, the struggle for the ultimate form of freedom— 'to live without anxiety.'" Without such a protest civilization can be defined only as a kind of slavery. The influence of civilization in this form is what renders sexuality dangerous. The explosive tendency within Eros is a product of the tension between sexuality as a binding force and sexuality as "nonadaptive" to its environment, in rebellion against the "supra-repressive organization of societal relationships under a principle which is the negation of the pleasure principle."[32] Eros is dangerous, in other words, only insofar as it exists under a regimen of surplus-repression: remove the surplus and you remove the danger.

Freedom Through Eros

Marcuse concedes that in order to be convincing this proposition is in need of considerable elaboration. "The hypothesis of a nonrepressive civilization," he writes, "must be theoretically validated first by demonstrating the possibility of a nonrepressive development of the libido under the conditions of mature civilization. The direction of such a development is indicated by those mental forces which, according to Freud, remain essentially free from the reality principle and carry over this freedom into the world of mature consciousness." The possibility of releasing nonrepressive libidinal energy would, as in the case of labor, involve a recapturing of an earlier, pregenital mode of sexual expression, a mode that was initially free and unlimited. "Originally," Marcuse explains, "the sex instinct has no extraneous temporal and spacial limitations on its subject and object; sexuality is by nature 'polymorphous-perverse.'" Freed from repression and from alienated labor, the body would be resexualized, would become "a thing to be enjoyed—an instrument of pleasure." This signal change would have an enormous impact on all other aspects of civilization; it would, among other things, "lead to a disintegration of the institutions in which private interpersonal relations have been

☆

[32] *Ibid.*, pp. 136, 139.

organized." "It would dissolve the institutions of society in which the reality ego exists."[33] It would, in short, bring about a total revolution.

And, despite the expectations of many, this revolution would lead neither to wanton promiscuity nor to cultural nihilism. Those who see a relapse into barbarism forget the influence of history, forget the fact that change would occur at the very height of civilization, "as a consequence not of defeat but of victory in the struggle for existence." Occuring *after* culture has reached its present level, after it had created a world which could in fact be free, revolutionary change, while it would clearly subvert the current process of civilization, would release progress from repressive influences and allow it to move in consonance with man's true needs and highest understanding. This dramatic stepping back in order to move in a genuinely forward direction is necessitated by the long history of increasing regression perpetrated in the name of progress. "If the guilt accumulated in the civilized domination of man by man can ever be redeemed by freedom, then," Marcuse insists, "the 'original sin' must be committed again: We must again eat from the tree of knowledge in order to fall back into the state of innocence."[34]

New knowledge of Eros released would require a reinterpretation of the sexual basis of civilization. Those who fear that instinctual liberation would lead to a sexual saturnalia are themselves victims of repressive reasoning, for the change Marcuse has in mind "involves not simply a release but a *transformation* of the libido." And this transformation, he believes, developing "within transformed institutions, while eroticizing previously tabooed zones, time, and relations, would *minimize* the manifestations of mere sexuality by integrating them into a far larger order, including the order of work. In this context, sexuality tends to its own sublimation: the libido would not simply reactivate precivilized and infantile stages, but would also transform the perverted content of these stages."[35] In order to understand the possibility of sexuality tending to its own sublimation, a closer look must be taken at the inner content of human instincts.

Marcuse holds that the strongest barrier to free civilization lies not in the conflict between instinct and reason but in the conflict that goes on within instinct itself. This conflict remains, moreover, even *after* the elimination of surplus-repression. It can be seen, for example, in the fact that the sex instinct, operating according to imperatives that

☆

[33] *Ibid.*, pp. 126, 44, 184, 181.
[34] *Ibid.*, p. 181.
[35] *Ibid.*, pp. 184, 185.

are beyond social ideas of good and evil, is not guided by reciprocity "in the choice of its objects," and thereby constitutes "a source of unavoidable conflict among individuals." This fact raises serious objections to the possibility of sexual self-sublimation. In considering such arguments Marcuse wonders whether perhaps there is "in the instinct itself an inner barrier which 'contains' its driving power. Is there," he asks, "perhaps a 'natural' self-restraint in Eros so that its genuine gratification would call for delay, detour, and arrest?" The answer is clearly affirmative. While we will not examine it here, Marcuse finds sufficient evidence, both within Freud's writings and elsewhere, to provide adequate verification for his hypothesis.[36]

Suffice it to say that if in fact Eros can exert self-control, the concern over conflict within the sexual instinct fades away. For "built-in" barriers to blind satisfaction are in the end personally productive rather than psychologically alienating. "No longer employed as instruments for retaining men in alienated performances, the barriers against absolute gratification would," Marcuse asserts, "become elements of human freedom; they would protect that other alienation in which pleasure originates — man's alienation not from himself but from mere nature: his free self-realization." And since self-realization would still occur as a function of alienation — albeit "healthy" alienation — the new civilization would by no means represent the achievement of heaven here on earth. Marcuse observes that "the ascendency of the pleasure principle would . . . engender antagonisms, pains, and frustrations — individual conflicts in the striving for gratification." But freed of repression "these conflicts would themselves have libidinal value: they would be permeated with the rationality of gratification. This *sensuous* rationality contains its own moral laws." Even more than this, the rationality of gratification "creates its own division of labor, its own priorities, its own hierarchy,"[37] in brief, its own civilization.

A New Reality Principle

From this perspective Marcuse occasionally warms to his argument and carries it to a point of absolute regeneration where necessity no longer yields even minor repressions. At this point the release of new positive energies is seen as giving rise to an entirely new mental outlook. "The striving for *lasting* gratification," writes Marcuse, "makes not only for an enlarged order of libidinal relations ('community') but also for the perpetuation of this order on a higher scale. The pleasure principle extends to consciousness. Eros redefines

☆

[36] *Ibid.*, pp. 206-207.
[37] *Ibid.*, pp. 208, 205.

reason in his own terms. Reasonable is what sustains the order of gratification." Under the old system reason could justify repression because reason itself was a function of repression, "the rationality of the performance principle." But now reason can be associated with entirely novel principles; redefined by Eros, reason demonstrates the reality of the new civilization. "Utopias," Marcuse argues, "are susceptible to unrealistic blueprints; the conditions for a free society are not. They are a matter of reason." In a free society one's understanding of reality itself will be dramatically altered. Liberated instincts, Marcuse concludes, will "generate a *new* reality principle."[38] And with reality constructed *de novo,* a different conception of everything that flows from the idea of reality is rendered possible.

The sense of time in particular will be transmuted. As things stand, "the flux of time is society's most natural ally in maintaining law and order, conformity, and the institutions that relegate freedom to a perpetual utopia." Time works insidiously to vitiate the formative influence possessed by memory. Nothing distinguishes Marcuse from Hannah Arendt more clearly than his feelings on this issue. For Arendt, man's actions are essentially tragic. The best intended and most carefully worked out actions will inevitably run out of control, will ultimately hurt someone or some segment of society. Consequently the ability to forget previous transgression is absolutely necessary if political life is to continue.[39] For Marcuse, on the other hand, the loss of memory paves a direct route to oppression. "The flux of time," he writes, "helps men to forget what was and what can be: it makes them oblivious to the better past and the better future." While recognizing the positive role played by forgetfulness, Marcuse is disturbed by its negative aspects. "This ability to forget," he remarks, "itself the result of a long and terrible education by experience, is an indispensible requirement of mental and physical hygiene without which civilized life would be unbearable." But the price paid for this ability is extracted in the form of submissiveness and renunciation. "To forget," Marcuse insists, "is also to forgive what should not be forgiven if justice and freedom are to prevail. Such forgiveness reproduces the conditions which reproduce injustice and enslavement."[40] And since such forgiveness is a function of the passage of time, time itself must be overcome so that man may use his memory properly in the pursuit of justice.

Indeed, Marcuse cannot imagine the emergence of a nonrepressive society unless the repressed content of memory is released. He sug-

☆

[38] *Ibid.,* pp. 204-205, 144, 206, 180.
[39] Arendt, *The Human Condition,* p. 216.
[40] *Eros and Civilization,* p. 212.

gests that memory will perform the healthy function of recalling the earlier days of gratification and fulfillment[41] once human consciousness is permeated by Eros. "But," he contends, "insofar as time retains its power over Eros, happiness is essentially a thing of the *past*. The terrible sentence which states that only the lost paradises are the true ones judges, and at the same time rescues, the *temp perdu*. The lost paradises are the only true ones not because, in retrospect, the past joy seems more beautiful than it really was, but because remembrance alone provides the joy without the anxiety over its passing and thus gives it an otherwise impossible duration. Time loses its power when remembrance redeems the past."[42] As redeemer rather than dredger of the past, memory will no longer be exclusively tied to duty, guilt, bad conscience, and sin, but will now refer to pleasure, happiness, and the promise of human freedom. Although not entirely clear on this point, Marcuse apparently concludes that the recollection of repressed hostile feelings, directed against those who have committed injustices, makes possible at the same time the release of a remembrance affected by the pleasure principle, which brings into the present enjoyment derived from the past experience of Eros.

For Marcuse this is not merely a theoretical issue, for the call to defeat the tyranny of time represents a call to the realm of action. "Remembrance," he points out, "is no real weapon unless it is translated into historical action. Then, the struggle against time becomes a decisive movement in the struggle against domination."[43] And, although he does not specify a precise mode of action, it is clearly suggestive to Marcuse that at the outset of the July Revolution insurrectionists all over Paris simultaneously fired at the tower clocks. The conquest of time and the liberation of memory would constitute a revolutionary change in the nature of civilization, a change that perhaps can only be effected by means of revolution itself.

The Tyranny of Modernity

In his introduction to the paperback edition of *Eros and Civilization* in 1961, Marcuse strikes a more pessimistic note than is sounded in the original text. While the omnivorousness of repressed culture is taken into account in the earlier analysis,[44] the 1961 statement gives to culture a dominance bordering on total omnipotence. The dialec-

☆

[41] Marcuse seems to refer, as does Freud at times, to both individual and collective memory. Man recalls his childhood, mankind remembers its "childhood."

[42] *Eros and Civilization*, pp. 212-213.

[43] *Ibid.*, p. 213.

[44] *Ibid.*, pp. 83-84.

tical force of negative action and reason has been rendered virtually powerless. The possibilities for change must now be considered against the enormous capabilities of advanced industrial society for defining culture in its own terms and for maintaining a "reasonable" regimen leading to enslavement and destruction. With the appearance of *One-Dimensional Man* in 1964, the overwhelming ease with which society holds to its current direction becomes a major theme, and while Marcuse reiterates his earlier hypothesis that freedom from necessity and the advent of automation may "explode the society," he now concludes that "unless the recognition of what is being done and what is being prevented subverts the consciousness and the behavior of man, not even a catastrophe will bring about the change."[45] *One-Dimensional Man* is in large measure devoted to delineating the all-encompassing aspect, the unidimensional nature, of contemporary society.

Marcuse finds that no sphere of human activity escapes the formative impact of the larger irrationality. Within the ideology of one-dimensional thought and behavior all "ideas, aspirations, and objectives that, by their content, transcend the established universe of discourse and action are either repelled or reduced to terms of this universe. They are redefined by the rationality of the given system and of its quantitative extension." The many varieties of personal and quasi-religious protest which abound in society are neither controversial nor dangerous to the status quo. "They are rather the ceremonial part of practical behaviorism, its harmless negation, and are quickly digested by the status quo as part of its healthy diet."[46] Much the same is true in the field of art, where the antagonistic element is assimilated and thereby rendered innocuous.

As with art so with intellectual life in general. Philosophy, for example, tends either to be caught up in a kind of abstract analysis that bears no relationship to present historical circumstances or to be dominated by the methodology of ordinary language theory, which ignores the really important questions altogether. Scientific thought is even more directly sustaining of the system since its applications make possible the very affluence and production that allow one-dimensional progress to control all understanding of both the present and the future. Science and technology have, in Marcuse's words,

☆

[45] Herbert Marcuse, *One-Dimensional Man, Studies in the Ideology of Advanced Industrial Society*, Beacon Press, Boston, 1964 (hereafter referred to as *One-Dimensional Man*), p. xv. For the earliest statement of the theme in *One-Dimensional Man*, see the Epilogue to the second edition of Herbert Marcuse, *Reason and Revolution*, Routledge and Kegan Paul, Ltd., London, 1955, pp. 433-439.

[46] *One-Dimensional Man*, pp. 12, 14.

"become the great vehicle of *reification*—reification in its most mature and effective form."[47]

In the crucial area of sexuality Marcuse finds the same process at work. He notes the dramatic alterations in sexual mores but does not regard these as progenitors of genuine social change. Indeed, quite the opposite is true. The new generalization of sex is perverse in that it produces what Marcuse calls "adjusted desublimation," a state which supports the status quo and which therefore must not be confused with genuine sublimation. Marcuse contends that "in contrast to the pleasures of adjusted desublimation, sublimation preserves the consciousness of the renunciations which repressive society inflicts upon the individual, and thereby preserves the need for liberation." Not that sublimation *qua* sublimation is the embodiment of social freedom. "To be sure," he adds, "all sublimation is enforced by the power of society, but the unhappy consciousness of this power already breaks through alienation. To be sure, all sublimation accepts the social barrier to instinctual gratification, but it also transgresses this barrier."[48] In failing to reach the level of actual gratification, desublimation leads to a "happy consciousness" which in its simplemindedness is supportive of one-dimensional ideology and which, in failing to achieve true happiness, keeps unhappiness just below the surface of civil order. There is, moreover, the strong possibility that such "unconscious" dissatisfaction lurking so near the public surface will one day give rise to a politics of manipulation if not of outright fascism.

As far as the broadest assessment is concerned, society, both in its political aspects and in the way it is treated by scholars, rests on repressive assumptions. To describe society in the language of structural-functional analysis—that is, to end social analysis, as most academics do, with a description and catalogue of society's various parts and working relationships—is to ignore, indeed to suppress, the vital historical considerations that might offer grounds for serious reform. "The suppression of this dimension," Marcuse writes, ". . . is not an academic but a political affair. It is suppression of society's own past—and of its future, inasmuch as this future invokes the qualitative change, the negation of the present." The structure of contemporary politics, which is to say the practice of pluralism, has the identical effect. While pluralism is certainly to be preferred over rule without or above the law, it is also pernicious in its own right, for it systematically serves to mask actual conditions. Marcuse accepts the

☆

[47] *Ibid.*, pp. 168-169.
[48] *Ibid.*, pp. 75-76.

pluralist dictum that modern society is comprised of countervailing powers and interests. "But," he insists, "these forces cancel each other out in a higher unification — in the common interest to defend and extend the established position . . . The countervailing powers do not include those which counter the whole."[49] What is needed, then, is a political force that will operate from a point beyond the system and can address itself to the problem of industrial society in its generic sense.

The Political Dimension

Marcuse leaves no doubt that dealing with this issue is first and foremost a problem of *political* speculation and action. The inadequacy of science stems precisely from the nonpolitical character of science and its attendant technology. The correct goal of science, theoretical as well as practical, is human liberation, but in order to pursue this goal those involved in the discipline must first recognize "scientific consciousness as political consciousness and the scientific enterprise as political enterprise." Marcuse argues that "the technological a priori is a political a priori inasmuch as the transformation of nature involves that of man, and inasmuch as the 'manmade creations' issue from and re-enter a societal ensemble." Rightly conceived the scientific act is an act against oppression. "It is," Marcuse concludes, "an act of *liberation.*"[50]

   If this is true of science it is even truer with respect to philosophy. The very inconsequentiality of modern philosophic thought is a direct function of its self-consciously constructed methodology, an approach which even before the inquiry begins "shuts off the concepts of a political, that is, critical analysis." A really meaningful philosophy is involved in the negation of dominant standards, it seeks truth through the use of a novel logic and a different universe of discourse. It is a philosophy that emulates the critical stance of a man like Plato. "And inasmuch as this project involves man as 'societal animal,' the *polis*, the movement of thought has a political content. Thus, the Socratic discourse is political discourse inasmuch as it contradicts the established political institutions. The search for the correct definition, for the 'concept' of virtue, justice, piety, and knowledge becomes a subversive undertaking, for the concept intends a new *polis*." Such an intention, though confined to the realm of thought, brings philosophy into the area of ideology. This is as it should be. Philosophy, accord-

☆

[49] *Ibid.*, pp. 97, 51.
[50] *Ibid.*, pp. 154, 233.

ing to Marcuse, "is ideology, and this ideological character is the very fate of philosophy which no scientism and no positivism can overcome."[51] To take from philosophy its ideological character is to cut it off from the world of political affairs, and such a dissociation renders philosophy irrelevant to change. Philosophy only fulfills its function when it generates a critical, perhaps a revolutionary, political conscience, a conscience capable of entertaining visions of "a new *polis*."

However cogent Marcuse's infusion of philosophy with ideological content, it is precisely this issue, the meaning and dimension of a new polity, that raises questions about his own philosophical position. From a critical standpoint Marcuse's thought fully conforms to his personal paradigm for theoretical speculation. No one reading his works can have any doubt as to where he stands with respect to modern civilization. On the other hand, the same cannot be said for his conceptualization of a new polis, for his remarks in this area are either ambiguous or unclear.

On a methodological level he argues that in the face of one-dimensional domination the possibility of envisioning a new polity is essentially nonexistent. He acknowledges that new alternatives are perceived only as fragments, parts that do not add up to a coherent whole. He insists, however, that despite its fragmentary perception, the "dialectical theory is not refuted, but," he hastens to add, "it cannot offer the remedy. It cannot be positive . . . It defines the historical possibilities, even necessities; but their realization can only be in the practice which responds to the theory, and, at present, the practice gives no such response."[52] This formulation, while it conforms to Marxian standards by uniting theory with practice, is profoundly ambivalent, for the ability to "define historical possibilities, even necessities" strongly implies a positive assertion, suggests at least an attempt to offer salient remedies.

In his essay on "Repressive Tolerance"[53] Marcuse claims slightly less for his approach. He confines it to distinguishing "false solutions" but "never with the evidence of necessity, never as the positive, only with the certainty of a reasoned and reasonable chance, and with the persuasive force of the negative." The stress on negation is crucial, "for the true positive," Marcuse writes, "is the society of the future and therefore beyond definition and determination, while the existing positive is that which must be surmounted. But the experience and understanding of the existent society may well be capable of identify-

☆

[51] *Ibid.*, pp. 181, 134, 199.

[52] *Ibid.*, p. 253.

[53] In Robert P. Wolff et al., *A Critique of Pure Tolerance*, Beacon Press, Boston, 1965, pp. 81-117.

ing what is *not* conducive to free and rational society, what impedes and distorts the possibilities of its creation."[54] The latter explication is consistent with Marcuse's statement very early in *One-Dimensional Man* that new realization can be expressed only in terms that "would amount to the negation of the prevailing modes." With this in mind, conceptions of political, economic, and intellectual freedom are limited to the potentiality of man to extricate himself from those structures which define these concepts at present.[55]

Despite these limitations, Marcuse's deep appreciation of the need for change frequently drives his theory beyond its own methodological constraints. The critique of present institutions *does* suggest, both logically and psychologically, characteristics of institutions in the future. Yet at the same time the stress on theoretical restraint means that all such suggestions will be hesitant, attenuated, and will ultimately leave the reader uncertain as to their author's fundamental direction. This is particularly true with respect to the argument in *One-Dimensional Man*.

The Politics of Gratification

On its most important level the process of change has to do with man's needs and their proper satisfaction. Liberation depends on discerning the repressive "gratification" of needs under present social conditions and understanding the possibility of changing these conditions in order to meet genuine needs in a nondestructive fashion. "The process," Marcuse stipulates, "always replaces one system of preconditioning by another; the optimal goal is the replacement of false needs by true ones, the abandonment of repressive satisfaction." He admits that to posit such changes through the alteration of society is to hypostatize society, to transform "society" as a mental construct into "Society" as a comprehensive reality. This, he believes, is altogether appropriate. "Society," he writes, "is indeed the whole which exercises its independent power over the individuals, and this Society is no unidentifiable 'ghost.' It has its empirical hard core in the system of institutions."[56] To release man's true needs, then, would require a totally different set of social institutions.

But, in keeping with the idea of surplus-repression, beyond a certain level the alleviation of toil and poverty and the delineation of genuine needs are relative to time and place. While universally valid

☆

[54] "Repressive Tolerance," in Wolff et al., *op. cit.*, p. 87.

[55] *One-Dimensional Man*, p. 4.

[56] *Ibid.*, pp. 7, 191.

as general standards, "as historical standards, they . . . not only vary according to area and stage of development, they also can be defined in (greater or lesser) contradiction to the prevailing ones." Given this situation, "what tribunal," Marcuse asks, "can possibly claim the authority of decision?" Who, in other words, can make the necessary decision as to what are true and what are false needs? This is a critical question, the answer to which has important political implications for Marcuse's overall theory. His reply, however, is scarcely a model of verbal clarity. "In the last analysis," he states, "the question of what are true and false needs must be answered by the individuals themselves, but only in the last analysis; that is, if and when they are free to give their own answer."[57] The qualifying phrase is telling, for the "if and when" of it all could cause the last analysis to appear extremely late in the revolutionary game.

Again, following the theory of surplus-repression, Marcuse informs us that freedom is obtainable only after civilization has achieved some measure of material stability so that individuals are not tied to mere necessity. Beyond this, society must enable its citizens, "its slaves," to form a true perception of their context before they can act to change things. "And, to the degree to which the slaves have been preconditioned to act as slaves and be content in that role, their liberation," Marcuse suggests, "necessarily appears to come from without and from above. They must be 'forced to be free,' to 'see objects as they are, and sometimes as they ought to appear,' they must be shown the 'good road' they are in search of. But with all its truth, the argument cannot answer the time-honored question: who educates the educators, and where is the proof that they are in possession of 'the good?'"[58]

This, in essence, is the same question as that which asked about a tribunal for delineating actual needs, and Marcuse might have more properly inquired: who *are* the educators? His "answer," at any rate, is less satisfying here than was his first, for he responds in such a way as to avoid the question entirely. "The question is not invalidated," he asserts, "by arguing that it is equally applicable to certain democratic forms of government where the fateful decisions on what is good for the nation are made by elected representatives . . . elected under conditions of effective and freely accepted indoctrination. Still, the only possible excuse (it is weak enough!) for 'educational dictatorship' is that the terrible risk which it involves may not be more terrible than the risk which the great liberal as well as the authoritarian societies are taking now, nor may the costs be much higher."[59]

☆

[57] *Ibid.*, p. 6.
[58] *Ibid.*, p. 40.
[59] *Ibid.*, pp. 40-41.

Whatever risks may be involved, one is justified in asking Marcuse whether he does advocate the implementation of such a dictatorship.

Marcuse's reader is not to have an answer to this question, for the argument fails again to deal directly with the issue. "The dialectical logic," Marcuse continues, "insists . . . that the slaves must be *free for* their liberation before they can become free, and that *the end must be operative in the means to attain it.*"[60] [Emphasis added in final clause.] At this point in his discussion Marcuse alludes to Marx's insistence that the goals of the socialist revolution must be present in the act of revolution, in the very consciousness of those who carry it out. He then demonstrates the importance of this idea to Marxist theory and argues that it has not been honored by actual communist societies in the world today. But he does not tell us whether this discussion is an extension of his own theory or whether it is merely illustrative *obiter dicta*. Does the principle of initial freedom contradict the notion of an educational dictatorship? Is it also a defining characteristic of socialism and, if so, does this mean that socialism of this variety is the dialectical end-product? These are not simply academic questions, since in "Repressive Tolerance" Marcuse is prepared to advocate a number of specific actions that follow from his theory and advance its espoused goals.

Presentiments of the Future

Before turning to these recommendations for action, however, it is necessary to examine some of Marcuse's further views relating to visions of the future. Early in *One-Dimensional Man*, he lists what he calls the "preconditions of self-determination." These are: "distribution of the necessities of life regardless of work performance, universal all-sided education toward exchangeability of functions." With these in mind, Marcuse can conjecture that the process of change will first require a "superimposed administration" but, with the knowledge that under the new order, administration itself will eventually disappear. Even after its disappearance, however, an unequal division of labor will continue to exist. "Such inequality," Marcuse suggests, "is necessitated by genuine social needs, technical requirements, and the physical and mental differences among the individuals." But because the supervision involved in this process will not lead to one interest controlling the existence of others, the process itself will, in spite of its intrinsic inequality, have no serious negative effects upon society.[61]

☆

[60] *Ibid.*, p. 41.
[61] *Ibid.*, p. 44.

Near the end of the book, Marcuse outlines those criteria relevant to a "transcendent project" capable of effecting the total alteration of present-day society. The criteria, posited as rational measures of historical truth, are as follows:

1. The transcendent project must be in accordance with the real possibilities open at the attained level of material and intellectual culture.

2. The transcendent project, in order to falsify the established totality, must demonstrate its own *higher* rationality in the three-fold sense that

(a) it offers the prospect of preserving and improving the productive achievements of civilization;

(b) it defines the established totality in its very structure, basic tendencies, and relations;

(c) its realization offers a greater chance for the pacification of existence, within the framework of institutions which offer a greater chance for the free development of human needs and faculties.[62]

When put together with his "preconditions" and his other tentative remarks about the character of change, one begins to get from these criteria at least a vague idea of what Marcuse's new polis might look like. Furthermore, we are told that the "framework of institutions" necessary for free human development is remarkably already before us. Marcuse notes that "paradoxically . . . it is not the notion of the new societal *institutions* which presents the greatest difficulty." Indeed, "the established societies themselves are changing, or have already changed the basic institutions in the direction of increased planning. Since the development and utilization of all available resources for the universal satisfaction of vital needs is the prerequisite of pacification, it is incompatible with the prevalence of particular interests which stand in the way of attaining this goal. Qualitative change is conditional upon planning for the whole against these interests, and a free and rational society can emerge only on this basis."[63] And since the planning procedure is well on its way, the institutional part of the revolution, one assumes, will be complete when present trends in this regard are carried to their logical conclusion.

When these various ideas are aggregated a view of the future emerges that suggests a planned society based on preexistent institutional arrangements; a society that includes at least a minimal equalitarian distribution of wealth, a vastly reduced area of human labor, a

☆

[62] *Ibid.*, p. 220.
[63] *Ibid.*, p. 251.

universal and reformed educational system, and in general an eroticized culture that works to enhance the creative potential of all individuals. This will very likely be a socialist system whose method of
planning can already be seen in many nations today. The transitional
phase must be consistent with the ultimate goal of these institutions,
the liberation of man from repressive structures and traditions, although there is the possibility that temporary repressive means in the
form of an educational dictatorship and a superimposed administration
may be necessary. This last notion of temporary repression—roughly
analogous perhaps to Marx's concept of the evanescent dictatorship of
the proletariat—brings us to the call to specific actions made in "Repressive Tolerance."

Action and Intolerance

Because established society is so pervasive in its influence, Marcuse
believes that only the most concerted and direct action by those interested in achieving liberation will have any chance of success. "Democratic totalitarianism," while it is far more benign than its dictatorial
counterpart, must be combatted with force and energy. Indeed, because its very benign aspect has the effect of benumbing the critical
conscience, one-dimensional institutions must be attacked in ways
that involve "'cutting through,' 'splitting,' 'breaking asunder' . . .
the given material" of society in the quest for objective truth.[64] The
attack, moreover, need be neither wanton nor ill-informed, for the
actions which must be taken are, "at least in developed civilization,
comprehensible, that is to say, they can be identified and projected,
on the basis of experience, by human reason."

The seeming impartiality of existing society is just that, for within
the one-dimensional context the people have been indoctrinated to
the extent that they do not think beyond those "alternatives" the system itself offers. In order to free the masses from their mental prison
the whole contemporary trend must be not only brought to a stop but
entirely reversed. "For the facts," explains Marcuse, "are never given
immediately and never accessible immediately; they are established,
'mediated' by those who made them; the truth, 'the whole truth' surpasses these facts and requires the rupture with their appearance."
Without such a rupture of the imperious ideology all real freedom of
thought and speech is impossible.

Like impartiality, the notion of tolerance of deviant opinion is part
of the myth that seeks to justify current conditions. The rationale for

☆

[64] "Repressive Tolerance," in Wolff et al., *op. cit.*, pp. 81-117; all quotations are taken
from these pages.

tolerance drawn from liberal theory was based on the possibility that individuals would be able by their own efforts to arrive at objective truth through examining the conflicting claims to truth made by various protagonists. This rationale is now a meretricious illusion. "Universal toleration," Marcuse argues, "becomes questionable when its rationale no longer prevails, when tolerance is administered to manipulated and indoctrinated individuals who parrot, as their own, the opinions of their masters."

The practice of tolerance must consequently be abandoned, for it is not really adhered to by those who rule society. It must, just as civilization as a whole, be replaced by its opposite — that is to say, by intolerance. Because the development of a "subversive majority" is blocked by systematic repression and inculcation, it may be necessary to employ "apparently undemocratic means" in the effort to turn things around. Since it is possible to define the direction that progressive change must take, it is also possible, Marcuse insists, to identify those policies, opinions, and movements that constitute regressive factors. "Suppression of the regressive ones," he concludes, "is a prerequisite for the strengthening of the progressive ones." His conception of this process is worth quoting at length.

> [Positive action] would include the withdrawal of toleration of speech and assembly from groups and movements which promote aggressive policies, armament, chauvinism, discrimination on the grounds of race and religion, or which oppose the extension of public services, social security, medical care, etc. Moreover, the restoration of freedom of thought may necessitate new and rigid restrictions on teachings and practices in the educational institutions which, by their very methods and concepts, serve to enclose the mind within the established universe of discourse and behavior — thereby precluding a priori a rational evaluation of the alternatives. And to the degree to which freedom of thought involves the struggle against inhumanity, restoration of such freedom would also imply intolerance toward scientific research in the interest of deadly 'deterrents,' of abnormal human endurance under inhuman conditions, etc.

And in the attempt to eradicate inhuman conditions, the use of violence is by no means out of the question.

It is vital to keep in mind that at the core of every society, no matter how advanced, lies the use of violence by those in power. Violence in the form of police, mental institutions, racial suppression, and neocolonialism are but a few of the most obvious examples. Violence is of course reprehensible when practiced by either rulers or those whom they exploit but, notwithstanding our repulsion, its necessary use has been historically demonstrated. One must, Marcuse contends, differentiate between revolutionary and reactionary violence. "In terms of ethics, both forms of violence are inhuman and evil — but since when," he asks, "is history made in accordance with ethical standards? To start applying them at the point where the oppressed rebel against the oppressors, the have-nots against the haves, is serving the cause of actual violence by weakening the protest against it." Furthermore, an objective look at history reveals that revolutionary violence has had the effect, at least temporarily, of advancing the cause of justice and freedom and has therefore contributed to progress in civilization. The same objective examination reveals that "with respect to historical violence emanating from among ruling classes, no such relation to progress seems to obtain."

Tolerance, like progress itself, must be liberated from its context of repression. In practice this would mean intolerance of movements from the right with toleration afforded to those on the left. The extent of toleration and intolerance in both cases would cover "the stage of action as well as of discussion and propaganda, of deed as well as of word." The reason for this is that the distance between propaganda and mass action has become so small that devastation can be an almost immediate consequence of unchecked dogmatizing. This was amply shown by the short line running from Nazi doctrine to the appearance of Auschwitz and the outbreak of World War II, both of which could have been avoided "if democratic tolerance had been withdrawn when the future leaders started their campaign."

Liberal applications of the clear and present danger test to threats from the right are inadequate since the entire post-fascist period constitutes such a danger. Tolerance of repressive movements should, therefore, be withheld "before the deed, at the stage of communication in word, print, and picture." Marcuse admits that "such extreme suspension of the right of free speech and free assembly is . . . justified only if the whole of society is in extreme danger." But, he maintains, "our society is in such an emergency situation, and . . . it has become the normal state of affairs." The logic that Marcuse draws from this new normality leaves him but one option. "It should be evident by now," he writes, "that the exercise of civil rights by those who don't have them presupposes the withdrawal of civil rights from those who prevent their exercise, and that liberation of the Damned of the Earth presupposes suppression not only of their old but also of their new masters."

Who Makes the Decisions?

Behind all of these assertions looms the identical question encountered in *One-Dimensional Man*: Who delineates movements on the right, pinpoints repressive policies and opinions, isolates those standing in the way of progress, and determines when the application of violence is made in the interests of liberation? Again Marcuse is sensitive to the issue, but once again his answer leaves the reader in considerable doubt. The following paragraph constitutes his entire treatment of the problem.

> The question, who is qualified to make all these distinctions, definitions, identifications for the society as a whole, has now one logical answer, namely, everyone "in the maturity of his faculties" as a human being, everyone who has learned to think rationally and autonomously. The answer to Plato's educational dictatorship is the democratic educational dictatorship of free men. John Stuart Mill's conception of the *res publica* is not the opposite of Plato's: the liberal too demands the authority of Reason not only as an intellectual but also as a political power. In Plato, rationality is confined to the small number of philosopher-kings; in Mill, every rational human being participates in the discussion and decision — but only as a rational being. Where society has entered the phase of total administration and indoctrination, this would be a small number indeed, and not necessarily that of the elected representatives of the people. The problem is not that of an educational dictatorship, but that of breaking the tyranny of public opinion and its makers in the closed society.

The involutions in this prose make it impossible to determine Marcuse's exact meaning. The renewed but unexplicated references to "educational dictatorship" serve to cloud the issue further. At the very best we are left with the still more vexing problem of trying to know with some degree of certainty when an individual reaches the level of rational being.[65]

In the final analysis Marcuse provides us with no coherent way of connecting particular political actions with the expectations of total change, with the goals of his future polis. Repressive acts committed in the name of the pleasure principle are still repressive acts and must be judged by the age-old standard of consistency between

☆

[65] In his most recent statement Marcuse seems to equate rationality with morality, and with this equation he suggests a natural propensity in man to move in the right direction. He argues at one point that "political radicalism . . . implies moral radicalism: the emergence of a morality which might precondition man for freedom. This radicalism activates the elementary, organic foundation of morality in the human being. Prior to all ethical behavior in accordance with specific social standards, prior to all ideological expression, morality is a 'disposition' of the organism, perhaps rooted in the erotic drive to counter aggressiveness, to create and preserve 'ever greater unities' of life." At another point he wonders whether there is a "primary distinction between beautiful and ugly, good and bad — prior to all rationalization and ideology, a distinction made by the senses (productive in their receptivity), distinguishing that which violates sensibility from that which gratifies it." (Herbert Marcuse, *An Essay on Liberation*, Beacon Press, Boston, 1969, pp. 10, 32.) Of course, even if we grant the possibility of a predisposition to make such distinctions, we still have the difficulty of determining how or when the distinctions are to become apparent. The situation is further complicated when, later in the book, Marcuse states that he would always choose democracy of any kind over a dictatorship of any kind, but since such a choice is presently meaningless because there exists no real democracy, he can envisage a new elite, possibly the educated elite, assuming control. (*Ibid.*, p. 70.)

ends and means — which is no more than Marcuse himself demands. [66] Whereas Lenin could at least offer a reasonable case for the use of violence and for the need to utilize some of the illiberal mechanisms of capitalism, Marcuse's argument fails ultimately to be persuasive, and his prescribed methods of change stand logically disconnected from the triumph of Eros.

The Individual and Civilization

Marcuse's questionable treatment of political action does not constitute a mere analytical lapse on his part but is continuous with his inability to paint with clarity a more complete picture of the eroticized future. And the latter is more than simply a function of a dialectical reasoning process that can only speak in terms of negative responses to the contemporary monolith. The argument that the dialectic cannot describe a revolutionized world beyond our present experience [67] might be more compelling if Marcuse's previous representation of the redeemed individual had not been so detailed and so unhesitating.

Imagining an institutional construction of future society and rendering a judgment about means relevant to its realization are preeminently political considerations and, while Marcuse repeatedly places the political aspect at the center of his philosophy ("liberation," he writes in the preface to *Eros and Civilization,* "instinctual as well as intellectual, is a political matter"), his categories seem for the most part to stem from another focus entirely and to be devoid of political content. Thus, while in "Repressive Tolerance" he can criticize the ersatz rebellion of one-dimensional life on political grounds — "it isolates," he says, "the individual from the one dimension where he could 'find himself': from his political existence, which is at the core of his entire existence" — this dimension, political existence itself, is given very little meaning in most of his writings. [68]

☆

[66] In *An Essay On Liberation,* on the other hand, Marcuse comes close to rationalizing a disjunction between ends and means. He writes: "the proposition 'the end justifies the means' is indeed, as a general statement, intolerable — but so is, as a general statement, its negation. In radical political practice, the end belongs to a world different from the contrary to the established universe of discourse and behavior. But the means belong to the latter and are judged by the latter, on its own terms, the very terms which the end invalidates." (*Ibid.,* p. 73.)

[67] In an exchange with Norman O. Brown (Herbert Marcuse, "Love Mystified: A Critique of Norman O. Brown," *Commentary,* vol. 43, pp. 71-75, February, 1967; Norman O. Brown, "A Reply to Herbert Marcuse," *Commentary,* vol. 43, pp. 83-84, March, 1967), Marcuse suggests that a wholly new language would be necessary in order to describe the new order.

[68] "Repressive Tolerance," in Wolff et al., *op. cit.,* pp. xi, 14-15.

Marcuse's primary concerns carry him chiefly to two interrelated levels of analysis: that of civilization and that of the individual. The realm of politics, while it is not unrelated to these levels, is situated in an area somewhere between the two. It is territory occupied by nations, by governments, by the institutions, procedures, behavior patterns, and history of peoples in their collective status. Marcuse's essential focus begins and for the most part remains on the nature of civilized life, and this means that the consideration of politics is neglected in the interest of dealing perpetually with questions relating to the meaning of humanity itself. To the extent that these questions involve the understanding of human psychology—and this is a very large extent—he moves "beneath" the political stratum to the analysis of the individual psyche. Although the central term of discourse changes from "civilization" in *Eros and Civilization* to "society" in *One-Dimensional Man* (to "capitalism" in *An Essay On Liberation*), the meaning remains constant: civilization and society are generally interchangeable in his vocabulary.

Freudian categories allow Marcuse to dramatize, perhaps metaphorically, the enormous compass of his subject matter. He argues that the process of domination by the father of the child characteristic of the familial Oedipal cycle has now moved into society itself, thus exaggerating vastly the guilt of those who would seek to overcome society's pervasive influences. The revolt against civilization now becomes, in Marcuse's words, "the supreme crime again—this time not against the despot-animal who forbids gratification but against the wise order which secures the goods and services for the progressive satisfaction of human needs. Rebellion now appears as the crime against the whole of human society and therefore as beyond reward and beyond redemption."[69] While the idea of society as Oedipal father may be metaphorical, Marcuse's psychoanalytic treatment of time is clearly meant as argumentation with direct reference to human reality. In the end the attempt to break through the boundaries of time involves far more than remembering past injustices in order to exorcise them; it is ultimately concerned with the most critical considerations of individual existence: those of life and death.

Time Beyond Politics

Marcuse borrows from Nietzsche an existentialist approach to time. "The tyranny of becoming over being," he writes, "must be broken if man is to come to himself in a world which is truly his own. As long as there is the uncomprehended and unconquered flux of time—senseless loss, the painful 'it was' that will never be again . . . Man comes to

☆

[69] *Eros and Civilization*, pp. 83-84.

himself only when the transcendence has been conquered—when eternity has become present in the here and now." This conceptualization of time leads directly to a confrontation with the inescapable actuality that teaches us that for no man is time without limit. "The brute fact of death," Marcuse observes, "denies once and for all the reality of a nonrepressive existence. For death is the final negativity of time, but 'joy wants eternity.' Timelessness is the ideal of pleasure . . . The mere anticipation of the inevitable end, present in every instant, introduces a repressive element into all libidinal relations and renders pleasure itself painful."[70] From this broadest of all perspectives, repression becomes not merely the product of irrational political and social factors, but a phenomenon absolutely endemic to man's situation in civilized existence.

Notwithstanding this fact, Marcuse believes that once liberated from its repressive encrustation, civilization will look upon death from a wholly different vantage point. At the very least the "instinctual" will to death, the Nirvana principle, will be eliminated. "Death," Marcuse contends, "would cease to be an instinctual goal. It remains a fact, perhaps even an ultimate necessity—but a necessity against which the unrepressed energy of mankind will protest, against which it will wage its greatest struggle." In this struggle, energized by the unity of reason and instinct, crucial distinctions could at last be made. "Under the conditions of a truly human existence, Marcuse argues, "the difference between succumbing to disease at the ages of ten, thirty, fifty, or seventy, and dying a 'natural' death after a fulfilled life, may well be a difference worth fighting for with all instinctual energy. Not those who die, but those who die before they must and want to die, those who die in agony and pain, are the great indictment against civilization. They also testify to the unredeemable guilt of mankind." As he warms to the argument, Marcuse implies that even the struggle may take on a new complexion. He insists that "a philosophy that does not work as the handmaiden of repression responds to the fact of death with the Great Refusal . . . Death can become a token of freedom. The necessity of death does not refute the possibility of final liberation. Like other necessities, it can be made rational—painless. Men can die without anxiety if they know that what they love is protected from misery and oblivion. After a fulfilled life, they may take it upon themselves to die—at a moment of their own choosing."[71]

Whatever else can be said of Marcuse's discussion of this issue, it must be pointed out that it is not a political discussion. Neither the activities of governments nor the processes of political action can

☆

[70] *Ibid.*, pp. 110, 211.
[71] *Ibid.*, pp. 215-216.

respond meaningfully to the pentultimate questions of life and death. There is no political way of knowing whether death can be confronted ultimately as a nonrepressive force. Trite as it is to say it, death is an existential problem; it must be faced finally by men as individuals, apart from all others. And generally speaking it is man in this capacity, as an individual, the human psyche as the constituent subdivision of the civilized whole, that commands the major part of Marcuse's attention.

Individuality and Repression

When he said that Freud's theory of the individual was perforce a theory of the genus, Marcuse moved the focus of his lens from the individual to civilization, much as the astronomer adjusts his telescope from a view of the star to a view of the constellation. Similarly, when he contemplated civilization transformed, he narrowed to the individual once again. This shift in focus becomes clear when in *One-Dimensional Man* Marcuse notes that "self-determination will be real to the extent to which the masses have been dissolved into individuals liberated from all propaganda, indoctrination, and manipulation, capable of knowing and comprehending the facts and of evaluating the alternatives. In other words, society would be rational and free to the extent to which it is organized, sustained, and reproduced by an essentially new historical Subject."[72] While the idea of the liberated individual is salient, the reference to newly organized society is gratuitous, for Marcuse is unable to formulate a conception of unrepressed social organization. He leaves us with civilization altered via the Great Refusal, with the emergence of new historical man essentially unrelated to a social context.[73]

This new being rises as the result of a progressive disaffection from the negative present. The real objective, which the "negation of the negation" seeks, is the regenerated individual. This is why Marcuse insists that alienation rightly understood is not always a disease or a psychological malfunction, but a necessary step toward making man whole again. To be alienated from the system is to be against it and therefore in a position to move in the direction of its opposite, that is, in the direction of psychic health. Although Marcuse is quick to chide contemporary philosophy for its spurious perspectives, one of his criticisms of the discipline applies equally to his own intentions.

☆

[72] *One-Dimensional Man*, p. 252.

[73] In this connection Marcuse's occasional allusions to community, enclosed in both parentheses and quotation marks in *Eros and Civilization*, pp. 189, 204, are also somewhat gratuitous. The parentheses and quotation marks are necessary because nowhere is the content of community spelled out.

"The philosopher," he writes in *One-Dimensional Man*, "is not a physician; his job is not to cure individuals but to comprehend the world in which they live — to understand it in terms of what it has done to man, and what it can do to man."[74] But for Marcuse, the practicing philosopher, the two endeavors are actually interrelated and the comprehension of the world is attempted so that the complete cure of individuals might begin.

Had Marcuse's orientation been slightly different, he might have done a good deal more to bridge the gap between the concept of psychic repression and that of political repression. He might, in other words, have lent a political dimension to Freud's discussion of the nature of civilization. But one senses in Marcuse that politics is itself part of the problem. Politics is related always to institutional uses of power. Not only is Marcuse reluctant to speculate about new institutional forms of power, but he seems to see power in its very essence as a function of the contemporary social disease. "'Pacification of existence,'" he argues, "does not suggest an accumulation of power but rather the opposite. Peace and power, freedom and power, Eros and power may well be contraries!" In order to effect meaningful change, then, power must be reduced both quantitatively and qualitatively. "The notion of such a reversal of power," Marcuse explains, "is a strong motive in dialectical theory."[75] The implication one draws from this is that institutionalized power and thus political life itself will, as in Marx, be extirpated in the new civilization. Politics is reduced to a means that will be discarded once its revolutionary ends are achieved. The complete end of politics, as it turns out, is one of the main goals of political action.

Negations

An awareness of this goal is important not only for theoretical reasons, but also because the particular call to action in "Repressive Tolerance" is made with such uncompromising force — to say nothing of the fact that the call has to some degree been heeded by youthful political activists on three continents. Yet the actions, repressive in their own right, stand in theoretical isolation, substantiated in the end only by Marcuse's guarded faith in the dialectical process.

One wonders if the plea for energetic negative action is more a product of frustration and despair on Marcuse's part than an extension of his theory. So pessimistic is he of positive change that any action, even that of the most dubious variety, is perhaps acceptable so long as

☆

[74] *One-Dimensional Man*, p. 183.
[75] *Ibid.*, pp. 235-236.

it seeks the destruction of the powerful forces that be. Near the beginning of *One-Dimensional Man,* Marcuse notes that white collar elements have grown increasingly important in carrying out the processes
of technological society. For this reason "political radicalization
would have to be accompanied by the emergence of an independent
political consciousness and action among the white-collar groups—a
rather unlikely development," Marcuse observes, "in advanced industrial society." By the book's conclusion this unlikely development is
ruled totally out of the realm of possibility and Marcuse turns instead
to "the substratum of the outcasts and outsiders, the exploited and
persecuted of other races and other colors, the unemployed and the
unemployable."[76] It is apparently this substratum to which "Repressive Tolerance" is addressed.

But even as he alludes to those whose protest "hits the system
from without" and therefore cannot be absorbed or deflected, Marcuse
feels an overriding sense of powerlessness. The very consciousness of
repressive reality, critical as it is, is inadequate unless energized by
"the absolute need for breaking out of this whole." But, with material
wants taken care of, precisely this need goes unfelt. In light of this,
even the outcasts represent only the faintest of hopes. "Nothing,"
Marcuse laments, "indicates that it will be a good end. The economic
and technological capabilities of the established societies are sufficiently vast to allow for adjustments and concessions to the underdog,
and their armed forces sufficiently trained and equipped to take care
of emergency situations." In the concluding paragraph of *One-
Dimensional Man* he reiterates the theoretical dilemma. He reasserts
that his "theory of society possesses no concepts which could bridge
the gap between the present and its future; holding no promise and
showing no success, it remains negative. Thus it wants to remain loyal
to those who, without hope, have given and give their life to the Great
Refusal."[77] In the end the theory will be validated by the actions
involved in the Great Refusal, the actions themselves being justified
only by their negative force, only by the possibility that, in being
dialectically opposed to the status quo, they may lead to its opposite,
the good society. But what this opposite actually looks like or whether
the recommended actions have any chance of getting us there Marcuse
cannot tell us.[78]

☆

[76] *Ibid.,* pp. 38, 256.

[77] *Ibid.,* p. 257.

[78] An *Essay On Liberation* seems to represent something of a shift in Marcuse's thought.
Five years after the publication of *One-Dimensional Man,* Marcuse finds the revolution
at last underway, and the new essay is an explicit attempt to join the ideological conflict.
In this connection, while he cannot offer a "blueprint" for a "concrete alternative," he
recognizes the necessity of suggesting specific goals for the revolution. "The concept of
the primary, initial institutions of liberation is familiar enough and concrete enough:

The compelling quality of Marcuse's work lies more in its powerful critical penetration than in its inherent logic. By blending the perspectives of Marx and Freud and then using this combination as a point of departure for social analysis, he alerts us to the all-encompassing nature of the dominant culture, and by so doing he simultaneously makes us aware of the mighty barriers standing in the way of positive change. This is no small contribution. Few have been able to probe the depths of civilization with such imagination, and fewer still have been capable of operating at such a fundamental level of analysis. But the weaknesses in the analysis leave us wondering whether, when all is said and done, Freudian categories are really germane to such considerations.[79] More importantly, devoid of political relevance, Marcuse's philosophy not only seems to advocate actions which will increase the amount of social repression, it ultimately cannot reach beyond the point of negative opposition and we are consequently provided with no serious way of imagining a new community and no logical means of ascertaining the road to its realization. In the final analysis negation alone fails as sufficient grounds for a theory of revolution.

The New Left and the Great Society

As one looks back on the 1950's and 1960's one notes that Marcuse's difficulties were replicated to some extent by postwar American radicalism in general. This was especially true of those youthful radicals who comprised the New Left. Desirous of a regenerated society, but fearful on the one hand of ideological dogmatism and of organizational authoritarianism on the other, the New Left was forced to confront a series of painful questions. How does one state general ideals and ethical principles as goals for action without at the same time erecting a full-blown ideology? Without an ideology, how is it possible to know when or whether particular actions are related to long-term objectives? How is it possible to organize without really organizing; or, to put it differently, how does one coalesce people into effective political units without falling prey to the snares of bureaucratic rigidity and the iron law of oligarchy?

---

collective ownership, collective control and planning of the means of production and distribution" (p. 87). While this espousal of traditional Marxist ends is a little more specific here than in some of his other writings, it does not address itself directly to the question of action. Marcuse makes no attempt to relate it to the problem of the individual's ultimate liberation from repression.

[79] Philip Rieff, for example, argues that the application of Freud must be confined to the realm of the individual. (Philip Rieff, *Freud: The Mind of the Moralist*, Doubleday & Company, Inc., Garden City, New York, 1959, chap. VII.)

The New Left "resolved" these problems essentially by leaving them suspended. Political action would not wait upon elaborated theoretical responses. Ideology was thus rejected out of hand as too constricting, while ideals were stated in a highly abstract language that would not be applied to particular cases. Actions were justified simply on the grounds that they were opposite to manifestly immoral existing policies. Individuals were organized with an eye toward effectuating "participatory democracy," that is, in ways which would allow citizens to be involved in—at best, to initiate—those decisions which most affected their lives.

The results of New Left strategies have not been entirely positive. Without an ideological base, many programs and policies have been characterized by confusion and disagreement, with a consequent disillusionment on the part of numerous participants. Amidst this confusion participatory democracy has yielded ground while ideological dogma and authoritarian leadership have reappeared and have proven attractive to those who have become discouraged. In other words, those very modalities which the New Left began by eschewing have gained a new viability in recent years. The dedication of the true believer and the dynamism of committed leadership elements have taken on a new appeal for those who either cannot give intellectual shape to their political dissatisfactions or are consistently frustrated by the serious deficiencies found in other approaches.

While the protests and rebellion of the younger generation held, and continue to hold, enormous political promise precisely because the attack is launched from a point outside of the system, radicalism has not been able, either in its most general sense or in its crystalization in New Left thinking, to work its ideas into a meaningful political theory. And although the movement has exhibited a keen awareness of American purposelessness and a deep commitment to feelings of community, these characteristics tend to remain at the verbal or emotional level and have not provided either a useful point of departure for political action or an intellectual foundation for a radically new political theory.

Though typically far less penetrating, there has come from within the mainstream itself evidence of self-criticism sometimes very close to that of the New Left. Thus, echoing Clancy Sigal, Senator William J. Fulbright could state that "if one probes beneath the chrome-plated surface, he comes inescapably to the conclusion that the American people by and large are not happy . . . America's trouble is basically one of aimlessness at home and frustration abroad."[80] To a large degree

☆

[80] Quoted by William A. Williams, *The Great Evasion,* Quadrangle Books, Inc., Chicago, 1964, p. 18.

a perception somewhat akin to Fulbright's was shared by many who were active in mainstream politics during the Kennedy-Johnson years.

Indeed, it seems fair to say that the Great Society program extended from principles that, as *theoretical* formulations, contained strong overtones of community and purpose.[81] The idea of the Great Society embodied a vision of something more than a people held together by consensus. It described a nation in which none would suffer the degradation of want, where all would enjoy equally the advantages of education, progress, and public service. Its vision presupposed that citizens could link arms as brothers and strive together to achieve a nationhood whose greatness was not only material but aesthetic and spiritual as well, a society in which equality and justice would not be regarded as cynical expressions of institutionalized hypocrisy. And the War on Poverty was a perfect device to make the quest for the Great Society operational, for the reference to warfare suggested a total mobilization of the nation's resources against an enemy common, in one way or another, to every segment of society. The Great Society, in short provided a national purpose to which American citizens and public officials alike could dedicate themselves; the War on Poverty provided a framework within which Americans could work together as a community to achieve their national purpose.

The presidential call to seek the Great Society was certainly far clearer and more compelling than that of its twentieth century predecessors. It was, again on the level of theory, farther reaching and more open to fundamental change than the New Frontier, the New Freedom, the New Nationalism, and even the New Deal. Had Great Society doctrines been taken at their word and been implemented with even partial success, the resultant accomplishment might have constituted a genuine triumph for democratic politics and guaranteed for Lyndon B. Johnson an illustrious place in American history.

There were reasons at the outset for not accepting these doctrines at face value. For one thing, Johnson's rhetorical style generated serious doubts. His speeches, alternately saccharine and mail-fisted, raised grave questions about the President's sincerity. More dubious, although not clearly perceived by many, was the paradoxical nature of a call for community arising from the political mainstream in the first place. Traditional politics had always settled for a sufficient modicum of consensus based upon the preservation of law and order. As indicated frequently in this book, consensus suggests a system in which individuals or groups pursue their own specific goals, where interests

☆

[81] The following discussion of the Great Society first appeared in a slightly different form in "Requiem for the Great Society," *The Nation*, vol. 206, no. 20, pp. 627-629, May 13, 1968.

must compromise with other competing interests in order to realize at least part of their objectives, and where all interests are expected to agree to the same "rules of the game." Community, on the other hand, brings men together in common enterprise and engenders in each a concern for the well-being of all citizens. With this in mind, it seemed odd that Johnson, a consensus practitioner of long standing, should transcend his background in political brokerage for a new position of such radical dimension.

The truth is that Johnson never really exceeded his past experience. His political style was fixed, and it was probably inevitable that his program should disintegrate so easily in the face of foreign adventurism in Southeast Asia. While the Great Society's stated objectives were equal to our highest aspirations, its practitioners failed to understand that these goals could never be reached by the usual methods of interest politics. The Johnson administration preached equality, justice, and brotherhood, but engaged in a political enterprise whose blatant motto seemed to be: "Jump on board, there's something here for everybody — everybody, that is, who agrees to play the game."

Purpose and Understanding

The inability not only of the Great Society program but of American society as a whole to engender a viable national purpose has had a strange effect on our comprehension of social and political reality. The consideration of purpose requires an unfiltered confrontation of institutions and practices as they now exist so that they might be measured in terms of national goals. Such a confrontation makes it necessary to reconstruct the philosophy underlying these institutions in order to understand them fully. Because a new purpose has not emerged, this confrontation has not taken place, and as a consequence, America has moved in theoretical uncertainty, possessing no coherent philosophical statement that actually applies to the given situation, no formulation yielding even a general understanding of what in fact the society has been about for the past half-century.

If comprehension of the past has been in short supply, political theories entailing a remodeled future have been even scarcer. Awareness of the events surrounding World War II and the growing sophistication of intellectual criticism have combined to make it exceedingly difficult to "transcend" the imperatives of experience, to ascend to the level of myth-creation necessary in order to think creatively about novelty and change. A kind of functional innocence has always been useful in the endeavor to reach this level, innocence not in the form of ignorance or inexperience, but of the sort which allows the theorist mentally to suppress, at least temporarily, considerations that might cause him to deviate from his theoretical goal.

Innocence of this kind is above all denied to the political thinker today, especially to the academic political thinker. A scholarly appreciation of the other side to every argument, the realization that every "reform" seems to call forth still another dehumanizing aspect of contemporary culture, and a sensitivity to what appears to be an exponential growth in the complexities of modern technology and organization have caused intellectuals of the most radical persuasion to lower their sights as well as their hopes. The modern academy has always tended to stress the analytical as opposed to the creative side of social thought. More recently, its profound cynicism, along with the incentive in the social sciences to become genuinely "scientific" — that is, to focus on particular increments of subject matter that are susceptible to tests of verification — has relegated theoretical speculation to an isolated "normative" area, the province of idealists or ideologues. Meanwhile the scientists of the profession have sought to carry their discipline forward to increasing objectivity. This being the case, such concepts as community and purpose, manifestly normative in function and effect, have gone largely unattended.

The impact of pressures beyond the academy has been even more telling. The inescapable facts of Nazism, the bomb, and the general proliferation of violence have placed severe limits upon political speculation and have injected a note of despair into the most optimistic of philosophies. These facts have also had the effect of creating a preconceived bias in favor of existing institutions, institutions that, despite their obvious inadequacy and even injustice, may have remained free of the devastations of totalitarianism. Since World War II, intellectuals as a whole have seemed prepared to settle for the tenuous continuation of the status quo, even as they rail against it, for to do otherwise might be to risk the development of something far worse.

Many intellectuals, almost as a reflex action, have thought of community and purpose in strict conjunction with totalitarianism. Such an identification, though understandable, should not be made so simply or so automatically. The shape that community takes, for example, is dependent upon the existence of other traditions, and while it makes sense to be concerned that an ardent communalism can under certain circumstances lead to an antilibertarian dystopia, it is entirely improper to equate the two categories. Where a libertarian tradition exists, authoritarianism will likely find it difficult to make headway. Government dedicated to a collective purpose is in danger of becoming excessively paternalistic when there is no salient public sentiment that opposes such a development. It ought to be pointed out that in this day and age *all* modern political systems exhibit authoritarian tendencies, and all societies, communal or otherwise, must face the reality of this situation.

I pointed out in Chapter 2 that individuality might best be realized within a strong communal context, where citizens are secure enough to permit deviations from accepted norms. At the same time the communal principle, carried to an extreme, would tend to dogmatize collective norms and make idiosyncratic ideas and behavior difficult to maintain. We are faced here with a tension between possibly conflicting but beneficial propensities. Perhaps we must accept this tension as natural, necessary, and altogether healthy. Community and individuality may be seen as related in a complementary fashion, each depending on the other for vitality and each wary that the other will be carried beyond the point of complementarity.

It is possible to institutionalize this tension, at least to a limited degree. Part of the national purpose, part of government's *raison d'etre,* could be to advance the rights and liberties of groups and individuals. That this is possible we can already see in governmental action taken in behalf of racial minorities. As Croly pointed out, government must take sides in the enactment of public policy.[82] And if equality is a significant component of the national purpose, then government must choose its sides with respect to righting imbalances of equality wherever they occur. In other words, the national purpose should involve the recognition that true individuality for all citizens is only possible when a preexisting condition of genuine equality is firmly entrenched.

Equality in America has typically been defined either as equality of opportunity or as equality before the law. However useful these concepts may be, and they have occasionally been powerful liberating forces, they fail to get at the most basic meaning of equality: namely, the equal right of every person to be treated as a unique individual, one whose special needs and aspirations entitle him to a significant degree of respect and attention from all of his countrymen. Equality in this sense implies an individuality far more meaningful than that suggested by economic individualism. It means that the individual is deserving of a decent life irrespective of his ability to compete in the marketplace, regardless of whether or not he belongs to an active interest group, and, it should not be necessary to add, whatever his race, religion, or personal creed. The feelings of mutual concern and

☆

[82] The Report of the President's Commission on National Goals demonstrates this point exactly. Its various recommendations seek to delineate precisely those sides the government should take and why. President's Commission on National Goals, *Goals for Americans,* Prentice-Hall, Inc., New York, 1960.

mutual respect that underlie this notion of equality can only be sustained within a communal context. Without a communal base to rest upon, the equal right to dignity and security must for the most part remain beyond realization. Needless to say, America has seldom provided such a communal foundation.

On the other hand, as both Croly and Dewey pointed out, there is a minor current running throughout American history that gives expression to emotions and intentions other than those of economic individualism. Within this current there has often been the understanding of compassion, generosity, and social responsibility as part of what it means to be an American. In some measure this conception has been expressed by Paine, Jefferson, Brownson, Bellamy, and to a degree by Emerson, in addition to Croly and Dewey; and despite its caricature in Fourth of July oratory, its debasement in campaign propaganda, and its cynical manipulation by the promulgators of American foreign policy, it has somehow persisted through the generations. Its resuscitation and application to the present situation could yield both a better idea of what the nation is accomplishing and a clear pronouncement of American purpose.

Whether a contemporary national purpose can at this late date generate communal sentiments is, however, another question entirely. Interdependence, the essential attribute of community that avoids both the isolation of extreme independence and the authoritarianism of totally dependent relationships, is typically associated with proximity and commonality. The activities and effects of government tend to be remote from most people, or at any rate are perceived in this way, and are therefore without the emotional content possessed by a Gemeinschaft situation. While government might once have provided a functional vehicle for the overall realization of community, this is probably no longer the case. A national sense of community embodying the emotional involvement of Gemeinschaft seems beyond our grasp at this point in time. Too much has happened and society has gone too far in the opposite direction, both in its structure and in its practice.

The establishment of a national purpose could, however, have the beneficial effect of giving the nation coherence and direction, thereby mitigating the excessive isolation and estrangement generated by the present system. To the extent that individuals identify with their nation's goals they feel more a part of their society's future; consequently they will, as Dewey indicated, be more inclined to join with others in groups in order to pursue mutual objectives. The national purpose could thus make it far easier for groups of interdependent citizens to develop into communities at the local and neighborhood levels. Government could, moreover, take the nurture and protection of such groups as a part of its responsibility. This, too, would be part of its national purpose. The result would be a wholly new kind of pluralism, where groups and associations operate not within an interest-oriented system of rules of the game based upon established procedures, but for the first time as communal collectivities working within a context of shared purpose and meaning.

A new national purpose, then, would not be likely to produce a national sense of community. Such a sense may be finally beyond our grasp; the old interdependencies seem distant now and past the point of contemporary relevance. Political purpose, however, may be able to create a new concept of interdependence, demonstrating that now, more than ever before, what happens to one citizen is related to what happens to all citizens. At the same time, a vital purpose might also give the nation a new source of political meaning, some idea of possible goals and objectives suitable to a *free* society. Matthew Arnold could easily have had America in mind when he wrote: "Freedom . . . is a very good horse to ride, but to ride somewhere. You . . . think that you have only to get on the back of your horse Freedom . . . and to ride away as hard as you can, to be sure of coming to the right destination." Under the pressures of economic individualism, Americans have ridden freedom swiftly, recklessly, and without direction. Only an interdependent people, bound together in the pursuit of common objectives, can provide appropriate destinations — a destiny — for a society created in the name of freedom.

Whatever the chances of formulating a new national purpose, the possibilities of making use of such a formulation depend on the realities of the day. National purpose as a regenerative force presupposes that America is still susceptible to positive change, that we have not gone so far down the road of political elitism, organizational inflexibility, ecological blight, technological onanism, and racial and civil warfare that a change in course is beyond hope. In 1960, Archibald MacLeish believed that "we not only *have* a national purpose: we have a national purpose of such aspiration, such potentiality, such power of hope that we refer to it — or used to — as the American Dream." The problem is "not to *discover* our national purpose but to *exercise* it." But MacLeish was wrong. While for him the American Dream could be identified with "the liberation of humanity" and "the freedom of man and mind,"[83] for many Americans, perhaps for most, it has meant the personal promise of economic individualism, the par-

☆

[83]Archibald MacLeish, "We Have Purpose . . . We All Know It," Clinton Rossiter, Adlai Stevenson, et al., *The National Purpose*, Holt, Rinehart and Winston, Inc., New York, 1960, pp. 39, 47, 48.

ticular rewards offered by a nation blessed with material abundance. If in fact it is not too late for a dedication to national purpose, a new discovery of its meaning will have to be made, for the liberation of humanity and the freedom of the mind have not been the dominant goals of American society. An effective purpose defined in terms of liberation and humanity would bring America to an entirely new way of social and political life.

BIBLIOGraPHY

This bibliography is intended to be suggestive rather than exhaustive. A comprehensive listing of materials relevant to the concept of alienation alone could run to a book-length chapter. The following items include those works (chiefly books) that seem most germane to each chapter, as well as all the titles cited within the various chapters.

1. Purpose and Community

For the most general assessments of American political and social thought see the following. Arendt, Hannah: *On Revolution*, The Viking Press, Inc., New York, 1963. Arieli, Yehoshua: *Individualism and Nationalism in American Ideology*, Harvard University Press, Cambridge, Mass., 1964. Boorstin, Daniel: *The Genius of American Politics*, The University of Chicago Press, Chicago, 1953. Dorfman, Joseph: *The Economic Mind in American Civilization*, The Viking Press, Inc., New York, 1946–1959. Ekirch, Arthur A., Jr.: *The Decline of American Liberalism*, Atheneum Publishers, New York, 1967. Hartz, Louis: *The Liberal Tradition in America*, Harcourt, Brace and Company, Inc., New York, 1955. Hofstadter, Richard: *The American Political Tradition*, Alfred A. Knopf, Inc., New York, 1948. Young, Roland (ed.): *Approaches to the Study of Politics*, Northwestern University Press, Evanston, Ill., 1958. Morgenthau, Hans: *The Purpose of American Politics*, Alfred A. Knopf, Inc., New York, 1960. Parrington, Vernon L.: *Main Currents in American Thought*, Harcourt, Brace & World, Inc., New York, 1927–1930. Walter, Rush: *Popular Education and Democratic Thought in America*, Columbia University Press, New York, 1962.

The best available surveys of the history of American political theory are: Grimes, Alan P.: *American Political Thought*, rev. ed., Holt, Rinehart and Winston, Inc., New York, 1960. Minar, David W.: *The American Experience*, The Dorsey Press, Homewood, Ill., 1964.

The idea of community is treated in: Friedrich, Carl J.: *Community* (Nomos II), The Liberal Arts Press, Inc., New York, 1959. De Grazia, Sebastian: *The Political Community*, The University of Chicago Press, Chicago, 1958. Greer, Scott and David W. Minar (eds.): *The Concept of Community*, Aldine Publishing Company, Chicago, 1969. Toennies, Ferdinand: *Fundamental Concepts of Sociology (Gemeinschaft und Gesellschaft)*, translated by Charles P. Loomis, American Book Company, New York, 1940.

On the problems of national purpose see: Durkheim, Emile: *Suicide*, J. A. Spaulding and George Simpson (eds. and translators), The Free Press, Glencoe, Ill., 1951. Henry, Jules: *Culture Against Man*, Random House, Inc., New York, 1963. Mailer, Norman: *The Presidential Papers*, G. P. Putnam's Sons, New York, 1963. Potter, David: *The People of Plenty*, The University of Chicago Press, Chicago, 1954. President's Commission on National Goals: *Goals for Americans*, Prentice-Hall, Inc., Englewood Cliffs, N. J., 1960. Riesman, David, Nathan Glazer, and Reuel Denney: *The Lonely Crowd, A Study of the Changing American Character*, Yale University Press, New Haven, Conn., 1950. Rossiter, Clinton, Adlai Stevenson, et al.: *The National Purpose*, Holt, Rinehart and Winston, Inc., New York, 1960. Sigal, Clancy: *Going Away*, Houghton Mifflin Company, Boston, 1962.

2. The Conservative Expression
James Madison and John Adams

Documents and commentaries pertaining to the constitutional period in American history may be found in the following. Beard, Charles A.: *An Economic Interpretation of the Constitution of the United States*, The Macmillan Company, New York, 1961. Eidelberg, Paul: *The Philosophy of the American Constitution*, The Free Press, New York, 1968. Farrand, Max (ed.): *Records of the Federal Convention of 1787*, Yale University Press, New Haven, Conn., 1911–1937. Kenyon, Cecilia M. (ed.): *The Anti-federalists*, The Bobbs-Merrill Company, Inc., Indianapolis, 1966. Lewis, John D. (ed.): *Anti-Federalists Versus Federalists*, Chandler Publishing Company, San Francisco, 1967. Solberg, Winton U. (ed.): *The Federal Convention and the Formation of the Union*, The Bobbs-Merrill Company, Inc., Indianapolis, 1958.

The papers of the most important writers in early United States history are now being published in definitive scholarly editions. For James Madison see: Hutchinson, W. T. and W. M. E. Rachal (eds.): *The Papers of James Madison*, The University of Chicago Press, Chicago, 1962–. Until these compilations are completed it is necessary to make use of earlier published editions. In the case of Madison see: Cooke, Jacob E. (ed.): *The Federalist*, Wesleyan University Press, Middletown, Conn., 1961. Hunt, Gaillard (ed.): *The Writings of James Madison*, G. P. Putnam's Sons, New York, 1900–1910. Koch, Adrienne (ed.): *Notes of Debates in the Federal Convention of 1787 Reported by James Madison*, Ohio University Press, Athens, 1966. Worthington, R. (ed.): *Letters and Other Writings of James Madison*, New York, 1884.

A massive undertaking is now underway to provide definitive publication for the manuscripts of the entire Adams family. With respect to John Adams the following have already appeared. Butterfield, L. H. (ed.): *Diary and Autobiography of John Adams* (The Adams Papers, Series I), The Belknap Press, Harvard University Press, Cambridge, Mass., 1961–1966. Wroth, L. K. and H. B. Zobel (eds.): *The Legal Papers of John Adams* (The Adams Papers, Series III), The Belknap Press, Harvard University Press, Cambridge, Mass., 1965. For earlier compilations see: Adams, Charles F. (ed.): *The Works of John Adams*, Little, Brown and Company, Boston, 1856. Cappon, Lester J. (ed.): *The Adams-Jefferson Letters*, The University of North Carolina Press, Chapel Hill, 1959.

See the following for biographical and critical treatments of Adams and Madison. Brant, Irving: *James Madison*, The Bobbs-Merrill Company, Inc., Indianapolis, 1941–1956; and *James Madison and American Nationalism*, D. Van Nostrand Company, Inc., Princeton, N. J., 1958. Dauer, Manning J.: *The Adams Federalists*, The Johns Hopkins Press, Baltimore, 1953. Handley, Edward: *America and Europe in the Thought of John Adams*, Harvard University Press, Cambridge, Mass., 1964. Haraszti, Zoltan: *John Adams and the Prophets of Progress*, Harvard University Press, Cambridge, Mass., 1952. Howe, John R.: *The Changing Thought of John Adams*, Doubleday & Company, Inc., Garden City, N. Y., 1962. Also important are Ames, Seth (ed.): *The Works of Fisher Ames*, Boston, 1854. Oster, John E. (ed.): *The Political and Economic Doctrines of John Marshall*, New York, 1914.

3. Early Liberalism
Thomas Paine and Thomas Jefferson

The most compact collection of Paine's works can be found in: Foner, Philip S. (ed.): *The Complete Writings of Thomas Paine*, The Citadel Press, New York, 1945. See also: Conway, Moncure D. (ed.): *The Writings of Thomas Paine*, G. P. Putnam's Sons, New York, 1894–1896. Wheeler, Daniel E. (ed.): *The Life and Writings of Thomas Paine*, Vincent Parke and Company, New York, 1908.

Several volumes of the definitive Jefferson collection have already appeared. See: Boyd, Julian P. et al., (eds.): *The Papers of Thomas Jefferson*, Princeton University Press, Princeton, N. J., 1950–. Until this collection is completed, one must also consult: Ford, Paul L. (ed.): *The Works of Thomas Jefferson*, G. P. Putnam's Sons, New York, 1904–1905. Lipscomb, Andrew A. and Albert Ellery Bergh (eds.): *The Writings of Thomas Jefferson*, Thomas Jefferson Memorial Association, Washington, D.C., 1903. Padover, Saul K. (ed.): *The Complete Jefferson*, The Viking Press, Inc., New York, 1943; and *A Jefferson Profile, As Revealed In His Letters*, The Viking Press, Inc., New York, 1956.

For collateral reading on Jefferson and Paine see the following: Aldridge, A. O.: *Man of Reason*, J. B. Lippincott Company, Philadelphia, 1959. Boorstin, Daniel J.: *The Lost World of Thomas Jefferson*, Henry Holt and Company, Inc., New York, 1948. Chinard, Gilbert: *Thomas Jefferson, The Apostle of Americanism*, The University of Michigan Press, Ann Arbor, 1957. Conant,

James B.: *Thomas Jefferson and the Development of American Public Education*, University of California Press, Berkeley, 1962. Conway, Moncure D.: *The Life of Thomas Paine*, G. P. Putnam's Sons, New York, 1937. Elder, Brother Dominic: *The Common Man Philosophy of Thomas Paine*, University of Notre Dame Press, Notre Dame, Ind., 1951. Koch, Adrienne: *The Philosophy of Thomas Jefferson*, Peter Smith, Publisher, Gloucester, Mass., 1957. Levy, Leonard W.: *Jefferson and Civil Liberties*, Harvard University Press, Cambridge, Mass., 1963. Malone, Dumas: *Jefferson and His Times*, Little, Brown and Company, Boston, 1948–1962. Patterson, C. P.: *The Constitutional Principles of Thomas Jefferson*, University of Texas Press, Austin, 1953. Peterson, Merrill D.: *The Jeffersonian Image in the American Mind*, Oxford University Press, New York, 1960. Schacter, Nathan: *Thomas Jefferson*, Thomas Yoseloff, Ltd., London, 1951.

For valuable insights into late eighteenth century America see: de Crevecoeur, J. Hector St. John: *Letters from an American Farmer*, Fox, Duffield and Company, New York, 1904. Bourdin, H. L., R. H. Gabriel, and S. T. Williams (eds.): *Sketches of Eighteenth Century America*, Yale University Press, New Haven, Conn., 1925. Tyack, David: "Forming the National Character: Paradox in the Educational Thought of the Revolutionary Generation," *Harvard Educational Review*, vol. 36, winter, 1966.

4. A Vision of Glory
Alexander Hamilton

The definitive edition of Hamilton, as yet incomplete, is: Syrett, Harold C. (ed.): *The Papers of Alexander Hamilton*, Columbia University Press, New York, 1961–. At present one must also use: Hamilton, John C. (ed.): *The Works of Alexander Hamilton*, Charles S. Francis and Company, New York, 1851.

Useful supplementary material on Hamilton may be found in: Cooke, Jacob E. (ed.): *Alexander Hamilton, A Profile*, Hill and Wang, Inc., New York, 1967. Miller, John C.: *Alexander Hamilton: Portrait in Paradox*, Harper & Brothers, New York, 1959; and *The Federalist Era: 1789–1801*, Harper & Brothers, New York, 1960.

5. The Liberal Expression
Ralph Waldo Emerson and Orestes Brownson

The following should be consulted in order to obtain a good sense of the Jacksonian era in American history. Blau, Joseph L. (ed.): *Social Theories of Jacksonian Democracy*, The Liberal Arts Press, Inc., New York, 1954. Chevalier, Michael: *Society, Manners, and Politics in the United States*, John W. Ward (ed.), Doubleday & Company, Inc., Garden City, N.Y., 1961. Grund, Francis J.: *Aristocracy in America*, Harper & Brothers, New York, 1959. James, Marquis: *Andrew Jackson, Portrait of a President*, The Bobbs-Merrill Company, Inc., Indianapolis, 1937. Lewis, R. W. B.: *The American Adam*, The University of Chicago Press, Chicago, 1955. Meyers, Marvin: *The Jacksonian Persuasion*, Stanford University Press, Stanford, Calif., 1957. Probst, George E. (ed.): *The Happy Republic: A Reader in Tocqueville's America*, Harper & Brothers, New York, 1962. Rozwenc, Edwin C. (ed.): *Ideology and Power in the Age of Jackson*, Doubleday & Company, Inc., Garden City, N.Y., 1964. Schlesinger, Arthur M., Jr.: *The Age of Jackson*,

Little, Brown and Company, Boston, 1945. Trollope, Frances: *Domestic Manners of the Americans*, Donald Smalley (ed.), Vintage Books, Inc., Alfred A. Knopf, Inc., New York, 1960.

Works by and on Alexis de Tocqueville are crucial to a clear understanding of Jacksonian America. In this connection see: Drescher, Seymour (ed.): *Tocqueville and Beaumont on Social Reform*, Harper & Row, Publishers, Incorporated, New York, 1968. Lively, Jack: *The Social and Political Thought of Alexis de Tocqueville*, Clarendon Press, Oxford, 1962. Mayer, Jacob P.: *Alexis de Tocqueville, A Biographical Essay in Political Science*, The Viking Press, Inc., New York, 1940. De Tocqueville, Alexis: *Democracy in America*, Phillips, Bradley (ed. and revisor), Reeves-Bowen text, Vintage Books, Inc., Alfred A. Knopf, Inc., New York, 1957. Pierson, George W. (ed.): *Tocqueville in America*, Oxford University Press, New York, 1938. Zetterbaum, Marvin: *Tocqueville and the Problem of Democracy*, Stanford University Press, Stanford, Calif., 1967.

The writings of Ralph Waldo Emerson may be found in the following collections: Atkinson, Brooks (ed.): *The Complete Essays and Other Writings of Ralph Waldo Emerson*, Random House, Inc., New York, 1940. Emerson, Edward Waldo (ed.): *The Complete Works of Ralph Waldo Emerson*, Houghton Mifflin Company, Boston, 1904. Gilman, W. H. et al. (eds.): *The Journals and Miscellaneous Notebooks of Ralph Waldo Emerson*, The Belknap Press, Harvard University Press, Cambridge, Mass., 1960–1963. Rusk, R. L. (ed.): *The Letters of Ralph Waldo Emerson*, Columbia University Press, New York, 1939. Wicker, S. E. and R. E. Spiller (eds.): *The Early Lectures of Ralph Waldo Emerson*, Harvard University Press, Cambridge, Mass., 1959.

Most of Brownson's essays appeared in the *Boston Quarterly Review* and the *Brownson Quarterly Review* during the 1830's and 1840's. In addition, however, see the following. Brownson, Orestes A.: *The American Republic*, P. O'Shea, New York, 1866. Brownson, Henry F. (ed.): *The Works of Orestes A. Brownson*, Detroit, 1882–1887.

For material on Brownson and Emerson see Barzun, Jacques (ed.): *Selected Writings of John Jay Chapman*, Farrar, Straus & Cudahy, Inc., New York, 1957. Cabot, James Elliot: *Ralph Waldo Emerson*, Houghton Mifflin Company, Boston, 1893. Holmes, Oliver Wendell: *A Memoir of Ralph Waldo Emerson*, Houghton Mifflin Company, Boston, 1887. Konvitz, Milton R. and Stephen E. Wicker (eds.): *Emerson, A Collection of Critical Essays*, Prentice-Hall, Inc., Englewood Cliffs, N.J., 1962. Paul, Sherman: *Emerson's Angle of Vision*, Harvard University Press, Cambridge, Mass., 1952. Schlesinger, Arthur M., Jr.: *A Pilgrim's Progress: Orestes A. Brownson*, Little, Brown and Company, Boston, 1939. Wicher, Stephen E.: *Freedom and Fate, An Inner Life of Ralph Waldo Emerson*, University of Pennsylvania Press, Philadelphia, 1953.

The following works should be consulted to gain a balanced view of political thought during the Jacksonian era. Bassett, John Spencer (ed.): *The Correspondence of Andrew Jackson*, Carnegie Institution of Washington, Washington, 1926–1935. Holloway, Emory (ed.): *The Uncollected Poetry and Prose of Walt Whitman*, Doubleday & Company, Inc., Garden City, N.Y., 1921. Richardson, James D. (ed.): *A Compilation of the Messages and Papers of the Presidents 1789–1897*, vol. II, published by the authority of Congress,

Washington, D.C., 1900. Sedgwick, Theodore (ed.): *The Political Writings of William Leggett*, Taylor and Dodd, New York, 1840. Simpson, Stephen: *Working Man's Manual*, 1831. Skidmore, Thomas: *The Rights of Man to Property*, Burt Franklin, New York, 1829. Webster, Daniel: *The Works of Daniel Webster*, Little, Brown and Company, Boston, 1854.

6. The Southern Variation
John C. Calhoun and George Fitzhugh

The definitive edition of Calhoun's writings is currently being released. See: Meriwether, R. L. (ed.): *The Papers of John C. Calhoun*, The University of South Carolina Press, Columbia, 1959–. Consult also: Cralle, Richard K. (ed.): *The Works of John C. Calhoun*, D. Appleton & Company, Inc., New York, 1853. Jameson, J. Franklin: *The Correspondence of John C. Calhoun*, Annual Report of the American Historical Association for 1899, Government Printing Office, Washington, 1900. Calhoun, John C.: *A Disquisition on Government*, The Bobbs-Merrill Company, Inc., Indianapolis, 1953.

Fitzhugh's main ideas appear in: Woodward, C. Vann, (ed.): *Cannibals All! or Slaves Without Masters*, The Belknap Press, Harvard University Press, Cambridge, Mass., 1960; and *Sociology for the South, or The Failure of Free Society*, Burt Franklin, New York, 1965. Both works are collected in Wish, Harvey (ed.): *Ante-Bellum: Writings of George Fitzhugh and Hinton Rowan Helper on Slavery*, G. P. Putnam's Sons, New York, 1960.

Biographical and critical studies of Calhoun and Fitzhugh may be found in the following. Capers, Gerald M.: *John C. Calhoun, Opportunist*, University of Florida Press, Gainesville, 1960. Current, R. N.: "John C. Calhoun, Philosophy of Reaction," *Antioch Review*, vol. 3, June, 1943, pp. 223–234. Drucker, P. F.: "Key to American Politics: Calhoun's Pluralism," *Review of Politics*, vol. 10, October, 1948, pp. 412–426. Heckscher, Gunnar: "Calhoun's Idea of 'Concurrent Majority' and the Constitutional Theory of Hegel," *American Political Science Review*, vol. 33, August, 1939, pp. 585–590. Genovese, Eugene G.: *World of the Slaveholders Made*, Pantheon Books, a division of Random House, Inc., New York, 1969. Lerner, R.: "Calhoun's New Science of Politics," *American Political Science Review*, vol. 57, December, 1963, pp. 918–932. Merriam, Charles: "The Political Theory of Calhoun," *American Journal of Sociology*, vol. 7, March, 1902, pp. 577–594. Wiltse, Charles M.: "Calhoun and the Modern State," *Virginia Quarterly Review*, vol. 13, summer, 1937, pp. 396–408; and *John C. Calhoun*, The Bobbs-Merrill Company, Inc., Indianapolis, 1944–1951. Wish, Harvey: *George Fitzhugh, Propagandist of the Old South*, Louisiana State University Press, Baton Rouge, 1943.

Studies of slavery, of North-South rivalry and warfare, and of Reconstruction are extremely numerous. The following constitute a representative sample of those possessing particular relevance to political reorganization. Current, Richard N.: *The Lincoln Nobody Knows*, McGraw-Hill Book Company, New York, 1958. Cash, W. J.: *The Mind of The South*, Doubleday & Company, Inc., Garden City, N. Y., 1954. DuBois, W. E. B.: *Black Reconstruction: An Essay toward a History of the Part Which Black Folk Played in the Attempt to Reconstruct Democracy in America, 1860–1880*, S. A. Russell, New York, 1956. Eaton, Clement: *Freedom of Thought in the Old South*, The

Duke University Press, Durham, N.C., 1940. Elkins, Stanley M.: *Slavery, A Problem in American Institutional and Intellectual Life*, Grosset & Dunlap, Inc., New York, 1963. Franklin, J. H.: *From Slavery to Freedom*, Alfred A. Knopf, Inc., New York, 1947. Green, James J.: *Wendell Phillips*, International Publishers Company, Inc., New York, 1943. Jaffa, Harry V.: *Crisis of the House Divided: An Interpretation of the Issues in the Lincoln-Douglas Debates*, Doubleday & Company, Inc., Garden City, N.Y., 1959. Jenkins, William S.: *Pro-slavery Thought in the Old South*, The University of North Carolina Press, Chapel Hill, 1935. Nye, R. B.: *Fettered Freedom*, Michigan State College Press, East Lansing, 1949. Phillips, Wendell: *Speeches, Lectures and Letters*, New American Library, Inc., New York, 1969. Stampp, Kenneth M. (ed.): *The Causes of the Civil War*, Prentice-Hall, Inc., Englewood Cliffs, N.J., 1959. Taylor, William R.: *Cavalier and Yankee*, George Braziller, Inc., New York, 1961. Williams, T. Harry: *Lincoln and the Radicals*, The University of Wisconsin Press, Madison, 1941. Williams, T. Harry (ed.): *Abraham Lincoln: Selected Speeches, Messages and Letters*, Holt, Rinehart and Winston, Inc., New York, 1957. Wolf, Hazel C.: *On Freedom's Altar; The Martyr Complex in the Abolition Movement*, The University of Wisconsin Press, Madison, 1952.

7. In Defense of the National Purpose
   William Graham Sumner

There exists no complete edition of Sumner's works. Various pieces of his writings are included in the following. Keller, Albert G. (ed.): *The Challenge of Facts and Other Essays*, Yale University Press, New Haven, Conn., 1919; *Earth-Hunger and Other Essays*, Yale University Press, New Haven, Conn., 1913; and *War and Other Essays*, Yale University Press, New Haven, Conn., 1911. Persons, Stow (ed.): *Social Darwinism: Selected Essays of William Graham Sumner*, Prentice-Hall, Inc., Englewood Cliffs, N.J., 1963. Sumner, William Graham: *Collected Essays in Political and Social Science*, Henry Holt and Company, Inc., New York, 1885; *Folkways*, Ginn and Company, Boston, 1906; and *What Social Classes Owe to Each Other*, Harper & Brothers, New York and London, 1883. Sumner, William Graham and Albert G. Keller: *The Science of Society*, Yale University Press, New Haven, Conn., 1927.

For treatments of Sumner and his ideas see: Hofstadter, Richard: *Social Darwinism in American Thought*, rev. ed., Beacon Press, Boston, 1955. Keller, Albert G.: *Reminiscences of William Graham Sumner*, Yale University Press, New Haven, Conn., 1933. Page, Charles H.: *Class and American Sociology, from Ward to Ross*, The Dial Press, Inc., New York, 1940. Starr, Harris E.: *William Graham Sumner*, Henry Holt and Company, Inc., New York, 1925.

Consult the following for ideas that pertain to Sumner and his times. Carnegie, Andrew: *The Gospel of Wealth, and Other Timely Essays*, The Belknap Press, Harvard University Press, Cambridge, Mass., 1962. Cochran, Thomas C. and William Miller: *The Age of Enterprise; A Social History of Industrial America*, rev. ed., Harper & Row, Publishers, Incorporated, New York, 1961. Commager, Henry Steele: *The American Mind: An Interpretation of American Thought and Character since the 1880's*, Yale University Press, New Haven, Conn., 1950. Darwin, Charles: *The Descent of Man*, John Murray (Publishers), Ltd., London, 1871; and *The Origin of the Species*, John Murray

(Publishers), Ltd., London, 1859. Fine, Sidney: *Laissez Faire and the General Welfare State; A Study of Conflict in American Thought, 1865–1901*, The University of Michigan Press, Ann Arbor, 1956. Josephson, Matthew: *The Robber Barons*, Harcourt, Brace and Company, Inc., New York, 1934. McCloskey, Robert G.: *American Conservatism in the Age of Enterprise, 1865–1910*, Harper & Row, Publishers, Incorporated, New York, 1964. Miller, Perry (ed.): *American Thought: Civil War to World War I*, Rinehart & Company, Inc., New York, 1954. Spencer, Herbert: *The Man Versus the State*, Mitchell Kennerley, New York, 1916; and *Social Statics*, D. Appleton & Company, Inc., New York, 1864. Youmans, Edward L. (ed.): *Herbert Spencer on the Americans and the Americans on Herbert Spencer*, D. Appleton & Company, Inc., New York, 1883.

8. Ideological Revolt
Edward Bellamy

Edward Bellamy's main ideas may be found in: Bellamy, Edward: *Edward Bellamy Speaks Again*, The Peerage Press, Kansas City, 1937; *Looking Backward, 2000–1887*, Random House, Inc., New York, 1951; and *Equality*, D. Appleton & Company, Inc., New York, 1897.

Bellamy's biographers and commentators include the following. Bowman, Sylvia E.: *The Year 2000: A Critical Biography of Edward Bellamy*, Bookman Associates, New York, 1945. MacNair, Everett W.: *Edward Bellamy and the Nationalist Movement, 1889–1894*, The Fitzgerald Company, Milwaukee, 1957. Madison, Charles A.: "Edward Bellamy, Social Dreamer," *The New England Quarterly*, vol. XV, 1942, pp. 444–466. Morgan, Arthur E.: *Edward Bellamy*, Columbia University Press, New York, 1944; and *The Philosophy of Edward Bellamy*, King's Crown Press, New York, 1945. Walker, Francis A.: "Mr. Bellamy and the New Nationalist Party," *Atlantic Monthly*, vol. 65, February, 1890, pp. 248–262.

For an understanding of Populist, Nationalist, and other varieties of political thought and action during Bellamy's day, see the following. Crick, Bernard: *The American Science of Politics*, University of California Press, Berkeley, 1959. George, Henry: *A Perplexed Philosopher*, C. L. Webster and Company, New York, 1892; *Progress and Poverty*, Robert Schalkenbach Foundation, New York, 1937; and *Social Problems*, Belford, Clarke and Company, New York, 1883. Goldman, Eric F.: *Rendezvous with Destiny, A History of Modern American Reform*, Alfred A. Knopf, Inc., New York, 1956. Gronlund, Lawrence: *The Cooperative Commonwealth*, Stow Persons (ed.), The Belknap Press, Harvard University Press, Cambridge, Mass., 1965; *The New Economy*, H. S. Stone and Company, 1898; and *Our Destiny*, Lee and Shepard, Boston, 1890. Hicks, John D.: *The Populist Revolt: A History of the Farmers' Alliance and the People's Party*, University of Nebraska Press, Lincoln, 1961. Hofstadter, Richard: *The Age of Reform*, Alfred A. Knopf, Inc., New York, 1955. Lloyd, Henry Demarest: *Wealth against Commonwealth*, Thomas C. Cochran (ed.), Prentice-Hall, Inc., Englewood Cliffs, N.J., 1963. McVey, Frank L.: "The Populist Movement," *Economic Studies*, vol. 1, August, 1896. Pollack, Norman (ed.): *The Populist Mind*, The Bobbs-Merrill Company, Inc., Indianapolis, 1967; and *The Populist Response to Industrial America*, W. W. Norton & Company, Inc., New York, 1962. Tindall, George B.: *A Populist Reader:*

Selections from the Works of American Populist Leaders, Harper & Row, Publishers, Incorporated, New York, 1966. Ward, Lester: *Dynamic Sociology,* D. Appleton & Company, Inc., New York, 1883; and *Glimpses of the Cosmos,* G. P. Putnam's Sons, New York, 1913–1918.

9. Attenuated Vision
   Herbert Croly

Herbert Croly's political theory is contained in: Croly, Herbert: *Progressive Democracy,* The Macmillan Company, New York, 1914; and *The Promise of American Life,* Capricorn Books, G. P. Putnam's Sons, New York, 1964.

For materials on Croly, the following should be read. Chamberlain, John: *The American Stakes,* Corrick and Evans, Inc., New York, 1940. Dexter, Byron: "Herbert Croly and the Promise of American Life," *Political Science Quarterly,* vol. 70, June, 1955, pp. 197–218. Forcey, Charles: *The Crossroads of Liberalism: Croly, Weyl, Lippmann, and the Progressives,* Oxford University Press, New York, 1961. Noble, D. W.: "The New Republic and the Idea of Progress, 1914–1920," *Mississippi Valley History Review,* vol. 38, December, 1951, pp. 387–402.

Progressivism as a whole contained a great number of complex and sometimes conflicting political propensities. The following should be consulted to obtain an understanding of the diversity and richness in Progressive thinking. Bentley, Arthur F.: *The Process of Government,* Peter Odegard (ed.), The Belknap Press, Harvard University Press, Cambridge, Mass., 1967. Aaron, Daniel: *Men of Good Hope, A Story of American Progressives,* Oxford University Press, New York, 1951. Bryce, James: *The American Commonwealth,* The Macmillan Company, New York, 1915. Chamberlain, John: *Farewell to Reform: Being a History of the Rise, Life and Decay of the Progressive Mind in America,* Quadrangle Books, Inc., Chicago, 1965. Ely, Richard T.: *Property and Contract in their Relations to the Distribution of Wealth,* The Macmillan Company, New York, 1914. Faulkner, Harold U.: *The Decline of Laissez Faire, 1899–1917,* Harper & Row, Publishers, Incorporated, New York, 1968; and *The Quest for Social Justice, 1898–1914,* The Macmillan Company, New York, 1931. Filler, Louis: *Crusaders for American Liberalism,* The Antioch Press, Yellow Springs, Ohio, 1950. Girvetz, Harry K.: *From Wealth to Welfare: The Evolution of Liberalism,* Stanford University Press, Stanford, Calif., 1950. Ginger, Ray: *Altgeld's America; 1892–1905,* Quadrangle Books, Inc., Chicago, 1965. Godkin, E. L.: *Problems of Modern Democracy,* Archibald Constable and Company, Westminster, 1896. Kolko, Gabriel: *The Triumph of Conservatism: A Reinterpretation of American History, 1900–1916,* Quadrangle Books, Inc., Chicago, 1967. Lippmann, Walter: *Drift and Mastery: An Attempt to Diagnose the Current Unrest,* Mitchell Kennerly, New York, 1914; and *A Preface to Politics,* The University of Michigan Press, Ann Arbor, 1962. Madison, Charles: *Critics and Crusaders,* Henry Holt and Company, Inc., New York, 1947. May, Henry: *The End of American Innocence,* Alfred A. Knopf, Inc., New York, 1959. Noble, David W.: *The Paradox of Progressive Thought,* The University of Minnesota Press, Minneapolis, 1958. Resek, Carl (ed.): *The Progressives,* The Bobbs-Merrill Company, Inc., Indianapolis, 1967. Roosevelt, Theodore: *The New Nationalism,* William E. Leuchtenburg (ed.), Prentice-Hall, Inc., Englewood Cliffs, N.J., 1961. Steffens, Lincoln: *The Autobiography of Lincoln Steffens*, Harcourt, Brace and Company, Inc., New York, 1931. Weinstein, James: *The Corporate Ideal in the Liberal State, 1910–1918*, Beacon Press, Boston, 1969. White, Morton G.: *Social Thought in America; The Revolt Against Formalism*, The Viking Press, Inc., New York, 1949. Weinberg, Arthur and Lila Weinberg (eds.): *The Muckrakers*, Simon & Schuster, Inc., New York, 1961. Wiebe, Robert H.: *Businessmen and Reform: A Study of the Progressive Movement*, Harvard University Press, Cambridge, Mass., 1962. Wilson, Woodrow: *The New Freedom*, William E. Leuchtenburg (ed.), Prentice-Hall, Inc., Englewood Cliffs, N.J., 1961.

Of the many social and economic critics during the era of Progressivism, Thorstein Veblen is deserving of special notice. The following includes both his most important writings and those of scholars who have considered Veblen and his ideas. Dorfman, Joseph: *Veblen and His America*, The Viking Press, Inc., New York, 1935. Riesman, David: *Thorstein Veblen, A Critical Interpretation*, Charles Scribner's Sons, New York, 1953. Veblen, Thorstein: *Absentee Ownership*, B. W. Heubsch, New York, 1923; *The Engineers and the Price System*, B. W. Heubsch, New York, 1921; *The Instinct of Workmanship*, B. W. Heubsch, New York, 1914; *The Theory of Business Enterprise*, The New American Library, Inc., New York, 1958; and *The Theory of the Leisure Class, An Economic Study of Institutions*, Random House, Inc., New York, 1934.

Croly's period also marked the appearance of ideologies that ran far to the left of Progressivism. The following original and secondary works give some indication of the limits and depth of radical thinking in this era. Broderick, Francis L.: *W. E. B. DuBois: Negro Leader in a Time of Crisis*, Stanford University Press, Stanford, Calif., 1959. Debbs, Eugene V.: *The Writings and Speeches of Eugene V. Debbs*, The Hermitage Press, New York, 1948. Kipnis, Ira: *The American Socialist Movement, 1897–1912*, Columbia University Press, New York, 1952. Kornbluh, J. L.: *Rebel Voices: An I.W.W. Anthology*, The University of Michigan Press, Ann Arbor, 1964. Morgan, H. Wayne (ed.): *American Socialism, 1900–1960*, Prentice-Hall, Inc., Englewood Cliffs, N.J., 1964. Perlman, Mark: *Labor Union Theories in America: Background and Development*, Row, Peterson & Company, Evanston, Ill., 1958. Perlman, Selig: *A Theory of the Labor Movement*, The Macmillan Company, New York, 1928. Persons, Stow and Donald D. Egbert, (eds.): *Socialism and American Life*, Princeton University Press, Princeton, N.J., 1952. Quint, Howard H.: *The Forging of American Socialism*, The Bobbs-Merrill Company, Inc., Indianapolis, 1964. Renshaw, Patrick: *The Wobblies; The Story of Syndicalism in the United States*, Doubleday & Company, Inc. Garden City, N.Y., 1967. Shannon, David A.: *The Socialist Party of America: A History*, Quadrangle Books, Inc., Chicago, 1967. Tannenbaum, Frank: *The Labor Movement*, G. P. Putnam's Sons, New York, 1921.

10. The Great Community
   John Dewey

The monumental task of collecting Dewey's voluminous writings has recently been undertaken by a group of scholars at Southern Illinois University. The first installment appears as follows. Axtelle, George E. et al. (eds.): *The Early*

Works of John Dewey, 1882–1898, Southern Illinois University Press, Fiffer and Simons, Inc., London and Amsterdam, 1967–.

The following list is comprised of Dewey's most important political and philosophical studies. Dewey, John: *Characters and Events: Popular Essays in Social and Political Philosophy*, Joseph Ratner (ed.), Henry Holt and Company, Inc., New York, 1929; *Democracy and Education, An Introduction to the Philosophy of Education*, The Macmillan Company, New York, 1920; *Essays in Experimental Logic*, The University of Chicago Press, Chicago, 1916; *Experience and Nature*, Dover Publications, Inc., New York, 1958; *The Influence of Darwin on Philosophy, And Other Essays in Contemporary Thought*, Henry Holt and Company, Inc., New York, 1910; *Individualism Old and New*, Capricorn Books, G. P. Putnam's Sons, New York, 1962; *Liberalism and Social Action*, G. P. Putnam's Sons, New York, 1935; *Logic, The Theory of Inquiry*, Henry Holt and Company, Inc., New York, 1938; *Reconstruction in Philosophy*, Henry Holt and Company, Inc., New York, 1920; *Philosophy and Civilization*, G. P. Putnam's Sons, New York, 1931; *Problems of Men*, Philosophical Library, Inc., New York, 1946; and *The Public and Its Problems*, Henry Holt and Company, Inc., New York, 1927. For a good one-volume anthology of Dewey's thought see: Ratner, Joseph (ed.): *Intelligence in the Modern World*, Random House, Inc., New York, 1939.

The range, duration, and volume of Dewey's writings have engendered a critical literature that is itself very sizable. The following items are particularly relevant to a consideration of Dewey's political ideas. Bestor, Arthur: "John Dewey and American Liberalism," *The New Republic*, vol. 133, August, 1955, pp. 18–19. Cork, Jim: "John Dewey, Karl Marx, and Democratic Socialism," *The Antioch Review*, vol. 9, December, 1949, pp. 435–442. Frankel, Charles: "John Dewey's Legacy," *The American Scholar*, vol. 29, summer, 1960, pp. 313–331. Greger, George R.: *John Dewey in Perspective*, Oxford University Press, London, 1958. Haworth, Laurence: "The Experimental Society: Dewey and Jordon," *Ethics*, vol. 71, October, 1960, pp. 27–40; and "Dewey's Philosophy of the Corporation," *Ethics*, vol. 72, January, 1962, pp. 120–131. Hook, Sidney: *John Dewey: An Intellectual Portrait*, Northwestern University Press, Evanston, Ill., 1939; "John Dewey and His Critics," *The New Republic*, vol. 67, June 3, 1931, pp. 73–74; and *John Dewey's Philosophy of Science and Freedom*, The Dial Press, Inc., New York, 1950. Kallen, Horace: "Individuality, Individualism, and John Dewey," *The Antioch Review*, vol. 19, fall, 1959, pp. 299–314. Knight, Frank: "Pragmatism and Social Action," *International Journal of Ethics*, vol. 46, January, 1936, pp. 229–236. Lamont, Corliss (ed.): *Dialogue on John Dewey*, Horizon Press, New York, 1959. Murphy, Arthur E.: "John Dewey and American Liberalism," *The Journal of Philosophy*, vol. 57, June 23, 1960, pp. 420–436. Somjie, H. H.: *The Political Theory of John Dewey*, Teachers College Press, Columbia University, New York, 1968. Thomas, M. H.: *John Dewey, A Centennial Biography*, The University of Chicago Press, Chicago, 1962. White, H. B.: "The Political Faith of John Dewey," *The Journal of Politics*, vol. 20, May, 1958, pp. 353–367.

For expressions of New Deal thinking and for criticisms of the New Deal philosophy see the following. Arnold, Thurmond: *The Folklore of Capital-*

ism, Yale University Press, New Haven, Conn., 1937; and *The Symbols of Government,* Yale University Press, New Haven, Conn., 1935. Berle, A. A. and Gardiner C. Means: *The Modern Corporation and Private Property,* The Macmillan Company, New York, 1933. Burns, James M.: *Roosevelt: The Lion and the Fox,* Harcourt, Brace & World, Inc., New York, 1956. Cooke, Alistair: *A Generation on Trial,* Alfred A. Knopf, Inc., New York, 1950. Derber, Milton and Edwin Young: *Labor and the New Deal,* The University of Wisconsin Press, Madison, 1957. Fusfield, Daniel: *The Economic Thought of Franklin D. Roosevelt and the Origins of the New Deal,* Columbia University Press, New York, 1956. Lerner, Max: *Ideas for the Ice Age,* The Viking Press, Inc., New York, 1941. Leuchtenburg, William E.: *Franklin D. Roosevelt and the New Deal,* Harper & Row, Publishers, Incorporated, New York, 1963. Lippmann, Walter: *The Good Society,* Grosset & Dunlap, Inc., New York, 1943. Mitchell, Broadus: *Depression Decade,* Rinehart & Company, Inc., New York, 1947. Schlesinger, Arthur M., Jr.: *The Age of Roosevelt,* Houghton Mifflin Company, Boston, 1957–1960. Tugwell, Rexford: *The Democratic Roosevelt,* Doubleday & Company, Inc., Garden City, N.Y., 1957; "The Experimental Roosevelt," *Political Quarterly,* vol. 21, July, 1950, pp. 239–270; "The Fallow Years of Franklin D. Roosevelt," *Ethics,* vol. 66, January, 1956, pp. 98–116; "The Progressive Orthodoxy of Franklin D. Roosevelt," *Ethics,* vol. 64, October, 1953, pp. 1–23; and "The Protagonists: Roosevelt and Hoover, "*The Antioch Review,* vol. 13, December, 1953, pp. 419–442. Wilson, Edmund: *The American Earthquake,* Doubleday & Company, Inc., Garden City, N.Y., 1958. Zinn, Howard (ed.): *New Deal Thought,* The Bobbs-Merrill Company, Inc. Indianapolis, 1966.

11. Modernity and Purpose
   Herbert Marcuse and Robert Dahl

Herbert Marcuse's political philosophy is contained in the following volumes. Marcuse, Herbert: *Eros and Civilization, A Philosophical Inquiry into Freud,* Random House, Inc., New York, 1955; *Negations; Essays in Critical Theory,* Beacon Press, Boston, 1968; *An Essay on Liberation,* Beacon Press, Boston, 1969; *One-Dimensional Man, Studies in the Ideology of Advanced Industrial Societies,* Beacon Press, Boston, 1964; and *Reason and Revolution,* Routledge & Kegan Paul, Ltd., London, 1955, Marcuse, Herbert, Robert P. Wolff, and Barrington Moore: *A Critique of Pure Tolerance,* Beacon Press, Boston, 1968.

Many recent commentaries bear directly or indirectly on Marcuse's ideas. Among them are the following. Cranston, Maurice: "Herbert Marcuse," *Encounter,* vol. 32, March, 1969, pp. 38–50. Duclow, Donald: "Herbert Marcuse and 'Happy Consciousness,'" *Liberation,* vol. 14, October, 1969, pp. 7–15. Peretz, M.: "Herbert Marcuse: Beyond Technological Reason," *The Yale Review,* vol. 57, June, 1968, pp. 510–527. Rieff, Philip: *Freud: The Mind of the Moralist,* Doubleday & Company, Inc., Garden City, N.Y., 1959; and *The Therapeutic Vision, Uses of Faith after Freud,* Harper & Row, Publishers, Incorporated, New York, 1966. Robinson, Paul A.: *The Freudian Left: Wilhelm Reich, Geza Roheim, Herbert Marcuse,* Harper & Row, Publishers, Incorporated, New York, 1969. Roszak, Theodore:

The Making of a Counter Culture, Doubleday & Company, Inc., Garden City, N.Y., 1969. Wolff, Kurt H. and Barrington Moore (eds.): *The Critical Spirit, Essays in Honor of Herbert Marcuse*, Beacon Press, Boston, 1967.

Robert Dahl has authored a large number of well-known books and articles. The following is a list of those that are most speculative and most germane to theoretical reflection. Dahl, Robert: *Modern Political Analysis*, Prentice-Hall, Inc., Englewood Cliffs, N.J., 1963; *Pluralist Democracy in the United States, Conflict and Consent*, Rand McNally & Company, Chicago, 1967; (ed.), *Political Oppositions in Western Democracies*, Yale University Press, New Haven, Conn., 1966; *A Preface to Democratic Theory*, The University of Chicago Press, Chicago, 1956; and *Who Governs? Democracy and Power in an American City*, Yale University Press, New Haven, Conn., 1961. See also: Dahl, Robert and Charles E. Lindblom: *Politics, Economics, and Welfare*, Harper & Brothers, New York, 1953.

Many writers have endorsed pluralist doctrines and many others have been critical of the pluralist position. Included here are only a few of the most prominent from both categories. Arendt, Hannah: *Between Past and Future*, The Viking Press, Inc., New York, 1963; *The Human Condition*, Doubleday & Company, Inc., Garden City, N.Y., 1959; *Men in Dark Times*, Harcourt, Brace & World, Inc., New York, 1968; and *On Revolution*, The Viking Press, Inc., New York, 1963. Galbraith, John K.: *American Capitalism*, Houghton Mifflin Company, Boston, 1962. Ginzberg, Eli et al.: *The Pluralistic Economy*, McGraw-Hill Book Company, New York, 1965. Kariel, Henry S.: *The Decline of American Pluralism*, Stanford University Press, Stanford, Calif., 1961; and *The Promise of Politics*, Prentice-Hall, Inc., Englewood Cliffs, N.J., 1966. Lowi, Theodore J.: *The End of Liberalism, Ideology, Policy, and the Crisis of Public Authority*, W. W. Norton & Company, Inc., New York, 1969. McConnell Grant: *Private Power and American Democracy*, Alfred A. Knopf, Inc., New York, 1962. Morgan, Douglas N.: "A Postscript to Professor Dahl's 'Preface,'" with a rejoinder by Dahl, *American Political Science Review*, vol. 51, December, 1957, pp. 1040–1061. Nisbet, Robert: *Community and Power*, Oxford University Press, New York, 1962. Rose, Arnold: *The Power Structure, Political Process in American Society*, Oxford University Press, New York, 1967. Truman, David: *The Governmental Process*, Alfred A. Knopf, Inc., New York, 1951. Williams, William A.: *The Great Evasion*, Quadrangle Books, Inc., Chicago, 1964. Wolff, Robert P.: *The Poverty of Liberalism*, Beacon Press, Boston, 1968. Wolin, Sheldon S.: *Politics and Vision: Continuity and Innovation in Western Political Thought*, Little, Brown and Company, Boston, 1963.

INDEX